"Presence and connection are the double helix of our being. Without the belonging that is sustained by our relationships, we fade into a purgatory of loneliness. Without being present with the other, we cannot realise the loving interconnection that is the truth of our existence. Emma Donaldson-Feilder and Liz Hall offer the treasure of why, what and how – inspirationally, wisely and with profound compassion. Relational mindfulness must be the future for coaches, indeed for all of humanity. Here is how."

Professor Michael West CBE, *Professor of Organizational Psychology, Lancaster University; Senior Visiting Fellow, The King's Fund, London; Convenor, Health Impact Group, Global Compassion Coalition*

"Emma Donaldson-Feilder and Liz Hall have written a brilliant book on Relational Mindfulness and its significance for coaches and in coaching. In our mechanistic, utilitarian, digital, world it is rare truly to be listened to. And it is especially rare in the workplace context to have deep, meaningful, open and interactive conversations. It is too easy for coaches to fall for the merely instrumental and for the coaching relationship to be hollowed out in pursuit of goals, KPIs and targets. This book allows for a return of our essential humanity into the coaching context. More than almost anything today, we all need to be deeply heard and to be allowed to discover our own deeper purpose. Good coaching leads to that. This book can help us all coach more deeply."

Michael Chaskalson, *Founder, Mindfulness Works; Professor of Practice Adjunct at Hult EF Corporate Education*

"Clearly, mindfulness enhances our relational capacity. Clearly, well-crafted relational practice can strengthen mindfulness. This book contributes to how this synergy can be applied in coaching, leadership, and elsewhere. But the boldest assertion in this work is suggested on every page: our growth in relational capacity and awareness can yield the intuitive wisdom we so urgently need at this time. Wisdom is about human suffering and our higher potential as skilful and compassionate people. And profoundly wholesome results can be expected when this wisdom guides our lives – as coaches, leaders, citizens, and members of the human family. I hope you read this book carefully and let it touch you."

Gregory Kramer, *Meditation Teacher and Author of* Insight Dialogue: The Interpersonal Path to Freedom, A Whole Life Path: A Lay Buddhist's Guide to Crafting a Dhamma-infused Life *and other publications on Relational Dharma*

"We all want a better life. For some, it means more freedom. For others, it means more love. Sadly, for too many it means less fear and pain. An even more basic human drive is to want a better life for our children and our loved ones. For many, it may even extend to all of the others with whom we share our planet. As coaches or helpers, we want to inspire and invoke this hope and renewed capability in our clients. This book is about hope. But it is not fanciful hope, it is feasible hope. Liz and Emma focus on two major themes, mindfulness and caring for and with others. With their style and linguistic magic, they have created a book that is a feast of possibilities. Relational Mindfulness is what creates conditions in which you and coaching clients, friends, family or coworkers have special moments of caring, laughter, productivity, and ingenuity. That is what this book can help you seek and achieve. Enjoy reading it. Talk about it with others. Practice their exercises."

Richard E. Boyatzis, *Distinguished University Professor of Case Western Reserve University and Professor in Departments of Organizational Behavior, Psychology and Cognitive Science*

"For coaching to step-up to what is now needed in the world, it needs to not only develop an eco-systemic way of thinking, being, doing and perceiving but also a spiritual perspective grounded in mindfulness, compassion, non-attachment and gratitude. Liz Hall and Emma Donaldson-Feilder bring their many years of practice and supervision to provide an excellent practical and step by step practice approach to how we can all develop our spiritual source and resourcefulness."

Professor Peter Hawkins, *Global Thought Leader and Best-Selling Author on Systemic Coaching, Systemic Team Coaching and Supervision*

"*Relational Mindfulness for Coaches* is an important book. The last 30 years have seen a huge increase in people taking to intrapersonal mindfulness practice to support their own well-being, and growth. As a mindful coach, do we leave it there and simply bring our own mindful attention implicitly into the coaching relationship? Liz and Emma are pointing to another way – a way of bringing mindfulness more explicitly into the practice of dialogue. When we do so, not only do we create the psychological safety for new insight to emerge, but we may also help others on their vertical development journey toward self-authorship and for some, the self-transforming mind. Our world needs more leaders better able to navigate complexity and co-create solutions to some of our toughest global challenges. This book offers a way to accelerate that, ironically by slowing down. Helping others access courage, collaboration and wisdom will be key if we are to find meaningful solutions to our ecological and climate crisis. As Liz and Emma point out, relational mindfulness moves us in the direction of greater compassion – this may be the most powerful alchemical ingredient as we look to integrate our own shadow and rediscover our inherent wholeness as human beings."

Mark McMordie, *CEO of The Conscious Leader, Co-author of* Mindfulness for Coaches *and Contributor to* Ecological & Climate-Conscious Coaching

"Coaching an individual outside their context often does more harm than good. Every human is a cluster of systems nested within a multitude of other systems. Relational mindfulness is an essential tool for the mature coach, who wants to add more value than helping someone solve a complicated problem. It takes us to where coaching belongs – the world of complex adaptive systems."

Professor David Clutterbuck, *Founder and Practice Lead,*
Clutterbuck Coaching and Mentoring International

"Supported by compelling stories and testimonials, Hall and Donaldson-Feilder present us with a practical guide for how Relational Mindfulness can evolve our coaching practice. Not only can Relational Mindfulness unearth greater leadership insight and intelligence, by helping us welcome 'what is' with greater wisdom and compassion; but it also gives coaches a toolkit to make progress towards 'equality of outcomes', by providing coaching that creates the most needed benefits for clients, whatever their background or identities. This book is an inspirational invitation to coaches seeking more creative, inclusive, and transformational relationships with those they serve."

Will James, *Founder of With Diversity, Provider of Coaching*
and Consultancy Services, and Director of Inclusion and
Sustainability at APECS

"If we are to address the polycrisis we are facing, humans will need to evolve to find a different way of being. This book starts with the self work and the importance of mindfulness and non-judgement and then skillfully guides us into the relational space, providing a path to support individual change and tools for coaches to utilise and share. Emma and Liz share their personal passion for Relational Mindfulness with deep compassion, in a way which models their call to action."

Rita Symons, *Coach, Supervisor, Managing Director –*
Enhance Coaching and Consultancy, World Citizen and
Former EMCC UK President

"In these troubled times with so much calling for our attention, so urgently, it feels even more important than ever to remind ourselves that true stillness can help us to have profound movement in our thinking. That stillness is often achieved through practices like individual mindfulness or having a thinking partner who can offer the promise of sustained generative attention and deep listening. Relational mindfulness builds beautifully on these practices; slowing us down, transcending a focus on the self to re-learn to be fully present for another even whilst in dialogue: through this we can cultivate shared compassion, deep insight, wisdom and a remembering that we are all connected. This is "Systems work" with an important focus on the relationship. As a Time to Think teacher I know that the quality of our feeling, thinking and actions most depend on the way we are treated by others who around us; Liz and Emma's deeply thoughtful, highly accessible book brings new perspectives and many accessible systemic practices to anyone – not just coaches – embarking or continuing on this journey. Now is not the time to be alone – this book on relational mindfulness illuminates an inviting pathway of a whole new way of being together. Highly recommended."

Linda Aspey, *FBACP, Time to Think Faculty,*
Climate Psychology Alliance

"This book is a helpful and timely addition in coaching as we are seeing the signs of how social, economical and environmental factors are making it harder to cope while at the same time, we are becoming more aware of what our brains and bodies require to feel healthy. There is so often an incongruence between healthy, thriving functioning and the systems in which we operate which contributes to increased levels of stress on an individual and collective level. Tools like RM provide an accessible and practical way of working with coaching clients, and just 'being' with all the people we interact with! RM encourages us to apply awareness, self-compassion and empathy to ourselves and those we work with, or who are around us; recognising and honouring the value our diverse inner worlds and perspectives. Improving how we relate to others is something we can all benefit from, both practically and with the increased positive emotions and hormonal balance that occurs as a consequence of good relationships. As research often shows, it is also one of the most powerful aspects of a productive coaching relationship. This book draws on research and thinking from multiple fields and pulls it together in a way that brings it to life, and embedding that practice is the key!"

Lindsay Comalie, *Experienced Organisational Development Consultant,*
Coach, Coach Supervisor and Positive Psychologist, previously
responsible for Imperial College London's Coaching Academy and
an early adopter of RM for Coaches when she invited Emma to
offer an RM Programme for Imperial College's Internal Coaches

"*Relational Mindfulness for Coaches* is a transformative dialogue that blends scientific evidence, real-world examples, and practical guidance to introduce and integrate relational mindfulness into the realm of coaching. This book explores the depths of relational mindfulness both as a personal practice for coaches and as an invaluable tool in their professional toolkit. The authors' expertise and enthusiasm shine through, providing a well-rounded exploration that feeds the enquiring mind. Their insightful approach not only enhances coaches' presence and awareness but also fosters wisdom, compassion, and courageous collaboration. Whether you are an experienced coach or new to the field, this book will enrich your practice and elevate your impact. Highly recommended!"

Simon Dennis, *Head of Enterprise Platform Services*
and a Coaching Ambassador for Fujitsu, having previously been
Head of Coaching at Fujitsu UK & Ireland and established a Coaching
Community utilizing Internal and External Coaches within the business

"This timely book is an important addition to the canon of mindfulness literature. The tendency to conflate mindfulness with meditation has perpetuated the view that engaging in such practices is somehow narcissistic: we sit blissed out in our bubble, disengaged from real world problems. Liz and Emma dispel this unhelpful myth with this comprehensive introduction to Relational Mindfulness. In these times of polarisation and reactivity, it couldn't be more essential to bring self-aware, attentive and compassionate listening to our dialogues, relationships and workplaces. By including their own stories and accounts from practitioners in this thoughtful book, Emma and Liz bring warmth and an everyday quality to what is both a manual and an informative reference. I found it a mindful exercise in itself to read their calm and engaging prose and having used Insight Dialogue, the method they espouse, I know it works brilliantly! I hope this excellent book gets the widespread attention it deserves."

Hetty Einzig, *Leadership Coach, Author, Executive Editor of* Coaching Perspectives *and Director of Publications Strategy, Association for Coaching*

"The authors beautifully describe the growing awareness of the power of Relational Mindfulness – mindfulness expanded and deepened through the relational meditation practice of Insight Dialogue. Inspiring and practical, the book offers a progressive path for coaches' development in cultivating attuned relational presence, relational awareness, wisdom, courage, compassion and collaborative capacity. Clearly and warmly written, the book highlights illuminating interviews with coach-practitioners that unfold the professional and personal benefits of training and development in Relational Mindfulness."

Jan Surrey, *Senior Insight Dialogue Retreat Teacher; Clinical Psychologist; Faculty and Board Member of the Institute for Meditation and Psychotherapy in Boston, MA, USA*

"This book on relational mindfulness (RM) illustrates the amplifying power of embodied presence in relationship. We know and others know when someone is open and receptive, and this expanded relational capacity contributes to transformations of self and other views. With awareness, true change becomes possible. Habits and perceptual biases limiting our interactions can become sources of insight and wisdom as we deepen our understanding of the shared human condition. This application of Insight Dialogue and RM will benefit coaches and their clients and contribute to workspaces and personal relationships that are attuned, capable, flexible and compassionate. The book is an insightful overview of how the practices of RM enhance and expand relational capacity across various models informing coaching. It is a significant and heartfelt contribution to the field."

Phyllis K. Hicks, *Co-author and Trainer of the Interpersonal Mindfulness Program and Senior Insight Dialogue Retreat Teacher*

"If you want to harness the significant benefits of mindfulness in ways that are most pragmatic and relevant to coaching, relational mindfulness offers a richly elegant solution. The authors provide a clear, compelling and theoretically grounded understanding of the approach, enriched by practitioner accounts of its paradigm-shifting impact on their coaching relationships. Offering refined guidelines for deepening presence through interpersonal practice, the approach simultaneously cultivates self-awareness and relational attunement, essential ingredients for impactful coaching effectiveness. The book shows how relational mindfulness resonates with and augments the major coaching approaches, and offers an inspiring vision of how we can infuse more wisdom and compassion into our work, our lives, and in facing the challenges of our contemporary world."

Graham Lee, *Author of* Leadership Coaching, *and*
Breakthrough Conversations for Coaches, Consultants, and Leaders

"This book could not come at a more important time. We make vastly different, wiser, choices when we have the space for dialogue. In a world that is often too caught up in the busyness of instrumental, short-term, tangible targets, and at a time where speaking truth to power is critical, coaches are uniquely positioned to hold open this space for dialogue and insight with leaders. This book is an essential guide and resource to help coaches to do that well."

Professor Megan Reitz, *Associate Fellow, Saïd Business School,*
Oxford University; Adjunct Professor of Leadership and Dialogue,
Hult Business School

"*Relational Mindfulness for Coaches* invites readers on a transformative journey to deepen their presence in relational spaces. The book seamlessly integrates personal experiences, rigorous research, theory and practice to advocate for a deeper connection with oneself, thereby enhancing the coaching relationship. Presence, awareness, wisdom, compassion, and courageous collaboration are explored through exercises and practices aimed at fostering mindfulness and meaningful connections with clients. The authors also explore somatics, a field which is central to my practice and growing in reach every day. The book explores how embodied practices complement traditional coaching methods, enriching the coaching process with a deeper understanding of physical sensations and emotional states. Grounded in extensive research and enriched by the authors own learning, this book is an invaluable resource for coaches seeking to create impactful and transformative coaching experiences. It emphasises not just techniques, but also the profound importance of connecting deeply with oneself and others to bring about meaningful change."

Dr Eunice Aquilina, *Author of* Embodying Authenticity *and*
Stepping Into Your Power

Relational Mindfulness for Coaches

The quality of coaches' presence and awareness is key to the quality and success of their coaching relationships and interventions. *Relational Mindfulness for Coaches* supports coaches to co-create compassionate, psychologically safe yet courageous coaching spaces, generating profound insight, wisdom, and understanding in the client.

At the book's heart are powerful practices to expand mindful presence from the individual to the relational, bringing present-moment, non-judgemental awareness to self, others, and the relationship, whilst speaking and listening. The book provides understanding of Relational Mindfulness's (RM's) foundations in mindfulness, compassion, and Insight Dialogue. Drawing on their and other experienced coaches' experiences, the authors illustrate the benefits of engaging in RM practices and provide easy-to-follow guidance for bringing RM into coaching. They also situate RM in the wider field of theory and practice, including neuro-science, and explore RM in relation to a host of other coaching models. In these challenging times of polarisation and conflict, the climate emergency, and a crisis in mental health, this inspiring book addresses the urgent need to create trans-formational dialogue and interrelatedness in coaching and beyond.

This pioneering book will be essential reading for coaches, coaching supervisors, coaching psychologists, coaching academics, leaders, and other helping professionals.

Emma Donaldson-Feilder is a Relational Mindfulness and Insight Dialogue teacher, chartered coaching psychologist, coaching supervisor, leadership coach, and chartered occupational psychologist, who aims to support the development of kinder, wiser workplaces.

Liz Hall is the founding editor of *Coaching at Work* magazine, a leadership coach, and a mindfulness teacher, with clients including the NHS. Her other publications include *Coach Your Team* (2019), *Mindful Coaching* (2013), and *Coaching in Times of Crisis and Transformation* (with others, 2015).

Relational
Mindfulness
for Coaches

Enhancing Presence, Awareness, Wisdom, Compassion and Courageous Collaboration

Emma Donaldson-Feilder and Liz Hall

Routledge
Taylor & Francis Group

LONDON AND NEW YORK

Designed cover image: Photo taken by Liz Hall in July 2024 in New Hamlet, Plum Village France

First published 2025
by Routledge
4 Park Square, Milton Park, Abingdon, Oxon OX14 4RN

and by Routledge
605 Third Avenue, New York, NY 10158

Routledge is an imprint of the Taylor & Francis Group, an informa business

British Library Cataloguing-in-Publication Data
A catalogue record for this book is available from the British Library

ISBN: 978-1-032-47225-6 (hbk)
ISBN: 978-1-032-48716-8 (pbk)
ISBN: 978-1-003-39042-8 (ebk)

DOI: 10.4324/9781003390428

Typeset in Adobe Garamond
by Newgen Publishing UK

We dedicate this book to Mother Nature and all her creatures, including our dear partners, Ray and Malcolm, and beloved teachers, Thich Nhat Hanh and Gregory Kramer.

Contents

About the authors

Emma Donaldson-Feilder is a Relational Mindfulness (RM) and Insight Dialogue (ID) teacher, chartered coaching psychologist, coaching supervisor, and chartered occupational psychologist, who aims to support the development of kinder, wiser workplaces. In 2019 she completed a professional doctorate, in which she conducted research exploring the use of mindfulness and RM in leadership development. Building on this work, she developed a range of RM programmes to support leadership development and coach development. Her publications include numerous articles and book chapters and co-authorship of *Preventing Stress in Organisations: How to Develop Positive Managers* (2011). She trained as a mindfulness teacher with Bangor University's Centre for Mindfulness Research and Practice (UK) and as an ID teacher with the Insight Dialogue Community (USA). More about the author can be found at www.affinitycands.com.

Liz Hall is the founding editor of *Coaching at Work* magazine, a leadership coach, and a mindfulness teacher, with clients including the NHS. Her other publications include *Coach Your Team* (Penguin, 2019), *Mindful Coaching* (Kogan Page, 2013), *Coaching in Times of Crisis and Transformation* (with others, Kogan Page, 2015), and book chapters including 'Compassion Focused Coaching' (with Irons & Palmer, *Handbook of Coaching Psychology*, Routledge, 2019). She trained as a mindfulness teacher with Bangor University's Centre for Mindfulness Research and Practice (UK) and Solterreno (Spain) and has been practising mindfulness since 2004. More about the author can be found at www.lizhallcoaching.com.

There is a dedicated website accompanying this book, which can be found at www.relationalmindfulness.net.

Foreword

From the start of this outstanding book, it is clear that the authors Emma Donaldson-Feilder and Liz Hall bring us a wealth of experience and a deep and in many ways pioneering approach to coaching. Their book addresses their subject in a wide-ranging way, and its extensive outlining of both theory and practice will make it a truly invaluable resource for any coach who wants to take their practice to new levels, and to become an agent of genuine transformation for their clients.

As an experienced coach and trainer of coaches, I see that the great majority of coaching as it is currently practiced takes place at the cognitive level, and is therefore situated in the foothills of consciousness. While it may bring some benefits, it will rarely if ever penetrate the more hallowed ground of real transformation. As the book reminds us: "We cannot think our way to being different" (Eunice Aquilina).

How refreshing and inspiring therefore to hear so early in this book that:

> The quality of coaches' presence and awareness is key to the quality and success of their coaching relationships and interventions. *Relational Mindfulness for Coaches* supports coaches to co-create compassionate, psychologically safe yet courageous coaching spaces, generating profound insight, wisdom, and understanding in the client.
>
> In these challenging times of polarisation and conflict, the climate emergency and a crisis in mental health, this book addresses the urgent need to create transformational dialogue and interrelatedness in coaching and beyond.

And much later that:

> Some of us might say that the crux of our work as RMEC (RM-Enhanced Coaching) practitioners is to support individual and collective evolution of consciousness.

The book is rooted in their detailed and authoritative writing about the field of mindfulness. Thankfully this is not in the relatively shallow way that mindfulness has been colonised and reduced by the corporate world. We are not talking here about a technique to reduce stress, improve focus, etc., but rather the depth of practice that arises out of an ancient body of wisdom, a practice that massively expands the coach's consciousness and therefore their perceptual field.

The book clearly explains why this is such an essential foundation of the work, what the pillars are of the practice, and why it is a core of the coach's presence. A coach can either be sitting with their client trying to figure out what is happening and how to make something 'useful' happen by attempting to control the outcome or they can be holding a much deeper, emergent space through the depth of their embodied presence. This requires an enormous letting go of the desire to control, married with a deep trust in the intelligence of life that arises when we settle into truly embodied presence. As we hear in many ways in the book, including powerful testimonies from practitioners, this is how deep movement occurs in a client.

But mindfulness alone is not enough, and this is where, by bringing in the relational quality, the book touches new and immensely rich territory. To be fully present to oneself and the client at the same time is a high calling, a lifelong learning, and the book offers in depth and detailed ways to engage and develop this exquisitely refined practice. This is the human being at our shining best – deep presence, open heart, multi-dimensional attention, completely attuned to self, the client, and the relational field in all its richness.

As the coach learns to reside in this relational field, anchored through deep embodiment, the authors describe vividly the kinds of unfoldment that can open, not through cognitive intention but through profound 'beingness.' It is through the quality of this holding, and the natural sense of safety it generates, that layers of numbness can, for instance, start to melt in a client, that long suppressed tears may start to flow, or that light-bulb moments of self-awareness suddenly ignite. It is not surprising to hear practitioners describe such relational fields as 'blessed' or 'sacred.'

All of which is not to say that the coach steps back from being fearlessly truthful when that is the correct 'action' needed. Quite the contrary:

> There are lots of reasons why people do not want to or cannot listen to the 'truth', but we need discerning truth-sayers. We need people with courage to call things out. And we need this speaking up to be done wisely and compassionately.

The book is also rich in theory, with extensive material about how their approach connects with as well as differs from parts of other teachings already in place, consideration of the relevant neuroscience, and discussion about how this work can best be trained.

Through its depth of integration of the theoretical and the practical, I believe this is a landmark book in the field of coaching, one that holds itself to the highest standards, and invites you the coach to embark on a profound journey of your personal and therefore your professional development.

We are at a critical time in the world. Our civilisation is in deep crisis, starved of love, connectedness, and mutual care. Polarisation and war are creating tremendous suffering and separation, even among family and friends. We speak everywhere of 'connection', yet we have never been more disconnected from ourselves and others.

Every one of us deep down knows that the human heart must be connected – to self, others, nature, community, and a deeper field of unity – to be healthy, thrive, and experience life as meaningful. The many organisations failing to respond to this are the ones struggling to survive.

It is no longer enough to participate in and help people to make a broken system work better. It is time for coaches and coaching to play their part in birthing the highest possibilities for humankind.

For anyone who hears this calling and who aspires to reach their highest potential as a coach, to be of the deepest service not just to their clients but to humankind as a whole, this pioneering book is one you will return to over and over again.

Nicholas Janni
Author of UK Business book of the Year 2023,
Leader as Healer, A New Paradigm for 21st Century Leadership
Founder and CEO, The Leader as Healer Institute

Acknowledgements

This book would not have been possible without the help and support of so many people. We are very grateful to all who have contributed, including Rebecca Marsh at Routledge for her interest in our book idea, patience through our writing process, and support with the book's development.

We would like to offer our heartfelt thanks and appreciation to the 11 kind people who participated in our informal qualitative research. The book is infinitely richer and more meaningful as a result of all that we learnt from them and the quotes they provided. Thank you to:

- Becky Thoseby, Head of Workplace Wellbeing, Inclusive Culture Centre of Expertise, People Group, Ministry of Justice, UK
- Beth Clare McManus, Coaching Psychologist, UK
- Emma Reading, Coach and Coaching Psychologist, UK
- Jane Brendgen, Adult Development and Executive Coach, UK
- Malcolm Frow, Insight Dialogue Teacher, Management Consultant and Executive Coach, UK
- Pirjo Puhakka, Executive Coach, Coach Supervisor, Mentor Coach, Thinking Time, Finland
- Rhonda Miller, Chartered Coaching Psychologist, UK
- Saima Butt, Coach and Facilitator, Change Advantage, UK
- Shenaz Kelly-Rawat, Chartered Psychologist PsSI, Director, Learning Partnership, Ireland
- Stephanie Wheeler, Leadership and Team Coach, Lego® Serious Play® Facilitator, Author, UK
- One further interviewee (based in the EU) who asked to remain anonymous.

Emma

A huge thank you to my partner, Malcolm Frow, who has been my wonderful companion on the Insight Dialogue (ID) and Relational Mindfulness (RM) journey from the start. Our regular ID practice is foundational and all the ID teaching, retreats, and workshops we have shared have been a joy and an inspiration. Your support of my RM programmes and this book has been invaluable. I would not be where I am today without you: my gratitude and love are beyond words.

I am deeply grateful to Gregory Kramer for his genius in creating ID, his generosity in sharing it and helping others like me to teach it, and his support for my development – not to mention his friendship and wise guidance – over more than a decade. Enormous gratitude, too, to the other senior ID teachers, Phyllis Hicks, Mary Burns, and Jan Surrey, for their mentoring, care, and wisdom. Heartfelt thanks to Jane Brendgen, who introduced me to ID and has been such an integral part of my ID journey as well as a dear friend, and to the ID 6 for all the rich and developmental ID-based time we shared. And a big thank you to all the people in the ID community, including fellow teachers and participants, who have been part of this journey and given me a sense of belonging. I will be donating my royalties from this book to the Insight Dialogue Community, the organisation that supports the teaching and promulgation of ID around the world.

Many thanks to Michael Chaskalson and the late Cindy Cooper for skilfully teaching me mindfulness and nurturing my development as a mindfulness teacher. And a big thank you to Nick Smith for supervising my coaching supervision for nearly a decade and helping me grow as a coaching supervisor and a human being.

I also want to express my thanks to all the coaches who have participated in my RM programmes and helped me get this precious practice out into the world – particularly to the 4Ss, who have encouraged me and helped me create more and longer programmes through their engagement with the profound learning RM offers.

Lastly, but by no means least, to Liz, my co-author and dear friend: a deep bow and so much gratitude. I could not have written this book without you, it has been a great joy to collaborate with you on it, and I will be forever grateful for all we have shared.

Liz

I am profoundly grateful to all my mindfulness teachers over the years who include Thich Nhat Hanh, Brother Phap Huu, Geshe Tashi Tsering, Bodhin, Kate Gooch, Michael Chaskalson, Rosalie Dores, Gregory Kramer, and my co-author, Emma, who first introduced me to Relational Mindfulness (RM).

I thank Jane Brendgen for her friendship, for suggesting I undertake an eight-week RM programme with Rosalie, for all the relationally mindful, compassionate, and deliciously deliberately developmental conversations, and her support for being more courageous in speaking the truth.

I thank my beloved husband, Ray Freeman, for his loving commitment to being mindful and compassionate within our family and beyond, and for being open to embracing RM.

There are many other dear friends and colleagues whose support, compassionate wise presence, and shared commitment to growth continue to mean so much to me: my Dharma brother, Mark McMordie; Lindsay Wittenberg, with whom (along with Mark and others) I had the joy of rolling out Coaching through Covid, a compassionate response to the suffering of healthcare workers. This initiative offered us a sandpit in which to play with embodying mindfulness and compassion at the core of what we did and how we related, shining a light on what is possible when we show up with appreciation of our interconnectedness.

I thank my wonderfully wise coaching supervisors, Ian Mitchell and Eunice Aquilina, and IFS therapist, Mark Elton, who continue to help me to do my shadow work, and to heal and grow, so I can step more fully into the 'power with' that is our birthright.

I thank our three beautiful children, Molly, Emma, and Dylan, who inspire me to learn to truly embody mindfulness and compassion in our interactions.

Finally, I come back once again to dear Emma, my co-author, whose friendship, compassion, wisdom, and integrity I value so highly. I am deeply honoured to have shared this challenging, creative, and deeply relationally mindful journey and to have collaborated on this project. With heartfelt gratitude.

Section 1

Introduction

I just think now how can you do mindfulness without relational mindfulness? All these people out there who are doing mindfulness and they don't even know Relational Mindfulness exists. I didn't even know it existed. Oh my goodness, they're missing out. They really are. I feel like I need to go on the street and tell everyone because individual mindfulness is just the tip of the iceberg… it can be so much richer!

> Becky, an in-house coach and Relational Mindfulness
> practitioner, and one of our interviewees for this book.

Welcome to our book about how Relational Mindfulness (RM) can enhance our coaching. In this section – Chapters 1–3 – we introduce and put the book in context. Firstly, we set the scene, exploring what we mean by RM, why we wrote the book, why we believe it is important and what the book contains. We then establish the ground on which RM stands in terms of individual mindfulness and compassion and the benefits of these for coaching. Figure S1 shows where you are on your journey through this book.

DOI: 10.4324/9781003390428-1

You are here!

Introduction

Section 1
- Setting the scene
- Exploring mindfulness and compassion: definitions and origins
- Benefits of individual mindfulness and compassion in coaching

Origins, underpinnings and benefits of RM

Section 2
- Exploring Relational Mindfulness (RM)
- Insight Dialogue-based RM
- Benefits of bringing RM into coaching

Practice and application

Section 3
- Foundations for practice and application
- Exploring each of the six guidelines in turn

Section 4
- Different levels of bringing RM into coaching
- Preparing with, embodying, drawing on RM

Additional gems to further enhance RM

Section 5
- Becoming fully present and aware
- Relating and connecting
- Insight and wisdom

Next steps and beyond

Section 6
- Where next for you?
- Vision for the future

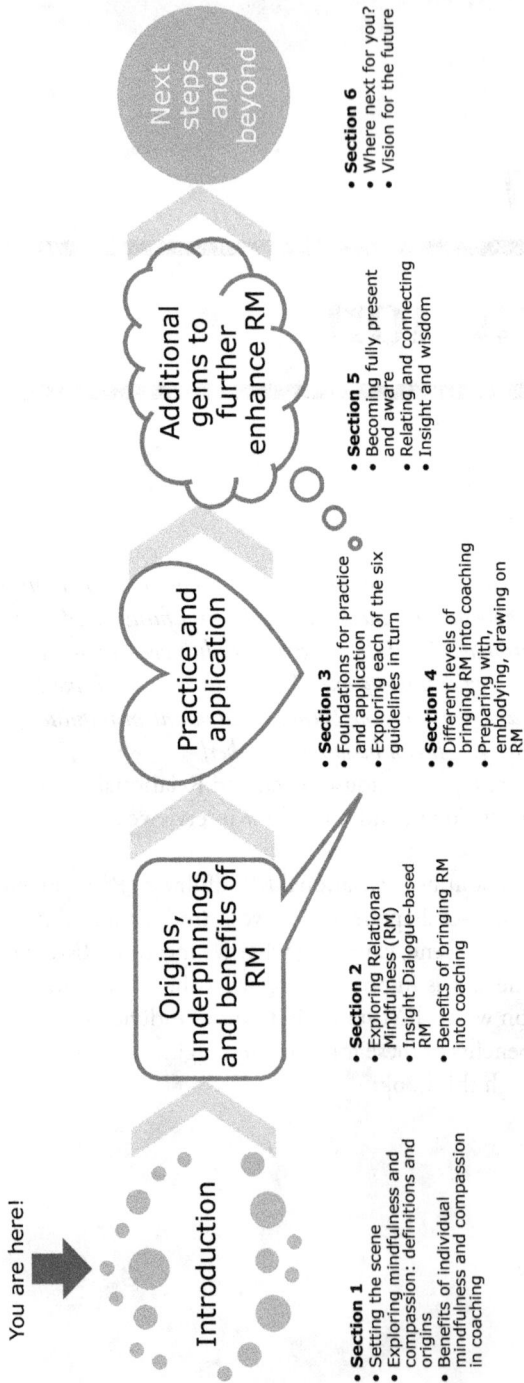

Figure S1 You are here!

Chapter 1

Setting the scene

The journey of a thousand miles begins with a single step.

Lao Tzu

We are delighted that you have opened this book! We believe Relational Mindfulness (RM) offers enormous potential for coaches and the wider world to bring much-needed greater levels of attention, kindness, and wisdom to our work and the rest of our lives, and those of our clients. In this chapter we briefly introduce the concept of RM, then set out our motivations and intentions for writing the book, and outline its content.

What are we talking about?

What we mean by RM

Put simply, RM shifts the practice of mindfulness from the individual into the relational sphere. RM takes the deliberate placing of attention and the non-judgemental attitude inherent in mindfulness and applies them as we interact with others. Thus, RM brings present moment, non-judgemental awareness to ourselves, to others, and to the relationship between us, whilst we are speaking, listening, or otherwise relating to others.

RM practices, such as the ones described in this book, are designed to support the development of relational awareness, presence, attunement, and insight. As with individual mindfulness, RM can be cultivated through formal and informal practice, with the aim of accessing a state of RM for increasing proportions of our daily interactions with others, until this becomes an embodied part of who we are

DOI: 10.4324/9781003390428-2

and how we function. As coaches, this means bringing RM to an increasing extent into how we are being and what we are doing in and between coaching sessions. (See Chapter 4 for more information on our definition of RM, and Chapter 5 for the background to the form of RM practices we outline in this book.)

Defining coaching

When we use the term 'coaching', we are referring to "*a conversation or series of conversations with the aim of helping people learn, grow and fulfil their potential*" (Hall, 2013, p.17). These conversations might involve one or more coaches and they might be about helping an individual, team, or group. Coaching may be provided by a designated coach or a manager or leader who has developed coaching skills. We use the term 'coach' to refer to anyone providing coaching.

The benefits of RM for coaching

As you will read later in the book, we believe, and our evidence suggests, that engaging with RM practice presents wonderful opportunities for the enhancement of coaching capacities in the coach and better outcomes for coaching clients. (See Chapter 6 for the benefits of bringing RM into coaching.)

More broadly, we believe that RM offers an exciting and much-needed invitation to bring mindfulness out of its largely individual focus (particularly in Western cultures) into the collective arena, not just of coaching, but also other relationships, leadership, teams, and beyond to community and the environment. Certainly, this invitation to bring more RM into the collective is part of our motivation for writing this book, and we hope you will help us do this too!

The coaches we interviewed as part of our research for this book showed similar enthusiasm, as we saw in Becky's quote at the beginning of this section's introduction. Becky points to a ramping up that RM offers beyond individual mindfulness. In addition, RM has the potential to make greater awareness and wisdom accessible to those who choose not to engage with individual mindfulness.

Stephanie, another of our interviewees, also a coach and RM practitioner, emphasises, "*...the importance of relational mindfulness being a thing in its own right and not being a progression from mindfulness.*" She continues, "*... RM has the capacity to be life-changing: it doesn't need to be restricted to those people who are interested in mindfulness and meditation...it feels much more expansive and possibly more accessible....*"

Other helping professions

We have written the book for coaches because that is the world we know and the water in which we swim. However, the more we talk to other helping professionals about RM, the more we realise that the journey we set out in this book is also relevant to many others who work with individual clients. Psychotherapists, counsellors, and psychologists could benefit from RM practice in the same way as coaches. Social workers, paramedics, and other health professionals could potentially do so too. We would encourage any helping professional to read this book and whenever we say 'coach' or 'coaching' replace that in their heads with their own professional domain.

Why we wrote this book

We have each travelled a long journey to get to the point of writing this book. During that journey our paths crossed at different points including through conferences, programmes, and journal articles. In late 2019, our paths converged with Emma accepting a request to write a series of articles about RM for *Coaching at Work*, the journal that Liz edits. We started having regular conversations about RM and coaching, from which the idea of writing a book together naturally emerged. By way of background, we share below our personal journeys before describing our process for writing this book and providing a map of what the book contains.

Emma's story

The first steps

My first encounter with mindfulness and meditation was in the late 1990s. Like many who found their way into meditation around that time, I started by learning Transcendental Meditation (TM) and found that daily meditation gave me a moment of calm that helped me feel better in the rest of my day. Soon after, I began my Masters in Occupational Psychology and discovered ACT (Acceptance and Commitment Therapy), which has mindfulness as a key element. Supported by my research supervisor, Frank Bond, I became really interested in how ACT could be applied in workplace settings and conducted my research dissertation looking at psychological flexibility, improvements in which are the key mechanism by which ACT enhances wellbeing (Donaldson-Feilder & Bond, 2004).

By the time I started working as an occupational psychologist and coach in the early 2000s, my appetite for mindfulness and meditation had been thoroughly whetted and I was keen to learn more. I discovered Jon Kabat-Zinn's work through reading books and using his guided audios and found mindfulness meditation a valuable alternative to TM. However, at this stage, if you had asked me, I would probably have categorised most of my mindfulness and meditation activity as 'personal development.' I was benefiting enormously from it in terms of my own wellbeing and life, but – other than running a few sessions of ACT for clients – I was not yet applying it in my work.

Integration

That separation between my mindfulness practice and my professional life changed in 2008, when I attended my first mindfulness for coaches course, with Michael Chaskalson. My understanding and enthusiasm about the potential benefits of mindfulness and meditation grew to a point where it seemed important to bring it into my work.

The research literature about the benefits of mindfulness and meditation had really blossomed in the late 20th and early 21st centuries (and has continued to grow exponentially). What was once firmly positioned in the spiritual and personal domain had moved, via significant applications in the clinical, medical, and psychotherapeutic worlds, into workplaces, and work-related applications. Research was starting to show positive outcomes from work-based mindfulness programmes, including improved employee health and wellbeing (e.g. Jamieson & Tuckey, 2017; Lomas et al, 2017).

However, my enthusiasm for mindfulness and meditation was sparked as much by my personal experience as the research literature. Seeing how mindfulness/meditation practice led to improvements in my own ability to be present in the moment, to quieten my self- and other-judgemental tendencies, to be calmer and kinder in relationships, and to live a happier, more grounded life, I wanted to see the benefits ripple out to others.

Initially, the main integration of mindfulness/meditation into my work was in terms of my presence as a coach and coaching supervisor. My own mindfulness practice helped me to be more present for my clients, more aware of different aspects of what was going on in the moment, better able to be grounded and 'hold' the client in the coaching or supervision process. As I attended further courses and stabilised my own mindfulness meditation practice further, I felt more able to embody mindful awareness and started to offer clients brief guided mindfulness practices, where this felt appropriate for the coaching or supervision. I subsequently trained as a mindfulness teacher to better enable me to guide clients in this way. (See Chapter 14 for our proposed model of levels of capacity for bringing mindfulness into coaching.)

Finding Insight Dialogue

When I discovered Insight Dialogue (ID) in 2010 and attended my first ID residential retreat in 2011, I knew this was something important. At that stage, I had no idea of the sea change ID would bring about not only in my meditation practice, but also in my relationships, my practice as a psychologist, and eventually my career direction. Initially, ID seemed to be just a further means of developing my own mindful presence and mindfulness guiding, but the more I delved into it, the greater my enthusiasm for it grew.

We will explain a lot more about ID later in the book, but to clarify the distinctive element of ID briefly: it adds a relational dimension to the process of meditation. ID practice involves mindful dialogue, in which participants meditate whilst speaking and listening about particular contemplation topics in dyads, small groups, or a large group. Developed by Gregory Kramer in the US (Kramer, 2007), ID has spread around the world in the last 25 years and now has an international community of teachers and facilitators, of which I have become a part (I was recognised as an ID teacher in 2021).

As I engaged with ID, I saw a marked increase in all the mindfulness benefits I had already noticed, particularly in my relational awareness, empathy, compassion, and kindness, and in how I could translate mindfulness into my day-to-day life. I also found my wisdom and understanding growing as a result of the contemplation topics and teachings offered in ID and the insight-generating possibilities of meditating in relationship. I saw too, over and over, the 'magical' shift in the room resulting from the connection and the shared sense of common humanity that emerges as people meditate in dialogue with one another whilst contemplating existential, wisdom-based topics and exploring experience in an embodied way.

Tumbling into a doctorate

By 2016, I was convinced that this relational take on meditation/mindfulness was a powerful approach and was keen to find ways to integrate it into my work. In discussions with fellow ID-practising coaches and leadership development professionals, I found agreement with my view that an ID-based approach, with its focus on the relational application of mindfulness, would be an ideal vehicle to support development for those for whom relationship is a central part of their role (including, for example, coaches, leaders, people managers, and psychologists). As an evidence-based practitioner, I looked for research evidence that could support this integration of RM into professional development programmes. Finding that the research literature was almost non-existent, I tumbled into doing a professional doctorate with that integration as its central theme (Donaldson-Feilder et al, 2019, 2021).

After completing the doctoral stage of my development journey in 2019, the logical next step was to run programmes based on RM, which I now do. As a result, I have seen RM provide benefits in coach development, leadership development, professional and personal development, and other contexts where building quality relationships is a vital component. Articulating the value of RM in writing for professional audiences also felt important, so I was delighted to find that Liz was interested in this work and supportive of publishing articles about RM in *Coaching at Work*.

Deciding to write this book

By this point, I was very aware of Liz's pioneering work on mindfulness for coaches and her excellent book, *Mindful Coaching* (Hall, 2013), and very much admired how she was integrating mindfulness with coaching. Her support in publishing the RM articles in *Coaching at Work* and other projects on which we collaborated was both relational and mindful. So, when Liz asked "…so when are you going to write the book about RM for coaches?" the natural response was to suggest we co-author. In that moment it became obvious to me that writing about RM needed to be a relational endeavour and I could not imagine anyone better than Liz with whom to write. The opportunity to engage in a collaborative exploration of the field was enormously appealing: I knew I would learn and grow in the process. It felt like the doorway to another developmental step on my journey.

Over this journey, my passion for ID and for ID-based RM has grown ever stronger. I believe that the way these dialogue practices bring together meditation, relationship and wisdom has the potential to change not only the way we coach, but all our relationships. I so want to get ID-based RM out into the world: I see the coaching community of which you, Liz, and I are a part as a starting point for making a real difference in the way people relate to one another.

Liz's story

My first encounter with mindfulness was in 1995 through a friend who witnessed my struggles as a working single mother of a young baby. I was feeling exhausted and overwhelmed as I tried to juggle meeting many different demands. Practising self-care seemed impossible – I felt I was not in a position to drop anything. However, this friend suggested I could just carry on doing whatever I felt I needed to do but in a different way – being more in the moment. I was intrigued. Could this be the answer? I was up for trying anything.

Although not formal meditation practice, this friend was inviting me to adopt a more mindful mindset – setting a conscious intention to be aware of what was happening as it unfolded, rather than fretting about the past or future. It felt very novel, and simple although not easy. Soon, however, I started to notice changes in how I was feeling and relating.

Bedtimes in particular had felt fraught; many working parents will recognise the sense of desperation one can feel when children take a long time to go to sleep. With this new approach, I now found myself being more present as I read bedtime stories or sat with my daughter while she played in the bath. I was laughing more with her, I was more patient. I was showing up more fully, and occasionally experiencing life – precious moments with my daughter – unfolding in the present moment.

I started to explore further, particularly through the lens of Buddhism, reading widely, meditating formally on a regular basis, and later participating in various programmes including in 2004–2005, a two-year *The Foundation of Buddhist Thought* course through the Jamyang Centre in London, and an eight-week Mindfulness-Based Cognitive Therapy programme at the Brighton Buddhist Centre.

Around the same time, with a background in journalism, I became the editor of a new journal on coaching, *Coaching at Work*, and trained as a coach in 2007, launching my coaching business in 2008. Mindfulness at this time was still viewed by many as a spiritual practice unsuited to the workplace, or at least merely a fringe activity. So I mostly did not mention my mindfulness practice in business circles.

I delved deeper into mindfulness including at retreats such as a number of those offered by the late Buddhist monk Thich Nhat Hanh in the UK and in Plum Village in France. And like Emma, I noticed many positive changes from having a regular mindfulness practice. I too became kinder and calmer, more aware of the patterns I hold when in relationship to others. I became more available to others, more present. I found it easier to focus at work, and better able to manage stress. In parallel, I started delving into drawing on the wisdom of the body in coaching, working with colleagues such as coach supervisor Dr Eunice Aquilina. I found adopting a somatic approach fuelled my individual mindfulness practice, building my and clients' capacity to work with the body as a crucible for transformation, to use self as instrument, including in relationships. We talk more about the role of the body in mindfulness later in the book, including in Chapter 19.

Given the benefits I was personally reaping and witnessing in clients, although at that time, the literature on mindfulness and coaching was sparse, along with others such as Emma, I was becoming increasingly convinced of the positive contribution mindfulness could make to coaches, their clients, coaching practice, and beyond.

I started carrying out research into the application of mindfulness within coaching, presenting my initial findings at the European Mentoring and Coaching Council's annual research conference in 2012. My first book, *Mindful Coaching*, was published in 2013. I trained as a mindfulness teacher at Bangor University's Centre for Mindfulness Research and Practice in Wales, and at SolTerreno in Spain, delivering Mindfulness-Based Stress Reduction programmes, and weaving mindfulness and compassion into other programmes and workshops, including leadership development for the UK National Health Service (NHS), and for coaches including through the Academy of Executive Coaching, i-coach academy, and Henley Business School.

Coaching as a profession has evolved and matured considerably since its early days. Early widespread concerns such as how mindfulness, which is primarily concerned with the here-and-now, can possibly be relevant in coaching, which for many is centred on goal-setting, no longer get aired so frequently. Many of us now embrace a 'goal-light' approach to coaching, for example, and do not focus solely on the future.

Mindfulness too – as a philosophy, a movement, an approach or set of approaches – has evolved. Whilst I was wholly convinced that there could be a positive impact on the wider system from individuals practising mindfulness, I could see this might be limited – by others' levels of emotional intelligence, maturity in terms of adult development, by organisational culture, and so on.

I became intrigued to explore with others what collective mindfulness might look like, and how we might address the potential limitations of individual mindfulness. I was part of a team at the Institute for Employment Studies collaborating with Cranfield University researching team mindfulness in the UK's Navy, and I interviewed people such as Rachel Lilley whose project with the Welsh Government explored how we might ramp up individual mindfulness within the collective (I explore both in Chapter 3).

And I came across Emma's work. I already knew of Emma as a fellow meditator who was pioneering the application of mindfulness in coaching, and colleagues spoke highly of her. When I got to know her, I understood why. Fascinated to hear about the work she was doing around RM, I participated in a masterclass Emma ran for *Coaching at Work* and commissioned her to write an inspiring and practical series on RM, which saw her win an accolade in the *Coaching at Work* annual awards in 2020 (Donaldson-Feilder, 2020a, 2020b, 2020c).

Curious to know more, I took part in a RM eight-week programme delivered by Rosalie Dores, via the Mindfulness Project in the UK, and in Emma's foundational RM for coaches programme, both online. I was hooked. I signed up for Emma's year-long RM deepening presence and awareness for coaches programme and took part in my first ID retreat with the founder of ID, Gregory Kramer, and other teachers including Emma and Rosalie. By now, I had let go of any lingering idea that having solely an individual practice was sufficient to enhance the quality of relationship and dialogue to the degree I felt was truly possible. Of course, having an individual mindfulness practice can positively impact how we interact with others. But RM takes us to a whole new and much-needed level.

Again, having experienced personally and witnessed in others the benefits of RM practice, including in coaching, I wanted to integrate this more into my own practice and spread the word so others may benefit. So, having collaborated with Emma on a few other projects, I was delighted when she suggested we co-author this book. I had a strong feeling that I would enjoy working with her, and that we would collaborate beautifully – as I have and we have. And that not only would we get a chance to share the gifts of RM, we would learn lots on the way. That has certainly been the case for me. As Brené Brown suggests in her book, *Dare to Lead* (2018), "*Write what you need to read*" (2018, p.5). With that motivation in mind, I have very much been writing what I need to read, but also what I think we all in these very difficult times need to read. And the learning goes on. Working with Emma has been a joy, with us embracing RM throughout. We set out our process below.

How we wrote this book

Our process

It felt congruent and important to both of us to put in place a process for collaboration which honoured the principles of RM. We wanted to ensure we worked in accordance with the RM foundations of awareness, compassion, and wisdom.

This included being kind to ourselves and each other about what we were able to commit to and when.

We wanted to work with the RM guidelines set out in this book (see Chapter 5). So each time we met to discuss the book, we would start by taking a pause, setting a timer for 5 minutes or so and sitting together in silence. We would then take it in turns to check in, pausing to notice and allow what was present to be there, opening to our internal experiences and to each other, attuning to what wanted to emerge, practising deep listening, and speaking our truth. Having spent time on our initial grounding and check-in in this way enabled us to bring these guidelines to our collaborative process as we worked together on the emerging project.

As we developed a book outline and worked it up into a proposal for Routledge, then started creating the manuscript itself, this mindful and relational approach made it easy to be open with one another about our wishes and concerns. Our time together felt spacious and generative. When difficulties arose, we found space to contemplate them together and invite each other's perspectives. We brought receptivity and kindness to whatever emerged and to each other. Our meetings were a chance to learn more about ourselves and each other as well as address the practicalities of who would do what and by when. Joy and mutual care arose naturally as we spent time together in this way: we felt and expressed deep gratitude for our collaboration and great appreciation for each other's contributions.

Broadening the relational input

As we developed our plans further, it became clear that the relational nature of this book was not just about our relationship with each other, but also about our relationships with other coaches who were practising RM. We are not isolated pioneers here, but part of a network of explorers engaging with RM and bringing their own perspectives and experience to the field. We connected with coaches who had been through one of our RM programmes and/or were seeing the benefits of RM for their coaching and their wider lives. Eleven of these kind people agreed to participate in our informal qualitative research (see Acknowledgements for a list of names).

Each interviewee generously gave an hour of their time to dialogue with one or both of us and share their experience of practising RM, drawing on the six RM guidelines, working with RM in their coaching, how RM had changed what they were doing/how they were being in coaching and elsewhere, the impact on their clients/others, and their views on RM's potential contribution to coaching and the wider world. These were rich and valuable conversations that provided us with new insights and data to weave into the book. Hearing about their experiences gave us even greater confidence and enthusiasm for getting this book out and spreading the word about how RM can support coaches in their work and beyond. As you will see, Chapter 6 was particularly shaped by their feedback, and their quotes, stories, and words of wisdom bring the content of the book to life. (See our dedicated website for more detail on the methodology for these interviews – link provided below.)

Why this book is important now

As is obvious from our individual stories, we both believe strongly that RM has something really important to offer to the world of coaching – and to the world more broadly. The qualities and capacities that we have seen emerge and strengthen through the RM practices, such as greater presence, awareness, empathy, compassion, understanding, and insight, are invaluable to coaches who wish to support growth and development in their clients.

We will say more about the benefits to coaches, coaching and clients in Chapter 6. At this point, we want to emphasise that we are not alone in highlighting the importance of more conscious and relational perspectives on coaching. Our exploration of applying RM in coaching is part of a building wave of writing, programmes, podcasts, and other communications that bring approaches such as dialogue, compassion, wisdom, vertical development, and relational focus to bear on what coaching is and can be (e.g. Boyatzis et al, 2019; Stelter, 2019; de Haan, 2008). We hope that this book can be a contribution to a wider movement towards greater awareness, relationality, and wisdom in coaching and in the people and communities that coaching serves.

In these challenging times of polarisation, climate emergency, health crises, and conflict, this book addresses the compelling need to create dialogue and inter-relatedness. In an organisational context, where toxic workplaces, a pandemic of mental ill health, and alienation threaten to destabilise the world of work, the book aims to offer timely support for positively transforming relationships, team dynamics, and organisational culture. Against the backdrop of continued global interest and growth in coaching and mindfulness, our intention is to support growing capability in both areas and the capacity to integrate the two with greater fluency and ease.

Given RM's foundations in the Buddhist practice of ID, we hope that this book and the practices it encourages can provide a bridge from the perennial wisdom of Buddhism to the modern world. The Buddha's teachings – around suffering, its causes, and the potential to free ourselves – are perhaps needed more than ever in the face of the consumerist, growth-seeking cultures in which so many of us are living and coaching. RM offers us the possibility of shifting how we experience the world, helping us to see more clearly and to release the constrictions and constructions that limit us, to free ourselves to live with greater compassion, care, and ease – and to help our clients do this too.

A route-map through the book

The way the book is structured is designed to take the reader on a journey. We have created a route-map – see Figure 1.1 – which aims to help you locate where you are as you progress on that journey.

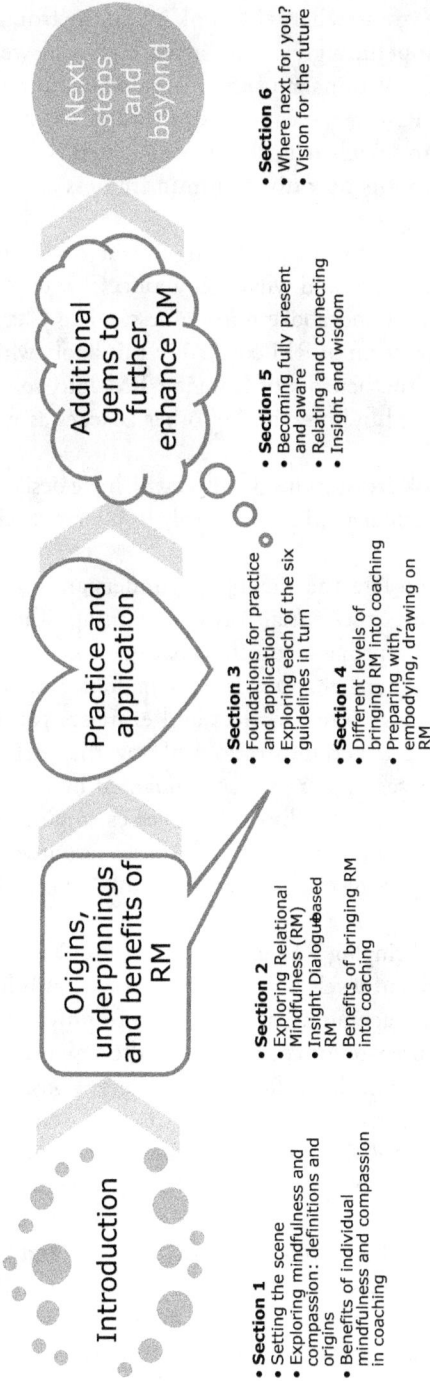

Figure 1.1 Route-map for this book.

Right now, you are in Section 1, which aims to provide an introduction to the field and orientate you to where the book is coming from. This 'Setting the scene' chapter has hopefully given you a sense of who we, the authors, are, our backgrounds, motivations, and intentions in writing the book. The next chapter aims to set RM in the context of mindfulness and compassion, on which it draws and to which it is closely connected. Chapter 3 extends this by looking at the benefits of individual mindfulness and compassion in coaching.

In Section 2, we aim to give you a grounding in where RM comes from, the foundations on which it is based and what it is about. Chapter 4 explores what RM is and what it adds over and above mindfulness, while Chapter 5 explains the origins of the particular form of RM covered in this book, which is based on ID. Chapter 6 elucidates the benefits of bringing RM into coaching, drawing on the evidence we collected by interviewing other coaches as well as our own experience.

At the heart of the book are Sections 3 and 4, which are designed to help you try out RM practices and understand how to apply it in your coaching and other relationships.

Section 3 aims to translate the theoretical understanding from the previous sections into a more experiential form of learning. The initial chapter in this section, Chapter 7, provides the foundations for practice and application of RM. The subsequent chapters from Chapters 8 to 13 take one of the guidelines each and delve into practices and exercises you can undertake yourself, together with quotes and illustrations of how this particular guideline has supported others. These chapters are accompanied by the resource sheets in Appendix 1, which provide step-by-step processes to guide your practice. We have also created an online library of audios and resources to accompany and support you on this part of the journey (available on our dedicated website – see link below).

Section 4 focusses on bringing RM into coaching. In Chapter 14, we introduce a model for the different levels of capability involved in bringing mindfulness and compassion into coaching. Chapters 15 and 16 provide suggestions and examples of how we can prepare for coaching with the support of RM and how we might embody the RM guidelines during coaching sessions. Chapter 17 goes a step further and offers illustrations for how we can offer mindfulness practices in coaching drawing on the RM guidelines. Chapter 18 rounds off this section with our thoughts on bringing elements of mindful dialogue into coaching and is accompanied by resource sheets in Appendix 2.

Section 5 takes a step back to explore how RM relates to and can be informed by other approaches and frameworks, and vice versa. It situates RM in the wider field of theory and practice, including neuroscience, and explores RM in relation to a host of other coaching models. As we mentioned, we see this book as a contribution to a much broader movement in coaching and beyond. Chapters 19–21 help illuminate this wider field and how RM fits into it.

Finally, Section 6 looks at what might lie beyond the book. In Chapter 22, we provide suggestions on how you, the reader, could take your own practice of RM further. Then in Chapter 23 we set out our vision for how RM can contribute to coaching and the wider world in the future.

Having set the scene for this book, we will now outline the mindfulness and compassion foundations on which RM is built.

References

Boyatzis, R., Smith, M., & Van Oosten, E. (2019). *Helping people change*. HBR Press.

Brown, B. (2018). *Dare to lead*. Random House.

de Haan, E. (2008). *Relational coaching*. Wiley.

Donaldson-Feilder, E. J. (2020a, March/April). Part 1. Relational mindfulness: why the enthusiasm and what is it? *Coaching at Work,* 15(2). www.coaching-at-work.com/2020/02/29/mindfulness-a-magical-shift/

Donaldson-Feilder, E. J. (2020b, May/June). Part 2. What does relational mindfulness mean for coaches, mentors and coaching supervisors? *Coaching at Work,* 15(3). www.coaching-at-work.com/2020/05/05/relational-mindfulness-part-2-an-anchored-connection/

Donaldson-Feilder, E. J. (2020c, July/August). Part 3. What does relational mindfulness mean for leadership development? *Coaching at Work*, 15(4). www.coaching-at-work.com/2020/06/29/developing-leadership/

Donaldson-Feilder, E. J., & Bond, F. W. (2004). The relative importance of psychological acceptance and emotional intelligence to workplace well-being, *British Journal of Guidance & Counselling*, 32(2), 187–203.

Donaldson-Feilder, E. J., Lewis, R., & Yarker, J. (2018/2019). What outcomes have mindfulness and meditation interventions for managers and leaders achieved? A systematic review. *European Journal of Work and Organizational Psychology*, 28(1), 11–29, published online November 2018, doi: www.tandfonline.com/doi/full/10.1080/1359432X.2018.1542379

Donaldson-Feilder, E., Lewis, R., Yarker, J., & Whiley, L. (2021/2022). Interpersonal mindfulness for managers: A Delphi Study exploring the application of interpersonal mindfulness to leadership development. *Journal of Management Education*. https://journals.sagepub.com/doi/10.1177/10525629211067183

Hall, L. (2013). *Mindful coaching*. Kogan Page.

Jamieson, S. D., & Tuckey, M. R. (2017). Mindfulness interventions in the workplace: A critique of the current state of the literature. *Journal of Occupational Health Psychology*, 22(2), 180.

Kramer, G (2007). *Insight Dialogue: The interpersonal path to freedom*. Shambhala.

Lomas, T., Medina, J. C., Ivtzan, I., Rupprecht, S., Hart, R., & Eiroa-Orosa, F. J. (2017). The impact of mindfulness on well-being and performance in the workplace: An inclusive systematic review of the empirical literature. *European Journal of Work and Organizational Psychology*, 26(4), 492–513.

Stelter, R. (2019). *The art of dialogue in coaching*. Routledge.

Information

Dedicated website accompanying this book: www.relationalmindfulness.net

Chapter 2

Exploring mindfulness and compassion

Definitions and origins

> *Do not be satisfied with the stories that come before you. Unfold your own myth.*
>
> Rumi

In this chapter, we explore the origins, definitions, and the establishment of individual mindfulness and compassion, and how mindfulness and compassion complement each other.

Origins and applications of mindfulness and compassion

Jon Kabat-Zinn is one of the leading figures responsible for mindfulness becoming more mainstream. In the late 1970s, Kabat-Zinn was working as a molecular biologist in a teaching hospital in the US. While on a meditation retreat, it dawned on Kabat-Zinn that the skills he was learning could perhaps help patients that healthcare professionals had not been able to cure. He recruited chronically ill patients who were not responding well to traditional treatments to participate in an eight-week stress-reduction programme, now called Mindfulness-Based Stress Reduction (MBSR), at the University of Massachusetts Medical Center (now UMass Memorial Health).

DOI: 10.4324/9781003390428-3

Even back then, however, Kabat-Zinn held far-reaching hopes for mindfulness: (2004): "*Meditation helps us wake up from this sleep of automaticity and unconsciousness, thereby making it possible for us to live our lives with access to the full spectrum of our conscious and unconscious possibilities*" (p.3).

The MBSR programme and many variations, including Mindfulness-Based Cognitive Therapy (MBCT), have since been rolled out all over the world including in workplace and healthcare settings (e.g. Jamieson and Tuckey, 2017). In the UK, for example, in 2022, the National Institute for Health and Care Excellence issued new guidelines on the management and treatment of depression in adults, expanding the potential application of mindfulness, including beyond the recommendation of MBCT purely as a treatment to prevent relapse in depression to also being for those currently suffering from depression.

Momentum has continued to gather in recent years, with mindfulness being adopted in sectors including education, government, and the armed forces. It has also been embraced in the world of business, such as within the technology company Google, and in coaching (e.g. Passmore & Marianetti, 2007; Spence et al, 2008; Silsbee, 2010; Hall, 2013, 2015a, 2015b, 2019; Chaskalson & McMordie, 2017). Mindfulness is increasingly included not only within coaches' toolkits of approaches to draw on with clients as appropriate, but also to help coaches become more present, for example. Mindfulness is at the core of some coaches' approaches – for example, those who draw on acceptance and commitment therapy (ACT), which is increasingly being successfully and widely adapted for coaching (Skews, in Hall, 2023), or Gestalt (we explore both in later chapters).

Compassion too is being embraced widely in secular contexts including as a core component of leadership (e.g. West, 2021), and in healthcare. Clinical psychologist Paul Gilbert has helped bring about the acceptance of compassion underpinning mental health interventions. Initially developed by Gilbert to work with clients with high shame and self-criticism, Compassion Focused Therapy (CFT) is now being used to address a range of issues including depression, and Post-Traumatic Stress Disorder. As its evidence base builds, CFT is increasingly being offered as a trans-diagnostic healthcare option in some National Health Service hospitals in the United Kingdom. And just as the acceptance of MBCT by NICE as a valid treatment option for mental health issues helped to 'legitimise' mindfulness, the growing acceptance of CFT also continues to legitimise compassion in non-spiritual quarters.

There has been an increase in the number of compassion-based initiatives in, for example, education, healthcare, and the workplace. In organisations, interest continues to grow (e.g. Atkins & Parker, 2012), such as in compassionate leadership through the Compassionate Mind Foundation, and the work of people such as Michael West (2021). Increasingly, compassion is being embraced within coaching too (e.g. Hall, 2015a; Palmer, 2009), such as with the development of Compassion-Focused Coaching (CFC) informed by CFT (Irons et al, 2018). We explore CFC and another compassion-based approach, coaching with compassion, in Chapter 20.

Nothing new

While the adoption of mindfulness and compassion development practices in the workplace is relatively recent, neither mindfulness nor compassion are new, of course. The ability to be mindful and to be compassionate are inherent human capacities, the cultivation of which have been central in many spiritual lineages, including Buddhism.

Although he was not the first spiritual teacher to recommend meditation, the roots of mindfulness as a mind-training technique – and as part of a spiritual development pathway – can be traced to the teachings of the Buddha (which means 'awakened one'), who lived some 2600 years ago in the region now known as Nepal. The word *mindfulness*, coined by Buddhist scholar T. W. Rhys Davids in 1910, comes from the Pali word *sati*, commonly defined as memory or retention.

In its original Buddhist context, as we can see in what is widely viewed as the seminal text on mindfulness in the Buddhist teachings, the *satipatthana sutta*, *sati* essentially captures a kind of present-moment awareness, a remembering of the present moment. However, there is a history of contemplation in all the major religions (not all view Buddhism as a religion – for many, it offers a secular psychological and philosophical framework).

Compassion for self and others are also core aspirations within Buddhism and being compassionate, to others at least, is central in many, if not all, world religions, including Islam, Christianity, and Judaism.

Having set the scene a little, we now explore what we mean by mindfulness and compassion.

Defining mindfulness and compassion

Many readers will already have a personal mindfulness practice, have experienced mindfulness, or at least have an idea of what is meant by mindfulness and compassion. You may be aspiring to develop compassion and, indeed, have a specific compassion development practice. However, to help orient our journey together in this book, it feels important to set out how we, the authors, understand these two fields and approaches. And we recognise some of you may be delving into mindfulness and compassion for the first time.

Defining mindfulness

One widely cited definition is that of Kabat-Zinn: "*Mindfulness means paying attention in a particular way; on purpose, in the present moment, and non-judgmentally*" (Kabat-Zinn, 2004, p.4).

Mindfulness is about waking up to "*the fact that our lives unfold only in moments*" (Kabat-Zinn, 2004, p.4). As Kabat-Zinn says (2004, p.4): "*If we are not fully present for many of those moments, we may not only miss what is most*

*valuable in our lives but also fail to realize the richness and the depth of our possibil-
ities for growth and transformation."*

Another definition of mindfulness is that of coaching researchers Cavanagh
and Spence (2013): *"A motivated state of decentred awareness brought about by
receptive attending to present moment experience."*

Mindfulness: philosophy, practice, state, or trait?

Part of the confusion around what is meant by mindfulness comes from it being
deeply experiential, but also because it can be described and expressed in a number
of ways.

Cavanagh and Spence (2013) distinguish between mindfulness as a:

- *Philosophy* (a set of beliefs about the nature of self, the world, and experience)
- *Deliberate intentional practice* (deliberate process or set of behaviours)
- *Present-moment state* (cognitive phenomena), and
- *Trait* (habitual predisposition towards experience)

Others, including Germer, Siegel and Fulton (2005) and Brown et al (2007), talk
about mindfulness as a particular state of awareness or consciousness. Brown et al
(2007) describe mindfulness as a distinctive state of consciousness which differs
from that of typical cognitive processing, with the individual allowing sensory
input, and noticing it rather than comparing, evaluating, or ruminating about it.

Brown and Ryan (2003) agree that the term mindfulness can be used to
describe a psychological trait (dispositional or trait mindfulness) which can be
measured and varies between individuals. Dispositional mindfulness is where
someone has a natural inclination towards a mindful way of being, which will
probably enhance their capacity to engage in mindfulness practices and achieve a
mindful state. Research suggests, for example, a link between dispositional mindfulness and adult attachment style, which may have implications for people's capacity for being relationally mindful. We explore attachment theory in Chapter 20.

What mindfulness looks like

Baer and colleagues (Baer et al, 2004, 2006, 2008) have identified five dimensions
of mindfulness in the development of questionnaire measures of dispositional
mindfulness:

- *Observing* (noticing internal and external stimuli)
- *Describing* (labelling one's experiences)
- *Acting with awareness* (attending fully to one's activity, without 'autopilot')
- *Non-judging* (refraining from evaluating one's experiences), and
- *Non-reacting* (experiencing one's thoughts and feelings without needing to
  immediately respond)

Attitudinal foundations for mindfulness

Kabat-Zinn (2004) identified seven core attitudes we need to cultivate in our mindfulness practice: letting go; non-judging; patience; 'beginner's mind'; trust; non-striving, and acceptance. He later added two more, gratitude, and generosity (Kabat-Zinn, accessed October 2023). Many of us seek to cultivate these in individual mindfulness practices, and with time, they become embedded. Like the RM guidelines we will set out in this book, they interweave and support one another. We will touch on these attitudes again in the next chapter on potential benefits of individual mindfulness and compassion development practice.

Next, we will explore what we mean by compassion.

Defining compassion

> *In India, they talk about the glance of mercy...that someone can look at you with such compassion for all the drama of your life, the suffering and successes and see you beyond that, and that changes everything, to see that secret beauty in another, that's all.*
>
> (Jack Kornfield, 2021)

The word compassion means 'suffering with another', stemming from the old French, meaning sympathy or pity, originating from the late Latin word *compassionem*, from the past-participle stem of *compati:* from *com* (with, together) and *pati* (to suffer) (e.g. Online Etymology Dictionary, accessed October 2023).

Gilbert (Gilbert & Choden, 2013) defines compassion as a motivation that orientates to: "...*a sensitivity to suffering in self and others with a commitment to try to alleviate and prevent it*" (p.94). Key is the wish to do something about the suffering one is faced with – our own or others.

What compassion looks like

Atkins and Parker (2012) propose that the core components of what they call 'compassionate responding' include acting, noticing, appraising, and feeling.

Taking appropriate action is one of five key attributes of a compassionate individual at work highlighted in research into compassion from leadership institute Roffey Park (Poorkavoos, 2016). The other attributes are being empathetic, being alive to the suffering of others, being non-judgemental, and tolerating personal distress.

Action taken is not always to do with others – in addition to extending compassion to others, we can extend compassion to ourselves (self-compassion) and be open to receiving compassion. Research (e.g. Jazaieri et al, 2013) has found that these three domains of compassion can be intentionally cultivated through training programmes such as the compassion cultivation training (CCT) programme developed by Thupten Jinpa and colleagues at Stanford University (Jinpa,

2015). However, some will find it easier to be compassionate than others, just as some will find it easier to be mindful, for reasons including lived experiences (we explore some approaches to understand what may be going on behind the scenes, in Chapters 19–21).

Self-compassion

Developing self-compassion tends to lead to compassion being rippled out to others. Being able to be compassionate to ourselves is also highly supportive of individual mindfulness, and Relational Mindfulness (RM), as we will explore in more depth later.

There is a large body of work focusing primarily on self-compassion, thanks to researchers such as Neff, Germer, and others.

Neff (e.g. 2015) highlights three core components in self-compassion:

- *Mindfulness*: Here it is about approaching our suffering and difficulties with awareness and acceptance, turning towards what is present rather than pushing it away
- *Self-kindness*: This is about being gentle and kind with ourselves as best we can, seeking to avoid being harsh, judgemental, and critical. As Neff says (2015, p.42), self-kindness

    "*means we stop the constant self-judgment and disparaging internal commentary that most of us have come to see as normal. It requires us to understand our foibles and failures instead of condemning them. It entails clearly seeing the extent to which we harm ourselves through relentless self-criticism, and ending our internal war.*"

    It is about enhancing our capacity to be kind to ourselves around what is tough, making space for it, reducing critical self-talk, and boosting kindly self-talk and self-care. It involves actively comforting ourselves, being in relationship with the suffering part or parts within us
- *Common humanity*: Self-compassion invites us to feel into our connection with others, knowing that we all suffer, accessing what it truly means to be a human being rather than feeling isolated and unique in our suffering. This aspect of self-compassion, in particular, offers a bridge into the relational sphere

Heartfulness: mindfulness and compassion as perfect companions

So far, we have explored separately what we mean by mindfulness and by compassion, and how we might these as traits. However, they are closely related. Compassion, or at least caring, is often implicit in mindfulness development for many people. Shapiro and Carlson (2009), for example, see mindfulness as the awareness that arises through intentionally attending in an open, caring, and discerning way, while Kabat-Zinn (2004, p.7) stresses that *"the overall tenor of mindfulness practice is gentle, appreciative and nurturing. Another way to think of it would be 'heartfulness.'"*

Much of the literature on mindfulness, including Buddhist literature, prescribes developing compassion, or qualities of kindliness, alongside mindfulness, seeing these as interdependent and as balancing one another (e.g. Brach, 2003; Germer & Siegel, 2012).

Many traditional MBSR and MBCT programmes, including workplace mindfulness-based interventions, do not teach compassion development *per se*, but do refer to kindliness. For both of us, our mindfulness practice has always included an aspiration to develop compassion for self and others. This aspiration has been fostered by our exposure to Buddhist teachings, but also by our personal experiences in our practice. The more we practise mindfulness, the more we feel kindly towards ourselves and others, more forgiving, more loving, more compassionate towards self and fellow beings, which enriches our coaching practice.

We are not alone – practising mindfulness can often lead naturally to the development of compassion, even if that is not an explicit intention. Research shows that mindfulness training increases self-compassion (e.g. Birnie et al, 2010; Shapiro et al, 2007) and compassion generally (e.g. Atkins & Parker, 2012; Lutz et al, 2008; Atkins, 2013). And the research summarised in the Mindfulness Initiative's reports (Bristow et al, 2020; Ormston & Bristow, 2023) highlights how mindfulness training promotes the conditions for both empathy and compassion including through regulating attention, reducing automatic judgement, encouraging perspective-taking and engaging a receptive attitude towards others.

While compassion and mindfulness are naturally linked, it is possible to generate one without the other; however, there are risks to developing either in isolation. For example, we can develop our 'muscles' of attentional control and decentred awareness without actively seeking to cultivate compassion. Type-A, highly driven, and competitive individuals, for example, may pick up mindfulness as an effective technique to help them become more focused and achieve more at work, but they risk becoming more competitive and ruthless or burnt out. In addition, practising mindfulness helps us shine a spotlight on whatever we choose to focus on. This typically includes physical sensations and emotions and may reveal the current impact of past challenging experiences, for example. This can be painful and may even come as a surprise.

We can benefit from the softening nurturing energy of compassion to help us avoid either worsening our situation or becoming more critical of ourselves or others.

As Brach (2003, p.29) says, *"Instead of pushing away or judging our anger or despondency, compassion enables us to be softly and kindly present with our open wounds."*

We can also have compassion without mindfulness. A parent instinctively seeking to rescue their child from their burning home may be profoundly motivated by compassion, but may not be mindful in their endeavours. In emergency situations, this may be appropriate and wise behaviour. However, in lower-stakes situations, compassion without mindfulness can lead to 'idiot compassion' where we lack the clarity to determine what is helpful versus what is unhelpful, over-indulgent, or unboundaried. And if we try to be self-compassionate without the clarity of mindfulness, we may tip into self-indulgence. Mindfulness helps us be discerning in our compassion. To quote Brach again (2003, p.29) *"If our heartfelt caring begins to bleed over into self-pity, giving rise to another story line – we tried so hard but didn't get what we so dearly wanted – mindfulness enables us to see the trap we're falling into."*

Thus, mindfulness and compassion support one another and combine to help us develop more fully. Quoting Gilbert and Choden again (2013, p.181):

> *Both mindfulness and compassion are vital to the process of growth and transformation, but while mindfulness is the servant of the awakening heart of compassion, it is the force of compassionate motivation that reorganizes the mind and sets in motion lasting change.*

For all the reasons set out above, it can be fruitful to explicitly seek to develop both mindfulness and compassion, which can give birth to wisdom – in Buddhist traditions such as Tibetan Buddhism, wisdom and compassion are seen as interrelated, as 'two wings of a bird.'

In the next chapter we will delve more deeply into the potential benefits of cultivating mindfulness and compassion.

References

Atkins, P. W. (2013). Empathy, self-other differentiation, and mindfulness training. In *Organizing through empathy*, 49–70. Routledge.

Atkins, P. W. B., & Parker, S. K. (2012). Understanding individual compassion in organizations: The role of appraisals and psychological flexibility. *Academy of Management Review*, 37(4), 524–546.

Baer, R. A., Smith, G. T., & Allen, K. B. (2004) Assessment of mindfulness by self-report the Kentucky Inventory of Mindfulness Skills. *Assessment*, 11(3), 191–206. doi: 10.1177/1073191104268029.

Baer, R. A., Smith, G. T., Hopkins, J., Krietemeyer, J., & Toney, L. (2006). Using self-report assessment methods to explore facets of mindfulness. *Assessment*, 13(1), 27–45. doi: 10.1177/1073191105283504

Baer, R. A., Smith, G. T., Lykins, E., Button, D., Krietemeyer, J., Sauer, S., & Williams, J. M. G. (2008). Construct validity of the five facet mindfulness questionnaire in meditating and nonmeditating samples. *Assessment*, 15(3), 329–342. doi: 10.1177/1073191107313003.

Birnie, K., Speca, M., & Carlson, L. E. (2010). Exploring self-compassion and empathy in the context of mindfulness-based stress reduction (MBSR). *Stress and Health*, 26(5), 359–371.

Brach, T. (2003). *Radical acceptance: Awakening the love that heals fear and shame within us.* Random House.

Bristow, J., Bell, R., Nixon, D. (2020). Mindfulness: developing agency in urgent times. The Mindfulness Initiative.

Brown, K. W., & Ryan, R. M. (2003). The benefits of being present: mindfulness and its role in psychological well-being. *Journal of Personality and Social Psychology*, 84, 822–848. doi: 10.1037/0022-3514.84.4.822

Brown, K. W., Ryan, R. M., & Creswell, J. D. (2007). Mindfulness: Theoretical foundations and evidence for its salutary effects. *Psychological Inquiry*, *18*(4), 211–237.

Cavanagh, M. J., & Spence, G. B. (2013). Mindfulness in coaching: Philosophy, psychology or just a useful skill. In *The Wiley-Blackwell handbook of the psychology of coaching and mentoring*, 112–134. John Wiley & Sons.

Chaskalson, M., & McMordie, M. (2017). *Mindfulness for coaches: An experiential guide.* Routledge.

Germer, C. K., & Siegel, R. D. (Eds.). (2012). *Wisdom and compassion in psychotherapy: Deepening mindfulness in clinical practice.* Guilford Press.

Germer, C. K., Siegel, R. D., & Fulton, P. R. (2005). *Mindfulness and psychotherapy.* Guilford Press.

Gilbert, P., & Choden. (2013). *Mindful compassion.* Constable & Robinson.

Hall, L. (2013). *Mindful coaching: How mindfulness can transform coaching practice.* Kogan Page Publishers.

Hall, L. (2015a). Nourishing the lotus flower: Turning towards and transforming difficulties with Mindful Compassionate Coaching. In *Coaching in Times of Crisis and Transition*, 192–221. Kogan Page Publishers.

Hall, L. (2015b), Mindfulness in coaching. In J. Reb & P. W. Atkins (Eds.), *Mindfulness in organizations: Foundations, research, and applications*, 383–408. Cambridge University Press.

Hall, L. (2019). *Coach your team.* Penguin UK.

Hall, L. (2023), ACT-based coaching supports goal attainment. *Coaching at Work*, 1(18), 9. www.coaching-at-work.com/2023/01/01/act-based-coaching-supports-goal-attainment/

Irons, C., Palmer, S., & Hall, L. (2018). Compassion focused coaching. In *Handbook of coaching psychology*, 206–216. Routledge.

Jamieson, S. D., & Tuckey, M. R. (2017). Mindfulness interventions in the workplace: A critique of the current state of the literature. *Journal of Occupational Health Psychology*, 22(2), 180.

Jazaieri, H., Jinpa, G. T., McGonigal, K., Rosenberg, E. L., Finkelstein, J., Simon-Thomas, E., Cullen, M., Doty, J. R., Gross, J. J., & Goldin, P. R. (2013). Enhancing compassion: A randomized controlled trial of a compassion cultivation training program. *Journal of Happiness Studies*, 14, 1113–1126.

Jinpa, T. (2015). *A fearless heart: Why compassion is the key to greater wellbeing.* Hachette UK.

Kabat-Zinn, J. (2004). *Wherever you go, there you are: Mindfulness meditation for everyday life* (retitled edition, original edition, 1994). Piatkus.

Kabat-Zinn, J. (2023, October). 9 Attitudes of mindfulness by Jon Kabat-Zinn. https://mbsrtraining.com/attitudes-of-mindfulness-by-jon-kabat-zinn/ (accessed October 2023).

Kornfield, J. (2021). 2021 Compassion in Therapy Summit, in the pain and reward of compassion. *Coaching at Work*, May/June 2021.

Lutz, A., Brefczynski-Lewis, J., Johnstone, T., & Davidson, R. J. (2008). Regulation of the neural circuitry of emotion by compassion meditation: Effects of meditative expertise. *PLoS One*, 3(3), e1897.

Neff, K. (2015). *Self compassion- stop beating yourself up and leave insecurity behind.* Yellow Kite Books (Hodder & Stoughton).

Online Etymology Dictionary. (2023). Compassion. www.etymonline.com/word/compassion (Accessed October 2023)

Ormston, R., Bristow, J. (2023). *Mindfulness in Westminster: Reflections from UK Politicians.* The Mindfulness Initiative.

Palmer, S. (2009). Compassion-focused imagery for use within compassion focused coaching. *Coaching Psychology International*, 2, 2.

Passmore, J., & Marianetti, O. (2007). The role of mindfulness in coaching. *The Coaching Psychologist*, 3(3), 131–138.

Poorkavoos, M. (2016). *Compassionate leadership: What is it and why do organisations need more of it*, 1–16. Roffey Park Institute.

Shapiro, S. L., Brown, K. W., & Biegel, G. M. (2007). Teaching self-care to caregivers: Effects of mindfulness-based stress reduction on the mental health of therapists in training. *Training and Education in Professional Psychology*, 1(2), 105.

Shapiro, S. L., & Carlson, L. E. (2009). *The art and science of mindfulness: Integrating mindfulness into psychology and the helping professions.* American Psychological Association.

Silsbee, D. (2010). *The mindful coach: Seven roles for facilitating leader development.* John Wiley & Sons.

Spence, G. B., Cavanagh, M. J., & Grant, A. M. (2008). The integration of mindfulness training and health coaching: An exploratory study. *Coaching: An International Journal of Theory, Research and Practice*, 1(2), 145–163.

West, M. A. (2021). *Compassionate leadership: Sustaining wisdom, humanity and presence in health and social care.* Swirling Leaf Press.

Chapter 3

The benefits of individual mindfulness and compassion in coaching

Yesterday I was clever so I wanted to change the world. Today I am wise, so I am changing myself.

Rumi

Scientific research has documented significant positive effects arising from practising individual mindfulness and compassion, not just for ourselves but those around us and beyond. In this chapter, we explore some benefits of relevance for coaching.

Research background

Since the early 2000s, research into mindfulness has been growing exponentially, including in the field of neuroscience. Much of the research on the impact of individual mindfulness practice has been carried out among participants on mindfulness programmes such as mindfulness-based stress reduction (MBSR), which have often included some form of compassion training. However, there has also been rapid growth in the scientific study of the impact of interventions and practices specifically focused on compassion cultivation.

The literature on the benefits of mindfulness in coaching is still relatively sparse although it is growing, with contributors including Hall (2013, 2015,

DOI: 10.4324/9781003390428-4

2019), Chaskalson and McMordie (2017), Cavanagh and Spence (2013), Silsbee (2010), Passmore and Marianetti (2007), Spence et al (2008), and Adamson and Brendgen (2021). There is also a growing body of literature exploring the benefits of compassion in coaching such as Irons et al (2018), and Boyatzis and colleagues (e.g Boyatzis & McKee, 2005, Boyatzis et al, 2019).

Given the extent and rigour of research into mindfulness and compassion in other disciplines and arenas, we will extrapolate implications for coaching from this broader research, rather than limit ourselves to the literature specifically on coaching and mindfulness and compassion.

If we look at the research in general, we can conclude that developing mindfulness and compassion can lead to benefits such as improvements in physical and psychological health, increased emotional intelligence, and better performance and productivity. There is often a link between different benefits, as they frequently support and amplify each other. Increasing emotional intelligence, for example, supports greater wellbeing and vice versa, including through increased self-awareness and self-regulation, which support both. Practising mindfulness and compassion can literally rewire our brains (see Box 3.1).

Box 3.1 The impact of mindfulness and compassion on our brains

The research suggests that individual mindfulness meditation practice:

- Increases activity and grey matter in the anterior cingulate cortex (ACC) and mid-cingulate cortex, cortical regions involved in attention regulation, emotion regulation, pain control, and self-control (Fox et al, 2014; Tang et al, 2015)
- Impacts the rostrolateral prefrontal cortex: a region associated with meta-awareness (awareness of thinking), introspection, and processing of complex, abstract information (Fox et al, 2014)
- Increases cortical thickness (Lazar et al, 2005) and greater grey matter concentration in the right anterior insula (Hölzel et al, 2008), part of the brain area which processes tactile information such as touch, pain, conscious proprioception (awareness of the position and movement of the body), and awareness of body sensations, thus improving capacity to pay attention to sensory experience
- Impacts the default mode networks, including the ACC, the ventro-medial prefrontal cortex, and posterior cingulate cortex, a region associated with emotion regulation and meta-awareness (the ability to observe thoughts, feelings, sensations, and impulses), introspection, and self-referential processing (reflections on personal identity) (Tang et al, 2015)

- Impacts the amygdalae – two almond-shaped brain structures associated with processing emotional stimuli and linking them to learning and memory. In regular meditators, the right amygdala (which responds immediately to perceived threats, sometimes creating an 'emotional hijack') becomes less active and has less grey matter density (Goleman, 2020)

Compassion cultivation training for individuals:

- Leads to activation across seven broad regions with wide-ranging functions, with the largest peaks in the:
  - periaqueductal grey matter, involved in autonomic function, motivated behaviour, and behavioural responses to threatening stimuli
  - anterior insula, which plays a core role in supporting subjective feeling states, and can regulate the introduction of feelings into cognitive and motivational processes
  - ACC, implicated in decision-making and evaluation processes, emotional regulation, preparation for tasks, error detection, and executive functions
  - inferior frontal gyrus, involved in language processing (Kim et al, 2020)
- Boosts altruism, with greater altruistic behaviour potentially emerging from increased engagement of neural systems implicated in understanding others' suffering, executive and emotional control, and reward processing, including:
  - altered activation in brain regions implicated in social cognition and emotion regulation, including the inferior parietal cortex and dorsolateral prefrontal cortex (DLPFC)
  - increased DLPFC connectivity with the nucleus accumbens (Weng et al, 2013)

Looking specifically at coaching-relevant benefits of mindfulness and compassion, in the following sections we will explore how mindfulness and compassion enrich our relationships and relational capabilities such as self-awareness and self-regulation, regulating nervous system activity, building trust and psychological safety, and attentional control. There are many other potential benefits which may positively impact relationships too, albeit indirectly, including boosting ethical behaviour, accessing meaning and purpose, shifting our relationship to goals, opening to emergence, and allowing creativity. However, we will stick to those which impact relationships more directly.

Relational benefits of individual mindfulness and compassion in coaching

Better relationships

As coaches, we know how important the relationship with our client is. Research carried out in the therapeutic arena points to the importance of the quality of the relationship – the working alliance – for successful outcomes (Ahn & Wampold, 2001). The same research suggested that when it comes to different theoretical approaches, none is better than the other in terms of effectiveness. Instead, the quality of the relationship seems to be a magic common ingredient. While research into coaching is at an earlier stage, it seems fair to assume that the relationship between coach and client is vital to successful coaching outcomes too.

As de Haan (2008, p.vi) says,

> *the most important effective ingredients are the capacity for learning of the persons conducting the conversation and the quality of the relationship between the interlocutors…how can we as coaches make the best possible use of the only genuinely effective ingredient that we are able to influence, the coaching relationship?*

For us, the answer to de Haan's question above is simple: draw extensively (although of course, not solely) on mindfulness and compassion – as a philosophy, practice, state, and trait (Cavanagh & Spence, 2013)!

Mindfulness and compassion's contribution

Improved relationships are a common benefit reported by those receiving mindfulness training (e.g. Allen et al, 2009; Bihari & Mullan, 2014; Rupprecht et al, 2019; Bristow et al, 2020). Studies from Allen et al (2009) suggest that mindfulness training leads to better communication, greater emotional closeness with friends and family, relating more constructively, reduced anger, and increased empathy. Mindfulness training has been found to increase forgiveness (Karremans et al, 2020) and reduce discrimination (Lueke & Gibson, 2016), and to increase conflict resolution (Alkoby et al, 2017). Mindfulness can help us become generally more emotionally intelligent (e.g. Chu, 2010; Cresswell et al, 2007; Lazar et al, 2005) which can in turn reduce workplace conflict (Boyatzis & McKee, 2005; Creswell et al, 2007).

Two studies carried out within government point too to the positive impact of mindfulness on relationships. The first Mindfulness Initiative report (Ormston & Bristow, 2023) highlighted that UK politicians trained in individual mindfulness experienced improved interpersonal relationships both within and outside of parliament and government, including more effective communication with constituents, colleagues, and family, more attentive listening and more empathy towards mental health concerns. Practising mindfulness and sharing experiences within a group appears to foster an environment in which politicians viewed each other more often as 'human beings', regardless of political affiliation.

The second study also saw individual mindfulness shift the nature of relationship, increasing connection and awareness, as well as supporting leaders to make complex decisions (Hall, 2019; Lilley et al, 2022). Between 2013 and 2019, more than 200 employees from the Welsh Government, including middle managers and senior civil servants, were trained in mindfulness and explored learning theories relating to emotion and cognition (including how these are not separable), decision-making and behavioural economics. Realising that they had incorrectly been making assumptions that others were seeing information in the same way as them, the participants started to listen more closely to one another, enhancing relationships and performance.

Compassion too improves the quality of relationships. Neff and colleagues (Neff et al, 2007, Neff & Germer, 2013) showed that self-compassion boosts happiness, optimism, and relationship satisfaction, while Dutton et al (2007) found that higher levels of compassion at work promote healing and build quality relationships, creating and building relational resources such as trust, and strengthening shared values of interconnectedness.

Next, we explore some of the ways in which mindfulness and compassion enhance relational capabilities of potential benefit in coaching, starting with increasing self-awareness and self-regulation.

Self-awareness

Many coaching clients will come to us seeking to increase self-awareness, and better harness the fruits of self-understanding. And we know as coaches that being highly self-aware is important for us to coach well. However, we all have blind spots, and risk getting caught by unconscious unhelpful patterns. Research (e.g. Brown et al, 2007) shows mindfulness grows self-awareness.

Broadly speaking, self-awareness is about the extent to which people are consciously aware of their internal states and their interactions or relationships with others (e.g. Sutton, 2016). Within that, we have *situational* self-awareness, an automatic process by which we compare our current actions to our internalised standards, making changes where necessary to reduce inconsistency (Silvia & Duval, 2001) and *dispositional* self-awareness, the trait-like tendency to focus on and reflect on personal psychological processes and inner experiences as well as relationships to others (Fenigstein et al, 1975).

Dispositional self-awareness can sometimes lead to rumination on negative self-perceptions. Rumination is associated with impaired interpersonal skills and increased negative affect, whereas reflection is associated with improved interpersonal skills (Takano et al, 2011). So, in coaching, we want to encourage reflection rather than rumination, and mindfulness can help grow attention to the present moment with an awareness that does not seek to react to or classify experience (Brown & Ryan, 2003). Sutton (2016) highlights this element of a receptive attitude as helpful in differentiating between mindfulness and other forms of self-awareness.

Mindfulness practice helps us recognise and disengage from our automatic thoughts and behaviour patterns. It helps us avoid being carried away into rumination and flights of potentially unhelpful fantasy, which can make it hard to be authentic, to stay present and connected with others, as well as being detrimental to our wellbeing. Mindfulness fosters more informed and conscious regulation which promotes positive functioning (Ryan & Deci, 2000) and improves connection with ourselves and others.

More choice

Increased awareness means more choice around what we pay attention to and how we respond. Mindfulness and compassion help us spot if/when we are, or a client is, struggling so we/they can respond accordingly in a kindly and wise manner. By enhancing interoceptive attention (awareness of what goes in our body), mindfulness helps us be more flexible in our cognitive appraisals, building capacity to reappraise adverse experiences and savour positive experiences (Garland et al, 2015). It helps us pick up early warning health-related signals from our body, and generally helps us tap into our body's wisdom. We explore tapping into somatic wisdom in the context of coaching and relationships in Chapter 19.

Practising mindfulness as coaches will help us deepen our self-awareness, which will benefit us, our clients, and the relationship. The more we embody mindful presence, the more we can role model and draw on our growing self-awareness in the moment in a coaching session, allowing us to offer potentially useful data to clients, for example, sharing what we might be noticing in ourselves when we think it may be the client's material.

Self-regulation

Self-awareness and self-regulation go hand-in-hand. Much coaching work is around helping clients self-regulate better as well as being more self-aware. As Cavanagh and Spence (2013, p.113) say, "*Coaching is fundamentally concerned with the enhancement of human self-regulation… The more detailed our understanding of mindfulness, the more effective we can be in using it to enhance our client's capacity to self-regulate.*" Perhaps a client has received poor feedback about how they are showing up at work, and recognise they need to be less reactive, for example, but they are not sure how. And to be an effective coach, we must get pretty good at self-regulation ourselves.

As Cavanagh and Spence (2013) point out, emotional reactivity is associated with a passive stance towards consciousness, where the person experiences themself as 'subject to' their perceptions. The emotions that arise from these perceptions are experienced as automatic and unchangeable. Mindfulness seemingly reduces emotional and behavioural reactivity, supporting adaptive, goal-directed self-regulation (e.g. Schultz & Ryan, 2015; Spence et al, 2008). With mindfulness, we aim to monitor rather than control the content of our minds, making it adaptive rather than maladaptive (Teasdale, 1999), supporting greater self-regulation. The decentred awareness of experience associated with mindfulness enables the individual to make their perceptions an *object* of attention, rather than being *subject* to them. Compassion too can improve emotion regulation (e.g. Diedrich et al, 2014).

Becoming aware of what is happening within, with a shift in subject–object relationship, allows people to opt to respond from a wiser, calmer place rather than simply react. This is a huge advantage when it comes to relationships, as well as improving health and wellbeing. The better we become at this as coaches, the greater will be our capacity to self-regulate, embody and role-model this for our clients, and support them to regulate their emotions. In these times we live in, this can be a huge gift.

Linked to self-awareness and self-regulation, understanding what goes on in our nervous system when we are triggered can be helpful for us and our clients, which we explore next.

Regulating nervous system activity

Mindfulness and compassion practice can reduce activity in brain areas related to the threat response, reactivating nervous system functions that relax the body after a period of stress and danger (e.g. Dutcher et al, 2021). Both practices activate the parasympathetic nervous system (PNS), counterbalancing the sympathetic nervous system, which helps us respond to threats through 'fighting or fleeing.' The PNS is in part to do with our 'rest and digest' relaxation response (although it also has another function – our capacity to 'freeze' or 'play dead' when under threat).

Fight, flight, or freeze are involuntary survival strategies in reaction to stress triggers. They have helped us survive as a species, but are not always helpful when coping with everyday stresses, and can be detrimental to our health and well-being, and our relationships, including in coaching.

Often our bodies do not get the time they need to return to the restorative rest and digest state, resulting in chronic stress leading to unhealthily high levels of cortisol and elevated heart rate over long periods of time. Our thinking becomes disordered and we experience perceptual narrowing (Weltman et al, 1971). When we are in fight–flight mode, we are more likely to react rather than respond from a place of choice, and we tend to be less empathic and less open to others' points of view. We become 'had by our experience' rather than 'having our experiences', get lost in our reactivity, and lose our sense of groundedness.

Mindfulness can help to lessen habitual impulsive tendencies to react, such as 'fight' or 'freeze.' The second study by the Mindfulness Initiative (Ormston & Bristow, 2023), for example, found that politicians who have undertaken mindfulness training report a reduction in such impulsions, which enhances their steadiness in the face of challenges and their capacity to keep an open mind on issues of complexity and helps them to navigate disagreement in a manner more conducive to active listening.

Mindfulness and compassion can increase our emotional bandwidth and repertoire, widening our 'window of tolerance' (Siegel, 2010) – the range of intensities of emotional experience we can process and integrate. If we or our clients find ourselves outside of our window of tolerance, we will be either hypo-aroused, where we may feel empty, flat, disconnected, and appear withdrawn and hard to reach, or hyper-aroused, where we may feel anxious, overwhelmed, fearful, and appear obsessive, or aggressive. Neither is supportive of the type of relationships we want in coaching.

Staying within our window of tolerance is important as coaches so we can avoid tipping into emotional and physical distress, remaining instead available to our clients and able to think clearly. It is therefore beneficial as coaches to widen this window if we can, for example, through mindfulness and compassion, to increase the range of emotions we can be with, including those we would perhaps rather push away. There is an argument that we can only coach as far as we have gone ourselves (emotionally), and that we 'coach from our wounds.' We can draw on mindfulness and compassion to build our emotional range by learning to notice, manage, and communicate our emotions, to feel safe in our body, and identify our triggers so we can up- or down-regulate when needed.

Holding the space mindfully for our clients, so that our regulated nervous system supports theirs to regulate, and being able to point clients to resources or directly impart mindfulness/compassion practices as part of our coaching offer, can be profoundly helpful for clients who are struggling. Being equipped to attend to clients' health and wellbeing in coaching has become increasingly important. Mental ill-health is on the rise, meaning coaches arguably do not have the luxury they perhaps once had of refusing to work with issues of health and wellbeing. We believe coaches need to be more psychologically informed than perhaps they have traditionally been expected to be, with an understanding of how human brains work and how to support greater mental health, and perhaps physical health to some degree too, as these are closely linked.

It is of course important to attend to our own health and wellbeing as coaches. Being resourceful, resilient, and well, so we can support our clients, requires us as coaches to attend to our own self-care, to recognise our own warning bells when it comes to personal health and wellbeing, and to take appropriate action to maintain our wellbeing. We need to take responsibility for our interior landscape and condition. As Bill O'Brien, the late CEO of Hanover Insurance (in Scharmer, 2009, p.27), so clearly said, "*The success of an intervention depends on the interior condition of the intervenor.*"

Mindfulness practice enhances presence, attunement (which we explore again in Chapter 19), and empathy (e.g. Shapiro et al, 1998; Shapiro et al, 2005). As coaches, cultivating mindfulness and compassion helps us become a more finely tuned 'self-as-instrument', better at being present, attuned, and resonant with our clients, and more able to meet them where they are.

Trust, psychological safety, and emotions

Mindfulness and compassion also support our capacity to cultivate trust and psychological safety (see Chapter 19). For example, research in the healthcare sector finds that patient perception of physicians' compassion levels is associated with higher trust in the physician (Kim et al, 2004; Weiss et al, 2017). Although concerned with the alliance between doctor and patient, these studies highlight the potential for compassion to strengthen the quality of relationship, including building trust, between coach and client too.

Developing a basic trust in ourselves and our feelings is an integral part of mindfulness training, and trust is one of the core attitudinal foundations for mindfulness. We start with trusting ourselves, building up to trusting others. As Kabat-Zinn (2004, pp.36–37), says,

> In practising mindfulness, you are practising taking responsibility for being yourself and learning to listen to and trust your own being. The more you cultivate this trust in your own being, the easier you will find it will be to trust other people more and to see their basic goodness as well.

Building trust and psychological safety requires changing our relationship with emotions. There is somewhat of a paradox here when it comes to the potential impact of mindfulness and compassion on how we deal with emotions. Yes, they can help us be less emotionally reactive, and at the same time they help us get more in touch with a wider range of emotions – 'positive' and 'negative' emotions.

A note here to readers: much of the literature, including on mindfulness and compassion, uses the terms 'positive' and 'negative' emotions. So we too will use these terms. However, we do not believe there is such a thing as a positive or a negative emotion. All emotions have their part to play, they mobilise energy and they are messengers. Failing to make space for certain emotions, pushing them away, refusing to acknowledge they exist, can lead to poor health and wellbeing, and poorer relationships. That said, let us now explore the role of so-called positive and negative emotions.

Positive emotions

Mindfulness increases our capacity to experience positive emotions (e.g. Lindsay et al, 2018; Frederickson et al, 2017; Garland et al, 2015), as does compassion (e.g. Förster & Kanske, 2022; Frederickson et al, 2017; Jazaieri et al, 2014).

Building our capacity to experience positive emotions promotes greater health and wellbeing, and better relationships. Frederickson and colleagues highlight how increasing positive emotion helps us flourish, supporting wellbeing, enhancing creativity, and increasing interpersonal resonance (e.g. Frederickson, 2013, see Chapter 19).

Tapping into positive emotions such as hope and optimism in coaching helps clients draw on their sense of self-efficacy, in addition to helping to build resonant relationships anchored in presence and attunement. Research by Boyatzis and colleagues (see Chapter 19), which has included longitudinal studies about behaviour change and almost 20 years of hormonal and neuroimaging studies, has highlighted the importance of harnessing mindfulness, compassion, and hope in anchoring clients in positive emotions which boost their capacity to change.

To quote Boyatzis et al (2019, p.45):

> *When we use a compassionate approach to help people move forward toward a self-defined ideal image of their future, our research shows they'll likely change in a sustainable way – far more than when they are told or feel they have to change… The key here is that the desire to motivation for change has to outweigh the obligation or motivation.*

Negative emotions

Also important for relationships, as well as health and wellbeing, is being able to navigate 'difficult' emotions. Mindfulness helps us be more accepting, reducing unhelpful emotional sensitivity (e.g. Cavanagh & Spence, 2013) and emotion suppression. People with higher levels of self-compassion are significantly less likely to suppress unwanted thoughts and emotions than those who lack self-compassion, and more likely to accept the validity of their feelings (Neff, 2003).

As Neff (2011, p.117) says, "*the beauty of self-compassion is that instead of replacing negative feelings with positive ones, new positive emotions are generated by embracing the negative ones. The positive emotions of care and connectedness are felt alongside our painful feelings.*"

Research by Jazaieri and colleagues among people who have engaged in compassion cultivation training (CCT) (Jazaieri et al, 2014; Jazaieri et al, 2018) also points to this aspect of compassion. They found that not only did CCT participants experience less anxiety, and more calmness, they were more likely to choose to accept experiences of stress and anxiety, and less likely to seek to hold onto other affective experiences.

Bringing mindfulness and compassion into our coaching will support us to build a psychologically safe coaching environment and build trust with the client. By being more skilful around 'positive' and 'negative' emotions ourselves, we can support clients to do the same.

Cavanagh and Spence (2013) point to the combination of reduced emotional sensitivity and greater attentional control that comes from developing mindfulness as being what potentially helps coaches and clients self-regulate. Next, we explore the latter.

Attentional control

Our ability to select and retain information requires attention control and 'working memory', the brain system that temporarily stores and manipulates information necessary for complex cognitive tasks such as decision-making, communicating, and guiding behaviour (Williams, 2018; Baddeley, 1992). Attention is a limited resource and in these times, for many of us, there are unprecedented demands on our attention.

Over time, chronic stress depletes working memory and increases the likelihood of intrusive thoughts, poor mood, psychological disorders, and performance errors (Jha et al, 2017). High stress levels also impair long-term, explicit memory (Sandi, 2013). Chronic stress and anxiety can lead to perceptual narrowing, meaning we miss important information on the sidelines (Prinet & Sarter, 2015), including in our coaching relationships. There is an implication here when it comes to self-care. At times when we or our clients have more on our plate, we might want to step up the amount of individual mindfulness practice even if this is counter-intuitive. As the Zen saying goes, *"You should sit in meditation for 20 minutes a day. Unless you're too busy, then you should sit for an hour."*

Individual mindfulness practice enhances 'executive control' (Cásedas et al, 2020), an ability that is vital for intellectual performance. Training the 'muscle of attention' through mindfulness helps us choose and control more easily where we place our attention, and to redirect our attention when we feel it is appropriate, including in relationship with others.

As Bristow et al (2020) point out, attention is vulnerable to capture from within, as well as from outside. We easily drift into 'autopilot', carrying out activities automatically and engaging in excessive mind-wandering. We spend about half of our waking life in mind-wandering (Killingsworth & Gilbert, 2010) – too much can lead to excessive rumination, rehearsal, and worry, so again, there are mental health implications. However, mindfulness' potential for reducing mind-wandering is important for coaching relationships too, helping us stay present to what is here in the moment, the person we are with, ourselves, and the relationship in between, and more able to listen deeply.

Greater attention control can also enable healthier use of technology, which in turn can have a profound impact on our relationships – most of us know only too well how addiction to smartphones can hinder connection, for example. Those who are typically more mindful tend to be more able to withstand the temptation to mindlessly browse social media (Reina & Kudesia, 2020). As coaches, we are not immune to unhealthy attachment to technology, which can negatively impact our coaching efficacy and relationships.

So, looking at all the research, individual mindfulness and compassion practices appear to have a lot to offer coaches and their clients. The thesis of this book is that Relational Mindfulness (RM) takes mindfulness and compassion to a whole new level, offering great benefits. However, before we move on to explore RM in more detail, we would like to note potential risks associated with individual mindfulness and compassion.

Potential risks of mindfulness and compassion

We are passionate advocates of mindfulness and compassion, and we hope the research highlights we have included above compellingly point to the impressive range of potential positive applications. However, we do not believe mindfulness and compassion are panaceas for all and it would feel remiss to not mention some potential risks associated with cultivating mindfulness and/or compassion, in addition to those we highlighted in Chapter 2 when we explored the need for cultivating both together.

Risks to individual practitioners

Willoughby Britton is known for her research into the possible negative effects of meditation. As a clinician, she trained as an instructor in MBSR and mindfulness-based cognitive therapy (MBCT) and has taught mindfulness to clinical and non-clinical populations. However, she now specialises, including through non-profit organisation Cheetah House, in helping meditators experiencing meditation-related difficulties, providing meditation safety training, and disseminating information on potential risks associated with meditation.

Britton and colleagues' ten-year study (Lindahl et al, 2017) on the varieties of contemplative experience (VCE) investigates the full range of experiences that can arise with contemplative practices, including those that could be considered difficult, challenging, or adverse. It is the most comprehensive research study on meditation-related challenges and adverse effects to date, drawing on more than 100 interviews with Western Buddhist meditators and teachers to create a taxonomy of phenomenology, influencing factors and remedies.

Positive effects included enhanced meta-cognition, increased cognitive processing, and greater clarity. Negative effects included fear, anxiety, panic, or paranoia; delusional or irrational beliefs; loss of ability to feel pleasure and intense lack of motivation; loss of sense of agency; depression, dysphoria, or grief; re-experiencing of traumatic memories; agitation or irritability; and even suicidality. Other effects – which may be negative or positive – included change in worldview; disintegration of conceptual meaning structure; distortions in time or space; changes in somatic energy; changes in self, other, or self-world boundaries; affective flattening or emotional detachment; and perceptual hypersensitivity.

It is worth noting that the study deliberately sought out meditators who had challenging meditation experiences, so the frequency of challenging experiences is an artefact of sampling and not a reflection of the actual frequency among Western Buddhist meditators. However, it does reveal that not everyone's experience with meditation will be positive.

In terms of risks associated with compassion, there can be resistance to focusing on developing compassion when people believe that this will lead to compassion fatigue – in other words, that you can have too much compassion. We, like many leading compassion researchers, do not believe this to be the case, but people *can* tip into empathic distress. We explore compassion fatigue versus empathic distress in Chapter 20, including some antidotes. Also, as we said in Chapter 2, some people can experience difficulties around being compassionate to self and others. Again, we will pick this up later.

Risks in the wider setting

Beyond individual experience, what about the perception of mindfulness in the wider setting? Once mindfulness' star had risen, there was a backlash, as is so often the case after initial widespread enthusiasm about something. Some have spoken out against what they saw as mindfulness being used in toxic cultures, rather like a sticking plaster to treat a gaping wound.

One vocal critic has been Ronald Purser, who popularised the term McMindfulness in an article for the Huffington Post with David Loy. In his subsequent book, Purser (2019) called out what he saw as the shadow side of the mindfulness movement. He argued that mindfulness has become a banal form of capitalist spirituality that mindlessly avoids social and political transformation, reinforcing the neoliberal status quo. He suggests that mindfulness is often taught to awaken individuals to a source of inner self-comfort, when it should also be awakening them to the outer conditions that make their existence difficult to bear in the first place.

We believe it is important as coaches to be aware of critiques such as Purser's and to stand in our personal integrity when integrating mindfulness and compassion into our coaching and other work. This includes not over-promising on what these might deliver, being aware of potential obstacles for individuals, teams, and organisations, being highly sensitive to the wider context, and being aware of our professional boundaries.

Potential antidote: widening the focus explicitly to relationship

An argument for mindfulness having been co-opted in business as a pretend easy-fix that ignores systemic issues is compelling, and undoubtedly worth considering on a case-by-case basis. This might particularly be the case where mindfulness programmes have been reduced to much shorter formats that do not provide enough input to embed mindfulness for participants. However, we believe that combining mindfulness with compassion helps, and bringing mindfulness explicitly into the relational sphere can be a powerful tipping point, moving beyond the individual to integrate the power of these practices into day-to-day interactions and, potentially, the relational culture.

We need to do our own work as coaches, as human beings, and that is foundational to what we offer as coaches. However, we do not have to do it alone, which is the premise and promise of this book: what becomes possible when we come together mindfully and compassionately?

In summary, we have outlined a number of benefits that can arise from practising individual mindfulness and compassion. But that well-known phrase comes to mind: 'if you think you're enlightened, spend a week with your family.' Being mindful and compassionate may be easy when practising alone but much more challenging when we come into relationship. Yet we believe that it is in relationship that profound growth and development truly happens. In the next section of the book, we explain what RM is, a particular form of RM practice, and the benefits of bringing RM explicitly into coaching.

References

Adamson, F., & Brendgen, J. (2021). *Mindfulness-based relational supervision: Mutual learning and transformation*. Routledge.

Ahn, H. N., & Wampold, B. E. (2001). Where oh where are the specific ingredients? A meta-analysis of component studies in counseling and psychotherapy. *Journal of Counseling Psychology*, 48(3), 251.

Alkoby, A., Halperin, E., Tarrasch, R., & Levit-Binnun, N. (2017). Increased support for political compromise in the Israeli-Palestinian conflict following an 8-week mindfulness workshop. *Mindfulness*, 8, 1345–1353.

Allen, M., Bromley, A., Kuyken, W., & Sonnenberg, S. J. (2009). Participants' experiences of mindfulness-based cognitive therapy: "It changed me in just about every way possible". *Behavioural and Cognitive Psychotherapy*, 37(4), 413–430.

Baddeley, A. (1992). Working memory: The interface between memory and cognition. *Journal of Cognitive Neuroscience*, 4(3), 281–288.

Bihari, J. L., & Mullan, E. G. (2014). Relating mindfully: A qualitative exploration of changes in relationships through mindfulness-based cognitive therapy. *Mindfulness*, 5, 46–59.

Boyatzis, R. E., & McKee, A. (2005). *Resonant leadership: Renewing yourself and connecting with others through mindfulness, hope, and compassion*. Harvard Business Press.

Boyatzis, R. E., Smith, M. L., & Van Oosten, E. (2019). *Helping people change: Coaching with compassion for lifelong learning and growth*. Harvard Business Press.

Bristow, J., Bell, R., Nixon, D. (2020). Mindfulness: developing agency in urgent times. The Mindfulness Initiative.

Brown, K. W., & Ryan, R. M. (2003). The benefits of being present: Mindfulness and its role in psychological well-being. *Journal of Personality and Social Psychology*, 84(4), 822.

Brown, K. W., Ryan, R. M., & Creswell, J. D. (2007). Mindfulness: Theoretical foundations and evidence for its salutary effects. *Psychological Inquiry*, 18(4), 211–237.

Cásedas, L., Pirruccio, V., Vadillo, M., & Lupiáñez, J. (2020). Does mindfulness meditation training enhance executive control? A systematic review and meta-analysis of randomized controlled trials in adults. *Mindfulness*, 11(2), 411–424.

Cavanagh, M. J., & Spence, G. B. (2013). Mindfulness in coaching: Philosophy, psychology or just a useful skill. In *The Wiley-Blackwell handbook of the psychology of coaching and mentoring*, 112–134. John Wiley & Sons.

Chaskalson, M., & McMordie, M. (2017). *Mindfulness for coaches: An experiential guide*. Routledge.

Chu, L. C. (2010). The benefits of meditation vis-à-vis emotional intelligence, perceived stress and negative mental health. *Stress and Health: Journal of the International Society for the Investigation of Stress*, 26(2), 169–180.

Creswell, J. D., Way, B. M., Eisenberger, N. I., & Lieberman, M. D. (2007). Neural correlates of dispositional mindfulness during affect labeling. *Psychosomatic Medicine*, 69(6), 560–565.

de Haan, E. (2008). *Relational coaching: Journeys towards mastering one-to-one learning*. John Wiley & Sons.

Diedrich, A., Grant, M., Hofmann, S. G., Hiller, W., & Berking, M. (2014). Self-compassion as an emotion regulation strategy in major depressive disorder. *Behaviour Research and Therapy*, 58, 43–51.

Dutcher, J. M., Boyle, C. C., Eisenberger, N. I., Cole, S. W., & Bower, J. E. (2021). Neural responses to threat and reward and changes in inflammation following a mindfulness intervention. *Psychoneuroendocrinology*, 125, 105114.

Dutton, J., Lilius, J. M., & Kanov, J. (2007). The transformative potential of compassion at work. In S. K. Piderit, D. L. Cooperrider, & R. E. Fry (Eds.), *Handbook of transformative cooperation: New designs and dynamics*, 107–126. Stanford University Press.

Fenigstein, A., Scheier, M. F., & Buss, A. H. (1975). Public and private self-consciousness: Assessment and theory. *Journal of Consulting and Clinical Psychology*, 43(4), 522.

Förster, K., & Kanske, P. (2022). Upregulating positive affect through compassion: Psychological and physiological evidence. *International Journal of Psychophysiology*, 176, 100–107.

Fox, K. C., Nijeboer, S., Dixon, M. L., Floman, J. L., Ellamil, M., Rumak, S. P., ... & Christoff, K. (2014). Is meditation associated with altered brain structure? A systematic review and meta-analysis of morphometric neuroimaging in meditation practitioners. *Neuroscience & Biobehavioral Reviews*, 43, 48–73.

Fredrickson, B. L. (2013). *Love 2.0: Creating happiness and health in moments of connection*. Penguin.

Fredrickson, B. L., Boulton, A. J., Firestine, A. M., Van Cappellen, P., Algoe, S. B., Brantley, M. M., ... & Salzberg, S. (2017). Positive emotion correlates of meditation practice: A comparison of mindfulness meditation and loving-kindness meditation. *Mindfulness*, 8, 1623–1633.

Garland, E. L., Farb, N. A., Goldin, P., & Fredrickson, B. L. (2015). Mindfulness broadens awareness and builds eudaimonic meaning: A process model of mindful positive emotion regulation. *Psychological Inquiry*, 26(4), 293–314.

Goleman, D. (2020). *Emotional intelligence*. Bloomsbury Publishing.

Hall, L. (2013). *Mindful coaching: How mindfulness can transform coaching practice*. Kogan Page Publishers.

Hall, L. (2015). 16: Mindfulness in coaching. In *Mindfulness in organizations: Foundations, research, and applications*, 383. Cambridge University Press.

Hall, L. (2019). *Coach your team*. Penguin UK.

Hölzel, B. K., Ott, U., Gard, T., Hempel, H., Weygandt, M., Morgen, K., & Vaitl, D. (2008). Investigation of mindfulness meditation practitioners with voxel-based morphometry. *Social Cognitive and Affective Neuroscience*, 3(1), 55–61.

Irons, C., Palmer, S., & Hall, L. (2018). Compassion focused coaching. In *Handbook of coaching psychology*, 206–216. Routledge.

Jazaieri, H., McGonigal, K., Jinpa, T., Doty, J. R., Gross, J. J., & Goldin, P. R. (2014). A randomized controlled trial of compassion cultivation training: Effects on mindfulness, affect, and emotion regulation. *Motivation and Emotion*, 38, 23–35.

Jazaieri, H., McGonigal, K., Lee, I. A., Jinpa, T., Doty, J. R., Gross, J. J. & Goldin, P. R. (2018). Altering the trajectory of affect and affect regulation: The impact of compassion training. *Mindfulness*, 9, 283–293.

Jha, A. P., Morrison, A. B., Parker, S. C., & Stanley, E. A. (2017). Practice is protective: mindfulness training promotes cognitive resilience in high-stress cohorts. *Mindfulness*, 8, 46–58.

Kabat-Zinn, J. (2004). *Wherever you go, there you are: mindfulness meditation for everyday life* (retitled edition, original edition, 1994). Piatkus.

Karremans, J. C., van Schie, H. T., van Dongen, I., Kappen, G., Mori, G., van As, S., ... & van der Wal, R. C. (2020). Is mindfulness associated with interpersonal forgiveness?. *Emotion*, 20(2), 296.

Killingsworth, M. A., Gilbert, D. T. (2010). A wandering mind is an unhappy mind. *Science*, 330 (6006), 932.

Kim, J. J., Cunnington, R., & Kirby, J. N. (2020). The neurophysiological basis of compassion: An fMRI meta-analysis of compassion and its related neural processes. *Neuroscience & Biobehavioral Reviews*, 108, 112–123.

Kim, S. S., Kaplowitz, S., & Johnston, M. V. (2004). The effects of physician empathy on patient satisfaction and compliance. *Evaluation & the Health Professions*, 27(3), 237–251.

Lazar, S. W., Kerr, C. E., Wasserman, R. H., Gray, J. R., Greve, D. N., Treadway, M. T., ... & Fischl, B. (2005). Meditation experience is associated with increased cortical thickness. *Neuroreport*, 16(17), 1893.

Lilley, R., Whitehead, M., & Midgley, G. (2022). Mindfulness and behavioural insights: Reflections on the meditative brain, systems theory and organizational change. *Journal of Awareness-Based Systems Change*, 2(2), 29–57.

Lindahl, J. R., Fisher, N. E., Cooper, D. J., Rosen, R. K., & Britton, W. B. (2017). The varieties of contemplative experience: A mixed-methods study of meditation-related challenges in Western Buddhists. *PLoS One*, 12(5), e0176239.

Lindsay, E. K., Chin, B., Greco, C. M., Young, S., Brown, K. W., Wright, A. G., Smyth, J. M., Burkett, D., & Creswell, J. D. (2018). How mindfulness training promotes positive emotions: Dismantling acceptance skills training in two randomized controlled trials. *Journal of Personality and Social Psychology*, 115(6), 944.

Lueke, A., & Gibson, B. (2016). Brief mindfulness meditation reduces discrimination. *Psychology of Consciousness: Theory, Research, and Practice*, 3(1), 34.

Neff, K. (2003). The development and validation of a scale to measure self-compassion. *Self and Identity*, 2(3), 223–250. DOI: 10.1080/15298860309027

Neff, K. D., Kirkpatrick, K. L., & Rude, S. S. (2007). Self-compassion and adaptive psychological functioning. *Journal of Research in Personality*, 41(1), 139–154.

Neff, K. (2011). *Self compassion – Stop beating yourself up and leave insecurity behind.* Hodder & Stoughton.

Neff, K. D., & Germer, C. K. (2013). A pilot study and randomized controlled trial of the mindful self-compassion program. *Journal of Clinical Psychology*, 69(1), 28–44.

Ormston, R., Bristow, J. (2023). *Mindfulness in Westminster: Reflections from UK Politicians.* The Mindfulness Initiative.

Passmore, J., & Marianetti, O. (2007). The role of mindfulness in coaching. *The Coaching Psychologist*, 3(3), 131–137.

Prinet, J., & Sarter, N. (2015). The effects of high stress on attention. *Proceedings of the Human Factors and Ergonomics Society Annual Meeting*, 59(1), 1530–1534.

Purser, R. (2019). *McMindfulness: How mindfulness became the new capitalist spirituality.* Repeater.

Reina, C. S., & Kudesia, R. S. (2020). Wherever you go, there you become: How mindfulness arises in everyday situations. *Organizational Behavior and Human Decision Processes*, 159, 78–96.

Rupprecht, S., Falke, P., Kohls, N., Tamdjidi, C., Wittmann, M., & Kersemaekers, W. (2019). Mindful leader development: How leaders experience the effects of mindfulness training on leader capabilities. *Frontiers in Psychology*, 10, 1081.

Ryan, R. M., & Deci, E. L. (2000). Self-determination theory and the facilitation of intrinsic motivation, social development, and well-being. *American Psychologist*, 55(1), 68.

Sandi, C. (2013). Stress and cognition. *Wiley Interdisciplinary Reviews: Cognitive Science*, 4(3), 245–261.

Scharmer, C. O. (2009). *Theory U: Learning from the future as it emerges.* Berrett-Koehler Publishers.

Schultz, P. P., & Ryan, R. M. (2015). The "why," "what," and "how" of healthy self-regulation: Mindfulness and well-being from a self-determination theory perspective. In *Handbook of mindfulness and self-regulation*, 81–94. Springer.

Shapiro, S. L., Astin, J. A., Bishop, S. R., & Cordova, M. (2005). Mindfulness-based stress reduction for health care professionals: Results from a randomized trial. *International Journal of Stress Management*, 12(2), 164.

Shapiro, S. L., Schwartz, G. E., & Bonner, G. (1998). Effects of mindfulness-based stress reduction on medical and premedical students. *Journal of Behavioral Medicine*, 21, 581–599.

Siegel, D. J. (2010). *The mindful therapist: A clinician's guide to mindsight and neural integration.* WW Norton & Company.

Silsbee, D. (2010). *The mindful coach: Seven roles for facilitating leader development.* John Wiley & Sons.

Silvia, P. J., & Duval, T. S. (2001). Objective self-awareness theory: Recent progress and enduring problems. *Personality and Social Psychology Review*, 5(3), 230–241.

Spence, G. B., Cavanagh, M. J., & Grant, A. M. (2008). The integration of mindfulness training and health coaching: An exploratory study. *Coaching: An International Journal of Theory, Research and Practice*, 1(2), 145–163.

Sutton, A. (2016). Measuring the effects of self-awareness: Construction of the self-awareness outcomes questionnaire. *Europe's Journal of Psychology*, 12(4), 645.

Takano, K., Sakamoto, S., & Tanno, Y. (2011). Ruminative and reflective forms of self-focus: Their relationships with interpersonal skills and emotional reactivity under interpersonal stress. *Personality and Individual Differences*, 51(4), 515–520.

Tang, Y. Y., Hölzel, B. K., & Posner, M. I. (2015). The neuroscience of mindfulness meditation. *Nature Reviews Neuroscience*, 16(4), 213–225.

Teasdale, J. D. (1999). Metacognition, mindfulness and the modification of mood disorders. *Clinical Psychology & Psychotherapy: An International Journal of Theory & Practice*, 6(2), 146–155.

Weiss, R., Vittinghoff, E., Fang, M. C., Cimino, J. E., Chasteen, K. A., Arnold, R. M., Auerbach, A. D., & Anderson, W. G. (2017). Associations of physician empathy with patient anxiety and ratings of communication in hospital admission encounters. *Journal of Hospital Medicine*, 12(10), 805–810.

Weltman, G., Smith, J. E., & Egstrom, G. H. (1971). Perceptual narrowing during simulated pressure-chamber exposure. *Human Factors*, 13(2), 99–107.

Weng, H. Y., Fox, A. S., Shackman, A. J., Stodola, D. E., Caldwell, J. Z., Olson, M. C., Rogers, G. M., & Davidson, R. J. (2013). Compassion training alters altruism and neural responses to suffering. *Psychological Science*, 24(7), 1171–1180.

Williams, J. (2018). *Stand out of our light: Freedom and resistance in the attention economy*. Cambridge University Press.

Section 2

Origins, underpinnings, and benefits of Relational Mindfulness

It took me a little while to understand what RM did for me as compared to mindfulness. I suppose I've only realized in the last few months that what the RM practice is, is a way to really settle my mind [in relationship]. Whatever I'm hearing from a client, RM is a way of being with their experience, as well as being with my experience of whatever their narrative is. It is about noticing the automaticity of my response – of catching that much more easily than if I wasn't in RM practice, because RM really brings in the freshness of the other.

Shenaz, Chartered Psychologist PsSI, Director, Learning
Partnership, Ireland, and one of our interviewees for this book

Having set the scene and foundations for the book in the first section, in this section we focus in on Relational Mindfulness (RM), its origins, and the benefits it offers. In Chapter 4, we start by defining our terms and exploring the field of RM, including looking at what RM adds over and above individual mindfulness. In Chapter 5, we go on to clarify the background to the particular form of RM practice, mindful dialogue, that we are presenting in this book. We round up the section, in Chapter 6, by delving into the benefits RM offers for coaching according to our informal research.

DOI: 10.4324/9781003390428-5

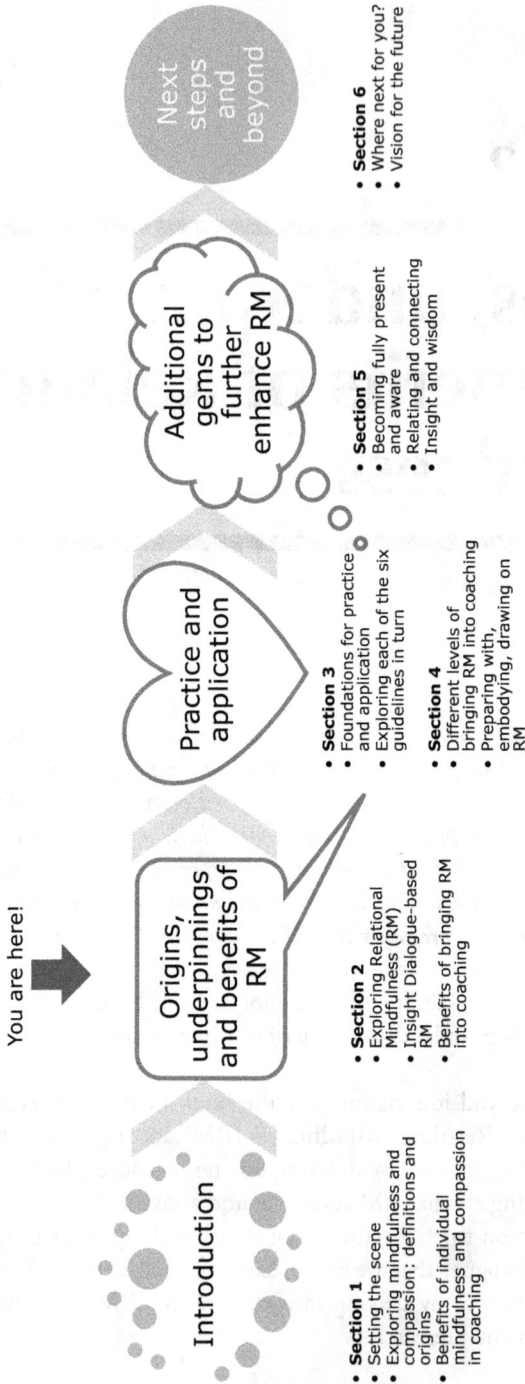

Introduction

- **Section 1**
- Setting the scene
- Exploring mindfulness and compassion: definitions and origins
- Benefits of individual mindfulness and compassion in coaching

You are here!

Origins, underpinnings and benefits of RM

- **Section 2**
- Exploring Relational Mindfulness (RM)
- Insight Dialogue-based RM
- Benefits of bringing RM into coaching

Practice and application

- **Section 3**
- Foundations for practice and application
- Exploring each of the six guidelines in turn

- **Section 4**
- Different levels of bringing RM into coaching
- Preparing with, embodying, drawing on RM

Additional gems to further enhance RM

- **Section 5**
- Becoming fully present and aware
- Relating and connecting
- Insight and wisdom

Next steps and beyond

- **Section 6**
- Where next for you?
- Vision for the future

Figure S2 You are here!

Chapter 4

Exploring Relational Mindfulness

The beginning of wisdom is the definition of terms.

Socrates

This first chapter in Section 2 defines the terms we use to talk about Relational Mindfulness (RM), gives a brief outline of the current range of perspectives on RM, and clarifies what RM offers over and above individual mindfulness (bearing in mind that RM practice is not limited only to those who have an individual mindfulness practice).

Defining our terms

As mentioned in Chapter 1, RM is about taking mindfulness practice into the relational sphere.

We define RM as:

> *paying attention on purpose, non-judgementally (or dispassionately) in the present moment, whilst speaking, listening or otherwise interacting with others; it is about awareness of self, the other(s) and the relationship.*

As explained in Chapter 2, there are multiple definitions of mindfulness and these variously present it as a state, trait, philosophy, or practice(s). Our view is that RM is a state, which can become a trait as the frequency and intensity of an individual's engagement with states of RM increase (see Jamieson & Tuckey, 2017, for an exploration of mindfulness in terms of state, trait, practice, and intervention).

We use both the terms 'non-judgemental' and 'dispassionate' within our definition of RM to help make it accessible to all. Some may find the term 'non-judgemental' off-putting on the basis that we are actually making judgements all the time – because we need to judge or discern what to do in any particular moment. For this reason, the word 'dispassionate' may be more meaningful for some, giving that sense of decentring or non-attachment implicit in definitions of mindfulness.

RM practice

We regard the exercises and activities presented in Section 3 of this book as *RM practices*, designed to increase the frequency and intensity with which we are in a state of RM. As we will explain in more detail in Chapter 7, these practices can be formal or informal. We will use 'RM practice' to encompass all forms of RM practices, both formal and informal. We will refer to formal RM practice as 'mindful dialogue' or 'relational meditation' (terms we will use interchangeably). The distinction between individual mindfulness practice and RM practice is that the latter includes interacting with others – speaking and listening mindfully.

The common thread in all RM practices is that they are designed to help us try out, rehearse, or 'practise', bringing our full attention into moments in relationship with a non-judgemental attitude. In the same way that repetitions in the gym build our capacity for certain physical activity, so repetition of RM practice builds our capacity for paying non-judgemental (dispassionate) attention in our relationships. Because it is a meditation practice, formal RM practice (relational meditation/mindful dialogue) also offers opportunities for insight and gaining wisdom.

Other perspectives on RM

We are by no means the only ones using the term 'relational mindfulness.' Marek Vich and colleagues conducted a research programme that explored RM training at a business school in the Czech Republic (Vich & Lukes, 2018). Deborah Tull, a meditation teacher based in the US, has written a book and created a four-week online programme for individuals, entitled RM (Tull, 2018). Meanwhile, Roberto Aristegui and colleagues have produced an edited volume of work (Aristegui et al, 2021) that *"proposes a new approach to mindfulness-based interventions, presenting them not as individual, but as relational practices."*

We also know of organisations and teachers who are using relational forms of mindfulness as a part of their development programmes. Some mindfulness courses now include some form of RM exercise and we know of mindfulness eight-week courses that build mindful dialogue into session six. In his work with Google, and the book he wrote about it, Chade-Meng Tan (2012), for example, sets out formal and informal practices of mindful listening and mindful conversations.

A YouTube search on 'relational mindfulness' brings up an array of videos offering different slants on the topic. Vich and Tull both appear in the list and the American Psychological Society provides a webinar video on RM as part of an online programme on mindfulness. There are trainers and experts exploring the relational potentials of mindfulness from a range of directions, many of them offering guided practices as well as practical advice. A number of them focus on bringing RM into professional spheres, particularly psychotherapy.

In the research and academic fields too, there is increasing interest in how mindfulness may affect relational variables (Pratscher et al, 2018). Over the last decade the concepts 'interpersonal mindfulness' and 'relational mindfulness' have started to appear in the literature, referring to the capacity to be mindful during interpersonal interactions, with the term 'interpersonal' often used as an equivalent to the word 'relational.' Most of the theory and research in this field has been in psychotherapeutic settings (e.g. Morales-Arances, 2021) and personal contexts (e.g. Kelley & Nichols, 2023). For example, Larissa Duncan and colleagues identified the importance of applying mindfulness in parenting relationships. They created a questionnaire measure, the Interpersonal Mindfulness in Parenting scale (Duncan, 2007), and a model of mindful parenting (Duncan et al, 2009) indicating the value to both parent and child.

Broadening out the enquiry, Steven Pratscher and colleagues have developed a widely applicable Interpersonal Mindfulness Scale. Initially, they explored the value of interpersonal mindfulness in the context of friendship (Pratcher et al, 2018) then moved on to undertake a more extensive process of scale development and construct validation (Pratscher et al, 2019). To frame their scale development, these researchers conceptualised interpersonal mindfulness as being mindful during interpersonal interactions and paying attention in the present moment while with another person, including being aware of internal and external experiences. Their Interpersonal Mindfulness Scale includes four sub-scales: presence, awareness of self and others, non-judgemental acceptance, and non-reactivity.

Meanwhile, Bassam Khoury and colleagues have created a different measure of interpersonal mindfulness, the Interpersonal Mindfulness Questionnaire, which operationalises interpersonal mindfulness in terms of four dimensions: detachment from the mind; body anchored presence; attention to and awareness of the other person; and mindful responding (Khoury et al, 2022). Each of these dimensions is designed to represent an embodied set of skills or abilities that can be cultivated through training and practice. In a work-related context, Lingtao Yu and colleagues introduced the concept of team mindfulness, created a measure of this construct, and looked at its value in teams (Yu & Zellmer-Bruhn, 2018). This latter research conceptualises team-level mindfulness as indicated by team members' collective perceptions of their interactions.

While not using the term 'relational/interpersonal mindfulness', Christopher Reina and colleagues' work also points to bringing mindfulness into relationships. In a theoretical paper with Mills and Sumpter (2023), Reina proposes a model of 'mindful relating', which teases out the mindful qualities of attention and decentering and their application in interpersonal interactions at work. Taking another but related angle with different co-authors, the qualitative study set out in Reina et al (2022) uses data gathered from multiple sources to develop a model of 'mindfulness infusion', which they describe as *"the process whereby individuals instil their mindfulness into their workplace interactions and relationships"* (p.1).

We must also mention our dear friends Fiona Adamson and Jane Brendgen, whose book (Adamson & Brendgen, 2021) explores their journey of bringing a RM approach to their coaching supervision relationship and the implications for developing relational practitioners in supervision, coaching, and related fields.

Overall, our review of the literature around relational and interpersonal mindfulness points to a growing interest in the applicability of mindfulness in relationships. As far as we can make out, the application of RM to coaching has not yet received coverage. We hope this book will change that and that we will start to generate research literature in the future!

What RM adds over and above individual mindfulness

As explored in Chapter 3, practising mindfulness and/or compassion has powerful benefits for us and our relationships, including our coaching relationships. Our key proposition in this book is that practising RM takes the benefits of mindfulness to a whole new level. As mentioned in Chapter 1, RM could also provide benefits for coaches who are not interested in practising individual mindfulness.

As we have made clear, the distinction between RM and individual mindfulness is that RM is *explicitly about bringing mindfulness into relationship*. Thus, formal RM practices include interaction with another person/other people in relational meditation or mindful dialogue – speaking and listening become meditative, contemplative activities. We might stretch this to embrace the application of RM to working with inner parts of ourselves, as we explore in Chapter 19, but essentially RM assumes relationship or relationships between various parties. The explicit introduction of relationship into meditation and mindfulness practice offers benefits (a) for how our practice translates into benefits in our everyday relationships and coaching and (b) for the quality of our mindfulness and our meditation practice. We will look at each of these in turn.

Benefits for translating RM practice into everyday relationships and coaching

Our own experience and that of the coaches we interviewed suggests that engaging in RM practices 'supercharges' what we gain in our daily lives as a result of our practice. This is particularly the case for the benefits our practice provides for how we function in relationships, including coaching relationships. The following overview of benefits is based on our own experience and what the coaches we interviewed said about what RM practice has changed in our/their lives and coaching.

Whilst individual mindfulness and compassion practices help us develop capacities and insights that we can take out into the world (see Chapter 3), meditating in dialogue gives us direct experience of relationally relevant capacities and insights whilst we are actually in a relational setting. This addition of a relational element in formal RM practices, such as mindful dialogue, gives rise to several benefits over and above those offered by formal individual mindfulness and compassion practices.

Because relational meditation/mindful dialogue is practised with another person, it is more similar to daily life than individual meditation. This confers two overarching benefits. Firstly, capabilities developed in formal RM practice are more easily translated into our daily interactions with others in our lives. Secondly, insights gained in mindful dialogue are directly applicable to our way of being in all our relationships, not just those with our meditation partner.

In addition, drawing on our own experience, and from the interviews we conducted, it appears that RM offers benefits by developing a number of capacities and qualities. These capacities and qualities can be grouped into four types (two of which can be classed as forms of insight):

- Relational meditation practice offers an opportunity to practise ways of being with another or others, which is not possible when meditating alone: through this practice we learn to be *more fully present* with another person
- A natural heart-opening or connection happens in real time during RM practice, allowing us to experience relationship together in ways we arguably cannot experience either through meditating alone or through relationship without mindfulness: this in turn helps us *find deeper connection* in our daily lives
- Slowing down our interactions through meditating in dialogue allows us access to insights that arguably would not be possible in individual mindfulness or compassion practice:
    - We become aware of and can observe our relational habits in the moment they emerge, which can enhance our *awareness of our habits* in our life more generally and give greater choice about whether to continue with habitual patterns or choose new ways of being and behaving

■ The power of two or more minds meditating together provides opportunities for **new ways of thinking and perceiving** to emerge that are unlikely to arise from one mind alone. This can shift our way of seeing the world from then on and open us to other new perspectives in our daily life and our coaching

We will explore each of these benefits a little further here and look at the implications for coaching in Chapter 6.

Becoming more fully present in relationship

In a very literal sense relational meditation is a chance to practise – to 'try out' or 'rehearse' – bringing present-moment, non-judgemental awareness to our speaking and listening. In mindful dialogue, we are guided to pause and notice what is arising moment-by-moment whilst speaking and listening. With the support of meditation guidelines, we are invited to release unnecessary tension that might get in the way of our being fully present with ourselves and our dialogue partner, and to bring a receptive attitude to whatever is arising in that moment internally and externally. We learn to be with and attune to whatever is emerging and vanishing in the relational space, to be with the constant flux and flow of experience without trying to control, plan, or avoid it.

Thus, by engaging in relational meditation, we are building the attentional process of bringing mindfulness into our interactions with others. We are strengthening the neural pathways that allow us to place our attention on relating and being with others. Our experience and that reported by others who practise relational meditation is that it develops our ability to be more present and bring a kindly receptivity to our relationships. This gives us a much greater capacity to 'be with' challenging moments, such as a difficult interaction in a coaching session or a stressful family situation. We establish greater presence in relationship with clients and others.

Let us hear what the coaches we interviewed have to say about RM and presence. Beth says, *"...really being present with the self and then bringing that to others... when I think of relational mindfulness and the gifts it's given me, that's the biggest piece... how to be really present in my work, in my coaching and elsewhere."* And Pirjo says. *"...[RM] is about improving my presence... it's not only about my working relationships; it can benefit my other relationships as well. So it's about my presence overall in any relationship."*

Finding connection

As mentioned in Chapter 1, practising and offering relational meditation reliably gives us an experience of a 'magical' shift in the room resulting from the connection and the shared sense of common humanity that emerges as people meditate in dialogue. The combination of relational presence and awareness with exploring direct experience of existential contemplation topics seems to open our hearts to one another naturally. Gently releasing the conventions of 'normal' conversation in mindful dialogue and bringing our full attention to one another taps into our sense of being fellow human beings and engenders compassion and care – for ourselves as well as each other.

Our experience is that even in quite short periods of mindful dialogue, we can feel a sense of connection that is quite rare in daily life. With practice, the capacity for empathy and compassion developed in relational meditation can extend beyond the formal practice of RM and into daily interactions. We have found that, the more we practise RM, the easier it has become to bring patience, kindness, and care to others, from our nearest and dearest, to our clients, to those with whom we only briefly interact.

To quote fellow RM-practising coaches, Shenaz says "...*deeply embedded in RM is the collaboration, the compassion and the kindness...*" Stephanie adds "...*in my vulnerability, I am creating the space for deeper relationships and more connection and compassion....*" And Jane explains "*RM has brought me home to the beauty of what it means to be a human being.*"

Insights: awareness of relational habits and choices

Part of the power of mindful dialogue is that it explicitly invites us to slow down and become more aware of what is happening moment-by-moment in the inter-action with our meditation partner. The experiences we have during relational meditation help enhance our self-awareness by enabling us to observe and learn about our habitual patterns in relationship. For example, in a relational medi-tation, I might notice my tendency to want to please others or my aversion to silence in the dialogue.

Becoming familiar with our internal drivers and behavioural tendencies in relational meditation can help us choose whether to act on them or not. The self-awareness and understanding generated in mindful dialogue seems to widen the space between stimulus and response (to paraphrase Viktor Frankl, 1946).

In our daily life, both the greater familiarity with our habits and tendencies and the developing capacity to find more space between stimulus and response can benefit our personal and work relationships. In combination, these factors can help us make wiser choices about whether to continue to act on our habits or choose different ways of relating. Where we might have jumped in, we can choose to hang back; where we might have got frustrated, we can find our way towards patience. We can shift how we experience and interact with the world, releasing constrictions and potentially freeing ourselves from struggles.

Emma R, one of the RM-practising coaches who took part in our research explains how RM has given her greater awareness and choice "...*relational mind-fulness has absolutely played a massive part in... me being able to take control and...*

not just react, to have power over the way that I respond to these very tricky situations." And Saima explains how RM has changed her response *"…in moments when I would have just blurted something out… I'm more mindful of the moment and the content and context, and of the impact of what could have happened had I blurted it out."*

Insights: new ways of thinking and perceiving

Providing appropriate agreements are in place (see Chapter 7), mindful dialogue can provide a psychologically safe space in which participating dialogue partners are supported towards generative ways of thinking (see Chapter 21). In addition, mindful dialogue involves shared exploration of contemplation topics, which can support new ways of perceiving and thinking about ourselves, others, our relationships, and the world. Because RM practice involves mindful listening to another person's views, it provides the chance either to see how we share common human concerns and challenges, or to gain a different perspective on a topic/ question, or both. This can emphasise both our shared humanity and the rich diversity of the human experience. It can reveal that our way of seeing the world is just one of many and is part of a complex interrelated system.

Shifts in perception and thinking can also arise through the contemplation topics used in mindful dialogue. The topic chosen for a dialogue can help us explore fundamental questions of human existence. As we mindfully explore our present-moment experience on the topic, we can gain in-the-moment insights into the nature of being human. Together with our dialogue partner, we can investigate the human experience from different perspectives, find new angles, and follow unexplored trains of thinking and feeling.

Taking this a step further, in line with work on dialogue from scientists such as David Bohm (1996), when we meditate together in dialogue, we find that a synergy and opening happens that allows us to access a more interconnected, interrelated way of thinking that move beyond individual paradigms to a larger whole.

This step into new more expanded perspectives and a greater sense of inter-connectedness has the potential to free us from some of our unhelpful ways of thinking, perceiving, and constructing our experiences. As we release the struggles of our old patterns, we can open to a clearer view of the world and let go of some of our stress-inducing tendencies to contract, want and not want, and seek happiness in external conditions.

To illustrate this, let us hear again from a couple of our interviewees. Beth says, *"…understanding that every perspective has something to add, and you don't have to listen to respond or judge or solve, has built a space for me to really allow what is emerging for the person or people I'm working with to be there, and for me to hold it in the same regard as I would my own thoughts. And I think that's been a big shift for me that I owe to relational mindfulness."*

And Jane adds, *"...there is something also about the collective intelligence that emerges in this practice. We're sitting in a field together with this shared intention to be present and then there's this emerging that happens and we have access to something that is greater than the sum of the parts. And, insight, understanding and wisdom, these qualities come with enhanced maturity, increased awareness, and increased capacity to be with the complexity of the world that we're living in. There is increasing capacity to hold it."*

Benefits of RM for our mindfulness practice

Whilst this book's focus is on RM for coaches, it is also worth noting that practising RM appears to have benefits for our mindfulness practice. The addition of a relational element to our meditation can enhance our practice in similar categories to the benefits named above:

- ▪ ***Sustaining and deepening our mindful awareness:*** in mindful dialogue, the presence of a meditation partner can enhance our capacity to bring our attention into the moment and reduce our distractibility. Sitting opposite someone in meditation provides a strong anchor for awareness: if my mind wanders off or my awareness wavers, my dialogue partner's presence can help bring me back into the moment. Meanwhile, neurobiological research points to the human capacity for interpersonal resonance and mirroring (see Fredrickson, 2013, for a summary). This means that, when meditating together, each dialogue partner's state will affect the state of the other. So, if I am agitated and my dialogue partner stays calm and stable, their stability can support me to calm down and increase the likelihood of finding a sense of tranquillity and mindful awareness. Our coach interviewees reported reaching a depth of mindfulness in RM practice that they had not attained in individual mindfulness practice. With practice, the presence of another person become an 'anchor' that reminds us to bring our attention fully into moment-by-moment experience
- ▪ ***Access to compassion and sense of common humanity:*** our experience and that of those we interviewed is that mindful dialogue practice consistently gives rise to a level of compassion for self and each other that is less easy to achieve in individual mindfulness practice. While compassion practices can introduce this kindly, caring attitude through visualisations and guidance, the presence of a dialogue partner regularly seems to elicit a compassionate response without the need to direct it or try to achieve it. The RM guidelines have kindly receptivity built into them, particularly the guideline Relax/allow (see Chapters 5, 8–13 for more detail). Sharing our felt experience with another who is giving their full attention and resonating with us, in unconstructed intimacy (see Chapter 7 for more), appears to generate a sense of common humanity and care for one another

■ ***Opportunities for insight:*** we have already mentioned how mindful dialogue allows us access to insights that arguably would not be possible in individual mindfulness or compassion practice. The aim of individual meditation practices, such as Insight Meditation, is to generate insight through calming the mind and paying close attention to moment-by-moment experience. In mindful dialogue, we not only have the calming and attentional elements, but also a relational element that can provide additional sources of insight as described above

By defining RM, exploring different perspectives, and looking at what RM adds over and above individual mindfulness, this chapter provides the foundations for delving deeper into RM. In Chapter 5, we will examine the origins of the particular form of RM we are presenting in this book.

References

Adamson, F., & Brendgen, J. (2021). *Mindfulness-based relational supervision.* Routledge.

Aristegui, R., Campayo, J. G., & Barriga, P. (2021). *Relational mindfulness: fundamentals and applications.* Springer.

Bohm, D. (1996). *On dialogue.* Routledge

Duncan, L. (2007). Assessment of mindful parenting among parents of early adolescents: Development and validation of the Interpersonal Mindfulness in Parenting Scale. *Doctoral dissertation,* The Pennsylvania State University, USA.

Duncan, L., Coatsworth, J. D., & Greenberg, M. (2009). A model of mindful parenting: Implications for parent–child relationships and prevention research. *Clinical Child and Family Psychology Review,* 12(3), 255–270.

Frankl, V. (1946). *Man's search for meaning.* Beacon Press.

Fredrickson, B. (2013). *Love 2.0.* Hudson Street Press.

Jamieson, S. D., & Tuckey, M. R. (2017). Mindfulness interventions in the workplace: A critique of the current state of the literature. *Journal of Occupational Health Psychology,* 22(2), 180.

Kelley, D. L., & Nichols, H. M. (2023). Relational mindfulness themes in descriptions of intimate encounters across six interpersonal contexts. *Journal of Social and Personal Relationships,* 40(5), 1495–1519.

Khoury, B., Vergara, R. C., Spinelli, C., & Sadowski, I. (2022). Interpersonal mindfulness questionnaire (IMQ). In O. N. Medvedev, C. U. Krägeloh, R. J. Siegert, & N. N. Singh (Eds.), *Handbook of assessment in mindfulness research.* Springer.

Morales-Arandes, E. (2021). Mindfulness as an embodied relational resource in psychotherapy. In R. Aristegui, J. Garcia Campayo, & P. Barriga (Eds.), *Relational mindfulness.* Springer

Pratscher, S. D., Rose, A. J., Markovitz, L., & Bettencourt, A. (2018). Interpersonal mindfulness: Investigating mindfulness in interpersonal interactions, co-rumination, and friendship quality. *Mindfulness,* 9(4), 1206–1215.

Pratscher, S. D., Wood, P. K., King, L. A., & Bettencourt, A. (2019). Interpersonal mindfulness: Scale development and initial construct validation. *Mindfulness,* 10(6), 1044–1061.

Reina, C. S, Kreiner, G. E., Rheinhardt, A., & Mihelcic, C. A. (2022). Your presence is requested: Mindfulness infusion in workplace interactions and relationships. *Organization Science*, 34(2), 722–753.

Reina, C. S., Mills, M. J., & Sumpter, D. M. (2023). A mindful relating framework for understanding the trajectory of work relationships. *Personnel Psychology*, 76(4), 1187–1215.

Tan, C.-M. (2012). *Search inside yourself.* HarperOne.

Tull, D. E. (2018). *Relational mindfulness: A handbook for deepening our connection with ourselves, each other, and the planet.* Wisdom Publications.

Vich, M., & Lukes, M. (2018). Development of mindfulness in relational context: construction and validation of relational mindfulness training (RMT). *Ceskoslovenska Psychologie*, 62(3), 244–257.

Yu, L., & Zellmer-Bruhn, M. (2018). Introducing team mindfulness and considering its safeguard role agains conflict transformation and social undermining. *Academy of Management Journal*, 61(1), 324–347.

Chapter 5

Insight Dialogue-based Relational Mindfulness

Find friends who love the truth.

The Buddha (from the Dhammapada)

As we saw in Chapter 4, there are various proponents of Relational Mindfulness (RM), with different slants on RM practice and how to develop greater mindfulness in relationship. Our definition of RM specifies that it involves speaking and listening, and that formal RM practice includes mindful dialogue with a meditation partner (or partners).

What distinguishes the form of formal RM practice that we set out in this book (and offer in the programmes we run) is that it incorporates a particular form of relational meditation that is based on Insight Dialogue (ID, Kramer, 2007). In this chapter, we seek to provide an understanding of what ID is, its characteristics and foundations, and how these shape the form of RM practice we are offering in this book.

Insight Dialogue

ID shares the orientation of the Buddhist Insight Meditation tradition, aiming to enable insights into the human condition, suffering, and the end of suffering. The intention is that developing present-moment awareness and gathering the mind in calm concentration support investigation into the nature of experience, enabling clear seeing and leading to greater compassion and wisdom, and freedom

DOI: 10.4324/9781003390428-7

from suffering. The difference between silent Insight Meditation and ID is that ID has the added element of meditating in relationship with another, which can further support insight by enabling us to investigate together. As Gregory Kramer, the creator of ID, explains, "*Because interpersonal meditation works with the moment-to-moment experience of interacting with another, it brings the liberating dynamic of meditation into our interpersonal lives*" (Kramer, 2007, p.4).

Having developed a strong Insight Meditation practice, Kramer collaborated with his colleague, Terri O'Fallon, to study the approach to dialogue developed by theoretical quantum physicist David Bohm. Bohm had developed a form of dialogue that aimed to broaden participants' thinking and their capacity to think beyond existing paradigms (Bohm, 1996). Kramer and O'Fallon's innovation was to bring their meditation practice into the dialogue, and thus ID was born. Over the years, Kramer has developed ID through many iterations and offered it to many people across the globe.

The RM practices that we describe in Chapters 7–13 of this book are grounded in ID, which gives them some key characteristics that distinguish them from other forms of meditation or relational process. In particular, ID-based RM practice is a dialogic form of meditation, underpinned by a set of six guidelines that anchor the meditative nature of the practice, and supported by contemplation topics that steer the meditative sharing.

Dialogic form of meditation: What distinguishes ID from most meditation and mindfulness practices is that it is explicitly relational. Whilst there is usually an initial period of silent/individual meditation to settle and ground us, and mindful pauses to bring us back into the moment, the central practice in ID – and ID-based RM practice – is engagement in meditative dialogue.

Sitting in a pair or small group with another person/people, we are invited to speak and listen to one another as meditation, rather than as conversation. There is often a separate speaker and listener initially, allowing the speaker to speak without fear of interruption and the listener to listen without needing to prepare a response. Subsequent phases of the dialogue will often release the form of separate speaker and listener, offering us the opportunity to meditate whilst in the dance of shared dialogue. Thus, an ID-based RM practice session will include meditation/mindfulness practice whilst silent, speaking, listening, and in shared dialogue.

Underpinned by six guidelines: The feature that perhaps most sets ID-based RM practice apart from other dialogic and RM practice is the use of the six ID guidelines, crafted by Kramer to anchor the meditative nature of the dialogue. Kramer describes the six guidelines as "*the scaffolding for ID*" (Kramer, 2007, p.107). These guidelines are:

■ Pause
■ Relax/allow

- Open
- Attune to emergence
- Listen deeply
- Speak the truth

An overview of these guidelines is provided below, and each guideline is explored in more depth in Chapters 8–13.

Supported by contemplation topics: To help focus the dialogue within ID/ID-based RM practice, we have a contemplation question or topic such as noting and naming out loud our present-moment experience, or exploring experiences such as change/ impermanence, generosity, or the roles we play in life.

Because ID is a Buddhist practice, the content of these contemplations in ID itself is informed by Buddhist wisdom teachings, aiming the dialogue towards wholesome qualities, and providing a reference point outside of our cultural norms around the causes of suffering and dissatisfaction. ID contemplations offer an opportunity to explore how the Buddha's profound and yet remarkably accessible teachings help us see more clearly the way we construct our world. This clearer seeing offers the possibility of freedom from that constructing process and all the stress, struggles, and suffering it brings.

In non-Buddhist ID-based RM practice, the explicit reference to Buddhist teachings may be removed and a wider range of wisdom sources may inform the topics explored. However, the contemplations still perform a function of inviting in perennial wisdom, establishing a purpose to the practice that is not just about development, but also potential liberation.

Dialogue on the topics chosen offers the opportunity to explore experientially the questions raised, and to examine aspects of the human experience moment-by-moment. The approach encourages us to re-evaluate our assumptions, habits, and patterns and reflect on how our experiences illuminate the nature of being human and human relationships. Because we are contemplating in a meditative state, we are providing and co-creating a powerful environment in which this exploration can unfold. As Kramer says, *"With [ID] practice the mind becomes sensitive and powerful. Introducing a topic into this ecosystem is like placing a seed in rich tropical soil. It quickly blossoms into a conversation laden with fruit"* (Kramer, 2007, p.186).

For example, contemplating a topic such as change or stress together can enable us to understand at a deep visceral level the way the body, heart, and mind contract, construct, want, and do not want. When this is experientially felt in mindful dialogue, with the support of mindful awareness and relational contact, there is an opportunity to see these stress-inducing tendencies more clearly, shift how we experience the world, and even let go.

These three characteristics are shown in Figure 5.1, with relational meditation at the core, the guidelines anchoring the mindful awareness, and contemplations supporting dialogue.

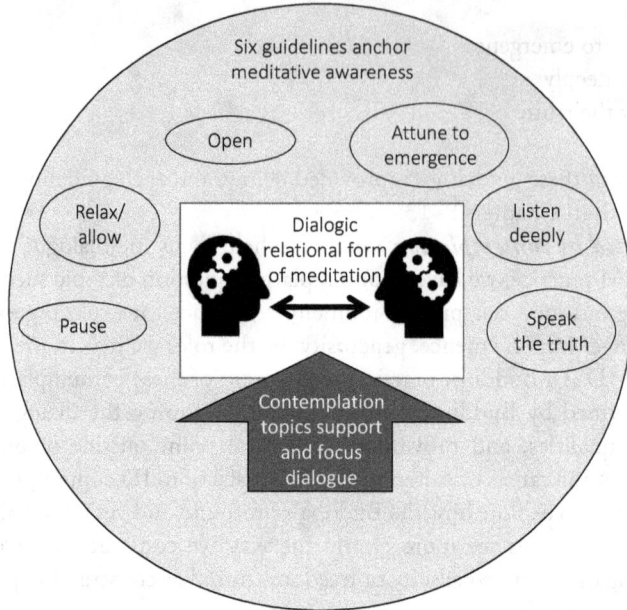

Figure 5.1 Characteristics of ID-based RM practice.

The three characteristics have parallels in the three foundations of ID-based RM practice that we describe next. To a degree, the relational nature of the meditation underpins the relational aspect of RM practice, the guidelines provide meditative anchoring, and the contemplations support the wisdom element. However, each of the characteristics contains strands of all three of the foundations.

Three foundations of ID-based RM practice

To elucidate how ID practice functions, Kramer and Ebert (2018) identify three 'bases' or foundations on which ID sits:

■ Meditative awareness
■ Relationship and
■ Wisdom

Because the RM practices that we set out in this book are based on ID, they sit on these same three foundations. As well as linking to the three characteristics of ID-based RM (set out in Figure 5.1), these foundations also underpin the qualities or capacities that RM practice develops, which were explained in Chapter 4 and will be explored further in the context of coaching in Chapter 6. See Figure 5.2

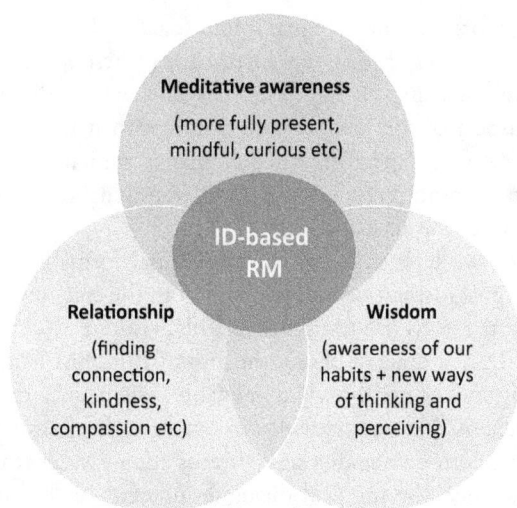

Figure 5.2 Foundations of and qualities developed by ID-based RM practice.

for a visual representation of how ID-based RM sits at the nexus of these three foundations and contributes to their development.

Now let us explore these three foundations in turn:

■ *Meditative awareness:* Formal RM practice is a meditation: speaking and listening are meditative activities and part of contemplative, mindful dialogue. The six guidelines that make ID/ID-based RM distinctive are the foundation for the meditative nature of the practice. They aim to enhance not only mindfulness, but also the other meditative qualities of investigation, energy, joy, tranquillity, concentration or gathering of the mind, and equanimity (set out in Buddhist teachings as the seven factors of enlightenment or awakening). Bringing these qualities together creates a form of awareness that is fully in the moment-by-moment experience and open to seeing clearly and gaining insight

■ *Relationship:* RM practice is conducted in relationship: in ID and ID-based RM sessions, you will be reminded regularly that 'you cannot practise ID/RM alone.' This foundation points both to the physical reality that mindful dialogue is practised with another person (or other people) and to the relational qualities that arise when we have a shared intention to meditate together and bring care to our meditative speaking and listening. These qualities are both an expression of intention about how we want to be with one another and a naturally arising experience when we bring meditative awareness and wisdom to our relationships. They can be characterised as goodwill and kindness, compassion for each other's struggles, joy in each other's good fortune, and an equanimous (balanced, even-tempered) stance towards the vagaries of relational interactions (these qualities are set out in the Buddhist teachings as the four Brahmaviharas or divine abodes). The relational aspect of the practice also brings with it the benefit of hearing another person's perspective, whether that is similar to ours (enabling a recognition of common humanity) or different (enabling a recognition that ours is just one view of the world)

■ *Wisdom:* As we have said, ID, in its original form, is a Buddhist practice, drawing its inspiration and purpose from the teachings of the Buddha, particularly the early Buddhist texts. This wisdom aspect of ID has two facets. Firstly, the practice shares the aim of Buddhist Insight Meditation to establish states of mind/body that enable insights into the human condition and the possibility of release from our struggles. It can help us become more aware of our own habits and patterns and of wider realities of human nature. Secondly, the mindful dialogue inherent in the practice involves exploration of a contemplation topic, designed to support the meditators to gain new perspectives on aspects of the human situation, and the structure and function of our mind/body, and to move towards a more wholesome life. As mentioned, dialogue founded on Buddhist wisdom teachings also brings wholesome qualities and intentions into focus and can take us beyond the cultural norms and construction processes that usually colour our view, aiming the practice towards freedom from suffering. Whilst formal ID-based RM practice may not make explicit reference to Buddhist teachings and may draw on a wider range of sources of wisdom, it still has this dual intention to create insight and to engage participants in contemplation of wisdom-generating topics to gain new and potentially liberative perspectives

These individual foundations are profound and powerful in and of themselves. In addition, they synergise with one another:

■ *Relationship and meditative awareness:* Chapter 3 has already explored how mindfulness can support our relationships, including our coaching relationships. At the same time, as mentioned in Chapter 4, relationship can also support mindfulness. When practising mindful dialogue, the presence of a meditation partner enhances my capacity to bring my attention into the moment, reduces my distractibility, and increases the likelihood of my finding a sense of calm and tranquillity. If I am practising opposite a fellow human being and my mind wanders off or my awareness wavers, their presence can help bring me back into the moment. In line with neurobiological research around interpersonal resonance and mirroring, the state of my meditation partner will affect my state (Fredrickson, 2013; Chapter 20). So, if I am agitated and my dialogue partner stays calm and stable, their stability can support me to calm down. Similarly, if I am curious when investigating a particular experience, my curiosity will ignite that in the other. Bringing together relationship and meditation helps us to attune to another person with present-moment, non-judgemental awareness, generating the meditative qualities mentioned above (mindfulness, investigation, and so on) and also building the relational qualities (such as kindness and compassion) for both participants. Through repeated practice, regularly experiencing these qualities in relationship establishes interacting with another person as a prompt or 'anchor', 'conditioning' us to bring greater presence, awareness, investigation, stability, and so on into all our relationships. However, without the input of the wisdom and insight aspect, this could just be a tool for improving relationship and communication, missing the opportunity the practice offers for gaining insight, developing the capacity for wisdom, and liberating our minds

■ *Meditative awareness and wisdom/insight:* Insight Meditation and many other meditative traditions/approaches are based on the value of calm, gathered mind-states for creating deeper understanding and insight in our lives. For centuries, monastics of many spiritual and religious traditions – and lay people too – have recognised that contemplative and meditative approaches enable us to access insights and understand wisdom teachings about the nature of human existence in ways that are not possible when the mind is distracted, activated or running on grooves of habit and delusion. When we bring any form of wisdom teaching to a mind that is in a state of meditative awareness, there is the possibility for us to learn at a much deeper level than we can if we are not in a calm and gathered state. However, without relational contact, it can be hard for most of us to really engage with such wisdom and even harder to apply it to our daily lives. Indeed, the Buddha, when one of his senior followers commented on good friendship as being "*half of the holy life*", corrected his friend and emphasised that good friendship is the "*whole of the holy life*" (Upaddhasutta) (we might translate good friendship as supportive relationships and 'holy life' as psychological and spiritual development)

■ *Wisdom/insight and relationship:* Have you had the experience of fretting about an issue, going over it in your head, and finding yourself ever more stuck, then talking it through with a friend and getting a whole new, much clearer perspective that provided a different, more effective way of seeing and dealing with it? Such an experience shows the power of relationship to enable insight or wisdom. Any shared reflective learning – including coaching supervision, coaching, and action learning groups – is drawing on the power of being listened to and potentially accessing more than one perspective to generate new understanding and clearer seeing. If we bring some form of wisdom into the mix – be that a Buddhist or other spiritual teaching, a psychological or philosophical theory, or any wisdom-oriented religious or secular offering – then the benefits are potentially multiplied.

Now we are not just accessing different perspectives, we are drawing on the wisdom of teachers and/or thinkers who have explored life or a particular aspect of life in some depth and offer insights that we can elucidate together to bring them to life in our own experience. Our relationship is also likely to be enhanced by our shared experience of building understanding of things that really matter in our lives. However, without mindfulness and other meditative qualities, the risk is that this exploration can be just a good conversation, which can be quite 'heady', not support deep insight or liberation, and not get integrated in a meaningful way into our way of being

As you will see, each of these pair-wise synergies is beneficial but lacks the presence of the third foundation. Bringing all three foundations together multiplies the benefits to profound and powerful effect.

From a neuropsychological perspective, the combination of mindfulness, non-judgement, and the other meditative qualities with the relational qualities of kindness, compassion, empathy, and stability establishes a sense of psychological safety between dialogue partners that allows better access to potential insights (McMordie, 2019). Research by American psychologist and neuroscientist Stephen Porges (2017) and others has shown that safe, 'calm and connect' neurobiological states are a prerequisite for accessing the higher brain structures that enable us to be creative and generative.

Those familiar with Nancy Kline's Thinking Environment (Kline, 1999), whose work we touch on again in Chapter 20, will also hopefully see how ID-based RM provides the kind of space that her approach establishes in service of generative thinking, exploration, and challenging of assumptions. Combine this with contemplation of existential topics and meaningful questions and we can see that the openings for insight are rich.

As mentioned above, ID-based RM practice also draws on Bohm's work around dialogue. Bohm (1996) instigated group dialogues that offered opportunities to engage participants in fully listening to one another's views with the aim not only of understanding each other's perspectives and thereby broadening their way of viewing and making sense of the world, but also generating ways of thinking that move beyond existing paradigms to new ways of seeing the complex interrelated adaptive systems of which we are a part. ID-based RM potentially offers similar growth and potential for freedom for us as individuals and for the systems in which we operate.

Linking back to what we said in Chapter 2 about the potency of developing compassion and mindfulness together and the risks associated with developing one of these in the absence of the other, these three foundations ensure that ID-based RM does not develop either quality in isolation from the other. Mindfulness is supported by the softening receptivity of relational qualities such as compassion and is given an ethical, discerning direction through wisdom/insight. 'Idiot' compassion, self-indulgence, and self-pity are avoided through the awareness of mindfulness and the clarity of insight.

The six guidelines for ID-based RM

ID-based RM relies on the six ID guidelines for both our formal relational meditation practice and our informal practice of translating RM into our daily lives and relationships. In Section 3 of the book, we delve into each guideline in more depth and provide exercises, practices, and quotes from our interviewees to illuminate what they each contribute, how we can apply them formally and informally, and how others have experienced them. Here, we provide a brief overview to set the scene.

As mentioned, the guidelines are the foundation for cultivating mindfulness and other meditative qualities in ID-based RM practice. They are thus central to establishing the meditative awareness foundation for mindful dialogue. Individually and in combination, they offer ways to access greater mindfulness, awareness, curiosity, interest, courage, energy, enjoyment, calm, concentration, and stability. Each makes its own contribution to this process, and they work together in a beautiful symphony. Together, they support us into a relational process in which connection with another (or others) is both a part of the practice and at the same time a magical consequence of spending time in this way with a fellow human being.

The guidelines can be seen as a profound journey from individual to relational meditation – as shown in Figure 5.3. However, it is important to note the paradox that, while the guidelines offer a progression and build one upon another, at the same time, they are also non-linear and, to an extent, holographic, with each guideline pointing to and enfolding the other five. Thus, it is particularly important to recognise that the guidelines are *not* a set of steps, strategies, or techniques to be approached in a hierarchical manner.

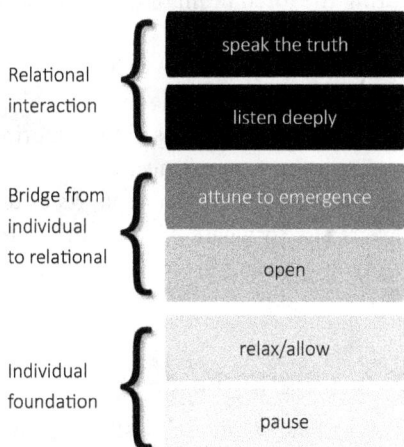

Figure 5.3 The six guidelines for ID-based RM.

It is also important to be clear that the guidelines are <u>not</u> designed to be a series of actions that we 'do', but instead an indication of how we can 'be' in our meditative dialogue – and in our relationships more broadly. They invite us to cultivate specific aspects of awareness. They are to be learned through experience and embedded at a somatic level, not purely understood at a cognitive level. The guidelines themselves are constructs expressed in language, but they aim to point to a felt experience, aspects of mind, and ways of showing up in the world.

The guidelines can also be a source of wisdom as they point to essential truths about the nature of being human, such as our interconnectedness with one another, how we and the world around us are in constant flux and change, and the vital importance of compassion, kindness, non-judgement, and receptivity. The purpose of the guidelines is thus not just to form a scaffolding for the practice of RM, but also to translate the three foundations that underpin RM into pragmatic, practical approaches to develop its potential.

Pause and Relax/allow

The guidelines Pause and Relax/allow establish the present-moment awareness and receptivity – or non-judgement – that make up the classic definition of mindfulness. In the RM context, these guidelines are about establishing an in-the-moment purposeful attention and a non-judgemental, dispassionate attitude whilst speaking, listening, and interacting with others.

Pause is about being fully present with our dialogue partner or, in daily life, with another person. It invites us to become aware of what is happening right now and to notice what is arising moment-by-moment. It is an invitation to remember to return our attention to this moment when our mind wanders off. It is a stepping back from the rush of doing, saying, or thinking – of our habits and patterns – in order to bring the torch beam of our awareness into our immediate experience.

Relax/allow counterbalances any tension that might arise or be noticed in the process of pausing, by inviting a calming and softening of the body, heart, and mind. It is about allowing whatever sensations, emotions, and thoughts are present, helping us to be with our experience, even if it is unpleasant, and to release the habit of resisting or avoiding it. It supports us to let go of judgement and bring a friendly awareness to whatever is arising, offering receptivity and kindness. It can also be about releasing the tension that can separate us from ourselves and others.

Open and Attune to emergence

While the guidance offered by Pause and Relax/allow might be familiar to anyone who has practised meditation or mindfulness, Open and Attune to emergence move us from the individual to the relational. These two guidelines are vital supports for maintaining meditative awareness whilst in relationship.

Open expands mindfulness to include not just the internal domain, but also the external world, both other people, and the environment. It offers us a more spacious awareness in which we can be with both internal and external and notice the relationship between the two – self and other, internal and external – how they influence and affect one another.

Attune to emergence invites a flexibility to be with the constant flux and flow of the relational moment, without preconceptions, planning, or trying to control. In individual mindfulness, this might be termed 'beginner's mind.' In RM, attuning to emergence is about cultivating the openness to be with complexity and continual change in the internal and external world, particularly when that external world contains other people. It supports us to be fully present with the ebb and flow of experience, and to let go of preconceptions, planning, and trying to control what happens next.

Listen deeply and Speak the truth

Listen deeply and Speak the truth support us to bring full presence and wise discernment to the activities of speaking and listening. They bring authenticity and full presence into each moment of dialogue in relational meditation – and each moment of interacting with others in daily life. In formal ID-based RM practice, the emphasis is on listening and speaking as meditative activities. This requires intention and energy: as Kramer and Ebert put it (Kramer & Ebert, 2018, p.100) *"meditating while speaking and listening is a challenge worthy of our finest attention."* Practising these guidelines in formal ID or RM practice can help us bring our presence and awareness into our conversations and interchanges with our fellow human beings in daily life.

Both Listen deeply and Speak the truth require us to draw on all the other RM guidelines and they are themselves reciprocal to one another: communication requires both a communicator and a receiver.

Listen deeply is about being fully present to the person who is speaking, to their words, body language, tone, energy, and context. It invites us to bring a stable, receptive awareness that provides kindness, empathy, and sensitivity.

Speak the truth involves a mindful discernment of the subjective truth of experience and sharing what is useful. At a gross level, this is about not lying, but rather telling things as we actually see them. At a more subtle level, it is about expressing what is true in the moment and discerning what is valuable, kind, and timely to be spoken.

These guidelines are very often taught together in ID/ID-based RM because they co-arise. The quality of the listener's attentive listening allows for and calls forth the depth and quality of the speaker's speaking and vice versa: the quality of the speaker's speaking calls forth attention and quality in the listening. There is a mirroring that happens that has its basis in our neurobiological systems, which are set up to support our connection with one another (see Chapter 20 for more on the neurobiology of connection). Indeed, listening deeply and speaking the truth are so reciprocal that one ID teacher suggested that they could also be called 'Speaking deeply' and 'Listening for the truth.' However, there is also value in exploring these guidelines separately as they each make unique and important contributions to ID-based RM practice.

Weaving the guidelines together

As we become more familiar with the six guidelines, we begin to see how they mutually support one another. The most obvious connections are between adjacent guidelines, for example, how pausing supports us to relax and allow, how listening deeply to ourselves and others is central to being able to speak the truth, and so on. At a more subtle level we can see how multiple guidelines work in synergy, for example, opening to internal, external, and both and attuning to what is arising in these domains is vital for listening deeply. And none of that can happen without the foundation of pausing.

Over time, we may begin to experience that the guidelines all merge and support one another as a fluid whole. One of our interviewees talks about how the guidelines are like the ingredients of a recipe in cooking, with the final result being much more than the sum of the parts saying, *"When I got to… listen deeply and to speaking the truth, there was an explosion of understanding and sensations… [like when] you cook something, you prepare different ingredients … you put everything together, the final result is completely different. The result of all the cooked ingredients was much richer, beautiful, deeper, [than] the individual ingredients."*

Brought together, the guidelines cease to be separate constructs and become something more fluid and experiential in nature. As another of our interviewees, Becky, expresses it, *"…all of [the guidelines] merging together and creating a way of being that I find very hard to describe because it's really just a felt sense… it's not a cognitive thing and if I describe it, I have to turn it into a cognitive thing and I can't do that, which is really fascinating…"*

Exploring each guideline individually is important at first, so that we understand the nuance and value each one offers. Maintaining awareness of the distinction between guidelines – even as they become familiar and the synergies are clear – can help us draw on the most helpful one in each moment. This is particularly beneficial for facing challenging moments in relationship. At the same time, accessing the rich confluence of the guidelines working together can help us find new ways of being and generate insights that require the support of multiple or all the aspects the guidelines introduce.

Adapting ID to non-Buddhist contexts

The Interpersonal Mindfulness Program (IMP)

Just as mindfulness and meditation have been increasingly used in secular and clinical settings (Jamieson & Tuckey, 2017), so too ID has been translated into a secular programme, the Interpersonal Mindfulness Program (IMP, Kramer et al, 2008). The IMP was created when Kramer brought together five Mindfulness-Based Stress Reduction (MBSR) teachers and trainers of teachers, to explore the creation of a program that draws from MBSR's teaching methodologies and ID's relational practices and wisdom basis.

The IMP mirrors other mainstream mindfulness-based interventions, such as MBSR, by having an eight- or nine-week structure, with weekly sessions and specified 'home practice' for participants to engage in between the weekly meetings. It is clearly defined through teachers' handbook and curriculum (Hicks et al, 2015-2019) and great care has been taken to ensure its fidelity to the ID practice on which it is based, while at the same time making it accessible in non-Buddhist contexts.

Because the IMP is a more recently developed intervention than most of the established mindfulness-based interventions (such as MBSR and Mindfulness-Based Cognitive Therapy), the current research literature about it is limited. However, recent research suggests that the IMP is considered highly acceptable and very useful and has positive effects on self-compassion, empathy, and compassion fatigue (Bartels-Velthuis et al, 2020).

IMP in leadership development

Meanwhile, my (Emma's) doctoral research explored the potential for applying the IMP, or a secular form of ID, in leadership and management development (Donaldson-Feilder et al, 2022). Having initially established that mindfulness had the potential to support leadership development (Donaldson-Feilder et al, 2019), the underlying proposition of this second piece of doctoral research was that a relational form of mindfulness would be potentially even more valuable approach to developing leadership qualities. Given the relational nature of leadership, we theorised that developing RM is likely to have even greater relevance and applicability than, and provide benefits over and above, those offered by individual mindfulness. The outcome of the research was a set of guidelines designed to help IMP teachers with the preparation, design, and implementation of an ID-based leadership development intervention.

The key messages from the research were that anyone developing an ID-based leadership development programme needs to:

- Ensure that the programme is true to its origins
- Intentionally gather information to determine the appropriateness of the programme for the 'audience' and communicate effectively to generate engagement
- Strategically determine the programme design, delivery, and messaging to make it accessible to and valuable for participants
- Recognise the importance of the facilitator's way of being and understanding of RM to the integrity and accessibility of the intervention

As explored further in Chapter 14, we strongly emphasise this last point about the significance of a facilitator's way of being. Our embodiment of RM is essential to our capacity to facilitate or coach others with and through this approach. My (Emma's) experience is that being taught RM by teachers who embody its foundations and qualities imparts the practice and develops my own qualities in a way that being taught by those who do not have this level of embodiment simply cannot touch.

The research also outlined facilitators of and barriers to ID-based leadership development. It suggested that such a programme will work best when there is senior-level buy-in and a champion/sponsor, and that there are cultural, attitudinal, and past-experience factors that may be helpful in creating a conducive environment for the programme. It also highlighted the knotty issue of whether and when such a programme can be offered to those who have not volunteered to attend and the sensitive handling needed when participants have pre-existing relationships (particularly hierarchical ones such as manager and direct reports). It identified individual characteristics that may be supportive for getting the most out of the programme, and those that may be contra-indications for participation (see Chapter 18).

Demand from coaches

I (Emma) am now applying these research findings when offering ID-based RM to leaders. However, the greatest demand for RM programmes is currently coming from coaches – both those providing coaching as external providers and those working in-house in organisations/workplaces (e.g. Donaldson-Feilder & Comalie, 2021).

More broadly, in terms of conferences, articles, and discussion, RM is generating mounting interest in the coaching community and in similar professions such as psychology, psychotherapy, and counselling. This is perhaps unsurprising: relationship is arguably even more central in coaching than in leadership, so a relational form of mindfulness is particularly relevant and applicable in the contexts of helping professions such as coaching. Add to that the pre-existing interest in mindfulness shown in the coaching world – evidenced by the popularity of books such as Liz's on mindful coaching – and it seems clear that RM is perfect for application in coach development and practice.

In retrospect, maybe my (Emma's) doctoral research should have focused on the potential for applying ID-based RM in coaching. As mentioned above, generating some research literature around this is certainly something we would like to do!

With an understanding of ID, its characteristics, foundations, and guidelines, we are in a position to explore ID-based RM in more detail and look at how to practise it (Section 3) and bring it into our coaching (Section 4). First, however, in the next chapter, we will set out the benefits of RM for coaching.

References

Bartels-Velthuis, A. A., van den Brink, E., Koster, F., & Rodier Hoenders, H. J. (2020). The Interpersonal Mindfulness Program for health care professionals: A feasibility study. *Mindfulness,* 11, 2629–2638.

Bohm, D. (1996). *On dialogue.* Routledge

Donaldson-Feilder, E. J., & Comalie, L. (2021). In the moment (case study article). *Coaching at Work,* 16(3), 48–51.

Donaldson-Feilder, E., Lewis, R. & Yarker, J. (2019). What outcomes have mindfulness and meditation interventions for managers and leaders achieved? A systematic review. *European Journal of Work and Organizational Psychology,* 28(1), 11–29.

Donaldson-Feilder, E., Lewis, R., Yarker, J., & Whiley, L. (2022). Interpersonal mindfulness for managers: A Delphi Study exploring the application of interpersonal mindfulness to leadership development. *Journal of Management Education,* 46(5), 816–852.

Fredrickson, B. (2013). *Love 2.0.* Hudson Street Press.

Hicks, P., Meleo-Meyer, F., & Kramer, G. (2015-2019). *Interpersonal Mindfulness Program: A teachers outline and resource guide.* Metta Programs.

Jamieson, S. D., & Tuckey, M. R. (2017). Mindfulness interventions in the workplace: A critique of the current state of the literature. *Journal of Occupational Health Psychology,* 22(2), 180.

Kline (1999). *Time to think.* Cassell Illustrated

Kramer, G. (2007). *Insight Dialogue: The interpersonal path to freedom.* Shambhala.

Kramer, G., & Ebert, L. (2018). *Offering the Insight Dialogue guidelines: A resource guide.* Metta Programs.

Kramer, G., Meleo-Meyer, F., & Turner, M. L. (2008). Cultivating mindfulness in relationship. In S. F. Hick & T. Bien (Eds.), *Mindfulness and the therapeutic relationship,* 195–214. Guildford Press.

McMordie, M. (2019). Be safe, be free. *Coaching at Work,* 14(4), 26–31.

Porges, S. W. (2017). Vagal pathways: Portals to compassion. In E. M. Seppälä, E. Simon-Thomas, S. L. Brown, M. C. Worline, C. D. Cameron, & J. R. Doty (Eds.), *The Oxford handbook of compassion science,* 189–202. Oxford University Press.

Upaddhasutta, e.g. translation by Bhikkhu Sujato on www.suttacentral.net.

Chapter 6

Benefits of bringing Relational Mindfulness into coaching

Sheer Awareness has the power to shatter all illusions.

Rumi

Having read the first few chapters of this book, perhaps you can already see how Relational Mindfulness (RM) practice could benefit your own coaching – and the world of coaching in general. We have certainly seen the value of RM in our own coaching and strongly believe coaching – and the wider world – can benefit from RM practice. However, we would not want you to take solely our word for its benefits! So, in this chapter we will be drawing largely from our interviews with fellow coaches, sharing what they said about the value RM has added for them. We also provide an exploration of how the Insight Dialogue (ID)/RM guidelines link to coaching competencies and the findings from a very small quantitative data set provided by participants in our RM for coaches programmes.

Coaches' experience of benefits

Although there are not yet empirical research studies from which we can draw to confirm what RM offers in coaching, we carried out our own informal qualitative research, interviewing 11 experienced coaches who practise RM and/or ID. In these interviews we gathered feedback and observations from these people on

DOI: 10.4324/9781003390428-8

their experience of RM and its impact on their coaching. The following is based on our analysis of what these people said when we asked them (a) what was different in what they were doing and how they were being as a result of their RM practice and (b) the benefits they had seen for their coaching from practising RM.

Our data suggest that practising RM and becoming more relationally mindful has provided profound benefits in how these coaches work. In most cases, the benefits of RM for coaching identified related to changes in what these coaches do and how they are showing up (their 'being') in their coaching. Interviewees also talked about benefits to their clients and others, including in their personal relationships, which we cover later in the chapter.

Where different interviewees said similar things about shifts in their ways of being/behaving in their coaching and other relationships, we grouped the data into themes. We then grouped these emerging themes into four overarching types of capacity or quality (these are the four we mentioned in Chapter 4 about what RM adds over and above individual mindfulness). For more information on the research and our analysis process, see our dedicated website: www.relationalmind fulness.net.

The results of our thematic analysis of the data are set out in Table 6.1 and each of the themes is explained below, grouped under the four types of capacity/quality.

Becoming more fully present

All the coaches we interviewed talk about the way practising RM has changed their capacity to be present in their coaching (and other) relationships. Many describe their 'presence' and the impact on their 'being' beyond what they are doing. They also talk about how they have slowed down and/or gained greater awareness in their coaching and the benefits of being more fully with coaching clients.

The majority talk about 'being present' and the quality of their 'presence.' They emphasise that practising RM has helped them improve their presence in relationship, supporting them to be more present, more open, and more aware of how they are showing up. For example, Shenaz says "*I think the quality of my presence is much better… just being open, tuned in, not trying so hard to have a result. There's much more quiet inside….*" And Becky describes how, through practising RM, she realised that "*the way that I show up is incredibly powerful and I was able to learn about… all the ways that it really does affect other people. And even in some really mundane encounters, it really enhanced my presence.*"

Stephanie talks about a particular experience when she and another team coach were coaching a team together: "*My co-coach is incredible, absolutely amazing, and has been meditating for decades, and is very skilled at being present in the room… I was really taken aback because I noticed that I felt like an anchoring presence in that room with the team and us as two coaches. And intellectually, I would have totally*

Table 6.1 Benefits of RM practice for coaching

Type of capacity/ quality	Themes from interview data
Becoming more fully present	■ Presence and being fully with the client ■ Level of awareness ■ Types of awareness e.g. aware of the body ■ Slowing down ■ 'Being' rather than 'doing' ■ Maturing and moving beyond tools and techniques
Finding connection	■ Relational aspect of coaching ■ Improved listening ■ Opening, allowing and resonating ■ Space for the client ■ Creating safety ■ Reciprocity
Insights: awareness of relational habits and choice	■ Making choices rather than reacting or acting habitually ■ Awareness of thinking and less buying into it ■ Having more choice over what we embody and aligning to values ■ Less clouded by own habit: more able to see client habits ■ Trusting experience/self/not knowing ■ Ease and self-acceptance
Insights: new ways of thinking and perceiving	■ Openness to other perspectives ■ Valuing others' views ■ New perspectives ■ Supporting insight, understanding, and wisdom for clients ■ Capacity to be with suffering and existential enquiries ■ Connection to a wider, collective intelligence

said that's her. And she said it afterwards, 'I really noticed that the energy was drawn to you.' And even when she was asking a question, the answers would come back to me, even though I was 'just' sitting there. How interesting. What was going on there?"

Awareness

The coaches also talk about their level of awareness, mindfulness, and capacity to get curious about what is happening. moment-by-moment. Practices such as mindful dialogue can help us bring greater awareness to what is arising in the moment in our relationships, which can be invaluable in coaching sessions. As Shenaz puts it, RM "*is helping me stay with the experience, and then noticing myself and bringing mindfulness to the act of speaking, to the act of coaching itself.*" Saima describes how RM "*evokes awareness… you find your client being – and you being – more curious, which is of value to the outcome.*"

Some coaches mention specific types of awareness, such as becoming aware of their own and other people's habitual twitches or facial expressions. One describes learning that he could identify when he was getting distracted because he would start doodling or sketching – something he had not noticed before practising RM. Others talk about the importance of becoming more aware of their body and bodily sensations and being able to use this awareness in their coaching. As Beth says, RM "*…is getting you out of your thinking brain and into your sense of knowing your bodily sense.…*"

For several, this enhanced awareness seemed to be partly down to RM helping them slow down, calm down, and give clients more space, not try to 'fix' them. For example, Pirjo says "*RM has kind of slowed me down in a positive way… giving more space to myself and to my clients as well.*" And Beth explains, "*I speak to a lot of coaches and feel like there's a sense of haste to propel people towards their best possible self or their goal or their actualisation. And actually, there's a real beauty in RM that reminds you that slowness and stillness and calmness can be just as, if not more, powerful than that kind of desire to work at pace and to really fix people's problems for them, [which] I think is the risk when you're working really quickly.*"

Malcolm also talks about how RM can help us avoid giving advice in coaching, saying "*I think [RM] restricts advice giving and therapising… it's okay to be silent. 'You don't have to do anything' is the default position. If you feel you need to be doing something and proving what a great coach you are [by] saying something, then it becomes advice.*"

Ways of 'being'

Linked to this aspect of being more present, aware, and spacious, at least half of the coaches talk about the distinction between 'doing' and 'being' in coaching and how RM has shifted their emphasis. For example, Pirjo says, "*The more I have worked in the coaching arena, the more I have noticed that coaching is so much more than 'doing'; more and more I feel it's the being of the coach that's important in coaching… [RM] definitely has had an impact on how I am being with my clients, and that has an impact on what I'm doing with my clients… my approach is less doing, more being.*"

This aspect of 'being' and moving beyond a focus on tools and techniques fits well with coaching maturity, which we explore later in this chapter. As Beth says, "*…[RM is] about you as a human being, how you are being rather than doing: being a coach versus doing coaching. I think there is a bit of coach maturity involved in that* *shift. I think we all probably start in a very 'doing' mindset because we're learning something new, and we want to get it... But I think RM... centres the coach not in terms of what they're doing, but how they're being. And I think that's super powerful."* And Stephanie talks about RM being a key part of moving into coaching mastery, saying *"...it really isn't around tools and everything else anymore. It is about the inner and outer workings of the coaching relationship and understanding the coachee. So it feels to me like RM is the missing piece... it's fine reading about 'it's the way of being that's really important', but you go, 'okay, great, but how do I get there?' And RM is, 'ah, okay, so this is how this could be.'"*

Finding connection

Back in 2008, Kramer and colleagues suggested that relational meditation could help those working with others, such as coaches, psychologists, and therapists, to be better able to collaborate with clients (Kramer et al, 2008).

Our interviews provided a firm endorsement of this, with many talking about the power of RM to improve the relational aspect of coaching. For example, Beth says, *"The fact that [RM is] relational definitely brings in that sense of connectivity to other people and that common humanity."* And Becky says, *"...how did I do coaching before I knew [about RM]?... We learn in coaching... that the primary lever for change is the existence of a coaching relationship and then it's the quality of the relationship and then it's... the methodology or whatever. ...if it's the existence of the relationship that is the primary driver for change, then wow! Because RM explicitly acknowledges the existence of the relationship as an entity and that, I think, has the potential to really enhance coaching for all coaches."*

Connecting through listening

Many of the coaches related this connection to an improved ability to listen. Despite listening being a core skill for all coaching, there was a sense that RM was enabling these coaches to listen in a deeper, more connected way to their clients and to others. For example, Emma R says, *"I'm using a lot more listening than I certainly would before. So a lot less of me having to take control of it and answer all the questions, actually using the kind of active listening elements to let them come up with the solutions. And that's been a profound change..."*

And Stephanie adds, *"[RM provides] a much more refined, careful attending to that relational aspect of coaching, which is key. The listening and the presence and all of that... It's always been a central aspiration, and also sits naturally with how I am in my work, but RM has given me the tools to do that with more intent and structure."*

Becky talks about RM changing the way she listens from listening to understand to listening for the sake of listening and the benefits of that. She says, *"It's like I'd discovered a whole new world that I didn't even know existed. And the next step on from that for me was being able to trust that if I don't listen to understand,*

I will understand and remember anyway. I will remember the bits that I need to remember. I will understand what I need to understand if I am listening in this new way just for its own sake. So that has really changed my coaching. I'm so much more relaxed. I'm not working so hard. And then… paradoxically, but of course, not really paradoxically at all, because I'm not working so hard, actually, the outcomes are better, they're more fluid and organic…"

The kind of listening these coaches talk about has a distinct flavour to it. It includes a greater sense of opening to and allowing the client/other person to be received, empathising and resonating with them, and deepening understanding at a somatic level. For example, Malcolm talks about resonating with his clients and says that RM *"was an invitation to a real pause and an investigation into what is really resonant here in this relationship."* Jane explains how RM has helped her work somatically: *"…there's an open space for things to emerge. It's open, it's receptive, it's present, it's tender, it's really intimate. I feel the person in my body, feel the connection, I feel the dynamics, I feel the energetic shifts. I feel the emotion and I see it on the client's face. I feel stuff before they've said it. I feel that my body is a receiver. If I feel something and the client doesn't name this, I might offer it and say, 'I'm noticing I'm feeling this and am wondering what might be around for you?'"*

The coaches also refer to the space that this RM-based form of listening provides and how that shifts the way the client responds. Rhonda says, *"I have been getting feedback like, 'you're giving me a chance to think', which is exactly what I'm trying to do: I'm trying to create a space for people where they can reflect for themselves and it's not just about me taking them down a road."*

And one of our other interviewees talks about bringing in RM when discussing difficult issues with someone: *"…I gave them more space, not in the coaching sense, but really in the RM sense… I felt that the person felt understood. There was less tension, less resistance in their behaviour and it went better, not only because they felt understood but also I understood better."*

Psychological safety

Building supportive, compassionate, collaborative relationships in coaching is important not just to build rapport, but also to create a safe space in which clients can think more generatively and stretch beyond their comfort zone. If we want to gain insight and wisdom, we need to feel safe and, if we want to support insight and wisdom for others, we need to offer compassionate listening, quality attention, and a psychologically safe space (see Chapter 20).

Our interviewees explicitly talk about how RM practice has helped them create a safer space in their coaching, where clients could be vulnerable and share things without fearing being judged, where there was a sense of trust that built quite quickly. For example, Jane says, *"I can see that my clients are able to be vulnerable because they really sense the depth of connection, that I'm really with them and they feel really safe. I think that the conditions that [RM] practice helps to create is that of deep psychological safety, so that people can do their best thinking, come to insights and access the wisdom that's in the field."*

And Beth explains, "*[Clients are] able to notice like 'oh, this has come up. I'm not really sure where that comes (from), but I am going to voice it and I am going to bring it to the space' and that vulnerability that's only really possible when someone either trusts you or the process and ideally both. I think that you can get there more quickly and more consistently through RM because you are really setting out a super safe and equal and open space for them to bring whatever comes up."*

Interestingly, the beneficial effects seem to flow both ways. The coaches report that the depth of connection RM helped them create made the work more rewarding and meaningful. As Jane puts it, "*It's really heartful. And it's reciprocal. The client is touched by what I might say and I'm touched by what the client says. So there's this beautiful process of human being to human being that happens. And there are moments of love that come, so many moments. It's exquisite. Truly, the connection with the clients as a consequence of this practice is exquisite at times."*

And Pirjo talks about the benefits of RM supporting "*…more meaningful relationships, harmony. And it can have a positive impact on the coach's own well-being."*

It is also important to note that the creation of safety and compassion does not mean settling into a comfortable agreement about how things are. Instead, this form of compassionate listening space is one in which self-awareness is fostered, new ways of thinking and perceiving are available, and courage is supported in service of wiser, kinder ways of being – as we explore next.

Insights: awareness of relational habits and choices

Another of the important changes coaches report after practising RM is an awareness of their habits and greater choice about whether they continue to behave according to habit or respond in new, more skilful ways. As coaches, as we noted in Chapter 3, we need to be aware of and manage our own relational drivers and patterns, to ensure that they do not get in the way of our being able to provide psychological safety, respond skilfully, or see clearly the relational 'dance' of the coaching.

Once we have identified our habits and are better able to spot them in the moment, we can choose not to follow the urging of our habitual patterns – for example, to please our client or to fill a silence – and instead hold the space for the client uncluttered by our own tendencies. In a coaching context, this self-awareness helps us 'get out of our own way.'

The coaches we interviewed talked about learning not to react in ways they would have done in the past. As Pirjo explains, "*…when there's a trigger, remembering to pause gives you a choice, you can choose what you are going to do. So there have been moments when I have been delighted that I haven't reacted in the normal way, but I have remembered to pause and then chosen something else."*

Our coach interviewees also mentioned greater awareness of their thinking patterns and less buying into the thoughts that arise. For example, one of them explains that "*Some thoughts have become already irrelevant/outdated, then…I have more choice about saying something or not.*" And Shenaz says "*I can watch my thoughts and initial reactions with some detachment and curiosity. Perhaps it is fair to say, I am not so attached to my way of seeing things….*"

This stepping away from our habits and patterns can give us greater choice over what we embody in our work. We have more flexibility to align our coaching with our intentions and values. As Stephanie puts it, "*…the power that comes with acknowledging what is here now in this moment and 'how do I want to be?'…I know what my drivers are pushing me to be – out of habit or learned behaviour or whatever – but how actually do I want to be in this space?*"

Noticing clients' habits

As we develop better moment-by-moment awareness of our own relational habits and patterns, we become better able to notice those of others, including our clients. We can provide a space that is less clouded by what draws us in or pushes us back, so our clients' patterns become more obvious. Jane talks about a coaching session in which she suggested something to a client, who disagreed and suggested something different, and Jane noticed that "*my mind didn't get caught in thinking about it, which would take me away from being present and connected to the client… So there is capacity to prioritise in awareness this person sitting with me and all of the stuff that's emerging in 'the between.'*"

And Shenaz says, "*…whatever I'm hearing from a client, RM is a way of being with their experience, as well as being with my experience of whatever their narrative is. It is about noticing the automaticity of my response – of catching that much more easily than if I wasn't in RM practice, because RM really brings in the freshness of the other.*"

Confidence and ease

Interestingly, the coaches report that this greater self-awareness and choice gives them a greater sense of confidence and trust in their capacity to coach, including being better able to tune into their own, their client's, and the system's wisdom. Malcolm says how RM has given him "*…the confidence to just really pause and be silent, be totally comfortable with that, and to be able to be more present and to really listen while being just silent and receptive.*" He explains he says less in coaching, but when he does speak, it is with more confidence. "*I think I just get close enough to the other person to really know, there is a deep knowing that arises… I think [RM] is a sort of step change in my confidence to trust my intuition and rely on what emerges.*"

Becky also mentions the impact of RM on her confidence as a coach, saying it has helped her be more flexible "*…to let go of a bit more of what I think good* *coaching is and meet the client a bit more where they are… it sounds a strange thing to say, that RM has made me more confident as a coach.*"

Some also talk about how practising RM has brought them a much greater sense of ease – with working with a group, with silences, in relationship – more self-acceptance and less anxiety. For example, Pirjo says, "*I have noticed that whenever I have been able to bring an RM attitude in a group context where I am a facilitator, for example, it helps to take the performance anxiety away from me.*"

There is a sense that these coaches are letting go of some of their constructions around who they should be and experiencing a freedom from the stress of that constructing and constructed existence.

Insights: new ways of thinking and perceiving

Many of the coaches refer to how practising RM helps them be more open to other perspectives in their coaching and their lives. They talk about RM reducing the force of their own views and expectations, opening them up to really hear what others have to say. For example, Beth says, "*Relational mindfulness reduces that clutter, that noise that you have from your own judgement and perspective, but also welcomes that you will have a different perspective and that's okay… being really open to other perspectives and not just as in 'well, you can say your perspective, but I'll still hold mine', but having that real openness to what someone's truth is [and] actually being able to reflect on that.*"

Another of our interviewees says that he noticed that when he was listening he was "*…waiting for the other to 'confirm' what I was expecting.*" He goes on to say, "*now I am more patient, listen more, try not to have expectations, and let the person finish….*"

They also talk about RM helping them to recognise that their own view is just one of many possible ways of seeing the world, that other people's perspectives are of value, and that dialogue can help them gain new ways of seeing. Beth again: "*… none of us really perceive reality as it truly is. We've all got our own experiences and values and things that inform the way we receive the world. I think that for me studying and practising RM has really built space for that perspective in me.*"

And another interviewee adds, "*I see the dialogue as a source of new ways of seeing differently from before… If you listen to a different opinion… now more and more I'm curious about that… I see that dialogue as an important element for a better understanding.*"

New awareness

Some talk about how RM practice itself can help us as coaches adopt new ways of looking and ways of seeing of which we were not previously aware. This links to adult/vertical development as we will mention again later in this chapter, and later in the book (see Chapter 21). As Jane explains, "*Given the nature of the RM process, it offers coaches the opportunity to work with uncertainty, volatility, ambiguity and complexity and to develop capacities to be more flexible, agile, to hold a broader perspective, to see things through different lenses... RM helps to disidentify, to come into relationship to our experience, to recognise it. We're not caught up in it. The principle in adult development is subject-object. When we're subject to our experience, we are caught up in it: it has us. When we can step out and see it, we have it, we are in relationship to it. It has become object. The RM guidelines also create the conditions for this, that we can see phenomena happening in the relational field rather than being identified with them."*

Similarly, mindful dialogue can help us find new perspectives within ourselves, as Becky describes: *"...it's almost magical. There have been times when I've been in [mindful] dialogue practice, where, as the words have come out and I've heard myself saying them, and I felt myself held by that other person, that I've kind of gone further. And I've said things which have been a surprise even to me, and I have thought, 'well!', and on occasion actually said to the partner, 'that would not have happened if I had been in individual [mindfulness] practice.' ...I would have gone so far and then no further, because I wouldn't have recognised that there was further to go, whereas in the dialogue I have gone further without realising that there was a further."*

Supporting insight

The access to new ways of thinking and perceiving we gain from RM practice gives us greater capacity as coaches to support insight, understanding, and wisdom for our clients. There is less 'ego' and more capacity to provide space for insight or, where appropriate, to offer a question, comment, or different perspective without attachment to being 'right' or 'a good coach.' For example, Rhonda says, *"I found that pausing and relaxing and opening myself more to what's emerging from the client... enables them to ask their own questions and identify their own insights rather than me coming up with all these great insights that I can give them. It's so much more powerful if they can see that themselves... sometimes just letting people talk and being a receptive listener can be such an amazing intervention... I think that's one thing RM has helped me with. It wasn't a new concept, but it's helped reinforce that concept... [Clients] will say 'this has all been in my head, but by expressing it now, I've just made this major leap' and I've never said a word. I was just sitting there or in front of a screen...."*

Jane describes it as *"...more capacity to attune to nuance, to notice, for example, that a question has come up and I'll hold it and then I might bring it into the dialogue at an appropriate time if it's still there. It's like a knowing in the body. It doesn't come from the head, it comes from this inner sense of 'this might be important, this might be relevant.' And then there is offering of that and at the same time, there's a humility. I often say to my client 'if I'm completely wrong here, you let me know.'"*

Existential questions and interconnectedness

Some also talk about how RM helps them support insight for clients by having a greater capacity to be with suffering and fundamental existential enquiries. For example, Stephanie describes, "*…holding paradoxes, being grounded, knowing that actually compassion is the driving force in everything, seeing our interconnectedness, all those rich Buddhist principles, moving you towards a way of being that is hopefully more effective in relationships and can hold more suffering, contain the suffering in a way that gives strength, enables joy, shares love… It all ties into these existential questions, 'if this is all we have, how do we make this the most meaningful little footprint that we leave during our time here?' And RM allows that footprint, I think, to be placed with more wisdom and awareness and care.*"

There is also a sense of RM connecting us to a wider, collective intelligence that can help us see the interrelated, interconnected nature of the world and coach from that broader perspective. As Malcolm puts it, "*[RM is] a way to empathise and identify with others and, through that, ultimately to reach a place of getting closer to connection with the whole rather than just with myself and with one other. It's a way of becoming part of something bigger.*"

Benefits for clients and others

The coaches we interviewed report a range of beneficial differences that their clients experienced when their coach started to practise RM. Some speak about feedback clients had provided about what had changed through the coaching. For example, Saima says, "*…folks will come back and say, 'my wife told me when I come back from your sessions, I'm a whole completely different person now'… And to me, that's the power of what happens [in RM].*"

Some talk about clients experiencing the coaching differently or responding differently in coaching. For example, Stephanie reports that "*…the tears seem to be happening much quicker… to the point where I had a coaching session recently and my client's tears started flowing within the first minute.*" She explains, "*RM is allowing me to create that space where as soon as you step in the room, something is different; you're allowing unconsciously, maybe the client is allowing something to emerge because I can't imagine she would have cried so quickly with a different coach… So I don't know, but I wonder whether there's a feeling from clients that they're almost stepping into a different sort of space with me now.*"

Others talk about how the shift in their coaching due to practising RM is opening up spaces for change. For example, Saima shares that there is "*…deep opening, deep listening, that deep sense of groundedness that means that… it feels like we're not having a superfluous, superficial conversation. It feels that change is possible from this so that that there are tangible conversations to be had.*"

And Jane explains how through RM practice she has developed "…*a grounded sense of trust in [my] capacity to hold what's here. This can be instrumental in shifting the conditions in a team, to support teams to move beyond fear because there is this anchor that feels safe and of course, in neurobiological terms it's going to have an effect on the whole system.*"

Coaches also talk about how RM helps them coach more powerfully. For example, Emma R says, "*I use lots of different models that I've integrated together… it feels like [RM is] kind of superpowering them… RM is my kind of backdrop, and then I'm using these approaches within it… it's surrounding the models that I am using. So I think the questions that I might ask might be the same, but I'm completely using the RM core techniques and the power of what I'm doing is so much stronger than it was before.*"

And Shenaz talks about how once she started to practice RM, things shifted and she is getting more repeat business: "*I began to listen in a very different way, working with these guys, and I noticed that the quality of the coaching changed, and it led to a lot more work. Because they said to me, 'oh, that was really interesting' – even though maybe I'd said ten words for the whole session! They asked me to do a lot more group work with their teams.*"

Benefits in personal relationships

Enhancing our capacity to be present, connect, be aware of our relational habits, and open to new ways of thinking will of course shift how we show up in all our relationships, not just our coaching. We can both attest to the difference practising RM has made to our personal, as well as our professional, relationships: helping us be kinder, more present, patient, open, and (we hope!) wiser. Many of the coaches we interviewed were keen to point out how RM had shifted their personal relationships.

Emma R shares an example of a close family relationship that has in the past been very problematic: "…*she would agree that she can be a very difficult person- ality. She is very open about that and has a lot of very difficult relationships throughout her life with people. And I was definitely one of them. …it was my intention then to use [RM] with this relationship… I have been kind of practising it [during phone conversations with her], obviously not known to her, but very much using it, and it has really utterly transformed (the relationship). …she will say our relationship has been transformed. We're now incredibly close. And I'm absolutely sure that it's because of using [RM]… I think there was a really heightened awareness of my own patterns… putting those aside and then deeply listening, I think has made a huge impact on that relationship. Just giving her that attention and that kind of deep kind of listening I think has been a huge part in it…*"

Saima talks about how RM has supported her through a challenging time in her private life: "*RM came into my life at a time when there was a major risk to the wellbeing of a significant other. RM gave me a moment to ask 'what's happening and how can I process this' rather than being in shock or sadness. And I genuinely believe that it's kept me sane. It brought me a level of patience and presence that was desperately needed in support of those significant others around me. It has meant holding that space for them to be in exploration of what they were experiencing, making space for it, and moving towards a more holistic recovery… Rather than, 'oh, for goodness sake, let's just fix this', it was 'just be with this and just take one little step forward, literally relax and allow… towards a path to recovery. Just give each phase an opportunity to live and breathe and speak its presence, however it needs to be noted. And then have it be released and see how that feels. Hold on to what you feel is precious and release what needs to be released.'"*

Links to coaching competencies

We firmly believe that ID-based RM practice aligns with core coaching competencies. And the feedback on benefits coaches were seeing for how they coached and the outcomes they saw from their coaching backs this up. Some of our coach interviewees explicitly mentioned RM as contributing to coaching competencies. For example, Stephanie says, "*If you look at the International Coaching Federation (ICF) competencies, or the other [frameworks], it's all about the things that RM is supporting you to do, isn't it? Really listening and non-judgement and even ethics… you can say this is what you want to achieve, but RM gives you a path to get there.*"

Saima, who is not only an International Coaching Federation (ICF)-accredited Master Certified Coach and facilitator but also runs an ICF-accredited coach training programme, says: "*[RM] captures so many competencies in the ICF core competency framework, across building trust and safety in a coaching conversation, establishing and maintaining presence in your relationship and then actively listening. RM as a tool is so valuable in enhancing the quality of these core competencies.*"

Saima also explains that she is already drawing out the links between the ICF core competency framework and RM – particularly the RM guidelines – in her coach training programme. She goes as far as to highlight a certain symmetry between the structure of the ICF core competency framework and the RM guidelines. The ICF core competency framework starts with foundational competencies around ethics and mindset, moves to relational competencies, and then to communication, awareness, and facilitating growth. The RM guidelines Pause and Relax/allow are foundational in building presence and receptivity, Open and Attune to emergence open us to the relational space, while Listen deeply and Speak the truth support listening and communication

Coaching competency frameworks and the RM guidelines

Inspired by Saima's work, we looked through coaching competency frameworks from the ICF and other coaching professional bodies (including the European Mentoring and Coaching Council (EMCC), Association for Coaching (AC), British Association for Counselling and Psychotherapy (BACP), and British

Psychological Society (BPS)). In line with what Saima was saying, we found that both the RM guidelines and the benefits of RM reported by coaches were relevant in some way to the competencies set out by the various bodies.

Some key examples of this include the following:

- *Maintaining presence:* The ICF includes 'Maintains Presence' as one of its eight core competency areas, defined as being fully conscious and present with the client and employing a style that is open, flexible, grounded, and confident. Most of the other frameworks also mention coaching presence and/or awareness in some way. This aligns well with the RM guidelines Pause and Attune to emergence in particular but is also supported by all the RM guidelines, which point to bringing our full awareness into the present moment as we speak and listen with another. This capability also clearly links to coaches reporting that becoming more fully present with their client and having a higher level of awareness was a key benefit of RM practice

- *Establishing and maintaining strong relationships:* All the coaching competency frameworks mention establishing, building, and maintaining a strong relationship with the coaching client. Research suggests that a big part of what we offer in interventions such as coaching is down to the relationship we establish with our client (e.g. Lee et al, 2021). Relationship is also a foundational element of mindful dialogue and all the RM guidelines can support enhancing our relational capacity. In particular, the guideline Open helps us bring awareness into the relational field, Relax/allow supports kindly receptivity, and Listen deeply is about high-quality relational listening. Our interviewees referred to how RM practice had helped with the relational aspects of their coaching through shifts such as finding greater connection, resonating, and reciprocity

- *Listening:* Allied to the relationship element of coaching, all the coaching competency frameworks also specifically mention listening. For the ICF, 'Listens Actively' is one of its eight core competency areas, and, for the other bodies, listening is included within their descriptions of one or more of their competencies. This clearly links to the RM guideline Listen deeply and is underpinned by all the RM guidelines. It was also mentioned as one of the areas of development/benefit for our coach interviewees

- *Cultivating insight and awareness:* Most of the frameworks include a competency related to insight and/or awareness, from the ICF competencies 'Evokes Awareness' and 'Facilitates Client Growth', to the AC's 'Raising awareness and insight', the EMCC's 'Enabling insight and learning', and the BACP's 'Facilitating awareness of self, others and situation.' Coaches reported how mindful dialogue and all the RM guidelines had supported their capacity for insight, awareness, and learning. They also indicated that practising RM and improving their own insight helped them to support insight, understanding, and wisdom for clients

- ■ ***Ethics:*** All the coaching competency frameworks mention ethics at some point and some of the professional bodies have additional ethical frameworks for coaches. Mindful dialogue and all RM practices also have a clear ethical foundation as we will explore further in Chapter 7

Interestingly, then, the RM guidelines and RM practice seem to align well to core coaching competencies, suggesting that they may be relevant to those setting out on their professional journey as a coach, as Saima's interpretation suggests.

Coaching maturity

At the same time, RM practice seems to offer the potential for developing coaching maturity for experienced coaches. As mentioned above, coaches we interviewed described how RM supports the shift from 'doing' to 'being' and how it can help coaches move beyond tools and techniques. This is in keeping with David Clutterbuck and David Megginson's model of coaching maturity (Clutterbuck & Megginson, 2011), which sets out four levels of coaching maturity. The most mature level, 'systemic eclectic', is reached when a coach has integrated a very wide array of ways of working into a self-aware, personalised way of being with the client.

Drawing from a sample of systemic eclectic coaches, Clutterbuck and Megginson (2011) observe that they have immense calm and confidence and that a critical question for them is *"Are we both relaxed enough to allow the issue and the solution to emerge in whatever way they will?"* (p.305). These characteristics align well with our own experience and with the developmental shifts our coach interviewees describe arising from their engagement with RM practice.

Clutterbuck and colleagues' later writing emphasises that coaching maturity is *"not a destination, but a continuous process"* (Willis & Garvey, 2024, p.5) and that *"developing into an experienced coach is not a straightforward or even a straight-line process"* (Garvey et al, 2024, p.8). This too aligns with our experience of RM practice and how engaging with mindful dialogue is a kaleidoscopic and ever-continuing journey aiming for wisdom and freedom.

The finding that RM helps coaches develop more aware, kinder ways of being, with insight into ourselves and others, and a broader, wiser perspective is also in keeping with models of vertical or adult development, which we will cover in greater depth in Chapter 21. We firmly believe that practising RM is potentially of particular value to those of us who want to provide coaching support for clients' vertical development and to work at depth with clients' mental models and meaning-making processes.

Quantitative data on the benefits of RM practice

We have not yet had the opportunity to carry out 'proper' quantitative research on the benefits of RM practice for coaches. However, we do have a small data set from coaches who have participated in our RM for coaches programmes. Some of the participants on programmes between 2020 and 2023 kindly agreed to complete a questionnaire before and after attending the programme.

For this data-gathering, we used Pratscher and colleagues' (2019) Interpersonal Mindfulness Scale, which includes four sub-scales:

- *Presence* – this includes being present and engaged in interactions with others, giving the other person our full attention, not being distracted, not multi-tasking/thinking of other things, and not on autopilot
- *Awareness of self and others* – this includes being aware of our own and other people's facial expressions, body language, gestures, and tone of voice. It involves awareness of our own feelings, moods, and emotions when interacting with others, and how these affect how we act towards others. It also includes getting a sense of how other people are feeling, the meaning behind their words and their intentions, and accepting that another person's situation or mood might influence their behaviour
- *Non-judgemental acceptance* – this includes accepting that others will have different opinions, listening carefully even when we disagree, not judging or criticising the other, and trying to accept how they are behaving without wanting them to be different
- *Non-reactivity* – this includes thinking about the impact of our words and taking time to form our thoughts before speaking. If we are upset with or in a tense moment with another person, this is about noticing how we are feeling before responding and not getting taken over by our feelings; trying to understand the other person's situation. It also includes being aware of our own intentions

Looking at the data from the 29 coaches who completed both 'before' and 'after' measures, we found improvements across all four of these areas, particularly Non-judgemental acceptance and Non-reactivity.

Interestingly, there were differences in the patterns of change between those who attended a four-session programme compared to those who attended a two-session programme:

- Presence improved more for those who attended four sessions than for those who attended two
- Awareness of self and others showed marked improvement for those who attended four sessions and little improvement for those who attended two

■ Non-judgemental acceptance improved for both groups, but considerably more for those who attended four sessions – for the latter, this was the area that showed the greatest increase
■ Non-reactivity showed marked improvement and improved to a similar degree for both groups

Clearly, this is not robust research as the data set is very small and we have no comparison or control group, so any conclusions need to be treated with extreme caution. Despite that, it is encouraging to see change in these areas following engagement with RM practice.

Having established RM as a potentially beneficial practice for coaches, we hope you are now eager to try it for yourself! The following section sets the foundations for practising RM (Chapter 7) and provides explanations, guidance, and suggestions for practice (Chapters 8–13).

References

Clutterbuck, D., & Megginson, D. (2011). Coach maturity: An emerging concept. In L. Wildflower & D. Brennan (Eds.), *The handbook of knowledge-based coaching: From theory to practice*, 299–313. John Wiley & Sons.

Garvey, B., Dierolf, K., & Clutterbuck, D. (2024). Suppose everything we knew about coach development was wrong? *Organisations & People*, 29(1), 8–19.

Kramer, G., Meleo-Meyer, F., & Turner, M. L. (2008). Cultivating mindfulness in relationship. In S. F. Hick & T. Bien (Eds.), *Mindfulness and the therapeutic relationship*, 195–214. Guildford Press.

Lee, G. C., Platow, M. J., Haslam, S. A., Reicher, S. D., Grace, D. M., & Cruwys, T. (2021). Facilitating goals, tasks, and bonds via identity leadership: Understanding the therapeutic working alliance as the outcome of social identity processes. *Group Dynamics: Theory, Research, and Practice*, 25(4), 271–287.

Pratscher, S. D., Wood, P. K., King, L. A., & Bettencourt, A. (2019). Interpersonal mindfulness: Scale development and initial construct validation. *Mindfulness*, 10(6), 1044–1061.

Willis, P., & Garvey, B. (2024). Coach development – Are we getting it all wrong? *Organisations & People*, 29(1), 3–7.

Information

Dedicated website accompanying this book: www.relationalmindfulness.net

Section 3

Practising Relational Mindfulness

RM can ground us in that space of being safe with uncertainty, trusting in our capacity to hold and be open to what's coming and work with the change principle – that change and transformation is happening right now, in this relational field. That's where the potentiality for change lies rather than it being associated only with the doing of tasks… The developmental opportunities are here now, alive now.

Jane, an adult development and executive coach,
and one of our interviewees for this book

Hopefully the first two sections of this book have whetted your appetite to engage with Relational Mindfulness (RM). You now know about the foundations and principles of RM, *but* knowledge can only take you so far. The real power of RM is not in understanding what it is about, but in practising it and applying the experiential learning from practice into your life and your coaching. This section aims to provide you with the foundations for RM practice (Chapter 7) and to guide you through applying each of the six RM guidelines in practice (Chapters 8–13). The forms of practice covered include both formal and informal practice and encompass both individual and relational practices.

DOI: 10.4324/9781003390428-9

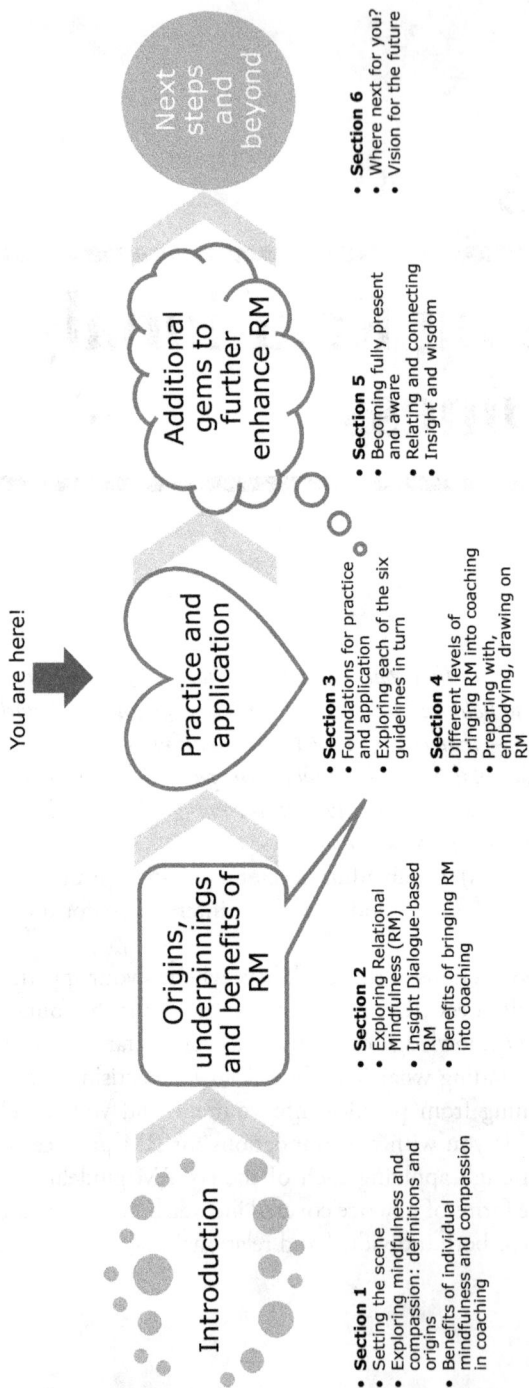

Introduction

- **Section 1**
- Setting the scene
- Exploring mindfulness and compassion: definitions and origins
- Benefits of individual mindfulness and compassion in coaching

Origins, underpinnings and benefits of RM

- **Section 2**
- Exploring Relational Mindfulness (RM)
- Insight Dialogue-based RM
- Benefits of bringing RM into coaching

Practice and application

- **Section 3**
- Foundations for practice and application
- Exploring each of the six guidelines in turn

- **Section 4**
- Different levels of bringing RM into coaching
- Preparing with, embodying, drawing on RM

Additional gems to further enhance RM

- **Section 5**
- Becoming fully present and aware
- Relating and connecting
- Insight and wisdom

Next steps and beyond

- **Section 6**
- Where next for you?
- Vision for the future

You are here!

Figure S3 You are here!

Chapter 7

Foundations for practising Relational Mindfulness

Awareness creates choice, practice creates capacity.

Amanda Blake

Cognitive or experiential learning

While we hope that reading this book proves insightful and beneficial for you, the truth is that just reading our words can only take you part of the way on the journey that Relational Mindfulness (RM) offers to us as coaches. The transformational part of the journey depends on a more experiential and embodied form of learning. The cognitive learning offered through reading – the knowledge and information we hope you have gained from the chapters so far – is valuable as a foundation and mental framework for developing new skills and behaviours. Such learning may provide new perspectives and alternative potential ways of seeing the world, but to shift to new paradigms and to embody new ways of being requires us to learn at an emotional and visceral level.

There is increasing awareness in the coaching world of the importance of somatic forms of learning. As Amanda Blake, an expert on embodied

DOI: 10.4324/9781003390428-10

self-awareness, puts it, "…*not all knowledge lies in the intellectual domain. There are other important ways of knowing, learning, and being…*" (Blake, 2022, p.211). Blake also points out that somatic forms of learning are very different to intellectual and cognitive learning, saying "…*the body learns through repetition, rehearsal, and practice over time (for example, consider how a musician builds the muscle memory to play a song by heart)*" (Blake, 2022, p.223). Because mindful dialogue and other RM practices are about embodied, experiential exploration whilst in relationship, we believe that they can offer this kind of somatic learning. However, such learning requires more than simply reading a book and understanding cognitively, and more than engaging in a single or small number of practice sessions. To access all that RM has to offer and make the kind of shifts our interviewees report in Chapter 6, we need to engage with RM at an experiential and embodied level and we need to practise (rehearse) repeatedly.

This section of the book is therefore designed to help you take the principles of Insight Dialogue (ID)-based RM and the RM guidelines from the printed page into your lives, with the aim of supporting learning at an embodied and experiential level through repeated practice. Each of the six chapters following this one will delve into one of the RM guidelines and provide exercises, practices, and examples from our coach interviewees. The aim is to illuminate what each guideline offers, and how we can apply it formally and informally. We hope that undertaking the practices suggested will give you an experience of how it feels to bring mindfulness into relationship. From that experiential level, a whole different world of learning can open up.

This chapter is designed to set the scene for Chapters 8–13, so that you know what to expect and, particularly, what formal RM practice/mindful dialogue/relational meditation is about. In Section 4, we will explore how to bring RM into our coaching, which is one way that our experiential learning in RM can be applied to important effect.

Note: We would also recommend considering attending an organised programme, such as the RM for coaches programmes we run. The benefits of attending such a programme include being part of a group of people all of whom are engaging in mindful dialogue, with a shared interest in this way of learning and in the potential RM offers for relationships in general and coaching in particular. You will also have the advantage of being guided in the mindful dialogue practices by a teacher who has deep understanding and experience of RM practice and of bringing RM into their coaching. The programme will give you an experience of practising with the ID-based RM guidelines in the group sessions (in pairs, small groups, and the whole group) and will provide support between sessions for practising individually and relationally – including helping you buddy up with other participants for mindful dialogue. Please see the dedicated website accompanying this book for details.

Table 7.1 Four categories of practice

	Individual	Relational
Formal	Formal individual practice e.g. individual meditation or mindfulness practice	Formal relational practice e.g. relational meditation or mindful dialogue
Informal	Informal individual practice e.g. engaging mindfully in daily activities	Informal relational practice e.g. engaging mindfully in daily interpersonal interactions

Four categories of practice

In the next six chapters, we will be providing you with four categories of practice. These four categories are illustrated in the 2×2 matrix shown in Table 7.1. You will find a mini version of this table before each type of practice in Chapters 8–13 to indicate where in the matrix the practice described lies. The two axes of the matrix are explained below.

Formal and informal practice

Practising mindfulness generally involves taking time on a regular basis to engage in a specific activity that develops mindfulness capability. The aim is, initially, to get into a state of mindful awareness and, in the longer term, to increase the frequency and duration of being in a mindful state, through which mindfulness can become a stable trait (Jamieson & Tuckey, 2017). Mindfulness practice activities are very often a form of meditation involving focusing attention on a chosen object, such as sensations in the body, the sensations of breathing, a mantra, sensations of walking, or other focus; and meditation can be practised sitting, walking, lying down, or in other postures.

As anyone who meditates knows, the human mind is not naturally good at maintaining focus on any particular object for any length of time, so the mind will wander off again and again. The practice is to notice that the mind is no longer where we intended it to be, then to return the attention to the chosen object. The word 'practice' is very appropriate as we need to practise this process of noticing and returning attention again and again to build the habit of being able to place and maintain our attention where we choose.

These practices, where we set aside time and engage in a specific mindfulness activity, are generally referred to as 'formal practice' (Birtwell et al, 2019). We step out of the other activities of our life intentionally to develop mindfulness, generally with the aim that, by doing so, we become more mindful at other times as well.

By contrast, 'informal practice' refers to engaging mindfully in our daily life (Birtwell et al, 2019). When learning mindfulness, we might be encouraged to choose a routine activity – for example, brushing our teeth, showering, eating, walking to work, or washing the dishes – and to make a deliberate effort to bring moment-to-moment awareness to the felt experience of engaging in the activity. We might also be invited to pause for a mindful moment at points throughout our day. This helps us build informal practices of mindfulness into our lives, developing our capacity to be aware of what we are doing while we are doing it as we go about our day.

Over time, a combination of formal and informal practice can enable us to be mindfully present in more and more of our day-to-day life, and less likely to be running routines and habits on 'autopilot' with little awareness or engagement.

Individual and relational practice

The descriptions of formal and informal practice given above focused on individual mindfulness and meditation practice. Whilst there may be other people around when we engage in individual practice, it does not involve directly interacting with others. For example, in formal individual practice, we may be sitting with a group of fellow meditators or following a mindfulness teacher's guidance, but we are not engaging with the other(s) as part of the practice. And in informal individual practice, we might be with family members or walking through a crowd, but again our focus is on our own experience, not on communicating mindfully with those around us. By contrast, RM practice – relational meditation or mindful dialogue – involves speaking and listening as part of the mindfulness or meditation activity.

In individual practice, the focus of attention tends to be on the sensations of our own body or its contact with the external world, whereas in relational practice, we broaden our focus of attention explicitly to include the interaction we are having with another or others. Thus, in RM practice, we choose to bring awareness right into the moment of interaction with another human being, imbuing our listening and speaking with intentional awareness. The ID-based RM guidelines (as outlined in Chapter 5 and described in more detail in Chapters 8–13) support us with different aspects of bringing mindful awareness to relationship.

Formal RM practice involves being in meditative dialogue with one or more dialogue partner(s), contemplating a particular pre-determined topic or question. Informal RM practice invites us to bring mindfulness to our interactions with others in our day-to-day lives. For coaches, the intention for learning RM practice may be to bring mindfulness into interactions with clients during coaching sessions. Having taught ID-based RM to many coaches over recent years, our experience is that the learning gained through RM can have benefits for our relationships way beyond our professional lives – an observation confirmed by the findings from the research we conducted with coaches.

Both individual mindfulness and RM practices are designed to help us choose where we place our attention and to enable greater discernment in our ways of being in the world. The aim is to help us pay attention moment-by-moment and bring a non-judgemental, dispassionate attitude to our experience. Mindfulness practices also aim to enable us to become more aware of our habits and reactions, and to allow us more space between stimulus and response in which to choose what we do. The distinction with RM practice is that we are explicitly looking to build these new capacities in our relationships. Thus, through RM practice, we can become aware of our relational habits in the moment in practice, enabling greater choice and flexibility in our speaking and listening.

The formal practice of relational meditation has the advantage of providing mutual support between dialogue partners, which can help with stabilising attention, as outlined in Chapter 4. This is underpinned by a range of neurobiological mechanisms that operate when we connect with one another, such as brain synchronisation, release of oxytocin, and vagal tone (see Chapter 20).

A potential downside of relational meditation is that interacting with another person can pull us into habitual patterns of conversation and, particularly when the interaction is stimulating, generate reactivity. In individual mindfulness practice, we spend much of our time noticing that our mind has wandered and choosing to bring it back. In RM practice, we are learning to notice when our mind has been drawn into habitual patterns and to build new habits of bringing our full attention and discernment to speaking and listening as it happens, even when emotionally charged interactions might tend to pull us into reactive states such as anger, fear, excitement, embarrassment (to name just a few!). In the process, we also learn about ourselves and our habits.

As mentioned in Chapter 4, Reina et al (2022) conducted qualitative research in which they looked at how individuals integrate their mindfulness into their day-to-day interactions with others, in a process that they call 'mindfulness infusion.' In this case, individuals were practising mindfulness individually and applying the capacities gained relationally. Multiple research studies have shown that individual mindfulness practice does have beneficial effects on relationships through promoting the conditions for empathy and compassion (see Chapter 3 and the Mindfulness Initiative's 2020 and 2022 reports for more details on this). We would certainly encourage coaches to engage in individual mindfulness as well as RM to enhance their capacity for awareness, empathy, and compassion in coaching and other relationships. Chapters 8–13 therefore include suggestions for applying the ID-based RM guidelines in our individual mindfulness practice (both formal and informal).

Whilst we encourage individual mindfulness and meditation practice and engage in it ourselves, our proposition, as set out in Chapters 4 and 6 and supported by the evidence from the coaches we interviewed, is that practising relationally will have an even stronger and more direct effect on our capacity for mindful awareness, empathy, compassion, and wisdom in relationship.

Chapters 8–13 and Appendix 1 therefore provide guidance designed to help you engage in formal and informal RM practices.

Kramer (2007) calls formal ID or mindful dialogue practice 'mutual interpersonal practice' because both (or all) people involved have agreed to engage in the dialogue, use the ID/RM guidelines, and support one another's meditation/contemplation. By comparison, he describes informal practice, where we engage one or more of the ID/RM guidelines in an everyday interaction, as 'unilateral interpersonal practice.' He emphasises the value of both – as do we. However, Kramer goes on to say, "*In truth, there is no such thing as unilateral practice, just as there is no practice separate from life: it is all life… Personal change brings about relational change… we share our practice with others through induction, or resonance, and they are naturally invited into their own greater capacity*" (Kramer, 2007, p.229).

Thus, the suggestion is that as mindful dialogue practice enhances our capability to be aware, compassionate, and wise, and we bring that into our daily relationships, others will respond differently to us and our relationships will change. Such shifts are in line with the neurobiological mechanisms described in Chapter 20.

Next, we will delve into RM practice in more detail, starting with formal ID-based RM practice, then looking at informal RM practice.

Formal ID-based RM practice

The elements of ID-based RM practice

As mentioned in Chapter 5, the formal practice of ID-based RM involves meditating together in dyads, small groups, or a large group. The meditative nature of the dialogue is anchored by six guidelines; and a contemplation topic or question steers the meditative sharing. See Figure 7.1 as a reminder of these core elements of RM practice.

The parameters for formal RM practice

The intention in RM practice is to bring our attention to the process of speaking and listening, becoming aware moment-by-moment of our relational interaction. Formal RM practice – relational meditation or mindful dialogue – invites us to slow down this interaction process and allows us to step out of the habitual rush of normal conversation. This, in turn, can help us discover things about ourselves, to notice relational habits and patterns that are out of awareness in our day-to-day, non-meditative lives: to spot such habits and patterns, we need to bring kindness and curiosity.

To help us suspend normal conventions of conversation and support the meditative quality of the mindful dialogue, we start formal RM practice with

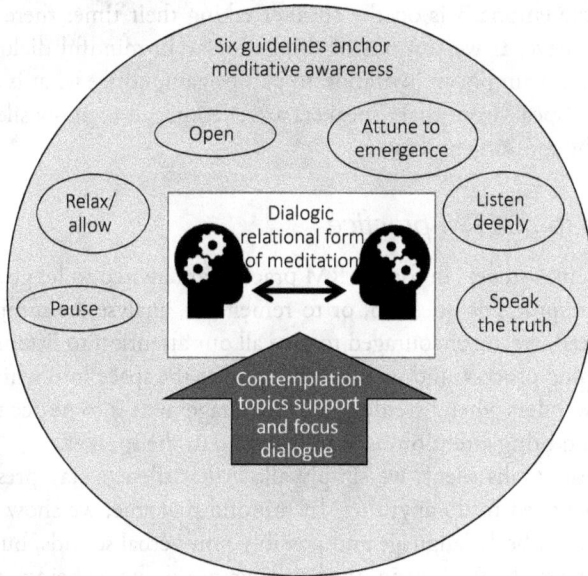

Figure 7.1 Characteristics of ID-based RM practice.

a period of silent or guided individual meditation, then usually have an initial period of relational practice with a separate speaker and listener(s). The individual practice helps settle and ground the co-meditators before engaging in dialogue. The separation of speaker and listener roles removes a layer of complexity in the dialogue as the meditators know their role is either purely speaking, with no need to listen to their partner, or purely listening, with no need to speak.

Once both/all speakers have spoken individually, there will generally be a period of shared dialogue, which gives the meditators an opportunity to become aware of the added elements the to-and-fro of speaking and listening introduces. Once participants are familiar with relational meditation, the teacher may introduce other formats of practice, such as inviting the listener to reflect back what they have heard or what has been evoked for them.

Speaking in formal RM practice

For the speaker in formal RM practice, the invitation is to let go of conventions such as feeling a need to create a coherent flow or fill the time/space. In this practice, it is OK to pause; in fact, pausing is positively encouraged as a foundation for bringing awareness to what is arising, and for speaking from that present-moment awareness.

A pause might take the form of a moment of silence in the speaking or simply an internal process of noticing and returning attention to the here-and-now.

Either way, the emphasis is on the speaker taking their time: there is no rush, nothing to achieve. If we run out of things to say in mindful dialogue, that is perfectly fine; it is simply an invitation to pause again, notice what is arising and, if/when ready, speak from that. Speakers are encouraged to allow silence to be a support for the speaking process.

Listening in formal RM practice

In a similar vein, listeners in formal RM practice are invited to let go of any need to prepare a response or question, or to remember, analyse, or summarise what we hear. Instead, we are encouraged to give all our attention to listening, to relax into the listening process, and to allow the speaker the space into which to speak. If our mind wanders when listening, the encouragement is to notice that as soon as possible, and bring attention back to listening to the speaker.

If the speaker falls silent, we simply allow that silence, stay present and let go of any urge/need to do anything. In mindful dialogue, we show that we are listening with our body language and possibly non-verbal sounds, but we do not intervene with words. We 'rest in' the listening, our only role being to receive the speaker's speaking. Even if we are asked to reflect back what we have heard as a listener, the encouragement is not to treat the listening as an exercise in storing up what we are hearing and then regurgitating it. Instead, we bring full awareness to the moment of listening and trust that, in this way, the speaker's words and broader communication will be received and will be available to us when we are invited to reflect back.

A note about the significance of the bell/timings in formal RM practice

As well as the characteristics set out above, one of the practical distinctions between formal ID-based RM practice and informal RM practice or everyday conversations is that there is a defined amount of time available for each part of the dialogue. During in-person practice, these timings and transitions between the phases of a dialogue will generally be indicated by the teacher ringing a bell. The teacher may also ring the bell during a contemplation to invite the meditators to pause before returning to dialogue. In online organised RM practice sessions, these timings will generally involve moving in and out of breakout rooms and receiving notifications from the teacher to indicate transitions between speakers and into shared dialogue. For mindful dialogue outside of a formal session, as you will see below, we recommend having a mindfulness bell to hold these timings.

However the timings are held, the fact that they are there is in itself an important support for practice. Sometimes the end of a phase of mindful dialogue practice may be a relief and a welcome opportunity to release whatever is happening. At other times the bell/banner/end of phase may be perceived as an unwelcome interruption and give rise to frustration or a sense of loss. Whatever the immediate response, the significance of these transitions is not simply to indicate the formal nature of the practice and the safety that structure provides. They also invite us to notice and interrupt any habits that might be running in that moment, creating an opportunity for change; and they remind us of the reality of impermanence, that nothing lasts and that we can learn to remain stable in the face of constant change and transition.

Practising online or in-person

You might imagine that RM practice would be largely an in-person activity. However, even when ID was initially created, online practice was part of the picture (Kramer, 2007) and, due to its international nature, the ID community has always included online mindful dialogue offerings. Whilst I (Emma) initially practised and offered mindful dialogue in-person, since the Covid-19 pandemic sent most of us online in 2020, I have moved to mainly offering online programmes. In our experience, videoconferencing services such as Zoom provide a good platform for online RM practice, though Kramer also shares examples of people practising ID in synchronous and asynchronous chat formats.

There is a wonderful richness about being together in the same physical location in mindful dialogue, so we would encourage you to experience that when you can, and we continue to seek out in-person opportunities ourselves. However, online practice also has a lot to recommend it. Firstly, practising relational meditation online allows you to dialogue with people who may not be near you geographically, giving access to a wider pool of potential dialogue partners. Secondly, not having to travel to mindful dialogue sessions means that you can fit practice opportunities into your day with more ease, as well as reducing your carbon footprint! Thirdly, engaging in mindful dialogue from your own home or office can give a sense of building RM into your everyday life rather than it being something apart. Finally, if your life involves online interactions, the experience of mindful dialogue online can help you connect more deeply with people over videoconferencing in those other contexts. One of the participants in an online RM for coaches programme in July 2020 reported that engaging in mindful dialogue gave her an experience of connecting with another human being in a way that she had not been able to do since starting to do all her work online in March 2020.

Discomfort and learning in formal RM practice

Whilst it may sound simple, formally practising RM is often hard to do. We are moving into unfamiliar ways of operating, which may feel uncomfortable for some people. It can also be a powerful and unfamiliar experience to be fully present with a fellow human being: we are invited into 'unconstructed intimacy' (see Box 7.1). Meanwhile, relational meditation may enable us to become aware of habits and patterns that were previously unconscious – another potential source of discomfort.

Box 7.1 Unconstructed intimacy

If we really look closely at our interactions with other people, we can see that they generally involve socially constructed selves: I have constructions in my mind about who I am and you are; you have constructions in your head about who you are and I am; we both have constructions (which may or may not be similar) about what is OK and not OK to say and do, social norms, habits, culture, and so on. These constructions are a natural part of how we operate in the world, they give us short-cuts and heuristics to help us live our lives. However, our constructions are also out of awareness most of the time: we take them for granted and believe that they are true.

The invitation in relational meditation/mindful dialogue is to slow down and bring full awareness to what is arising internally, externally, and in the relationship with our meditation partner. With practice, we can begin to see the constructions from which and through which we operate, and even the constructing process itself as it unfolds. We can potentially free ourselves from this 'magic show' of continual constructing, and instead interact with our meditation partner in a way that is free of these constraints, that is 'unconstructed.' We can find the wisdom, compassion, and love that lie within us all – and potentially even see that the duality of separate selves is also a construction.

This raises interesting distinctions between the intimacy we experience in the day-to-day world of friendships, marriage, family, and work relationships as compared with the intimacy we can experience in mindful dialogue. The intimacy that we experience in our relationships 'out in the world' is constructed, often over a period of time. It is built of shared experiences, agreements (whether implicit or explicit), wishes, and intentions and is deeply woven into our neurological structure. We have created familiarity, closeness, understanding, and safety in these relationships, which supports us to be open and intimate in the usual sense of the word.

By contrast, the intimacy we experience in relational meditation arises because we are in direct contact with our experience whilst present with another person. This directness of experiencing can help us step outside the constructed sense of self and other. The more we can let go of wanting things to be a particular way and simply be present with the immediacy of the moment, the greater the intimacy we have with everything in our experience, including our dialogue partner. Kramer (2007) calls this 'unconstructed intimacy' because it is not constructed by a 'hungry personality.' The term 'hungry personality' refers to the natural habit we all have to build a personality, an identity, a solo, separate self (Siegel, 2022). This sense of a separate self results in, and feeds, a range of 'hungers', such as a hunger to be seen in a particular way and not to be seen in other ways – see more below.

The potentially uncomfortable and unfamiliar nature of formal RM practice is normal and probably even helpful: it is taking us out of our comfort zone. To learn, we probably need to move into our discomfort zone: this space where we are challenged, and faced with new circumstances and new perspectives is where we learn. See Figure 7.2.

In formal RM practice, we are offered the opportunity to notice – and see if we can stay present with – discomfort, with the aim of learning and growing. For example, in mindful dialogue, we may notice particular 'hungers' arise, natural human habits in which we want things to be a particular way. We may observe any of the following arising:

- *Wanting pleasure:* we may want to feel enjoyment such as finding the dialogue entertaining, interesting, fun, or we may want the pleasure of connection and rapport with our dialogue partner(s)
- *Wanting to be seen:* we may want be seen in a particular light by our dialogue partner(s), for them to find us entertaining, impressive, funny, interesting, or empathetic, or we may want them to like and respect us

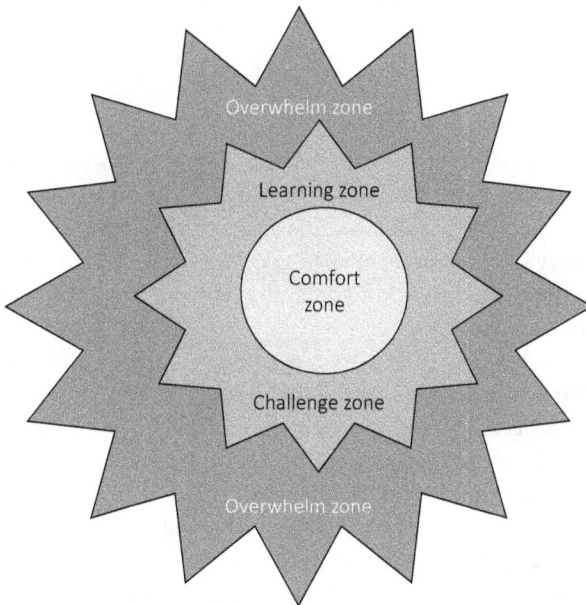

Figure 7.2 Finding our learning zone.

Note: The Learning Zone Model was originally developed by psychologist Lev Vygotsky, but has since been developed and popularised by others, most notably educator Tom Senninger.

■ *Wanting to disappear:* we may feel vulnerability, shyness, or embarrassment whilst in dialogue with another, fearing being seen as 'ignorant', 'boring', or 'unlikeable', wanting the earth to swallow us up when we have said something we regret or a sense of overwhelm at the intimacy of being together in this way

As well as experiencing these natural human hungers, we will generally find that we are more at ease with some people than others. Perhaps due to differences in values, approach, and/or background, we may find we have less of an affinity with some dialogue partners, which can lead to a sense of disconnect or confusion. Thus, there may be pleasure or discomfort in dialoguing with certain others.

These hungers, differences, and challenges are always operating in our lives. The invitation in relational meditation is to become more aware of them arising, and to practise being with the thoughts, emotions, and sensations. We can begin to see how these things pull/push/urge us into behaving in certain ways: seeing this can help us make more discerning choices about how we respond. We are not trying to change or get rid of our natural tendencies, instead, we are slowing down enough to notice them, bringing kindness to ourselves and others, and allowing ourselves the space to act with wisdom rather than out of blind habit. In this way, RM practice helps us learn, develop, and even transform.

Establishing safety for formal RM practice

Whilst moving out of our comfort zone is important for learning, we need to be careful not to get pushed into our overwhelm zone, where we are stimulated into 'fight, flight or freeze' stress states and shut down to learning, moving out of our window of tolerance (see Chapter 3). The aim in formal RM practice is therefore to establish safety – just as we would in coaching or learning programmes. It is important to adopt an ethic of 'do no harm' and bring kindness to ourselves and our partners in dialogue.

This tone of safety and mutual care can be supported by establishing a set of agreements that create a commitment for dialogue partners to look after themselves and each other with care. In an organised RM programme, the agreements will typically be along the lines of those set out in Box 7.2.

Confidentiality is perhaps the most important of these agreements, so that we trust that anything we share in our dialogue will not be repeated to others. In an organised RM group programme or session, what others say in pair/small group practice is not even shared with other members of the larger group during whole-group practice, let alone shared beyond the session participants. However, if a participant in such a programme feels that their dialogue partner is breaking other agreements, particularly if they are speaking in a harsh or abusive way, the encouragement is to ask the teacher for help, and this may involve breaking confidentiality.

Box 7.2 Agreements to establish safety in formal RM practice

■ As a dialogue partner, I agree to…
    …keeping all content confidential – speaking only of my own experience, not about others

■ As a speaker, I agree to…
    …only speaking what feels comfortable to share.
    …not speaking what is divisive, harsh, abusive, or false, but instead speaking what is kind, honest, appropriate, and of goodwill

■ As a listener, I agree to…
    …listening with no need to comment, ask questions, or give advice

---

For those planning to practise RM formally outside of an organised programme, it is important to find someone with whom you are confident that you will feel safe enough to step beyond your comfort zone, and who you assess will not trigger you into your overwhelm zone (see further guidance below). When you have agreed to practise RM formally together, before starting the process, it will be important to put in place agreements such as those in Box 7.2 to support both parties' safety.

Trauma-sensitivity

During practice, we may find that emotions arise, in ourselves or in our partner. This is completely normal as mindful contemplation can bring up emotionally charged realisations or reflections. It is important to just notice any discomfort that this may arouse and not react to a need to rescue, advise, or support our dialogue partner. In relational meditation, we are invited to allow the emotions to flow through us, and to bring kindness to ourselves and each other.

However, it is important to bring trauma-sensitivity to the process (Treleaven, 2018). If one or other dialogue partner is triggered into a trauma response, we need to be prepared to interrupt the dialogue to re-establish stability and support the person to ground themselves. In an organised programme, the teacher or other designated stability support person will be available to help with this. For those practising outside an organised programme, the key step when someone is experiencing a trauma response is to help the person find a safe and stable place within themselves and to be sensitive to their individual needs rather than assuming we know what will help them. We recommend reading David Treleaven's work in this area (Treleaven, 2018).

Eye contact

One other point to be aware of as we start to practise mindful dialogue is eye contact. One of the ways we know that someone is listening to us is that they make eye contact and being in eye contact has powerful effects on our embodied state. However, relational meditation is definitely not designed to be a staring match and it is important to be aware that different people have different levels of comfort with eye contact, whether for cultural, historical, or personal reasons including neurodivergence. To establish a sense of safety as well as connection, it is important that we notice and manage levels of eye contact to suit our own needs, while also being sensitive to our dialogue partner's needs. Practising mindful dialogue on videoconferencing may disrupt eye contact, so it is important to notice the impact of that.

Ethics, integrity, and care in formal RM practice

At this point, we would like to make explicit what has perhaps been implied or underlying much of what we have said so far: ID-based RM depends on and develops a strong ethos of ethics, integrity, and care for one another and the wider world. The agreements that we establish at the start of an organised RM programme or before engaging in formal mindful dialogue outside of an organised programme are not a formality. The creation of an ethical basis and agreements around mutual care are an important part of the practice.

In the original Buddhist version of ID, particularly on an ID retreat, meditators are asked to agree to a set of 'precepts' or ethical principles as a basis for relational meditation. These would cover areas such as doing no harm (including not engaging in harmful or harsh speech), not taking anything that is not freely given (including not revealing another's sharing from a dialogue), speaking truthfully and with discernment, avoiding intoxicants (including putting away addictive technology for the duration of the practice), and avoiding sexual misconduct (including not taking the intimacy establishing in relational meditation as an invitation for sexual advances). Ethical standards and acting with integrity and care are intrinsic not only to the relational foundation of ID, but also to the wisdom/insight foundation. Ethical behaviour is fundamental to the Buddha's teachings and a *sine qua non* in developing wisdom.

ID-based RM has the same foundations and is based on the same ethical intention and attitudes as ID. Without ethical mutual care, we cannot establish the conditions for developing the qualities and capacities detailed in Chapter 6. As mentioned, RM practice offers the potential for learning and developing at an experiential and embodied level. It is not just about cognitive change or even behavioural and skill development – it goes deeper and broader into ways of being and ways of seeing. Practising with integrity and attitudes of care for one another are an essential part of that process.

In mindful dialogue and other RM practices, the agreements we make and the ethical principles we establish are not rules to be obeyed but instead attitudes that help us grow. They bring a discernment and intentionality to how we bring mindfulness and compassion into our lives and our coaching, for the benefit of ourselves, our clients, and the wider world. The intention is that we not only espouse, but also embody a sense of care for self, other, and the interconnected whole.

Choosing a dialogue partner for formal RM practice outside of an organised programme

Given all that we say above about learning and safety in formal RM practice, it will not be a surprise to learn that we recommend you think carefully about who you practise mindful dialogue with. Participants in our RM programmes have the benefit of being able to practise with each other, ensuring that both partners have already demonstrated an interest in RM, had an introduction to mindful dialogue, and signed up to a set of agreements designed to keep the practice safe and supportive.

If you have not attended an RM programme and are looking to practise with someone from your existing circle, we recommend you identify someone who:

■ Shares your interest in bringing mindfulness into relationships
■ Will sign up to a set of agreements to establish safety during the practice (particularly an agreement to keep all that is said in mindful dialogue confidential – see Box 7.2 for a suggested list of agreements)
■ You trust not to judge you or what you say in dialogue and with whom you feel safe
■ Has sufficient awareness and mindfulness to engage with mindful dialogue: they do not need to be super-meditators or perfectly mindful at all times (!) but they do need at least some capacity to bring their attention into the moment and understanding of what mindfulness and meditation are about

Process for formal ID-based RM practice outside of an organised programme

When engaging in a formal ID-based RM practice (mindful dialogue or relational meditation) with one or more other people, we suggest the following process. Once again, we emphasise that this is not just about a set of 'doing' activities or an intellectual exploration. Instead, it is about exploring a way of 'being' and investigating at an embodied level, with an intention to bring mutual care at all times.

■ ***Setting agreements:*** You will need to create agreements to establish safety for the RM practice. These may be based on those set out in Box 7.2 and/ or your own agreements that are meaningful to the two (or more) of you

- ■ *Agreeing logistics:* You will also need to agree:
  - ■ How you will manage time – you will probably find it helpful to have a mindfulness bell app to support you with timings and setting it to ring at regular/specified intervals. (Examples include Meditation Timer, Mindfulness Bell, and Insight Timer, but there are no doubt others and you may already have your own favourite!) This will save you having to set and reset a timer for each section of the practice
  - ■ How long you will each speak for – initially, it may be good to start with relatively short time slots, for example, 5 minutes. You may want to increase this as the practice becomes more familiar
  - ■ Who will be the first speaker (and second speaker if there are three of you)
- ■ *Agreeing the contemplation question or topic and format for the dialogue:* The resources accompanying Chapters 8–13 (see Appendix 1 and the dedicated website accompanying this book) provide a range of contemplation questions and topics that you can use as the focus for dialogue. You will also find different formats for the dialogue in the later chapters
- ■ *Individual mindfulness practice to settle and ground:* It is important to take some time in silence (or guided individual practice) to settle and ground yourselves and anchor the RM practice in mindful awareness – included as Step 1 below
- ■ *Pair/small group formal RM practice:* Now you are ready to engage in the relational meditation/mindful dialogue itself. In your initial practices, we recommend you have a designated speaker, and the other person is/people are the listener(s), and keeping to a simple speaker 1, then speaker 2, then shared dialogue format. Assuming you are practising in a pair, the process could be as follows:
  - ■ *Step 1:* As mentioned above, you start with an individual practice: you can bring a particular RM guideline silently in your mind or use one of the audios provided in the resources on the dedicated website accompanying this book to guide you both through a practice (see link below)
  - ■ *Step 2:* After the silent practice, the first speaker takes 5 minutes to speak, during which the intention is that…
    - ■ …the speaker pauses to attend to sensations in the body and speaks from the felt sense of what arises in response to the chosen contemplation topic, drawing on further pauses to support mindful speaking
    - ■ … the listener rests in receptive awareness, staying connected to the sensations in the body and receiving the speaker's sharing, pausing internally to support mindful listening

- *Step 3:* After 5 minutes, you both pause briefly to settle into moment-to-moment experience in silence
- *Step 4:* Then, the second speaker takes 5 minutes to speak with the same intentions for both speaker and listener as set out for the first speaker's turn
- *Step 5:* After 5 minutes, you both take a further pause
- *Step 6:* Then, you release the form of separate speaker and listener and take a further 5 minutes to engage in shared dialogue, either continuing the same contemplation or developing the contemplation question slightly, with the same intentions for speaking and listening as when the roles of speaker and listener were separated out
- *Step 7:* Finally, you round off your dialogue and, unless you are continuing into a further dialogue, express your appreciation of one another (recognising that you could not do this practice without each other)

Once you are familiar with mindful dialogue, you may want to engage in formats of practice different to the one above, for example, inviting the listener to reflect back what they have heard or what has been evoked for them. Suggestions for these formats are set out in the resources accompanying Chapters 12 and 13 (see Appendix 1 and dedicated website). We encourage you to spend some time practising with the above format before doing this as it takes a while to establish familiarity with the process of meditating in relationship in this way.

Informal RM practice

Informal RM practice is about weaving RM into our relationships in our daily lives by bringing mindful awareness and the ID-based RM guidelines into our interactions with other people, including our coaching clients. Chapters 8–13 offer suggestions for this for each of the guidelines: bringing the guideline Pause into daily interactions, bringing the guideline Relax/allow into daily interactions, and so on.

As we become more familiar with the guidelines, and particularly as we practise formal mindful dialogue, it becomes easier to draw on the support of the ID-based RM guidelines for all our relationships. It becomes natural to pause and bring mindfulness as we listen and speak, to release tension and bring receptivity to what others are sharing, to maintain a sense of internal awareness as well as being present to the other. With practice, we get more adept at recognising and letting go of our preconceptions and assumptions so that we can listen fully and deeply to what others have to say. As we begin to embody the wisdom inherent in the ID-based RM guidelines, we can be more discerning about what we do and do not say, better able to choose the right tone and content when we talk about difficult topics, and kinder to ourselves and others in how we speak and what we communicate.

However, it is worth remembering that what we are aiming to do here may be changing habits built up over a lifetime. Bringing RM into relationship is likely to be particularly hard when an interaction is particularly charged – either with challenging emotions such as anger or fear, or with excitement and joy. Changing our way of being in these situations is especially difficult as the high emotional intensity makes it more likely for us to fall into habitual patterns of reactivity and we may get carried away on the waves of emotion. So, we cannot expect change to be immediate or easy – it takes time to build up the new neural pathways. As Kramer says, "*Our everyday relational life is the most difficult place to practice – and the most fruitful... we must be patient with ourselves... rest in kindness to ourselves*" (Kramer, 2007, p.229).

Kramer (2007) makes some suggestions for informal (or "unilateral") RM practice that are worth considering across all the guidelines:

■ Start with a focus on just one RM guideline. The guideline Pause is the easiest starting point, but we can focus on any of the guidelines and may find that some are particularly helpful in particular situations (bringing in Relax/allow when we are stressed, for example, or Attune to emergence when we know we might resist change, want a clear plan, or get stuck in our preconceived notion of how things should be)

■ Bring a guideline in for a time-limited situation or encounter. It may be less daunting to apply an RM guideline to a particular meeting, coaching session, or social interaction – where there is a beginning and end – rather than to aim to apply it open-endedly

■ Choose to experiment with bringing the RM guidelines to support us according to whom we encounter, how difficult we find interacting with that person, the purpose of being with them and/or the emotional tone of the interaction. (For example, we might choose to play with bringing Open and Listen Deeply into our coaching to help us stay in touch with our embodied internal experience whilst also listening attentively to the external experience of what our client is sharing.)

■ Mentally rehearse bringing one or more RM guidelines into a particular relationship or encounter before meeting that person. Just as athletes and sportspeople can enhance their performance by mentally rehearsing their movements, so too we can build our relational 'muscles' by integrating the guidelines into our thinking about interactions. In place of rehashing past encounters we regret or fearing a negative outcome from future ones, we can intentionally think through new potential repertoires. (For example, imagine bringing Pause into an interaction with a family member or client we find challenging.)

All these suggestions rest on a foundation of intention. Knowing the benefit that this way of being offers, we set an intention to apply our RM practice in our relational life. This helps us to bring the energy and application needed to remember and actively bring our RM practice to everyday relational moments.

One specific form of informal RM practice – arguably the purpose of this book – is bringing RM into coaching. We have dedicated the whole of Section 4 to considering this. Before getting to that, in Chapters 8–13, we delve more deeply into each of the RM guidelines and how to apply them in formal and informal, individual and relational practice.

References

Birtwell, K., Williams, K., van Marwijk, H., Armitage, C. J., & Sheffield, D. (2019). An exploration of formal and informal mindfulness practice and associations with well-being. *Mindfulness*, 10(1), 89–99.

Blake, A. (2022). *Embodied awareness, embodied practice: A powerful path to practical wisdom.* PhD Thesis, Case Western Reserve University.

Jamieson, S. D., & Tuckey, M. R. (2017). Mindfulness interventions in the workplace: A critique of the current state of the literature. *Journal of Occupational Health Psychology*, 22(2), 180.

Kramer, G. (2007). *Insight Dialogue: The interpersonal path to freedom.* Shambhala.

Mindfulness Initiative (2020). *Mindfulness: Developing agency in urgent times.* Mindfulness Initiative.

Mindfulness Initiative (2022). *Reconnection: Meeting the climate crisis inside out.* Mindfulness Initiative.

Reina, C. S., Kreiner, G. E., Rheinhardt, A., & Mihelcic, C.A (2022). Your presence is requested: Mindfulness infusion in workplace interactions and relationships. *Organization Science*, 34(2), 722–753.

Siegel, D. (2022). *IntraConnected.* W. W. Norton & Company.

Treleaven, D. A. (2018). *Trauma-sensitive mindfulness: Practices for safe and transformative healing.* W. W. Norton & Company.

Information

Dedicated website accompanying this book: www.relationalmindfulness.net

Chapter 8

Practising Pause

The quieter you become, the more you are able to hear.

Rumi

The guideline Pause is the fundamental starting point for engaging in ID-based mindful dialogue. Without pausing, we cannot engage the other Relational Mindfulness (RM) guidelines. As Stephanie says, "...*the pause seems to me to be the cornerstone of practising RM.*" In this chapter, we explore how to practice with the guideline Pause.

What is Pause?

The guideline Pause invites us to become fully present moment-by-moment, whilst speaking and listening, and reminds us to return our attention to the present moment when our mind wanders off. Pausing helps us to become more aware, to notice what is happening right now. It might involve an actual 'temporary stop' in the dialogue process, or it might be a more subtle interruption of the flow of habit and mental activity as we become aware of that flow and make the choice to bring our attention to what is happening in this moment.

In individual meditation, we might aim to focus our attention on the breath, the body, or another meditation object. When the mind wanders, we return the attention to our chosen focus to dwell in the immediate experience of here-and-now. In the same way, in RM practice we pause to return our attention to our immediate experience in relationship, while speaking, listening, or just being together. In both individual and relational meditation, as the sensations in the body or of breathing are always in the present moment, these can provide an

DOI: 10.4324/9781003390428-11

anchor to which we can 'come home' when our minds wander off or we get caught in habit.

Most of the time we bowl along with the momentum of 'automatic pilot', our minds busy ruminating on the past, worrying about the future, planning what we will do, and missing most of what is happening in the moment. When in conversation with another person, many of us spend a lot of time planning what we are going to say rather than fully listening to the other, and rolling out familiar stories rather than speaking of what is new, fresh, and true right now. Pause invites us to remember to bring attention to our in-the-moment experience, be that speaking or listening or simply being with a fellow human being. As Shenaz says, "*I realised that Pause was like shining a beam of light on 'where are my thoughts right now and how am I feeling in the present moment?'*"

Awareness means choice

In the relational domain, we all have habitual patterns around who we are trying to be with other people. Speaking and listening with others can trigger these patterns and habits strongly, so pausing is especially needed in relationships. A Pause can help us notice our automatic reactions and is the first step towards having choice over our subsequent actions. Once we become aware of our tendencies, instead of doing what we have always done, perhaps following the urging of our reactivity, we can bring discernment to what would be the wisest, kindest thing to do or say in these specific circumstances.

However, interacting with and being in relationship with others offer perhaps the most challenging situations into which to bring awareness of the present moment. Breaking old habits, not reacting to triggers, and redirecting our attention to immediate experience require intention and energy. Practising pausing repeatedly in formal RM practice – and in all the ways set out below – can help us train the 'muscle' of intentional present-moment awareness. In neurobiological terms, these practices are building stronger neural pathways for bringing and returning our attention towards present-moment awareness throughout our life. This is a powerful shift to make. As Beth says, "*I know [Pause is] like the entry into [RM], but I would say that's like the biggest thing. If you only went that far and really considered that relationship around pause and pausing together... I think that's been the biggest influence on my work....*"

Reducing suffering and opening to wisdom

The profound result of establishing a habit of pausing is that it can help us release clinging and reactivity, which are a source of so much suffering for ourselves and those around us. Pause can become a touch point and help release us from the buffeting of daily life into something that is calmer and happier. While pausing can initially feel like a disruption of conversational flow, over time it becomes a natural way of letting go of the urging of habit and instead being in contact with the flow of present-moment awareness.

Pausing in this way runs counter to our culture of busyness, speed, and constant activity. It is in stark contrast to the distraction and attention-shifting encouraged by social media. By disrupting these patterns, the guideline Pause can start to shake us out of the cultural norms of our individualistic, constructed view of self/other towards the wisdom of interrelatedness and seeing things as they actually are.

Supporting ourselves to pause

Before we suggest specific practices for Pause, we want to set out a few ways we can support ourselves to pause in both formal and informal RM practice:

■ *Literally stopping*: Initially, pausing may require us to literally stop to interrupt the flow of our habits. In formal RM practice, we are encouraged to do this explicitly, either by pausing while speaking or requesting a pause with our dialogue partner (provided we are doing this for ourselves, not because we think *they* need to pause). In informal RM practice, we can find ways to pause in our daily interactions with others: phrases such as 'let me think for a moment...' or 'good question...' can help; simply consciously taking a breath before speaking can also be a powerful pause. We can also support others, including our coaching clients, by inviting them to pause at relevant moments, for example, if they are getting dysregulated, agitated, or 'caught'
■ *Silently saying pause:* We may find it helpful silently to say 'Pause' to ourselves, particularly when we feel the urge to react habitually to a particular trigger or cue, or to fall into a familiar narrative
■ *Body as anchor:* As mentioned, we can use the body as an anchor – feeling our feet on the floor, the sensations of breathing, our posture. Bringing awareness to the sensations of the body can give us the stability to return our full attention to the dialogue in which we are engaged – be that formal RM practice or daily interactions. We can also notice whether we experience these sensations as pleasant, unpleasant, or neutral. Intentionally moving our attention in these ways helps us to be more intimate with our experience and brings an immediacy to our awareness
■ *Supporting each other to pause:* In formal RM practice, noticing when our dialogue partner pauses can help us to pause – and similarly, our pause will help our partner to pause too. In informal RM practice, we can also become more aware of when another person pauses and of the benefit of our pausing for them. Research shows that we are neurologically built to

mirror one another in this way (Fredrickson, 2013; see Chapter 20 for more on the neurobiology of connection)

■ *Noticing mind-states:* As we become more adept at choosing where to place our attention, we can make noticing our mind-states (wanting, aversion, confusion, distraction, sleepiness...) a cue for inviting a pause. We can also become aware that we are aware – turning attention to the 'observer' that is doing the noticing. This supports the more subtle internal form of pausing mentioned above, where Pause is about interrupting habits and patterns and opens us to clearer seeing and the potential to move beyond cultural norms to a more interrelated, liberated view

Over time, through repeated practice, we learn to pause with greater ease. The Pause can be a natural internal movement of remembering and becoming fully present, without the need for explicit support. It starts to be a part of our 'way of being' in daily life as well as in formal mindful dialogue practice. As Jane says, "...*the sense of Pause is like a platform... Pause helps to reconnect to the flow... There will be moments when I recognise that I'm disconnected from the flow. Then I pause. Then there is this reconnection with a sense of the body, the sense of speaking from the body. Pause is the ground... the embodiment... the attending here in the present moment.*"

	Individual	Relational
Formal		
Informal		

Individual formal practice: individual mindfulness or meditation with Pause

Almost any mindfulness or meditation practice is likely to help you develop your capacity to pause. Sitting meditation, body scan, yoga, walking meditation, loving-kindness meditation, and simply following the breath, for example, all have at their centre the invitation to bring awareness into the present moment. As we have noted, this is what the guideline Pause is about.

Weaving Pause into an existing practice

If you already have an individual mindfulness/meditation practice, we invite you to explore how it relates to the RM guideline Pause. Is your practice essentially about pausing in one way or another? We also invite you to start linking your existing practice more closely to RM. For example, is it possible to introduce add-itional pauses into your practice, and what is the result of doing so?

Establishing a practice

If you do not already have a mindfulness/meditation practice, we strongly encourage you to establish one. Even if you only practise for 5–10 minutes a few times a week, that is a good start in terms of 'building the muscle' of choosing where you place your attention. On the dedicated website accompanying this book we provide an audio download to help you pause, together with links to meditation apps to help you establish a practice.

During an RM programme we invite participants to engage in individual practice daily, if possible. If you need support to help you practise more regularly, you could consider setting an alarm or asking someone to check in with you to prompt you to practise. Finding a regular practice group can also be helpful, including through online 'drop-in' meditation sessions.

In addition to helping you be more present and aware in your relationships, individual mindfulness/meditation practice has all sorts of benefits. Research suggests that even 10 minutes' practice a day can improve wellbeing (Chaskalson & Reitz, 2018). The same research also found that it is better to establish a regular 10-minutes-a-day practice than to practise less frequently but for longer, so it seems that regularity is important and 10 minutes a day may be enough! In the context of enhancing RM, this individual practice is a valuable element. As Pirjo says, "…*individual mindfulness practice has been an essential part of relational mindfulness.*"

If you do not already do so, you might find it helpful to keep a practice diary/record. This can help you see patterns of when you do and don't practise, which conditions do and do not support your practice, how you feel after practising, and so on.

Integrating practice

If you struggle to establish a regular mindfulness/meditation practice that involves setting aside separate time, you might consider taking on a practice that can be done whilst engaging in another activity (walking, household chores, exercising…). The Healthy Minds app offers the option of doing any of its meditation practices whilst engaged in an activity. There are also meditation teachers who offer guidance on taking a light-touch, life-integrated approach to practice, such as Alexis Santos. (See our dedicated website for links to these resources.)

Even if you have decided that formal mindfulness/meditation is not for you, please do read on and continue to explore RM. Some people find that RM is a huge support despite not engaging in regular individual formal practice. As mentioned in Chapter 1, Stephanie encourages coaches to consider RM saying, "…*even if you don't have a mindfulness practice or that's not something that you think you might want or you actively definitely don't want… RM has the capacity to be life-changing.*"

	Individual	Relational
Formal		
Informal		

Relational formal practice: relational meditation/mindful dialogue with Pause

In the resources provided in Appendix 1 and on our dedicated website, we provide a step-by-step process to help you undertake mindful dialogue with the guideline Pause. Before you start, it is vital to read Chapter 7 and follow the guidance around choosing a dialogue partner, setting agreements to establish safety, and agreeing logistics for the practice.

Suitable contemplation topics for a mindful dialogue with Pause emphasise present-moment awareness, perhaps of sensations in the body, of sounds and sights, of energy levels, or of whatever is arising (specific suggestions are provided in Appendix 1). This may seem strange and uncomfortable at first, particularly if we have a habit of seeking content in our conversations, in which case simply naming what is arising in the moment may seem 'pointless' or 'boring.' If you notice that, great! You are learning something about your habits in relationship. Can you get curious about what is going on for you in the moment – the sensations of that response, the emotions…? If your mind tells you to do something different – engage in a non-meditative conversation, for example – can you invite the attention back to what is happening right now and pause, then reengage with the contemplation topic in its full simplicity?

We recommend following a simple flow from first speaker to second speaker to shared dialogue for this practice. Practising with Pause is an essential foundation for establishing mindful awareness whilst speaking and listening.

	Individual	Relational
Formal		
Informal		

Individual informal practice: bringing Pause into daily life

If you have done a mindfulness course, you will be familiar with the invitation to bring that mindfulness into your daily life in general, not just in formal practices. To support your RM capacity, we encourage essentially the same process: we invite you to practise pausing at regular intervals throughout your day. As you may have already discovered, pausing is not actually that hard, it is remembering to pause that is challenging! As Pirjo says, "*I thought 'that's easy, to pause.' It is very easy to pause once you remember to pause, so it has been kind of funny to notice how difficult it is to remember to pause.*"

So, our suggestions are, firstly, to find ways to help yourself to pause and then to choose how you practise pausing in that moment:

- Remembering to pause – may be helped by one or more of the following:
  - Setting a clear intention to pause regularly
  - Setting a bell on your phone or computer that rings every so often to remind you to pause
  - Identifying particular moments in your day when you will pause – for example, when you change from one task to the next, each time you make yourself a drink, when you get up from and sit down at your desk…
  - Buying some small sticky dots and placing them in locations that you will see regularly (on your phone, a door handle, your kettle, your computer…), then each time you see the dot, taking a moment to pause
  - Putting post-it notes up on or behind your computer screen – as Pirjo recommends, "*I have used post-it notes behind my video camera, because most of my work is virtual nowadays… and one of them is 'pause.' So whenever I move my gaze, I notice that*"

- Pausing – could include some or all of the following:
  - Bringing your attention consciously to sensations in your body
  - If you are sitting, noticing feet on floor, backside on chair
  - Observing the sensations of breathing in and out for a few breaths – or even just one breath!
  - Noticing any pleasant, unpleasant, or neutral sensations that are present in the body, heart, and/or mind

The more you do it, the easier it gets. Emma R suggests "*…just stop and focus on what is happening, throughout the day… the more you do it, the more you [get] better at being able… to do it more often.*"

	Individual	Relational
Formal		
Informal		

Relational informal practice: bringing Pause into daily interactions with others

Perhaps the most valuable – and most challenging – ongoing practice is to build the habit of pausing in our daily interactions with others. In my (Emma's) experience, learning to bring the guideline Pause into my relationships has been transformational, giving me space to bring my values and intentions around kindness and awareness to life even when faced with relational challenges.

The invitation is to use interactions with other people as a prompt to invite in the guideline Pause. Some ideas to help you do this are:

▪ At the point of encountering/meeting someone, whether on screen or in-person, taking a brief moment to pause, to feel your feet/body and take a breath, before speaking

▪ Bringing in Pause when you are finding a relationship difficult or facing a challenging moment with someone. This can be particularly beneficial, though not always easy. As Becky says, "*I'm applying it in my professional relationships, particularly when there's a difficult relationship… when I'm having difficulty understanding the other person, or they're behaving in a way that I'm finding difficult, I find it useful to look at that through the lens of RM*"

▪ Noticing the presence of pleasant, unpleasant, or neutral sensations associated with interpersonal contact – which thoughts or feelings reverberate

▪ If an interaction is becoming high-speed or high-emotion, inviting both yourself and the other person to pause for a moment before continuing the conversation. This can help you both slow down and make wiser choices. As Stephanie explains, "*The fact of being with another affects us physically… maybe they're agitated or upset or whatever, and then there is our reactivity to whatever is going on… then the pause is totally invaluable*"

▪ When you are asked a question or invited to comment, using that as a prompt to pause and slow down, rather than feeling you need to rush into responding

▪ You may want to try what Malcolm suggests and use eye contact as a reminder to help you bring awareness into interacting with another person: "*…when I began to practise [RM] I found that eye contact with some-body was… an anchor reminding me to Pause and Open*"

▪ If it feels like pausing is disruptive of 'natural' and spontaneous ways of interacting, it may be helpful to notice that, to quote Kramer, "*what we call spontaneous and natural is usually habitual and conditioned… Pause, on the other hand, paradoxically opens the door to true spontaneity. By stepping out of reactive habit, we enter the moment afresh*" (Kramer, 2007, p.115)

Box 8.1 provides a vignette of how one of our interviewees found bringing Pause into her family life extremely valuable.

Box 8.1 The benefits of bringing Pause into family life

One of our interviewees shares a touching personal story about how bringing Pause into her relationship with her teenage son has helped her – and him – get through a difficult period: "*I have a third child… who has been very dysregulated, has been very unwell and left school: he is back to school now, but still can be quite, at times, quite explosive. I started RM when he was 15 – he's now 18 – and it has become a bridge for me. The Pause has become the absolute foundational emotional space for me. The process of relational engagement with him necessitates for me to pause nearly all the time. It's fantastic training ground: he's my 'pause coach', literally. And from there, everything is possible. It astounds me how, if I don't remember to pause, I could say the wrong thing: I could go into what I might say to my other two adult kids, and that would be completely okay for them, but is not at all what he wants to hear and then he might respond or react.*"

She also shares how she has established a formal practice with her husband to help them both navigate challenges: "*…about eight months ago, [my husband and I] started some Pause Saturdays (especially because with our son, things could be really difficult) where we would just literally put a timer on, and we'd do the five-minute pause, then I would speak for three to five minutes, and then he would speak for three to five minutes. It has become a way for us to check in around some difficult areas. So that's quite a formal practice now.*"

Having established foundational practices based on the RM guideline Pause, we are ready to build from there to the other five guidelines, starting in the next chapter with the guideline Relax/allow.

References

Chaskalson, M., & Reitz, M. (2018). *Mind Time*. Thorsons.
Fredrickson, B. (2013). *Love 2.0*. Hudson Street Press.
Kramer, G. (2007). *Insight Dialogue: The interpersonal path to freedom*. Shambhala.

Information

Dedicated website accompanying this book: www.relationalmindfulness.net

Chapter 9

Practising Relax/allow

Make the best use of what is in your power and take the rest as it happens.
Some things are up to us and some things are not up to us.

Epictetus

As mentioned, both individual mindfulness and Relational Mindfulness (RM) have two aspects: an awareness aspect of intentionally becoming aware of present-moment experience; and an attitudinal aspect of bringing non-judgement, dis-passion, and 'decentring' to that experience (Reina et al, 2023). In RM practice, these two aspects are supported by the combination of the guidelines Pause with Relax/allow. As Malcolm says, "...*putting pause and relax/allow together, it's an invitation to be mindful in the moment, in relationship.*" In this chapter, we delve into the second of these guidelines and what it means to bring Relax/allow into our practice and our lives.

What is Relax/allow?

When we pause, we will often notice tension, habitual patterns of wanting or not-wanting, and even discomfort, pain, and/or reactivity. Relax/allow invites us to be with these elements of our experience in a non-judgemental, kindly way.

In its most obvious form, Relax/allow is an invitation to release tension where we can: to notice tight muscles, for example, and gently soften and relax them to the extent that this is possible; to become aware of our racing thoughts and release the tension of chasing them, again to the extent possible. In its more subtle form, Relax/allow encourages us to shift our relationship to our experience: instead of wanting to push away tension, agitation, or discomfort, we allow it to be there. As

Kramer puts it, with Relax/allow *"we recognise tension and choose ease"* (Kramer, 2007, p.119).

Instead of reacting with aversion or grasping, we bring receptivity and open-hearted acceptance that 'this is how things are right now.' In this way, Relax/allow builds a further layer of wisdom to that provided by Pause, potentially helping us move towards greater freedom and clear seeing.

This combination of relaxing and allowing helps us reduce the tension and discomfort that get in the way of staying with our present-moment experience: we become better able to be with things as they are. The discomfort, pain, and/or reactivity may not go away, but we are holding it in a wider space of awareness, which gives us more stability and ease. This shift in perspective interrupts our tendency to react to experience. Whilst pausing and noticing is the first step towards having choices over how we respond, relaxing and allowing gives us much greater capacity to release our automatic reactions and choose how we act. Kramer describes how Relax/allow *"gives stability and continuity to Pause"* (Kramer, 2007, p.124).

Importance in relationship

In RM practice, this release of tension, letting go of judgement, and allowing things to be as they are is extended to other people. It is almost always beneficial to notice tension and invite it to release and this can be particularly true when we are in relationship. When we encounter another person, we may become excited and/or tense, for example. Pausing to notice that, then relaxing and allowing what we find, can help us to bring greater calm to our interactions with others, creating greater likelihood of a 'choiceful' interaction.

In formal mindful dialogue practice, we let go of judging our dialogue partner, trying to control them, or wanting them to be a particular way. This willingness to be with our own experience and with another human being and their experience engenders a natural flow of kindness and compassion that is extended both to ourselves and to the other. The benefit of practising in dialogue with another is that their stillness can support ours and vice versa. As Jane puts it, *"The guideline Relax is allowing of the tenderness, the vulnerability, the pain, a real tender allowing of my experience. It's the ground of unconditional love. It's a compassionate acceptance of what's here. Compassion is an enabler. With compassion there's this softening, there's this yielding, there is this 'oh, it's like this', just noticing it with a tenderness."*

Building this habit of allowing and receiving in formal RM practice enables us to take the same approach in our relationships in daily life. We can recognise when tension arises in an interaction and invite that to release, offering ourselves and the other person acceptance, kindness, and ease.

Relaxing/allowing runs counter to our human instinct for vigilance and our culture of excitement, stimulation, and activity: Kramer describes it as "subversive" for this reason (Kramer & Ebert, 2018). To resist our instinct in this way requires some effort so making Relax/allow a habitual response requires a clear intention, implemented with energy. Engaging in formal RM practice can help us to overcome our natural tendencies and take this counter-cultural approach to our relationships.

Settling and releasing

The positive news is that relaxing and bringing kindly receptivity feels good, helping to make the practice more enjoyable, which in turn means we are likely to stick with it! In addition, relaxing/allowing helps us become more mindful and settles the mind. The calmness of relax/allow and the mindfulness of pause are mutually supportive. Relaxing/allowing opens up the possibility of supporting us to pause for longer.

As our capacity to relax and allow deepens, we can see our reactivity to discomfort as another layer of tension, enabling us to meet our reactivity as well as the discomfort itself with an attitude of allowing and accepting. We no longer judge our thoughts and feelings and can be fully present with them. Paradoxically, that very allowing and accepting, enables thoughts and mental tensions to become less troublesome. We can tap into the liberative wisdom of seeing thinking as a constructing process and become less attached to it. As Saima says, "...*Relax/allow for me has become about being permissive of the thoughts that are still in my mind and just acknowledging, metaphorically bowing to knowing that that is something I want to pick up and then just letting it go. And so I sort of have this visual sense in my mind's eye of seeing the bubbles of thoughts get smaller and smaller...*"

In addition, tension in the body or mind separates us from others and tightens us into our individuality, so Relax/allow can support us to access a more interconnected way of being and of seeing the world. Pausing, relaxing, and allowing can also help us become aware and step out of our tendency to identify or 'fuse' with our own and others' stories and, instead, connect with others in 'unconstructed intimacy' (see Chapter 7). As we are less blocked or distracted by the tensions, resistances, and automatic reactions, we are better able to focus and gather our mind and to see things as they actually are. We can see beyond our conditioned perspective with greater clarity and wisdom and access new insight and learning.

Supporting ourselves to relax and allow

Before we suggest specific practices for Relax/allow, we want to set out a few ways we can support ourselves to relax and allow in both formal and informal RM practice:

- ▪ *Body as anchor:* In the same way as the body is an anchor for the guideline Pause, the body is also an access point to experience Relax/allow (see Box 9.1 for a little exercise you can do right now!). Whether practising formally

---

Box 9.1 Exercise to get a feel for Relax/allow

As you read this, we invite you to try out this little exercise:

- Create a fist with one of your hands
- Really hold that fist tight and keep doing so for at least a minute – pay attention to how that feels
- After a minute or so, release the fist, let the tension go, soften your hand muscles, and notice how that feels
- That movement of relax, release, soften is analogous to the guideline Relax/allow

---

or informally, bringing our attention to the body, noticing where there is tension and choosing to relax that tension, where and to whatever extent is possible, helps to bring a sense of softening both physically and psychologically. It is important that this be not about striving to relax – which will simply add another layer of tension – but instead responding to a gentle invitation to soften and release

■ *Body and mind:* We can also bring greater awareness to the relationship between the body and the mind. In relational moments, whether in formal or informal RM practice, we can notice how some interactions seem to result in us tensing muscles in different parts of the body. For example, when we talk about something challenging, practise with/meet someone new, or receive uncomfortable feedback, we might notice a tensing in our belly, our neck, and/or our hands. By noticing this and releasing the physical tension, we can help ourselves counteract the build-up of mental tension. As Emma R puts it, "…*the real power of being able to relax/allow and just what that does to your brain… so powerful in being able to stop whatever has been happening and completely kind of transport myself into my body*"

■ *Feeling the discomfort:* A key element of bringing in this guideline is to recognise that there will be challenges in both formal RM practice and daily interactions that cannot be avoided, where release of physical tension is not enough. As best we can, when faced with these situations, the invitation is to acknowledge that 'this is how things are right now' and to release the resistance to feeling the discomfort. This realisation is a doorway to allowing whatever is here to be here

■ *Using silent reminders:* It may be helpful silently to say 'Relax', 'Allow', 'Receive', 'Accept', or similar words to gently remind and invite ourselves to soften

	Individual	Relational
Formal		
Informal		

Individual formal practice: individual mindfulness or meditation with Relax/allow

Engaging with the practices recommended for individual formal practice of Pause is the foundation of noticing the way things are, which is a precondition to allow us to choose to soften any tension we notice and/or allow things to be just as they are.

Whatever practice you chose for Pause, the invitation now is to explore adding the guideline Relax/allow. For example:

- Consciously taking a few deep breaths at the start of your practice to release tension and calm the body and mind
- Introducing some progressive muscle relaxation into your practice or doing an additional practice focusing on relaxing tense muscles
- Including an element of 'being with the difficult' in your practice: bringing a challenge to mind and inviting a sense of turning towards, allowing, and receptivity to it, not trying to change it or 'solve' it in any way, letting it be just as it is
- Introducing some self-compassion practices, which encourage a softening towards and care for ourselves that has similarities to and synergies with Relax/allow

On the dedicated website accompanying this book we provide an audio download that brings together the guidelines Pause and Relax/allow, which you can use as part of your practice. We also provide suggestions of meditation teachers/sites that offer self-compassion practices.

	Individual	Relational
Formal		
Informal		

Relational formal practice: relational meditation/ mindful dialogue with Relax/allow

In the resources provided in Appendix 1 and on our dedicated website, we provide a step-by-step process to help you undertake mindful dialogue with the guideline

Relax/allow. Once again, before engaging in formal RM practice, do please read Chapter 7 and follow the guidance around choosing a dialogue partner, setting agreements to establish safety and agreeing logistics for the practice.

Suitable contemplation topics for mindful dialogue practice with the RM guideline Relax/allow include inviting a kindly receptivity to whatever is arising in the moment, exploring how it feels to allow things to be as they are. To access how it feels to be fully present in relationship in a non-judgemental way, it may be helpful to reflect on and touch back into experiences of receiving this kind of attention from another or moments when we have experienced ease, gratitude, and/or contentment in relationship. Knowing how that sense of ease and receptivity feels helps us to bring it to our more challenging moments.

We recommend following a simple first speaker, second speaker, shared dialogue process for this practice. Keeping the practice simple is really helpful in these initial stages of learning the form of mindful dialogue and establishing familiarity with these foundational guidelines.

	Individual	Relational
Formal		
Informal		

Individual informal practice: bringing Relax/allow into daily life

To help integrate Relax/allow into your way of being, we invite you to practise relaxing and allowing at regular intervals throughout your daily life. Some ideas to help you do this are:

- Using the prompts that you set up to help you pause (bell, sticky dots, particular moment in your day…) to prompt you not just to pause, but also to relax and allow. Each time you encounter the prompt, taking a moment to pause and notice any tension you have in your body or mind, then exploring whether this tension can be released, and bringing a friendly receptivity to whatever tension will not release
- Whenever you start a new task or transition between activities, consciously taking a few deep breaths and noticing whether that helps reduce tension and/or gives you greater ease with which to engage with the next moment
- Whenever you notice feelings of agitation or excitement, taking a moment to pause and relax any tension you notice in the body, softening gently, not forcing anything or striving to relax

- Exploring how best to quieten and calm your mind. We each have our own triggers for tension and for release. What is your favourite calming, relaxing activity? Hearing a particular piece of music, visiting a place in nature, stroking a pet, being with someone dear to you, or something else? Identifying these doorways to relaxing and allowing builds a resource we can draw on to access that sense of softening and receptivity when we need it – or as a way to bring more of that into our day-to-day life

	Individual	Relational
Formal		
Informal		

Relational informal practice: bringing Relax/allow into daily interactions with others

As with Pause, perhaps the most valuable – and most challenging – ongoing practice is to build habits of relaxing and allowing in our daily interactions with others. The invitation is to use interactions with other people as a prompt to invite in the guideline Relax/allow. Here are some ideas to help you do this:

- When speaking with someone, bringing awareness to the interaction, and monitoring any tension in your facial muscles, jaw, belly, and so on. Then inviting a relaxation of that tension and seeing how it affects the conversation
- Intentionally bringing Relax/allow into challenging relational moments – arguments, difficult conversations, social gatherings. This will become easier to do as you get more familiar with this guideline. But it is usually hard in the heat of the moment, so it is important to be kind to yourself and not expect too much. Even if you recognise only after the event that it would have been good to pause and relax/allow, that is a step in the right direction and makes it more likely that you will be able to do so in the future. As Becky says, "*I would specifically then think, 'okay, well, how could I apply Relax/allow to this situation? How can I practise…?' Or then reflecting, 'if I'd remembered to practise Relax/allow, how might that have turned out?'*"
- Consciously inviting Relax/allow in relationships where you want to access greater kindness and compassion. As Malcolm puts it, "*Relax/allow is a doorway to kindness, to acceptance, to loving kindness. It is not just about accepting yourself… it's also a voice which says, 'And here's somebody else who needs time and care and attention. Let's accept this is what's going on here in this relationship…'*"

Now that we have explored Pause and Relax/allow, we have the foundations to take our mindfulness fully into the moment of interacting with another person. We are ready to bring in the guideline Open to support us to be with internal and external experience, as we will explore in the next chapter.

References

Kramer, G. (2007). *Insight Dialogue: The interpersonal path to freedom*. Shambhala.

Kramer, G., & Ebert, L. (2018). *Offering the Insight Dialogue guidelines: A resource guide*. Metta Programs.

Reina, C. S., Mills, M. J., & Sumpter, D. M. (2023). A mindful relating framework for understanding the trajectory of work relationships. *Personnel Psychology, 76*(4), 1187–1215.

Information

Dedicated website accompanying this book: www.relationalmindfulness.net

Chapter 10

Practising Open

Looking after oneself, one looks after others.
Looking after others, one looks after oneself.

The Buddha (Acrobat Sutta)

In this chapter, we get into the heart of Relational Mindfulness (RM) practice with the guideline Open, which takes our mindfulness explicitly into the external as well as the internal world. As Jane says, "*Open is an arriving in the relational field.*"

What is Open?

The guideline Open invites us to extend the awareness and acceptance established through Pause and Relax/allow beyond the boundaries of our own skin. Thus, Open marks a key transition in which we expand our mindfulness to include not just the internal world but also the external environment and our relationship with it. It offers a broadening of the attentional field and an awareness of our interrelatedness with the world around us, moving us from the individual to the relational.

At its simplest, Open is asking us to be aware of whether the mind is attending internally or externally. In a relational situation, this already helps us to be conscious of whether we are listening to our own body sensations, emotions, and internal dialogue (reacting, preparing, planning) or to the other person's words, body language, gestures, etc.

At a more sophisticated level, Open provides the possibility of a more spacious awareness in which we can hold what is occurring both internally and

DOI: 10.4324/9781003390428-13

externally. Both in relational meditation and in daily interactions, with Open we can be aware of the person we are with and our internal reaction to that and the interconnected flow between the two. We can potentially see the reality that the internal and external are not separate, but are interrelated, and that the boundaries we perceive to be there are constructions of our minds and our cultural norms. Emma R talks about the value of this "...*opening up from your experience inside your mind and your body ... to the wider environment. I've found that really powerful.*"

Practising Open supports us to develop a greater malleability of mind, where we can flex our attention between focusing on one aspect of experience (internal or external) and widening out to be aware of a greater range of stimuli. Using the analogy of a torch beam, Open invites us to be aware of whether we have a narrow beam of light that illuminates one small area, or a wider, more diffuse beam that shows us a much broader view. As Jane explains, "*It begins here in my own sensitive body. Then there is an opening to include the other, to include the environment, to include whatever's here and again it's those open loving arms of inclusivity. And the key piece is the embodied connection with self and a moving from that place to include the other. It's not leaving that place, it's including everything....*"

Relatedness and safety

The capacity to be present to ourselves and others developed through Open enhances the experience of relatedness. Once we can establish mindful awareness of both internal and external, we can become aware of the relationship itself, the constantly changing dynamic of self and other and what is happening between us. This corresponds to what Nicholas Janni describes as "dual attention", learning to pay inner and outer attention at the same time (Janni, 2023).

This stable attending to internal and external experience in relationship can give a sense of safety. We are no longer either captured by our internal reactions or captivated by the other person's speech/actions, so can attend to both more freely. This safety, stability, and freedom can support the courage to see more clearly and can help us let go of habits of wanting things a particular way.

This awareness and the choice Open offers over how and where we place our attention is the basis for relational meditation and mutuality in the meditative process. In formal RM practice, both dialogue partners are extending awareness to encompass each other and the relationship. Our attention can move between the internal, external, and both, as we mutually support one another to navigate these domains with less sense of boundary. We can help one another avoid getting caught either in narrow-focus awareness or in spacious awareness.

As Kramer points out, "*practising only focused mindfulness can tend to leave us narrow and tight, while cultivating only wide, spacious mind states can leave us ungrounded and spaced out. [ID/RM] is a way to become familiar and move between different qualities of awareness – internal and external – not privileging one over the other*" (Kramer, 2007, p.134).

Counter-cultural

In the same way that Relax/allow has a 'subversive' aspect, Open too has wisdom-enhancing, counter-cultural implications. It runs contrary to the prevailing culture of self and individualism, and by revealing the interconnected and interrelated nature of our existence, Open offers the possibility of revealing the myth of separation, healing our isolation, and our identification with a distinct 'I/me/mine' that needs to be defended from 'other.' Building on the foundations of pausing and relaxing/allowing, opening can deepen connection in the 'unconstructed intimacy' we referred to in Chapter 7.

It is natural to experience a resistance to this open way of being. Such resistance is a pattern many, if not all, of us have established as a defence mechanism. So, we need to be kind to ourselves and practise patiently to build new habits over time.

The release of isolation and defences, and the experience of interconnectedness made possible as we practise Relax/allow and Open, is a foundation for the natural arising of kindness and compassion. Observing people engaging in relational meditation, we regularly – indeed reliably – see a 'magical' shift in the group as a sense of mutual care and understanding arises between the meditators. As Saima explains, "*Open means there's a heartfelt sense of opening... There's an opening that then feels an allowance that connects me to everything that is precious to me.*"

As we will explore further in Chapter 23, this release of defences and the understanding of interconnectedness it enables means that RM has the potential to have much wider benefits in the world, not just in coaching.

Supporting ourselves to open

Before we suggest specific practices for the guideline Open, we set out a few ways we can support ourselves to open in both formal and informal RM practice:

- *Noticing focus on internal, external, or both:* The simplest level of Open is about noticing whether our attention is focused internally or externally. When we are with another person in formal RM practice or in everyday life, we can ask ourselves, 'Am I focused internally, externally, or holding both internal and external in my awareness?'
- *Exploring broadening awareness:* If we notice a tendency to hold a narrow focus on either internal or external sensations/stimuli, we can invite a gentle widening of our attention to see whether we can hold both. In an interaction with another, the invitation is to explore broadening our awareness

to hold both our internal sensations and the person/people we are with – whether in formal RM practice or informal daily contact with others

■ *Attuning to interactions:* As we become better able to hold a spacious awareness in which we are attending to both the internal and the external, we can attune more to the interactions between the two. For example, exploring how what another person says and does gives rise to internal reactions, how our internal state affects our experience of another person, and how what we say and do influence another person's response. We can begin to observe how deeply interconnected and interrelated everything is. We may notice that this is particularly true when the external includes another person: we are incredibly sensitive to one another!

■ *Settling when overwhelmed:* This exploration of internal, external, and both can become overwhelming at times, so it is important that we bring in the guideline Pause to notice when that happens. Once we are aware of overwhelm, we can choose to settle ourselves by focusing attention on the sensations of the body. This settling can help us to stabilise our mind and then, when we are ready, engage again with gently opening our awareness to the external, and to the interrelated nature of internal and external

■ *Non-striving:* It is also important not to try to force Open or strive for spacious awareness. The tension that such forcing/striving evokes will prevent the spaciousness and relatedness we are seeking. Building Open on the guideline Relax/allow is therefore vital to offer ourselves the kindliness and acceptance that enables spaciousness

	Individual	Relational
Formal		
Informal		

Individual formal practice: individual mindfulness or meditation with Open

Building on your individual practice with the guidelines Pause and Relax/allow, the invitation is now to bring in the guideline Open. For example:

■ Choosing practices that support you to bring your attention externally as well as internally. For example, practices that invite awareness of sounds and/or opening to the visual field

■ Choosing practices that extend awareness from being focused on a particular object of attention (such as breathing, body sensations, etc.) to a broader, expanded attentional field (for example, 'choiceless awareness', where the attention is spacious and open to take in whatever arises)

■ Engaging in walking meditation as a way to practise bringing awareness to the internal (the sensations of muscles moving the legs and body) and the external (the solidity of the ground beneath your feet, the movement of air against your skin, the various stimuli from your environment). Whilst walking, you can also bring awareness to the relationship between the internal and external as the walking body interacts and is interconnected with the world in which it is moving

■ Introducing some loving-kindness, compassion-for-others, and 'just like me' practices to encourage an appreciation and care for others, emphasising the interconnected, interrelated nature of all things, which supports the wide, compassionate awareness intrinsic to Open

On our dedicated website we provide an audio download that guides the listener through a brief practice supported by the guideline Open, which you can use as part of your practice. We also provide suggestions of meditation teachers/sites that offer loving-kindness, compassion, and 'just like me' practices.

	Individual	Relational
Formal		
Informal		

Relational formal practice: relational meditation/mindful dialogue with Open

In the resources provided in Appendix 1 and on our dedicated website, we provide a step-by-step process to help you undertake mindful dialogue with the guideline Relax/allow. As we will continue to repeat in each of these chapters about the RM guidelines, before engaging in formal RM practice, it is vital to read Chapter 7 and follow the guidance around choosing a dialogue partner, setting agreements to establish safety and agreeing logistics for the practice.

To get to grips with the complexity of attending to internal experience, external experience, and both, it can be helpful initially to engage in mindful dialogue simply noticing and naming these experiences. As this expansion of awareness becomes more familiar, contemplation topics relating to compassion or gratitude can help to explore the felt experience of interconnectedness between our internal world and the wider system of which we are a part. Topics relating to collaboration and connection in relationship can also help us explore this sense of how interrelated we and our lives really are.

As for the formal RM practices with Pause and with Relax/allow, we recommend continuing with the simple flow from first speaker to second speaker to shared dialogue for practising Open.

	Individual	Relational
Formal		
Informal		

Individual informal practice: bringing Open into daily life

To help integrate Relax/allow into your way of being, we invite you to practise opening at regular intervals throughout your daily life. Some ideas to help you do this are:

- Taking time to pause and open during your day, initially focusing your attention on specific sensations in your body (for example, the physical sensations of breathing or of your feet on the floor), then broadening out your field of awareness to include who and what is around you in that moment. Noticing how it feels to be with your internal sensations and/or the external surroundings: is it possible to be aware of both? You may find it helpful to set a timer to remind you to do this two to three times each day – you only need to take a minute or two each time
- One of the easiest ways to access the sense of spacious awareness that is part of the guideline Open is being in nature: the natural world helps us spontaneously expand our awareness to include the environment as well as our internal experience. By taking time in woodlands, open fields, near a river, or by the sea, allowing a natural flow of internal and external attention and letting a sense of ease, receptivity, and broad awareness naturally emerge. As Pirjo explains, "*...moving from what's going on in me and what I'm hearing or sensing or whatever is happening externally and then coming back to me and actually having that simultaneously: noticing my feet are on the ground and at the same time I can see the trees moving...*"

	Individual	Relational
Formal		
Informal		

Relational informal practice: bringing Open into daily interactions with others

Again, perhaps the most valuable – and most challenging – ongoing practice is to build habits of opening in our daily interactions with others. The invitation is to use interactions with other people as a prompt to invite in the guideline Open. Some ideas to help you do this are:

- When in conversation with others, exploring how it is to be fully present with them, listening deeply to what they have to say, whilst also being aware of the internal sensations and processes. You can use being with another person as a prompt to remind you to do this. You may find it easier initially to bring in the guideline Open with one other person. As you get more adept at being with internal, external, and both, you can begin to bring this into group situations too
- Using these conversations when you are applying Open to engage in an enquiry: can I continue to practise RM even when my conversation partner(s) is not practising as well? Does it need to be a shared practice or can I practise 'unilaterally'?
- Noticing where you get 'caught' in relationships and particularly where you tend to want to control what is happening – perhaps wanting the other person to be a certain way or say particular things. Seeing if it is possible to bring in the guideline Open as an invitation to be fully with the other person, allowing them to be just as they are, giving your attention to what is going on internally for you and externally for them, seeing if you can hold both with a kindly awareness. This brings with it a certain vulnerability, as Stephanie explains, "*[Open is] connected with this acceptance piece, especially in the personal relationships where I want the response to be a certain thing… that is the opposite of Open. That's all about me and my expectations and my values and my fears and whatever. And there's something very vulnerable… because it is letting go of being the expert. It is letting go of… knowing best… When you're not open, even though you'd probably be embarrassed to acknowledge it or admit it, what you're really doing is writing that other person's script for them based on what you want it to be*"

Having experienced the power of the RM guidelines Pause, Relax/allow, and Open, we are ready to add the rich and insightful value of being present to the flux and flow of experience that is invited when we attune to what is emerging in each moment, continuing to deepen wisdom through RM practice. In the next chapter, we bring this in with the guideline Attune to emergence.

References

Janni, N. (2023). *Coaches rising workshop on Unlocking your own evolution.* www.coachesrising.com

Kramer, G. (2007). *Insight Dialogue: The interpersonal path to freedom.* Shambhala.

Information

Dedicated website accompanying this book: www.relationalmindfulness.net

Chapter 11

Practising Attune to emergence

Those with wisdom… see change in what is changing.

The Buddha

The truth of impermanence is a profound and ultimately freeing wisdom teaching embedded in Relational Mindfulness (RM), one that can point us towards the preciousness of relationships and life in general. The RM guideline Attune to emergence brings this truth right into the moment of relating with another and helps us step beyond our preconceptions. In this chapter, we explore what this means and how we can take it into our practice and our lives.

What is Attune to emergence?

In the context of RM, attuning to emergence is an opening of awareness to the reality of constant change and complexity and bringing flexibility to allow us to be with it all. Both our internal experience and the world around us are always changing; sensations, thoughts, emotions, and stimuli from the environment arise and pass. This can be particularly noticeable when we are interacting with another person. The guideline Attune to emergence supports us to be fully present with the ebb and flow of experience, not trying to hold on to, control or predict what is happening. It is another invitation to open up to the wisdom beyond constructs.

Let us examine the phrase 'Attune to emergence':

DOI: 10.4324/9781003390428-14

- Emergence refers to the process by which the complex things we experience arise from underlying contributing factors
- Attune refers to the receptivity and openness which help us be present with this instability, this constant flux and flow

Letting go of trying to control

With Attune to emergence we are invited to step into what mindfulness teachers often call 'beginner's mind', as mentioned in Chapter 2. We are pointed towards letting go of preconceptions and of trying to control what happens next. Combined with the guideline Relax/allow, Attune to emergence offers us the prospect of 'surfing the waves', rather than trying to 'control the waves.' It opens the possibility of yielding and being with the process as it unfolds. This helps us to have the insight that we cannot really know what will happen next and supports us to be with what is actually happening now.

Thus, attuning to emergence is an invitation to see things as they are – i.e. constantly changing – and to make this impermanence itself the object of awareness. To do this, we need to, as best we can, let go of any agenda or goals, and simply be curious about what is arising and vanishing moment-by-moment. To attune to the ever-changing ebb and flow of experience, the mind must release or at least loosen resistance to what is arising or to not knowing what will arise. This releasing or loosening allows us to become more flexible and move with the experience.

Paradoxically, putting change and impermanence centre stage in our awareness gives us a degree of stability that is not possible if we are resisting or trying to control what happens. Once the object of our attention is change itself, because change is always present, we no longer need to shift attention from one focus to another. The effort we might have expended in resisting or trying to control what happens can be more fruitfully and wisely used in tracking the flow as it happens.

Attuning to emergence in relationship

Being with another person brings many layers of flux, change, and complexity. Attuning to what arises in relationship invites us to be present with this complexity and the changing landscape both within ourselves, in our sense of the other person, and of the space in between. When attuning to emergence, we listen fully to ourselves and our interlocutor moment-by-moment, rather than spending our 'listening' time preparing what we are about to say or spending our 'speaking' time predicting the impact of our words. This supports an alertness and receptivity to what might emerge in the relational space. As Jane puts it, "... *to sit in not knowing, to reside in the process of attuning to emergence: what is the client saying? What's showing up in the body?*"

This form of relational awareness involves letting go of trying to control where the dialogue (or informal conversation) will go. We are attentive to the thoughts, mind-states, emotions, sensations, and urges that arise for us, and allow them to come and go, rather than being driven by them. We become more in touch with the truth that it would be impossible to predict, let alone control, what will emerge in any particular interaction.

Learning, growing, and seeing more clearly

By attuning to emergence, we provide opportunities to learn and grow beyond our existing worldview. At the same time, we develop the insight that our perspective will always be conditioned to some degree by our previous experiences, culture, and upbringing, and that this conditioning gives rise to hopes, fears, and expectations about how we and others can and should be. And the more we hold onto our existing mindset, the more we place limits on what we can perceive.

As Gregory Kramer says, "*To think we can understand, let alone predict, what will emerge in any given conversation is a folly with a price. Prediction fills us with assumptions rather than the truth… Thinking we know costs us all we don't know – which is nearly everything*" (Kramer, 2007, p.144).

Becoming fully present in relationship

Attuning to emergence helps us release the assumptions, agendas, and tensions that get in the way of us being fully present with one another. Once we can relax into not knowing what will happen next and allowing the truth of change, we are open to greater possibility and connection. As Kramer puts it, the combination of the guidelines Open and Attune to emergence "*call us to release short-term attachments and personal agendas that hide us from each other*" (Kramer, 2007, p.142).

Thus, we see more clearly the unknowable and unplannable nature of relationship: we yield to the mystery of that. We do not let go of responsibility for our role in the relationship; however, we do release the delusion of stability and control, accessing instead the wisdom of knowing that everything is changing all the time. With Attune to emergence, we recognise that mindfulness is essential for us to be fully open to the unexpected and the potential of ourselves, the other, and the relationship.

Supporting ourselves to attune to emergence

Before we suggest specific practices for the guideline Attune to emergence, we set out a few ways we can support ourselves to attune to emergence in both formal and informal RM practice:

■ *Body as anchor:* As for the other guidelines, awareness of the body is a great way to help us to attune to emergence. The body is changing moment-by-moment, so when we attune to our experience, we can become aware of a constant flow of sensations – breathing, muscles, sensations on the skin, energy levels. These shifting body sensations can also help us attune to what is happening in a relational space, in formal RM practice, or daily interactions. As Jane puts it: *"There's an emergence that's happening [in the body], a constant flow of change, and attuning to emergence happens through connecting to the body"*

■ *Attuning to sound:* Attuning to the constantly changing music of another person's voice – or our own – can help us notice that the soundscape, and someone speaking in particular, is a source of awareness of arising and vanishing. In Kramer's words: *"Attune to the speaking voice as a song of impermanence. Let [Attune to emergence] remind you to come ever closer to the unplanned and unknowable aspects of this relationship"* (Kramer, 2007, p.146)

■ *Attuning to the relational field:* We can also turn our attention to what is emerging in the relational domain: how the experience of being with another person keeps changing. Getting curious about the flow of energy, focus, speaking, and listening can help us bring a flexible attention to ourselves and others

■ *Letting go of planning:* Inviting ourselves to let go of any need to plan what we are going to say and trusting that, when it is our turn to speak, the words will emerge, frees up our energy to tune in to the other person and listen fully to them, and also to notice what emerges for us. We can miss so much of this if we are preoccupied with shaping our response, question, or reflection

	Individual	Relational
Formal		
Informal		

Individual formal practice: individual mindfulness or meditation with Attune to emergence

Building on all the practices suggested in previous Chapters, the invitation here is to find ways to bring the guideline Attune to emergence into your mindfulness/ meditation practice. For example:

■ Choosing practices that help you bring your attention to the constantly changing nature of experience such as, practices that invite awareness

of the flux and flow of the breath, the changing soundscape, the flow of thoughts
■ You may find walking meditation a valuable activity in which to explore attune to emergence as walking brings a myriad of changing sensations and experiences associated with the process of moving
■ Any practice that brings in awareness of impermanence and 'not knowing' could be of benefit. For example, meditations that bring attention to how our bodies and everything around us is always changing, and those on how we cannot know, let alone control, what will happen next

On our dedicated website we provide an audio download that guides the listener through a brief practice supported by the guideline Attune to emergence, which you can use as part of your practice.

	Individual	Relational
Formal		
Informal		

Relational formal practice: relational meditation/ mindful dialogue with Attune to emergence

In the resources provided in Appendix 1 and on our dedicated website, we provide a step-by-step process to help you undertake mindful dialogue with the guideline Attune to emergence. Again, before engaging in formal RM practice, make sure you have read Chapter 7 and follow the guidance around choosing a dialogue partner, setting agreements to establish safety and agreeing logistics for the practice.

The guideline Attune to emergence is a powerful support for exploring the experience of change, both in the present moment and in longer time periods. Contemplation topics for mindful dialogue with Attune to emergence can therefore include speaking in the immediacy of the shifting moment and sharing experiences around change. They can also draw out the aspect of letting go of assumptions, preconceptions, and predictions.

As before, a simple first speaker, second speaker, shared dialogue process is supportive for this practice to help us 'hold' the complexity, uncertainty, and vulnerability of change.

	Individual	Relational
Formal		
Informal		

Individual informal practice: bringing Attune to emergence into daily life

The invitation is to practise attuning to emergence at regular intervals throughout your daily life. Some ideas include the following:

- Taking time to pause, relax into your direct experience, and broaden your field of awareness to include who and what is around you in that moment. Then inviting yourself to attend to each moment of experience with nothing to accomplish, experimenting with observing what arises, allowing certainty to fall away and beginner's mind to emerge. Not trying to control or achieve anything, just allowing the 'wisdom of not knowing.' You may find it helpful to set a timer to remind you to do this a few times a day (perhaps alternating practising Open and Attune to emergence) and spend just a minute or so engaging with it
- Occasionally turning attention to your thoughts and emotions to help you become aware of the never-ending shifting of the mental landscape. Bringing in Attune to emergence as an invitation to let these shifts come and go, rather than hold onto or pursue any of them
- Using the sense of being open to whatever emerges and not knowing what will happen next to frame your outlook day by day. Becky explains how Attune to emergence has become part of how she sets herself up for the day: *"At the beginning of every day, I have a set of intentions that I look at and remind myself of, and some are more relevant than others, depending on what I'm going to be doing that particular day. And Attune to emergence has become a sort of meta intention, actually an enabler for the other intentions"*
- Becoming aware of how everything is altering all the time and is made up of many different parts and factors. When you rest your attention on anything, you can identify ways in which it is shifting, be that subtly or more obviously.
- Exploring your reaction or response to changes that happen in your life. Are you aware of resisting or celebrating change? What do you notice about your emotions, body sensations, and thoughts when changes occur?

	Individual	Relational
Formal		
Informal		

Relational informal practice: bringing Attune to emergence into daily interactions with others

As with other guidelines, our daily interactions with others offer potentially the most valuable and most challenging opportunity to practice the guideline Attune to emergence. The invitation is to use interactions with other people as a prompt to invite in this guideline. Here are some ideas to help you do this:

- When speaking with someone, exploring whether you can bring an attitude of beginner's mind, letting go of any assumptions about what the other person is going to say or do (particularly if you know them really well!). Instead, being fully present to what emerges in the moment
- In daily conversations, letting go of any need to control the course of the conversation or achieve a particular goal. This does not mean that we do not set intentions, and hope for wise relationships, compassion, and good outcomes. Instead, it means we recognise that we do not know how these things are best attained: we allow that to emerge
- Bringing Attune to emergence as a form of inquiry that prompts us to explore our experience with other people through the lens of how things are changing and how the flux and change of other people's behaviour influences our internal landscape. As Jane puts it, *"When I'm [with other people] my inquiry is 'what's emerging?' … I'm curious about what is in the system that is emerging in this body, or that's taking shape in the form of thought. Thoughts or feelings are showing up [internally] and what is happening out there that they're showing up [here]? It's subtle. It's fascinating to be able to play in that field of emergence, to attune to the flow of what's coming up"*

Attune to emergence is intrinsic to mindful listening and speaking. So, with this guideline as our support, we can now move on to exploring the final two RM guidelines, Listen deeply and Speak the truth, in the next two chapters.

Reference

Kramer, G. (2007). *Insight Dialogue: The interpersonal path to freedom.* Shambhala.

Information

Dedicated website accompanying this book: www.relationalmindfulness.net

Chapter 12

Practising Listen deeply

Give every man thine ear, but few thy voice.

Shakespeare (Polonius in Hamlet)

The practice of Relational Mindfulness (RM) has listening and speaking at its heart. With the RM guideline Listen deeply, we turn attention to listening as meditation. In this chapter we explore what that means.

What is Listen deeply?

The guideline Listen deeply invites a stable, receptive awareness that provides kindness, empathy, and sensitivity, as a support to being fully present to the person who is speaking. To listen deeply in this sense, we need to draw on all the other RM guidelines. We need to pause and bring our attention to our listening: listening in the present moment and noticing what the speaker is communicating now, rather than letting our mind wander off into planning what we are going to say, working out how best to intervene or, perhaps worse, pondering what we will have for supper!

Listening deeply also involves setting aside our tendency to judge or analyse what the person is saying, and instead really seeking to understand, with generosity. It also draws on the capacity to be with what is being said – whether we experience that as pleasant, unpleasant, or neutral – bringing the kindly receptivity that arises with the guideline Relax/allow.

As Kramer puts it, with Listen deeply, "*We are a receptive field touched by the words, emotions and energies of our fellow human beings, grounded in clear awareness and sensitive to the speaker's offering*" (Kramer, 2007, p.150).

DOI: 10.4324/9781003390428-15

Whole body listening

When we listen deeply, we are using our eyes and other senses as well as our ears. We attend to the speaker's verbal expression, and to their body language, tone, and energy. Their gestures, facial expressions, and the music, volume, and intonation of their voice may communicate as much as – if not more than – their words and phrases. Taking in the rhythm, timbre, pauses, and volume of the speaking enables us to pick up the emotional tone of what the speaker is saying. Attending to the visual cues of body language can help us discern the speaker's mind-state. As Malcolm puts it, *"...listening includes facial expression, bodily movements, tapping the fingers... tone of voice, speed of voice, breathing, all of that information. It's like 'what is here in this breathing and living individual opposite?'"*

Whilst listening deeply invites our attention to rest on the speaker, it is not entirely an external exploration. It is also about allowing ourselves to be touched by the experience of another. As well as attending to what we see and hear in the speaker, we open to what is evoked internally. Our physical sensations, emotions, and what arises for us are a part of how we resonate and empathise with the speaker. Thus, the guideline Open is also an important foundation for listening deeply.

Receiving the truth of experience

Listening deeply is not just about hearing and comprehending another's words but about receiving the truth of their experience. We can only do this if we are fully immersed in the experience of listening as a total priority and listening with the wide awareness of Open that includes ourselves as well as the other. Malcolm again, *"I already knew about listening, but this is listening more deeply. This is listening to myself as well as to the other...."*

This whole body, fully present form of listening means attending to what is arising in the moment, and being with the person in front of us, unclouded by our expectations. If we are not attuning to emergence moment-by-moment, we will probably be reacting to our preconceptions, roles, and habits, not to the reality of this speaker and what they are communicating right now. Thus, the guideline Attune to emergence also underpins our capacity to listen deeply. When listening deeply, we can be aware of all that comes up for us, but not fall into it. For example, we may notice a habitual reaction arise and, instead of engaging in it, we let it pass.

Maintaining meta-perspective

While listening deeply involves our full attention, it does not mean getting absorbed into the speaker's stories and points of view. We see how compelling our own and each other's stories are and generate empathy through that understanding, but also retain a meta-perspective that can hold the other person, our own resonant response, and the broader context in our awareness. We are dwelling *"at the boundary of empathic response and non-identified awareness"* (Kramer, 2007, p.152). We are not 'buying in' to any particular narrative or worldview and instead allowing the listening to help us understand another's perspective in a way that expands our capacity to see different angles and, ultimately, see more clearly, beyond any one mindset. This helps us develop both flexibility and calm concentration in our listening, and to tap into wisdom that lies beyond self and relational constructs.

This combination of empathy and availability to the other without identification allows us to feel compassion when the speaker is expressing discomfort, pain, or suffering, and to feel resonant joy when they are sharing positive experiences. We avoid getting caught in our own internal dialogue or reactivity, so our hearts can be open to the other with kindness and goodwill and with an equanimity that can hold all that arises with stability and balance. We listen from a foundation of inner silence.

Balancing exploration and receptivity

Listening deeply involves us being both exploratory and receptive. The exploratory aspect of listening is about seeking to understand what is being expressed. We can be listening at a number of levels: the content and meaning conveyed in words; the emotion and energy transmitted in facial expressions, gestures, and the prosody, rhythm and timbre of the voice; and the nuanced sense of the person's presence we pick up through embodied awareness of the whole. However, if we get too caught in exploration, we can become tense and distant, so we need to balance that with receptivity that brings a stable and sensitive awareness, simply being present to what is unfolding.

Building on the foundations of Relax/allow and Open, Listen deeply can also be a point of access to a sense of common humanity, compassion, and loving kindness. As our listening becomes more receptive and boundless, we may also experience a liberating sense of oneness and connection to a wider interconnected whole.

Supporting ourselves to listen deeply

Before we suggest specific practices for the guideline Listen deeply, we set out some ways to support ourselves to listen deeply in both formal and informal RM practice:

- *Body as anchor:* Once again, the body is a key support in helping us to listen deeply. Attending to what is arising in our body can help us resonate with and fully receive another person's communication

■ *Setting intention:* Remembering the power of listening and how beneficial it is for our relationships can help us set an intention to listen deeply as much as possible and to bring the guideline Listen deeply into play in both formal RM practice and our daily interactions. As Emma R says, *"[RM is] really helping my listening, and the power of giving that listening to somebody else in lots of different circumstances is really impacting in a positive way in my coaching, in my relationships...."*

■ *Drawing on all the RM guidelines:* This helps us attend fully to the other person's communication and our own resonance. We are inviting patience and care: our listening becomes an act of generosity and kindness. We are bringing a softness to our listening that enables us to feel compassion and empathy, while at the same time having the stability to be with whatever arises

■ *Being flexible:* Not feeling that there is a 'right' way to listen deeply. As soon as we are caught in right/wrong dichotomies, we lose flexibility. Listening deeply is about finding agility in our listening that enables us to listen right now, not according to a formula. We may find it helpful to practise different types of listening: for example, wide spacious listening or specific-focused listening; listening more to verbal content or more to the non-verbal communication; listening to different aspects such as words, meaning, emotion, energy

	Individual	Relational
Formal		
Informal		

Individual formal practice: individual mindfulness or meditation with Listen deeply

Continuing the theme from previous chapters, the invitation is to find ways to bring the guideline Listen deeply into your mindfulness/meditation practice. For example:

■ You may find mindfulness of sounds a particularly valuable practice in this context, giving your full attention to each sound that arises, bringing interest and receptivity, exploring how it is to listen with mindfulness. Noting the rising and falling away, tone, rhythm, duration, etc. of the sound

■ Whatever your practice, bringing an attitude of deep listening to yourself. For example, mindfulness of breathing and/or body can be engaged with an attitude of giving full attention to listening to the sounds and sensations of your breath and/or body

On our dedicated website we provide an audio download that guides the listener through a brief practice supported by the guideline Listen deeply, which you can use as part of your practice.

	Individual	Relational
Formal		
Informal		

Relational formal practice: relational meditation/ mindful dialogue with Listen deeply

In the resources provided in Appendix 1 and on our dedicated website, we provide a step-by-step process to help you undertake mindful dialogue with the guideline Listen deeply. As always, before engaging in formal RM practice, please read Chapter 7 and follow the guidance around choosing a dialogue partner, setting safety agreements and agreeing practice logistics.

With the introduction of Listen deeply, we bring the focus squarely onto ways of listening. For those who have built a familiarity with mindful dialogue, this is a good moment to introduce opportunities for the listener to feed back on what they have 'received' from the speaker. Instead of simply having a first speaker, then shifting to the second speaker, then engaging in shared dialogue, the suggestion is to follow a pattern whereby, once the speaker has spoken, the listener takes a short time (much shorter than the speaker's) to reflect back what they have received in the speaker's communication. The speaker then has time (even shorter) to 'close the loop' in case there is anything that needs adding, correcting, adjusting, or whatever.

The listener's feedback can have different flavours depending on the focus of the listening. For example, the practice provided in the resources suggests engaging in two different forms of listening:

- Firstly, the listener is invited to listen for **content such as words and phrases**. When the speaker has spoken for the allotted time, the listener gives feedback on the words, phrases, and content they heard
- Secondly, the listener is invited to listen for **body language and the music of the voice**. This time, when the speaker has spoken, the listener gives feedback on these more embodied elements of the speaker's communication

It is vital to ensure that this process is a relational meditation, rather than a 'feedback exercise.' To support this, the listener is encouraged not to treat listening as a memory test, but instead to allow the speaker's communication to land fully in each moment. When listening in this way, the significant elements will be easy to recall later.

It is important to remember that listening deeply encompasses listening for resonances in our own body as well as listening to our dialogue partner, maintaining both empathy and non-identification, and balancing exploration with receptivity.

	Individual	Relational
Formal		
Informal		

Individual informal practice: bringing Listen deeply into daily life

The invitation is to practise listening deeply to yourself as much as possible in your daily life. Some ideas to help you do this are:

- As before, taking time to pause, relax into your direct experience and this time, bringing your attention to what is emerging in your internal dialogue, including any emotions and physical sensations arising. You may find it helpful to choose specific moments to do this, such as when you are making a decision or starting a new activity
- Noticing how it is to bring your attention to hearing, how sounds resonate in the body and give rise to sensations and emotions. Inviting curiosity and receptivity to whatever arises with this 'sense door'

	Individual	Relational
Formal		
Informal		

Relational informal practice: bringing Listen deeply into daily interactions with others

Interactions with other people are a particularly good prompt to invite in the guideline Listen deeply. This is where your practice of all the other guidelines bears fruit.

We suggest the following ideas for drawing on Listen deeply when speaking with someone:

- Inviting yourself to pause, relax, open, and/or attune to emergence as a basis for bringing attention to what the other person is communicating
- Attuning to the other person with your eyes as well as your ears, so that you are 'listening' for their words, gestures, facial expressions, body language, tone of voice, volume, rhythm, and so on

- Being mindful of listening for meaning, emotion, and energy levels
- Exploring bringing the generosity of full attention with curiosity and spaciousness, unhurried by internal or external agendas
- Seeing if you can avoid interrupting your listening with internal dialogue or preparing a response. Instead, aiming to notice how you receive and resonate with what the speaker is communicating. As Beth puts it, "... *understanding how powerful the role of listener is, like truly listening and not listening for your own agenda, or even listening to understand, just listening to listen...*"
- Listening to yourself as well as the other person to help with understanding what is happening in the relational space. Exploring how what is arising in your own body relates to what the other person is communicating, verbally or otherwise
- When preparing to speak, inviting yourself to pause so that you can listen deeply to what is arising for you and speak from that

Box 12.1 provides an example of how applying the guideline Listen deeply can support a more loving form of connection in our personal relationships.

Box 12.1 Listening deeply as a source of love

Some years ago, my (Emma's) mother was diagnosed with dementia. At the time of writing, she is now very frail and lives in a nursing home. Listen deeply has been a profound support to me through the process of being with someone who is confused and disconnected from 'reality.'

When I speak to my mum on the phone or visit her, she very often doesn't know where she is or remember that my dad and grandparents all died many years ago. In the first few years, when she asked me whether I had seen my dad or my grandparents recently, I would feel deeply uncomfortable and not know what to say. With the support of Listen deeply, I have learnt to listen beyond her words to the emotion and needs that lie beneath. If I can be really present in that moment and attentive to what she is communicating, I find I can hear her in a different and hopefully more beneficial way.

When she asks these questions now, I listen deeply to myself and acknowledge that there is a part of me holding onto the facts as I see them, then I can let the need to express that 'reality' pass. At the same time, as I listen deeply to my mum, I can discern the need for connection to others expressed in her tone of voice. I can bring a sense of love to my interaction with her, a receptivity and capacity to let her know that she is heard, loved, and connected to others, even if many of her nearest and dearest are no longer with us in bodily form.

In many ways, Listen deeply is profoundly entwined with Speak the truth. The two guidelines support and reinforce one another. In the next chapter, we delve fully into Speak the truth.

Reference

Kramer, G. (2007). *Insight Dialogue: The interpersonal path to freedom*. Shambhala.

Information

Dedicated website accompanying this book: www.relationalmindfulness.net

Chapter 13

Practising Speak the truth

It takes two to speak the truth – one to speak and another to listen.

Henry David Thoreau

As mentioned in Chapter 5, Listen deeply and Speak the truth are profoundly reciprocal. Having explored the former in the previous chapter, here we turn to the latter and explore the unique contribution Speak the truth brings to our practice of Relational Mindfulness (RM).

What is Speak the truth?

As an RM guideline, Speak the truth is about mindful discernment of the subjective truth of experience in the moment and sharing with another what is beneficial in the present context. At a gross level, this is about not lying and instead telling things as we actually see them. At a more subtle level, it is about expressing what is true in the moment and discerning what to speak according to whether it is valuable, kind, and timely.

'Truth' in this context means speaking what we believe to be accurate in that moment, recognising that our experience is always subjective, filtered by our senses, and coloured by our past experiences. We are aiming to share the subjective truth of our experience, to the extent that language allows, acknowledging that language will always be an imprecise vehicle to some degree. We are also aiming to express what is emerging now rather than speaking out of habit

DOI: 10.4324/9781003390428-16

or speaking words and phrases we prepared earlier. Speaking the truth is about bringing moment-by-moment awareness to our choice of words, expressions, gestures, and body language.

As we draw on the wisdom embedded in all the RM guidelines to support us to speak the truth, we can potentially touch into and express a truth beyond our individual experience. In a process that has similarities to Scharmer's 'presencing' (Scharmer, 2018), we can connect to the wider, interconnected system and the future potential. Our words can then include speaking the truth of the wider system and environment – expressing what wants to be spoken in an interrelated, connected whole.

Supporting awareness and wisdom

The guideline Speak the truth points to an intention to speak what is useful in supporting awareness and wise understanding. Speaking the truth requires us to draw on all the other RM guidelines. It involves pausing to be conscious of our evolving experience and speaking from the emergent moment: knowing that everything is changing moment-by-moment, and not getting stuck in any particular experience or expectation.

We can recognise that our truth changes in each moment as our experience unfolds. As Kramer puts it, "*When we Speak the truth, the story changes as we tell it, evolving in each Pause as subjective experience unfolds*" (Kramer, 2007, p.165). We open inwardly to know our own subjective truth and externally to understand the context into which we are speaking. This process needs to be supported by the kindly receptivity of releasing unnecessary tension and allowing whatever is experienced to be there.

Speak the truth is an invitation to listen deeply to ourselves with mindfulness, awareness, and presence, listening to what has the energy to be spoken and becoming more intimate with the process of speaking. As we pay attention to speaking, we can begin to see the way a thought arises in the mind, with an urge to express it, which then leads to the physical act of speaking, expelling air through our vocal cords to create sound, shaping words with our tongue and lips. Miraculously, these sounds can then be received by a listener's ear and comprehended as speech. Underlying all of this is the complex construction of meaning and language.

Care as well as wisdom

Speak the truth has the added dimension of communicating with care as well as wisdom. The aim is to speak with an attitude of kindness for both ourselves and the other. This does not mean avoiding saying difficult things, but instead ensuring that they are said with goodwill and consideration. We discern whether what we have to say comes from generosity, wisdom, and care (or from habit, grasping, aversion, and desire to control) and make wise choices in both what we say and how we say it. As Malcolm says, "*In many ways, the truth is hard to tell, because it is not any old truth, and it's not something that you might want to say reactively or without thoughtfulness… Speak the truth really involves… pausing and accepting and being open to this other human being you're with, and speaking the truth that's relevant to this moment and the context within which the work is taking place… sometimes truth is difficult and you don't have to say it, but the invitation can be to say quite difficult things [with an attitude of care].*"

Beyond the conceptual

Because it is about creating language, speaking involves conceptualising. Shaping words, phrases, and expressions that transmit concepts can make it hard to stay mindful: we tend to get tumbled into thinking. To remain in the moment – or return to it if we have got caught in the conceptual mind – we need the support of feeling the physical sensations of the body. By bringing mindfulness, investigation, and focus to the felt experience, we are better able to bring present-moment awareness into shaping language.

Even with this support, language cannot directly convey experience – it can only point to what we are feeling. As Kramer points out, "*we can never speak the whole truth, in the sense that the words are not the whole felt experience… When we use words, we wrap the coarse cloth of language around the subtly textured surface of experience*" (Kramer, 2007, p.165). So the invitation in mindful dialogue is to move back and forth between words and the felt experience, aiming to translate between the two.

Seeing our mind at work

Speaking in this way can help us to see our mind at work. It is a way of noticing, recognising, and investigating our stories, habits, drives, and assumptions. As well as discerning our truth, we can become aware of how we are constructing and making sense of the world. Awareness of this constructing process can help us deconstruct our meaning-making and perceptions, enabling us to shift and broaden our perspective and, potentially, release old habits and drives and form new, more supportive habits.

Of course, this realisation and release of constructs requires us to be emotionally and intellectually honest. So, Speak the truth is an opportunity to explore and refine our level of authenticity, aiming both to be more aware of our inner world and to create a stronger correspondence between that and our expression to others. When we meet another person authentically like this, we are better able to see each other's full humanity, helping us bring kindness, empathy, and mutual care to the dialogue. As Stephanie puts it, "*I thought truth and vulnerability were linked because it's me saying 'I'm angry' or 'I'm scared', but it's actually not… It's much deeper than that. That kind of peeling back the layers and then saying, this is almost the naked truth. 'Here I am'… it goes back to this common humanity… If*

I can access my truth, I have a much greater chance of seeing, enabling you perhaps to even try to uncover what your truth might be."

Not always easy

It is important to recognise that speaking and listening can lead to reactivity and misunderstandings as well as to clarity, calm, and connection. It is not easy to maintain awareness while speaking. Being with another person can trigger our emotions, habits, and yearnings. When this happens, at the very least, we get to see that clear communication is neither easy nor common. At best, difficult exchanges can help us learn how our reactivity can get in the way and, with awareness, this learning can help us discern how to speak and/or not speak with wisdom. If our tendency is to fall silent in these situations, awareness can help us explore whether being silent is an avoidance or a way of connecting to what is beneficial.

As with Listen deeply, Speak the truth has different layers. We can attend to the meaning and content of what we speak, the emotions and mind-states from which we speak, and the truth that lies beneath our thoughts and feelings. Our minds are generally flooded with thoughts and feelings, so discerning what lies beneath that takes practice and learning to attune to *"the source from which the words emerge"* (Kramer, 2007, p.175). In formal RM practice, we have the receptivity of our meditation partner's deep listening and the awareness built through their practice of the guidelines, to help us access this deeper level of dialogue.

It is important to recognise that language is always situated in a cultural background and a lifetime of conditioning and experience. RM practice can enable us to access greater clarity and kindness, helping overcome the inevitable differences between individuals and broaden our mutual understanding to encompass much more than is possible in everyday conversation.

Supporting ourselves to listen deeply

Before we suggest specific practices for the guideline Speak the truth, we share a few ways we can support ourselves to speak the truth in both formal and informal RM practice:

■ *Body as anchor:* As before, the body is a key support in helping us to speak the truth. As mentioned above, attending to what is arising in our body can help us to remain grounded in our moment-by-moment experience, rather than getting drawn into the cognitive world of language. Bringing attention to the physical act of speaking – how the breath, the throat, and the mouth are all intimately involved in forming speech – can help us bring awareness to the process

- *Pausing:* Pausing before, during, and after speaking: taking time to discern what is arising in the moment, rather than speaking out of 'automatic pilot' or pre-planned scripts. As one of our interviewees says, "*If it's not something that's being generated at that moment from the dialogue, well, I just don't say it anymore*"
- *Being wise and discerning:* Being aware that speaking the truth is a whole process from something arising in the mind, to an urge to speak, to a discernment of what is relevant, beneficial, and kind to speak, to finally choosing what to say and how to say it. If we are not mindful, the first two of these steps may happen quickly and words may tumble out without awareness, discernment, or choice; bringing mindfulness to the first two steps helps us engage the whole process with care and wisdom
- *Connecting to 'truth':* Regularly asking ourselves the question: what is true now? This can act as a prompt to help us bring in mindfulness and discernment
- *Being context-appropriate:* Considering not only what is factually true, but also what is skilful, useful, and kind in the particular context we are in. Drawing on all the RM guidelines can help us avoid speaking from reactivity or the urging of our habitual drivers. Even if our drivers are wholesome – for example, wanting to help or give advice – they can create tension, separate us from the moment, and take us away from discerning what is needed in this specific context
- *Checking intention:* Not avoiding saying difficult things, but instead checking out what our intention is in speaking and how we can speak in a way that will maintain receptivity and a sense of shared humanity for self and other
- *Practising:* Speaking the truth takes a lot of practice and care. Because it is so easy to get drawn into the thinking mind when speaking, we need to remind ourselves over and over to bring mindfulness in and draw on all the other RM guidelines. This takes intention and energy – and regular practice to build a new habit – but it is worth the effort!

	Individual	Relational
Formal		
Informal		

Individual formal practice: individual mindfulness or meditation with Speak the truth

As for the other guidelines, the invitation is to find ways to bring the guideline Speak the truth into your mindfulness/meditation practice. For example,

- ■ To speak the truth, you need to know the truth – your subjective reality in each moment. Paying full attention to your experience in each moment will help you know your reality when it comes to speaking it. So, whatever your practice, bringing an attitude of deep listening to yourself will support you subsequently to speak the truth
- ■ You may find mindfulness of thoughts a valuable meditation practice in this context: noticing your inner dialogue. Giving your attention to narratives that arise in the mind, allowing them to emerge and pass without engaging in them or getting carried away by them. The more aware you become of this mental activity, the more you can discern whether what this inner voice is saying is useful, beneficial, and kind – and whether it is part of a habitual pattern

On our dedicated website, we provide an audio download that guides the listener through a brief practice supported by the guideline Speak the truth, which you can use as part of your practice.

	Individual	Relational
Formal		
Informal		

Relational formal practice: relational meditation/ mindful dialogue with Speak the truth

In the resources provided in Appendix 1 and on our dedicated website, we provide a step-by-step process to help you undertake mindful dialogue with the guideline Speak the truth. As always, before engaging in formal RM practice, it is vital to read Chapter 7 and follow the guidance around choosing a dialogue partner, setting agreements to establish safety and agreeing logistics for the practice.

When practising with an emphasis on the guideline Speak the truth, we are invited to listen deeply to ourselves in order to discern the subjective truth in the moment and then to make wise decisions about what to verbalise. For those familiar with mindful dialogue, engaging in a practice with speaker/listener loops can support this process. While the 'loops' have a similar format to those suggested for Listen deeply, this time the listener's feedback focusses on what is evoked in them as they listen to the speaker.

Suitable contemplation topics for this practice could focus on the processes of speaking and/or of discerning what to speak. Alternatively, they could invite exploration of content about aspects of the experience of being human, such as our habit to seek pleasure or what we are learning about ourselves, thus offering the opportunity to access profound wisdom.

	Individual	Relational
Formal		
Informal		

Individual informal practice: bringing Speak the truth into daily life

The invitation is to listen deeply to yourself as much as possible in your daily life, taking time to pause, relax, and allow your direct experience, and bring full attention to your internal dialogue, to your emotions, and to physical sensations arising for you. Paying full attention to your experience in each moment will help you know your truth when it comes to speaking it. It will also help you discern whether what is emerging to be spoken is useful, beneficial, and kind.

As you become more aware of your urges to speak and your inner dialogue you can also better notice and investigate any habitual patterns, assumptions, and stories you tell yourself.

	Individual	Relational
Formal		
Informal		

Relational informal practice: bringing Speak the truth into daily interactions with others

The invitation is to use interactions with other people as a prompt to invite the guideline Speak the truth.

When speaking with someone…

- Inviting yourself to pause, relax, open, attune to emergence, and listen deeply to yourself as a basis for awareness of your subjective reality in each moment. Bringing mindfulness to notice what has the energy to be spoken, and where the energy comes from – you, someone else, the system, for example. Noticing how that changes from moment-to-moment
- Discerning whether what is emerging to be spoken comes from generosity, wisdom, and care. Will it be useful and beneficial (for whom and for what?) – and is this moment the right time to speak of it with the other person?

■ Setting a clear intention to pause before, during, and after speaking so that you have time and space to make wise choices about your speaking. Aiming to engage in speaking with courage, wisdom, care, and awareness

Box 13.1 provides a perspective on Speak the truth that emerged for Stephanie in her leadership development work.

Box 13.1 Transparency and responsibility

Stephanie shares how she was recently part of a team delivering a leadership development programme. In the section on communication, she felt compelled to bring in aspects of Speak the truth and the need to take responsibility in our choices of what to say.

When the programme emphasised being transparent with others about how we are feeling, she says, "*I couldn't help but stand up and say, 'actually, I think there's something missing'… It's not enough for me, for example, to realise, acknowledge, be open to the fact that, say, I'm angry, and just give you my anger. I think I do have a responsibility for looking beneath that and seeing how much of this has got anything to do with you at all.*"

"*How much of this has got to do with my past thoughts, experiences, beliefs? What I'm bringing into this conversation right now, in this minute?… maybe I just got a parking ticket two minutes ago or… this is triggering some real pain for me, which is bringing out all this anger. The truth in that moment isn't me sharing my anger with you… it's me acknowledging to myself what's here, what's present, and then having that discernment to say, 'okay, so what do I do with this, in this relationship, in this conversation?'… That anger may need to be parked and taken care of later.*"

As your practice deepens, you may also be able to tune into the truth of the wider system and speak from the interconnected whole of which we are a part. Box 13.2 sets out an exploration of Speak the truth from Liz's perspective.

Box 13.2 Speak the truth as a call to courage

The guideline Speak the truth has been and continues to be both a frequent wise companion and a compassionate yet uncomfortable disruptor of some of my (Liz) long-standing patterns. Patterns such as avoiding conflict, maintaining what on the surface seemed like harmony (ignoring the ripples below the surface), moulding myself to the context in which I find myself so I can feel I belong. It is helping to evolve my meaning-making and frequently takes me to a developmental edge I had previously shied away from.

Speak the truth encapsulates so much for me: a call to be courageous in naming what is present for me. It has helped me give feedback to certain family members on behaviour I find unsettling or unhelpful and supported me to mindfully, compassionately, and wisely, as best I can, share what is coming up and going on for me, whether I think that is coming from me or elsewhere. Yes, being careful to speak only with discernment but also ensuring I am not hiding behind a justification of not being sure if it is wise to speak up.

It is an invitation to feel into what 'truth' is – reminding myself that there is no such thing as absolute truth, which can be unnerving – and yet holding that there may be a 'truth' at times that might helpfully be shared. Accepting invitations to actively experiment so I can access deep learning, including around how my patterns of wanting to be liked, respected, and loved, show up and can get in the way. Helping me develop my 'self as instrument' – what do I notice that might be coming from the system, not from me but through me – yet reflecting too that I and the system are not separate?

Speak the truth has helped me deepen my listening too – to myself, to others, to the system. I have seen and experienced deep shifts away from fleeing and freezing patterns – having been bullied when I was younger and having had a wonderfully loving but controlling mother – towards greater freedom.

Speak the truth, for me, is also an invitation into profound authenticity, into really working out who and what 'I' am, what 'I' represent and offer, deeply aligning with that and speaking from that place. Helping clients do the same. Helping the system see itself, what it represents and how it might shift according to a new purpose.

Working my edge through Speak the truth is deep work, challenging, messy, yet highly rewarding as bit by bit I catch more and more glimpses of greater liberation, compassion, courage, and wisdom.

This chapter rounds off our exploration of the RM guidelines and how to practice them formally, informally, individually, and relationally. We hope you now have a strong sense of what these guidelines can contribute to our lives and how to build our capacity to embody each one. Since this book is particularly aimed at bringing the power of RM into our coaching practice, we have dedicated a whole section to exploring how to do this. The next section, Section 4, is therefore a chance to explore different aspects of bringing RM into coaching.

References

Kramer, G. (2007). *Insight Dialogue: The interpersonal path to freedom.* Shambhala.
Scharmer, O. (2018). *The essentials of Theory U: Core principles and applications.* Berrett-Koehler Publishers.

Information

Dedicated website accompanying this book: www.relationalmindfulness.net

Section 4

Bringing Relational Mindfulness into coaching

> *I've had one or two coaching conversations that seem to have had a massively disproportional impact. The feedback was that a single session was life changing... And I was thinking, 'Why? What is that?' Because if you looked at the words on paper, the questions might have been a bit more skilled now than they were six months ago, because you hope to always develop that side of things. But I did wonder if part of it was on a real nonverbal level, real visceral, somatic level... this grounded, spaciousness of, "We're in this together. I have no idea what's going to emerge by the end of our session, but whatever it is, it's all interesting and fine and how exciting!" I wonder whether [through RM] I'm bringing more of that quality into my work.*
>
> Stephanie, leadership and team coach, Lego® Serious Play®
> Facilitator, author, and one of our interviewees for this book

As we explored in Chapter 6, our experience and that of the coaches we interviewed is that practising Relational Mindfulness (RM) has enormous benefits for our coaching. As we become more fully present, find connection, and gain insights into our own relational habits and choices, and new ways of thinking and perceiving, we become better at relationships in general and coaching in particular. Whilst Section 3 was designed to help you develop a practice of RM, the purpose

DOI: 10.4324/9781003390428-17

of this section – Chapters 14–18 – is to explore how to integrate the experiential and embodied learning from our RM practice into our coaching. Through the combination of practising RM and then bringing it into coaching, we aim to help you realise the benefits we strongly believe are available for us as coaches and for our coaching clients.

You are here!

Introduction

Section 1
- Setting the scene
- Exploring mindfulness and compassion: definitions and origins
- Benefits of individual mindfulness and compassion in coaching

Origins, underpinnings and benefits of RM

Section 2
- Exploring Relational Mindfulness (RM)
- Insight Dialogue-based RM
- Benefits of bringing RM into coaching

Practice and application

Section 3
- Foundations for practice and application
- Exploring each of the six guidelines in turn

Section 4
- Different levels of bringing RM into coaching
- Preparing with, embodying, drawing on RM

Additional gems to further enhance RM

Section 5
- Becoming fully present and aware
- Relating and connecting
- Insight and wisdom

Next steps and beyond

Section 6
- Where next for you?
- Vision for the future

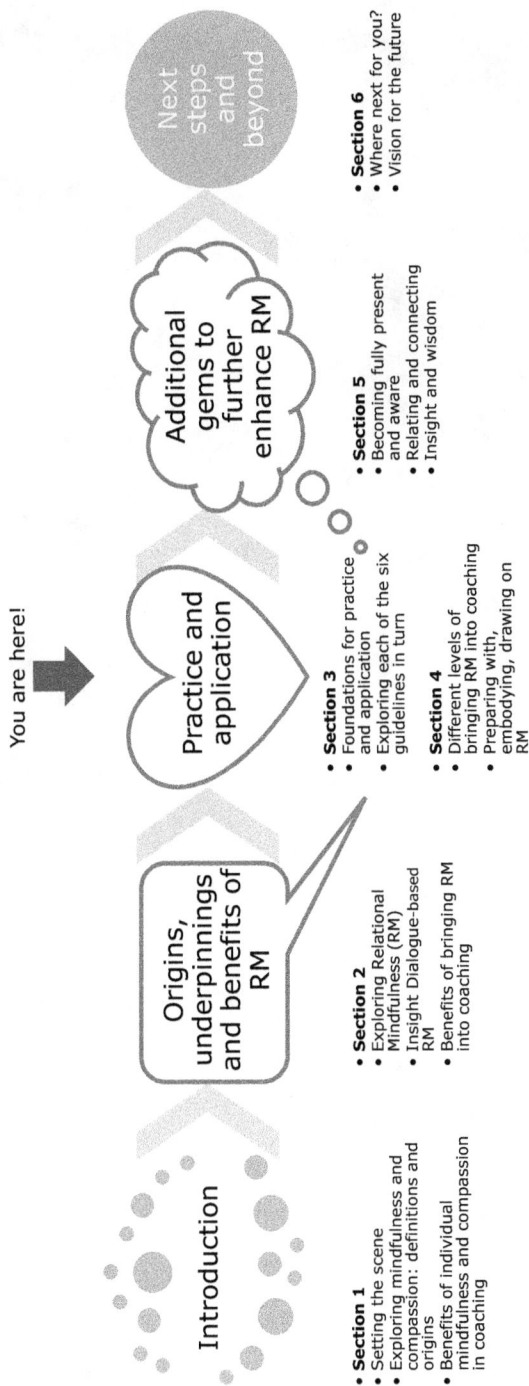

Figure S4 You are here!

Chapter 14

Different levels of bringing Relational Mindfulness into coaching

In preparation for the next few chapters (Chapters 15–18) that explore specific ways to bring RM into coaching, this chapter provides some important context and framing. As we contemplated our own journeys and all we have learnt about mindfulness and compassion applied to coaching, we felt that it was important to establish a sense of the capacity and competencies needed for this integration to be successful.

In the spirit of 'do no harm', we want to emphasise that the degree to which we bring mindfulness, compassion, and RM into coaching needs to be matched to the level of fluency and competence we have established with these approaches. We therefore start by proposing a framework of capacity, move on to define what we mean by RM-Enhanced Coaching (RMEC) and include our thoughts on the vital importance of embodiment in this work.

Coach capacity for bringing mindfulness, compassion, and RM into coaching

To set the scene for looking at the ways we can bring RM into our coaching, we would like to introduce a framework for understanding the different levels

DOI: 10.4324/9781003390428-18

at which coaches may be operating when it comes to bringing mindfulness and compassion into coaching relationships, and how RM fits in. While the research on applying these practices in coaching is still limited, we would like to suggest that operating at any of these levels will add benefits for the coach, client, and coaching process and outcomes.

We propose four levels of capacity at which a coach might operate when bringing mindfulness and compassion into coaching relationships:

- **Level One capacity: Basic competency enhances coaching capability.** Here the coach has some grasp of mindfulness and compassion, with or without experience of RM. They are able, at least on occasion, to enter into a mindful state (Cavanagh & Spence, 2013) and appreciate the benefit of doing so. They can build on this to some degree, for example, in helping them prepare before coaching sessions, and drawing on their own mindfulness and compassion during sessions. This will potentially enhance their coaching by improving their capacity to pay attention to and connect with the client with awareness and empathy. They have some understanding of how mindfulness and compassion development may benefit the client, with an idea of when and where to point the client to resources, so the client can potentially start to practise mindfulness/compassion and gain value from that. The coaches we spoke to all found that practising RM was enhancing their coaching in some or all of these ways

- **Level Two capacity: Embodiment adds role modelling/transmission.** Here, in addition to the above, the coach has embodied mindful and compassionate presence – mindfulness and compassion have become a trait or set of traits for them (Cavanagh & Spence, 2013). This will potentially have a greater effect on their coaching than Level One as they have now shifted their 'way of being', allowing them to bring greater awareness and compassion consistently and authentically into their coaching sessions. Their clients are likely to be able to pick this up, consciously or unconsciously, as the coach will be role modelling/transmitting to clients what being mindful and compassionate looks and feels like. This experience of mindfulness and compassion may enhance the capacity of the client to access these states themselves. The coach may also point the client to ways to start practising mindfulness/compassion with greater confidence and clarity, potentially adding further benefit for the client. Our informal research strongly suggests that practising RM can help coaches with this embodiment process

- **Level Three capacity: Competency to directly offer individual mindfulness/compassion practices.** At this level, the coach has not only embodied mindfulness and compassion, but also undertaken some form of mindfulness and/or compassion cultivation teacher training, enabling them to guide individual mindfulness/compassion practices safely, skilfully, and sensitively during coaching sessions. Their clients will benefit from accessing mindful and compassionate states not only by picking these up from the coach's embodiment, but also through the individual practices the coach guides. To support this level of capacity, the coach will need to have a regular mindfulness practice, spend time building their skills in offering mindfulness/compassion practices, and ideally attend mindfulness retreats from time to time. They will adhere to ethical/good practice guidelines such as those issued from the British Association of Mindfulness-based Approaches (BAMBA, accessed November 2023). Coaches at this level may find that practising RM helps them to offer individual mindfulness and compassion practices more skilfully. Once they are sufficiently familiar with RM, they can also weave the RM guidelines into the practices they offer (see Chapter 17)

■ *Level Four capacity: Competency to directly offer elements of mindful dialogue.* Whilst RM seems to be very supportive in enabling coaches to reach Levels One, Two, and Three, it is not essential to showing those levels of capacity for bringing mindfulness and compassion into coaching. In contrast, at Level Four, RM becomes an explicit part of the coaching process. Whilst coaches at Level Three might offer individual mindfulness/ compassion practices based on the RM guidelines, they are not bringing RM/mindful dialogue practice into coaching, whereas at Level Four capacity the coach is skilled enough to offer elements of mindful dialogue during the coaching session. To support this level of capacity, it is essential for a coach not only to embody the RM guidelines, but also to have a deep familiarity with RM practice and sufficient fluency with the guidelines to hold the space for mindful dialogue. Coaches who do this are not teaching RM, which would require training as an RM/Insight Dialogue (ID)/ Interpersonal Mindfulness Program (IMP) teacher, but they are bringing the form of RM directly into the coaching session (see Chapter 18)

The client's capacity

Just as the coach will be operating from a particular level when it comes to capacity for mindfulness and compassion, so too will the client. They may be completely new to mindfulness/compassion/RM, or they may have capacity at any of the levels mentioned above.

RM-Enhanced Coaching (RMEC)

We define RMEC as:

> *Any coaching in which the coach's effectiveness, skill or presence has been enhanced through their practice of and familiarity with RM.*

As mentioned in the descriptions of the levels above, RM can enhance coaching at any of the four levels of capacity. The benefits of RM practice for coaching outlined in Chapter 6 suggest that RM enhances the coaching practice of those we interviewed in a myriad of ways across the capacity levels.

Most of the coaches we interviewed in our informal research were using RM practice as a way to develop their coaching capacities (Level One capacity) and their 'way of being' or what they were embodying in coaching sessions (Level Two capacity). To support this, many of the coaches were using the RM guidelines to help them prepare for sessions, for example, practising with the guidelines Pause and Relax/allow to ground themselves before the start of coaching sessions (see Chapter 15). Our interviews also revealed many examples of how to embody the RM guidelines during coaching, for example using the guideline Open to help with dual awareness of self and client (see Chapter 16).

Some of the coaches we interviewed reported offering mindfulness practice in their coaching (Level Three capacity) and explicitly weaving one or more of the ID-based RM guidelines into the practices they offered. For example, these coaches might offer clients a guided practice underpinned by the guideline Pause at the start of the session or at relevant moments during the coaching. Bringing in the guideline Relax/allow can be used to help support the client to settle, let go of tensions they are holding, and bring a more spacious receptivity in which to 'hold' their experience and the coaching process. Indeed, any of the RM guidelines can be helpful as a source of guiding a coaching client to be more present and open in sessions (see Chapter 17).

In most cases, even those of us who are using the RM guidelines as an inspiration for supporting clients to pause and explore their experience are not actually using formal RM practice or mindful dialogue within our coaching. However, a couple of the coaches we interviewed have used elements of mindful dialogue/RM practice in their coaching (Level Four capacity). In both cases, these people were not only skilled, mature coaches, but also qualified as ID and/or mindfulness teachers. The direct application of RM in this way is a new and emerging area of applying RM in coaching, so our suggestions in Chapter 18 are still at pilot stage even in our own coaching work.

The vital importance of embodiment

Whatever our level of capacity, bringing RM into coaching is not about imparting knowledge or cognitive input, it is about RM's effect on our coaching capacity and how we are *being* as a coach, in other words, what we are embodying in our coaching. Embodiment means how our physical form and presence represent a quality or characteristic. If we are embodying RM, we physically represent the qualities of presence, awareness, compassion, kindness, and wisdom.

This physicality is important because our felt sense and how we move affect our perceptions and behaviour (e.g. Ziemke, 2016) and is central to learning and behaviour change (Zull, 2002). What we embody will be communicated to others with whom we interact through a range of the neurobiological mechanisms (see Chapter 20 and Frederickson, 2013). As a result, in coaching, our embodiment of a way of being and behaving that integrates the RM guidelines will be picked up by our clients at a visceral level. As explored in Chapter 7, RM practice is about embodied, experiential learning and we firmly believe that it is this embodied learning that is significant for our coaching. The suggestions in Chapter 16 are about embodying each of the RM guidelines in our coaching relationships.

Attaining embodiment before embarking on offering practices is vitally important. Amanda Blake (2022) puts this well in her writing about how coaches learn embodied self-awareness and integrate it into their coaching. She says, "*...attempting to share embodied ways of knowing without personal experience of [embodiment] risks misleading, confusing, or even doing damage to others and to [our] own reputation*" (Blake, 2022, p.222).

This is why we emphasise that only once we embody the RM guidelines and have undertaken training in how to teach mindfulness and/or compassion cultivation are we in a position to offer exercises/practices based on the RM guidelines directly in our coaching (capacity Level Three). Embodiment of the RM guidelines and a grounding in mindfulness/compassion teacher training are even more important if we want to introduce elements of formal mindful dialogue practice into our client work (capacity Level Four).

With our framework, definition, and clarification in place, we are ready to look at specific ways of bringing RM into coaching. We start this, in the next chapter, by looking at RM as a support for preparing for coaching sessions.

References

BAMBA. (2023). *Good practice guidelines for teaching mindfulness-based courses*. Accessed November 2023.

Blake, A. (2022). *Embodied awareness, embodied practice: A powerful path to practical wisdom*. PhD Thesis, Case Western Reserve University.

Cavanagh, M. J., & Spence, G. B. (2013). Mindfulness in coaching: Philosophy, psychology or just a useful skill. In J. Passmore, D. B. Peterson, & T. Freire (Eds.), *The Wiley-Blackwell handbook of the psychology of coaching and mentoring*, 112–134. John Wiley & Sons.

Fredrickson, B. (2013). *Love 2.0*. Hudson Street Press.

Ziemke, T. (2016). The body of knowledge: On the role of the living body in grounding embodied cognition. *Biosystems*, 148, 4–11.

Zull, J. E. (2002). *The art of changing the brain: Enriching teaching by exploring the biology of learning*. Stylus Pub.

Chapter 15

Preparing for coaching sessions with the Relational Mindfulness guidelines

We probably all know that it is good practice to take time before we start a coaching session to prepare and settle. Drawing on the Relational Mindfulness (RM) guidelines as we prepare for sessions ensures our RM practice enhances our coaching capability (capacity Level One – see Chapter 14). If we want to embody the RM guidelines in our coaching (capacity Level Two), both taking time to prepare and bringing the RM guidelines into this preparation are essential (and we can only operate at capacity Levels Three and Four if we are embodying the RM guidelines ourselves, so the same applies).

Here, we explore integrating each of the guidelines into our coaching preparation. On our dedicated website, we provide short audios for each of the RM guidelines that are designed to help with this. Alternatively, you may have your own favourite audio or practice to support you to access one or more of the guidelines.

DOI: 10.4324/9781003390428-19

Integrating Pause into preparing for coaching sessions

- *Mindfully pausing:* Making our preparation time an intentional pause with the support of the RM guideline Pause can be particularly beneficial in helping us embody mindful awareness for our coaching client. Taking a few minutes to engage in a mindful pause can help us sense into embodying pausing, which will flow into our subsequent interactions with our client. The key thing is to bring our attention to what is happening right now, noticing the felt sense of being here, and enabling the mind to settle out of distraction, and let go of what has come before or might happen later

- *Inviting Pause to help manage emotions:* Pausing can help us manage our emotions before a session, particularly at the start of a new coaching relationship when the grounding and settling offered by a pause can reduce anxiety and enable us to be more fully present with our client. Rhonda speaks about how when she is anxious, she draws on RM by "…*pausing and relaxing and just taking a deep breath before I begin…*"

Integrating Relax/allow into preparing for coaching sessions

- *Relaxing tension and allowing what is here:* Taking a moment as we prepare for coaching to intentionally relax any tension where possible, and to allow whatever remains to be here, can be a great way to prepare our hearts and minds to connect with our client. Setting a context of Relax/allow in our preparation and aiming to continue that into the session can help us be more skilful and support our client to resonate with our state, giving both of us greater access to awareness and receptivity

- *Thinking about the environment and set-up for coaching* in terms of what is going to best help our clients and us to relax and receive whatever arises. Stephanie shares how the beautiful surroundings and kindly set-up of a restorative yoga class she attended helped her to open to her emotions and be vulnerable in a way that she might not have done in a less supportive space. She says, "…*allowing isn't only about noticing something and then allowing it, but to actually intentionally set the scene, to allow things to arise…*"

Integrating Open into preparing for coaching sessions

- *Accessing the guideline Open:* Intentionally opening our awareness – bringing our attention to our internal experience, external experience, and both – before a session can help us hold both our client and our own responses and sensations in a spacious 'dual-attention' awareness

■ *Exploring the physical context:* It can be helpful to explore whether specific physical positions, postures, or environmental conditions help our awareness to be more spacious. Grounding ourselves with the guideline Pause, then bringing the kindly, allowing receptivity of the guideline Relax/allow are important foundations to this kind of opening. As Stephanie describes it: *"...physically putting my shoulders back and feeling open in my body: 'can I receive whatever is coming and stay this way and then see what happens?'... as you do that, your heart space opens up and you feel more grounded and there's more space...."*

Integrating Attune to emergence into preparing for coaching sessions

■ *Drawing on Attune to emergence* as we prepare for coaching invites us to notice and track how things are changing moment-by-moment, attuning to the arising and vanishing of our internal and external experiences. Sensations, thoughts, sounds, sights – all coming and going. This attunement can help us bring an attitude of beginner's mind to the coaching and a sensitivity to whatever emerges in the session

■ *Setting an intention to leave our preconceptions behind* as we prepare for coaching can also be a way of remembering the power of letting go of predicting, needing to control, and to plan whilst coaching, again helping us to attune to whatever emerges

Integrating Listen deeply into preparing for coaching sessions

■ *Drawing on all the guidelines and setting intentions:* To embody Listen deeply in our coaching, we will need the support of all the other RM guidelines, so practising with any or all of the guidelines before a session can help us listen deeply in coaching. It may be helpful to ask ourselves which of the guidelines we most need to strengthen and choose our practice accordingly. Slowing down and bringing both intention and application to our embodiment of mindful, receptive, spacious, attuned presence will support us to model and benefit from this form of listening

■ *Listening to ourselves:* Taking time to listen deeply to ourselves can help us to be aware of how the external environment – particularly another person – resonates within our system. As we review our notes or recall the previous coaching session with a client, it may be helpful to notice what comes up for us in terms of physical sensations and emotions

Integrating Speak the truth into preparing for coaching sessions

- *Drawing on all the guidelines and setting intentions:* Again, to embody Speak the truth in our coaching, we will need the support of all the other RM guidelines. Practising any or all of the guidelines before a session can help us to bring care, discernment, and freshness to our speaking when the session starts
- *Setting a clear intention to speak the truth* – in the full sense of the RM guideline – can also help set us up to bring wisdom and care to our speaking in the session. That intentionality allows us to speak with greater ease in the session. Saima reports how when she sets an RM-based intention before a conversation, *"…speaking the truth comes with flow and ease"*

Box 15.1 The power of preparing with RM

For many years I (Emma) would spend my preparation time before a coaching or supervision session re-reading my notes from the previous session, sketching out what I thought the session might cover, and clarifying what my intentions were. Since RM has become ever more central to my life, work, and way of being, it has dawned on me much more slowly than I like to admit that these activities may be a misdirection of my attention. Not that I am denigrating any of these activities – they all have their place and I still do them – but I have learnt that the last 5–10 (or more) minutes before a session are much better spent in settling my body, heart, and mind. Writing this chapter has helped me articulate some of the ways in which I do this. I choose my approach according to what feels most needed for my state at the time and the context, including my hypotheses of what to expect in the client(s). It has been remarkable to see how much more grounded this approach has enabled me to be and how much more flexible, effective, embodied, and connected my coaching and supervision has been as a result.

Integrating the RM guidelines into our preparation is the first step to bringing RM into our coaching at any of the capacity levels. Having integrated the RM guidelines into our preparation for a session, we are much better placed to embody them in the coaching itself. The next chapter offers further ideas of how to do this.

Information

Dedicated website accompanying this book: www.relationalmindfulness.net

Chapter 16

Embodying the Relational Mindfulness guidelines during coaching sessions

To realise the benefits of Relational Mindfulness (RM) at capacity Level Two and above, we need to embody the RM guidelines during sessions. This embodiment will enable us to be more fully present, better able to connect with clients, more aware of habits and choices, and more open to new ways of thinking and perceiving.

While integrating the RM guidelines into our preparation, as outlined in Chapter 15, will help with this embodiment, the suggestions in this chapter are designed to help coaches to explore and embed this way of being during coaching sessions.

Embodying Pause during coaching sessions

Pause is the fundamental starting point for embodying RM in coaching. It is the basis on which all the other guidelines sit, the '*sine qua non*.' Pausing and bringing our attention into what is here now is foundational for embodying presence and awareness in our coaching sessions.

- *Pausing deliberately:* In coaching or other client interactions, we can explore how it is to pause deliberately and invite a greater level of awareness and presence. We might actually pause our speaking or we might just pause internally to notice what is going on. We might invite our client to pause with us, or we might do it unilaterally

■ *Bringing intentions into the moment:* Pause can include becoming more intentional in our coaching. We can use a moment of pausing to remind ourselves of what we aspire to offer as a coach. As Saima puts it, *"...pausing for self, grounding for self, now with an expectation of it being for the service of others"*

■ *Pausing out of thinking:* When we notice that we are formulating hypotheses, questions, and/or reflections in a session, we can invite a pause and let go of the thinking to allow more space for listening. To quote Malcolm: *"... the pause is permission to be silent... to take time... I wish I'd got it when I began coaching... in the early days... I would have a hypothesis in my head and think... What's a good question? How do I intervene here, what do I do?' There's all this busyness going on... 'Pause' gives permission just to be present and just to listen and recognise what is here"*

■ *Framing coaching as a Pause:* The concept of pausing can be a way to frame coaching. In the rush of most modern-day workplaces and the challenging world in which we operate, many clients do not find the time to pause and reflect: coaching can offer them this. As Beth says: *"...inviting people to pause is a radical act... I refer to coaching as a pause for [my clients]. Sometimes all they need is to have the space in the diary and to be held accountable because it's with someone else"*

Embodying Relax/allow during coaching sessions

Relax/allow underpins a receptive, non-judgemental, empathetic approach in coaching. As we bring this attitude to ourselves and our client, we open up possibilities that are unavailable if we are in a tense, reactive, or striving state.

■ *Noticing and softening tension and inviting kindliness:* At any moment, we can choose to notice and soften tension in our body, then invite an attitude of kindliness – letting go of any sense of striving and allowing ourselves and our client to be just as we are, deliberately inviting a greater level of receptivity and non-judgement. Simply embodying relaxing and allowing through our presence is likely to help the client to be more open and receptive. The mirroring process described before (Frederickson, 2013) will enable a resonance between us and our client and our receptivity will be felt by our client. As Shenaz says: *"I'm now absolutely convinced that when I let go of the tension in my mind and in my body, my neural pathways are speaking to somebody else's neural pathways. I can actually visibly see this working with some clients: as I... <u>allow</u> the discomfort or whatever it is to be here – as I'm looking at the other person, they feel understood"*

- *Recognising and allowing difficult thoughts:* Inviting Relax/allow into our coaching approach can also be a way of calming our mind and getting out of our own way. For example, recognising a critical or anxious voice that could distract us from being present with our client, allowing that to be there, and releasing any need to bring that thinking into the coaching or let it separate us from what is happening in the moment with the client. As Malcolm puts it, *"…with Relax/allow, it's like, 'Okay, so you don't know what to do… you don't know what to say, you don't know what's going on. Okay, there is a little voice saying… you should be making some progress etc.' Relax says: '…This is the way it is. Isn't that interesting?' It is recognising and accepting all of this that the mind is thinking but not acting on that voice"*
- *Releasing resistance:* This guideline can also be a way to access greater compassion and connection with our clients. By releasing resistance to a client being the way they are, allowing what arises moment-by-moment in the coaching session, and not judging ourselves or our client, we can access a more compassionate attitude and not let our resistances get in the way of authentically connecting. As Jane describes, *"Compassion is really alive in the sessions. It's a resource, the loving arms of Pause, Relax[/allow]… it's so tender. I feel so connected to my client"*

Embodying Open during coaching sessions

Open is the key guideline for taking our mindfulness from an individual practice into the relational domain – bringing attention to internal, external, and the relationship between the two. This is central to being able to translate our RM practice into coaching and embody a presence that is relational and mindful.

- *Setting an intention:* As we start a session, it can be beneficial to set an intention to be as fully present as possible moment-by-moment to both the internal (our own sensations, responses, ideas, etc.) and the external (our client, their words, tone of voice, gestures, facial expressions, etc.). This intention will help enable us to set a context of spacious awareness for the client, as Beth says, *"…being really open to what someone's bringing into the space"*
- *Getting curious:* The guideline Open can be an invitation to curiosity. The stimulus might come from internal, external, or a combination of the two. By embodying Open, we can hold both these domains in awareness and let our curiosity encompass a wide space of enquiry. Pirjo describes how, when she notices something going on for herself or her client, *"I start to be curious about that"*
- *Opening to an equal enquiry:* Bringing Open into coaching includes inviting a dual awareness of our and our client's experience and being with the

client in an equal enquiry, exploring together and not having to have the 'answers.' When we embody Open in this way, we are better able to create a collaborative and inclusive approach based on common humanity and shared vulnerability. As Shenaz explains, *"Open... opened me up to my vulnerability and not knowing, and therefore the 'we' becomes possible... Because I don't know the answers, really. And isn't that the art of coaching at the end of the day? Isn't it that we're supposed to be part of this egalitarian conversational space where we both come together and explore and become creative?"*

- *Being with shared vulnerability:* Noticing when we see our own or the other person's physical and/or emotional vulnerability is another aspect of Open. We can access a sense of the shared human condition and how we respond to that. If habits of resistance arise, or a desire for it to be different, Open is an invitation to explore 'being with' the way things are, internally and externally, and bringing as much compassion, kindliness, and acceptance as we can to both. As Stephanie puts it, *"...there's something about Open being intrinsically linked to compassion and this idea of unconditional positive regard... that brings with it a bit of vulnerability..."*

- *Broadening attention:* Embodying the guideline Open involves broadening our attention and being with ourselves and our clients. This enables a combination of collaboration, curiosity, and letting go of the need to control the coaching, which can help us access a much more creative way of being. Shenaz again, *"I don't think we can be creative without being open... When I am in Open, I am definitely at the edge of myself. I don't really like being that open: I like to know my answers. So being open means being very present to whatever may emerge"*

- *Sensitivity and choice:* The wider, spacious awareness that practising Open invites can help us to be better in touch with what is happening for ourselves, our client, and between us. This can improve our choices about what we voice and when we voice it in coaching. As Jane says, *"With Open comes... greater sensitivity regarding what's appropriate to speak in the current context"*

Embodying Attune to emergence during coaching sessions

Attune to emergence is a powerful process in coaching as it supports a freshness of perspective and an attuning to what is possible in each moment of an encounter.

- *Bringing awareness to arising and vanishing:* Embodying the guideline Attune to emergence is about bringing awareness to the arising, emergent process of experience – to the 'tip of the moment.' Putting our attention on what is arising and vanishing, and tuning in to how things are constantly changing, can make us more sensitive to what is happening for and with our client

■ *Letting go of knowing what is best and inviting new ways of seeing:* We may be holding strong intentions of being in service to our clients and supporting them with their process, but the reality is that we cannot be sure ahead of time what will be the best way to do that. Instead, we can choose to attune to emergence and make wise choices about 'what next' based on the client and the context in front of us, in that moment. Allowing the process of coaching to emerge in this way can open us up to new possibilities and help our clients access new ways of seeing that are not possible if we abide by the conventional rules of conversation. As Malcolm says, "*[If] I don't know what to do, [I say to myself] 'Let's attune to emergence'... and it will inevitably evolve... this is where insights that go beyond ordinary conversation or individual meditation emerge*"

■ *Letting go of planning what to say* enables us to be fully with what is happening now. This is particularly important in coaching as it frees us up from formulating our next question, preparing to reflect back what our client has said, or choosing the perfect tool, technique, or analogy. Instead, all our energy can go into listening to our client and collaborating with them on their journey, giving them space to come to their own insights. Whilst that is probably what our training has encouraged us to do, the same training has probably also given us tools, techniques, ways to reflect back and ask questions that make simply being present hard. Reminding ourselves of the guideline Attune to emergence is a way of putting this letting go into practice. As Rhonda notes, "*...what I find is that people come to their own conclusions, people ask their own questions. All these wonderfully insightful questions that I feel like I should be asking them... it's so much more powerful if they come up with that themselves*"

■ *Getting curious:* Bringing an attitude of 'not knowing' and getting really curious about what will emerge in coaching frees us up to be fully with our client. Challenging ourselves to let go of a tendency to predict and instead open to what might arise gives us much more energy for listening and being in partnership with our client. All the energy and effort that would have been used for predicting and anticipating is now available for curiosity and openness to whatever comes up. As Stephanie puts it, "*...it can feel like there's strength and certainty if I can predict what you're going to say, and I know what to say after that... On the surface, that can feel safer and more secure, because our brains like to predict... [but getting curious is] so much more exciting and richer and more real... the possibilities are so much greater than the narrow vision of my predicting mind*"

■ *Letting go of preconceptions and of wanting to control:* Attune to emergence is an invitation to let go of preconceptions and of wanting to control a dialogue. Instead, we allow ourselves to be surprised by what arises (and vanishes) in the coaching and release the need to control what happens. As Rhonda puts it, *"Attune to emergence really is the most powerful element for me in my coaching because [it helps me let go of the]… preconceptions that are kind of lurking around the edges, even if they're not centre stage, trying to control how this conversation is going to go"*

■ *Stepping into a shared journey:* Stepping out of the formal role of coach and sharing the journey of exploring the emergent with our client can help us be more collaborative in our coaching. If we are attuning together to what is emerging, we have a more interconnected, unconstructed awareness, which offers a partnership-based, open space for the coaching to unfold. To quote Jane, *"[Attune to emergence] may support coaches to step out of the role of 'I'm the coach and you're the coachee' where there is a subtle power differential. The ability to let go of the role of coach comes from the groundedness of pause, relax. In turn, this facilitates the stepping into this wide open turbulent complex uncertain ambiguous space of attuning to emergence"*

Embodying Listen deeply during coaching sessions

In Chapter 20, we remind ourselves of the different levels of listening and how as coaches, we are expected to be good at listening. However, in different ways throughout this book, we have heard from coaches saying that, despite listening being a core skill they learnt in their training as a coach, practising the RM guideline Listen deeply takes listening to a different level. As Saima says, *"I thought I was listening deeply before I started RM. I thought I was a really active listener. I thought that's what I was being paid for for 20 years, until I arrived at Listen Deeply."*

As coaches, given our training, we are hopefully ideally positioned to develop this form of listening. We probably already have better listening skills than most. However, we believe it is in the interests of our clients and ourselves that we embody the RM guideline Listen deeply to enhance our listening skills even further.

■ *Drawing on all the RM guidelines:* To fully embody the RM guideline Listen deeply, we need to draw on all the other RM guidelines: pausing to be fully present, relaxing and allowing to release separation and be with whatever arises, opening to listen both internally and externally, and attuning to emergence to let go of preconceptions, planning and controlling, and be here now. With Listen deeply, these guidelines come together and support one another to make our listening fully relational and truly mindful

- ... *particularly Attune to emergence:* We are best able to embody Listen deeply when we let go of planning what to say next, so drawing on Attune to emergence is a key support for Listen deeply. While our coach training may have given us a wide range of models, tools, and approaches to enhance our coaching, Listen deeply encourages us not to be thinking about any of that as we listen to our client. If we are planning what to say next, we are not fully listening. As one of our interviewees puts it, "*The [opposite] of listening is preparing to reply.*" Instead, we trust that listening deeply to the client will help us choose what to say next – informed by all that we have heard and know – in a much more skilful way than half-listening-half-planning our response
- *Listening with our eyes and other senses as well as our ears:* While our client's words are important, we can often coach more powerfully – and access things that are outside of the client's awareness – when we attune to what is emerging in their non-verbal communication. Body language and facial expressions can help us support the client to tune into their emotions and assumptions. Meanwhile, the tone and volume of their voice, the speed at which they talk, the energy they give to particular words, and all the subtle-ties of their speaking can help us pick up and reflect a whole diversity of what they are communicating beyond their words. As Shenaz explains, "*... my eyes are listening... [I do] a lot of looking at people's faces and body language and tone of voice... if I see something on a face... I might say... 'I just saw you frown there. I'm just wondering what was happening for you'*"
- *Listening with the body:* Our bodies can pick up things that our minds might miss. Our client will be communicating in ways that resonate with us at an emotional and felt sense level. When we tune into our bodies as a way to listen, we can pick up on this communication. In addition, bringing in this felt sense can give what is said more significance and help us retain what we have heard. As Saima says, "*...listening with what sits in my heart and in my gut, rather than just what goes into my ear and sits cognitively in my head... I'm able to hold... even the littlest detail that someone would share with... that I might not have held before*"
- *Noticing when our mind wanders off:* Embodying Listen deeply depends on our capacity to attune to what is emerging, not only to help us let go of planning and preparing, but also to notice when our mind wanders off so that we can pause and bring it back. As Jane explains, "*...noticing that, because of what's happening in the field, the mind might go into thinking... to more constructing. So let's just pause and connect back to the base, to the ground and open up to listening deeply again*"
- *Listening internally as well as externally:* Embodying Listen deeply also depends on our capacity to build on the guideline Open so that we are listening internally as well as externally. As Malcolm puts it, "*...pointing*

the awareness to one's inner voice and to the voice of another." The spacious awareness of opening our attention in this way can enable us to listen to and receive both internal and external communication, without identifying or 'falling into' either our internal narrative or the stories/perspective of our client

■ *Listening beyond the words* is also important for embodying Listen deeply. Letting go of narratives and views allows us not to be constrained by any one perspective, to see more clearly and broadly, not limited by individual mindsets. We can listen 'between the words' and beyond the immediate in more creative ways. Shenaz says, "...*often listening deeply is saying 'what's not being said? What is it that you just haven't mentioned at all, or what we haven't even looked at?'*"

Embodying Speak the truth during coaching sessions

Our training as coaches probably taught us that speaking in coaching is largely about asking good questions, reflecting back what we have heard, and prompting the client to share their truth. It may not have given us a deep awareness of how we choose what to say in the moment. The guideline Speak the truth gives us greater insight into the speaking process as it unfolds and can help us make wise choices about which questions we ask, what we share, and how we speak.

If we believe that coaching is almost exclusively about listening, Speak the truth can help us think more about how our speaking may contribute to client outcomes. As Rhonda says, "...*sharing what's useful... rather than holding back."*

■ *Drawing on all the RM guidelines, particularly Pause:* Our capacity to embody Speak the truth in our coaching will depend on our being able to draw on all the other RM guidelines to help us stay mindful as we speak. Pausing is particularly important. As Shenaz puts it, "...*once the speaking starts, especially in coaching, I could lose my mindfulness in the words that I speak, but it's about staying alert and staying awake."*

■ *Bringing care and compassion* to our speaking is core to embodying Speak the truth. As we emphasised in Chapter 13, this does not mean avoiding saying things that might be challenging or difficult for the client to hear. Instead, it is about speaking with an attitude of goodwill and awareness that makes it easier for the client to hear. As Pirjo explains, "...*[RM] has brought more compassion and kindness towards myself and towards others as well. So, when I'm saying directly what I think, it... comes from a different, kinder place, or more compassionate place"*

■ *Bringing awareness to felt experience* helps us know what to say. Grounding ourselves in our bodily sensations can help us make wise choices about when to speak and what to say. As Rhonda puts it, "...*[Speak the truth is] really about that whole feeling of knowing when to speak."*

- *Couching our speaking as 'our truth'*, as a possible version, or a hypothesis, rather than anything more solid or absolute. In this way, we can keep the coaching flexible and allow choice to rest with the client. As Shenaz says, *"… what I often say is: 'look, this is my version of where I'm thinking this may be helpful, but it is only one version, having considered everything we worked on'… speaking the truth, for me, is very linked to the choice corollary, which is: 'what do you want to do next with this?'"*
- *Bringing flexibility:* Not grasping or holding onto a particular way of thinking or 'truth' can allow flexibility and awareness in how we intervene in coaching. When we embody Speak the truth in this way, we can draw on our subjective truth in the present moment in a discerning, wise, and kind way. As Stephanie explains, *"…my thinking on Speak the truth has shifted quite a lot in the last few months and I'm holding 'my truth' lightly… [the RM guidelines are] about not grasping at what I want, so much as to be connected to my truth…."*

Once we have reached the point where we embody the RM guidelines in coaching (capacity Level Two), if we have some training in offering mindfulness, compassion, and/or Insight Dialogue (ID)/RM, we can consider stepping into capacity Levels Three and Four as considered in Chapters 17 and 18.

Reference

Fredrickson, B. (2013). *Love 2.0*. Hudson Street Press.

Chapter 17

Directly offering individual mindfulness practices in coaching drawing on the Relational Mindfulness guidelines

---

As set out in the capacity levels framework in Chapter 14, once we embody a mindful and compassionate presence and have undertaken a mindfulness and/ or compassion cultivation teacher training, we have the skills and understanding to directly offer individual mindfulness and compassion practice in coaching (Level Three capacity). If we add understanding of and regular practice with the Relational Mindfulness (RM) guidelines to this level of capacity, we are in a position to weave the RM guidelines directly into the practices we offer in our coaching. This can be implicit or explicit.

Our interviews identified a few coaches who were using one or more of the Insight Dialogue (ID)-based RM guidelines to underpin the practices they offered in their coaching, such as guided practices at the start of the session or at relevant moments during the coaching. Based on the findings from these interviews, together with what we do in our own coaching, this chapter sets out a series of suggestions for offering practices in coaching that draw on each of the RM guidelines.

DOI: 10.4324/9781003390428-21

Bringing in the guideline Pause

- *Offering a Pause practice:* Using the guideline Pause can support clients to settle at the start of a coaching session, bring greater focus to the coaching process, and access deeper responses and new thinking. As Saima says, "*[I ask] 'Do they want a moment of just pausing to rid themselves of wherever they've been or whatever they've been doing and then invite the coaching conversation?' ... It's mostly been received with 'I needed that!'*"

  To support this pause, we might offer some practice guidance to point the client's attention to the physical sensations of being here now and/or ask them to become more aware of their state of mind. Alternatively, particularly if the person already has a mindfulness/meditation practice, we can just offer a few minutes of silence in which they ground and centre themselves.

- *Inviting a reflective pause to punctuate a client's speaking:* It can also be valuable to invite clients to pause at other points during a session. For example, inviting a client to pause before they respond to a question, or inviting a pause when the client seems to be speeding up or getting stuck. As Jane explains, "*I ask a question and invite them to pause for at least ten seconds before responding. And then I see them drop into the space so there's this deepening that happens and they have insights that are sometimes staggering. And I can feel it. I feel the pregnancy, the potency, or the potentiality in that moment, and then it starts to blossom and I just see it emerging*"

Bringing in the guideline Relax/allow

- *Offering a practice of Relax/allow:* Similar to our suggestion for the guideline Pause, we can explicitly offer our client practice guidance that integrates the guideline Relax/allow to help them bring a receptive attitude to whatever arises. It may be supportive to do this at the start of the session to help set the tone, intention, and attitudinal approach

- *Inviting awareness and release of tension:* If our client is getting particularly tense, agitated, or upset, we can draw on the guideline Relax/allow to invite them to notice the tension and acknowledge how things are in that moment, then release tension where possible and allow whatever is arising to be there. Gently offered at the right moment in a session, this can foster a kindly receptivity, enabling the client to shift their state to one in which they are better able to engage with the coaching process

Bringing in the guideline Open

- *Offering a practice that integrates Open:* We can draw on the guideline Open to guide a practice to help the client explore narrowing and broadening the focus of their attention and/or shifting attention between internal and external. This may be particularly useful when a client is stuck in their viewpoint and struggling to see other perspectives

■ *Using Open to help the client's exploration:* We may find it helpful to bring the guideline Open explicitly into coaching through the questions we ask. Pointing to the distinct experiences of the internal environment (felt sense, emotions, thinking, and so on) and the external situation – and the relationship between these two – can enable the client to widen their attention, awareness, and perspective. Shenaz uses the words internally and externally, for example "*'So internally, what's happening for you?'* ... *'When you say that, what is happening for you externally?'*"

In Box 17.1, Emma gives her thoughts on bringing the first three RM guidelines together to support an initial mindfulness practice at the start of a coaching session.

Box 17.1 The PRO start

Whilst a guided mindfulness exercise is not necessarily appropriate for all clients, we have both found that clients very often welcome a chance to take a moment to settle at the start of a coaching or supervision session.

I (Emma) have found that having the RM guidelines Pause, Relax/allow, and Open (PRO) in mind helps me guide a client to bring their attention into the moment and notice what is here now, let go of tension where possible and bring a kindly receptivity to their experience and, as I draw the practice to a close, widen their attention from a focus on the internal to taking in the external and touching into a sense of interconnectedness.

We need to be sensitive to what is going to suit different clients and check out with them what they want each time: gauging a client's familiarity with mindfulness, level of adult development (see Chapter 21) and mind-state will be important. For some clients, I find that a sentence or two that points to each of PRO is enough. For others, 5 or more minutes of mindfulness guidance is helpful. Depending on the situation, introducing Attune to emergence, Listen deeply, and/or Speak the truth adds further support.

Often, I will include an intention exploration as part of the practice – generally after Pause and Relax and before Open. This is an invitation for the client to look at what might be a beneficial focus for the session, explored from a range of angles, including not only the client's own perspective, but also what their stakeholders might say, and what society and the environment might want us to address. After this exploration, I invite a settling of the attention back into sensations in the body to help the client ground themselves in their embodied awareness for the session ahead and to open from there to connection and interconnection.

Bringing in the guideline Attune to emergence

■ *Inviting awareness of moment-by-moment change:* We can help clients attune to the emergent by encouraging them to become aware of change moment-by-moment. This could be through a formal guided practice, or through simply pausing with the client and sharing a process of letting go of trying to control or predict. By attending to what is emerging each moment ourselves and naming that, we can invite our client to bring attention to emergence with us

■ *Inviting awareness of the universality of impermanence:* When a client gets stuck or is struggling to accept an uncertain and unpredictable situation, we can invite them to recognise how everything is constantly arising and vanishing. From the sensations in their body and thoughts in their mind, to the sounds in their environment and the newsfeed on their phone, to the natural world and the seasons of weather, nothing stays the same. If we try to stop any of these changes, we are attempting the impossible. Instead, we can invite clients to 'surf the waves' and make this flux and flow the thing to trust. When they do this, they may find the stability they seek – the stability of knowing at an embodied level that 'change is the only constant.'

Bringing in the guideline Listen deeply

■ *Guiding practice:* Helping clients listen more deeply to themselves and to others is often an aim and/or outcome of coaching. The guideline Listen deeply gives us a way of knowing this as a felt experience that we can translate into direct support for our clients. We can guide them with one or more of the RM guidelines to support this capacity for deep listening to self and other. The aim is to give them an experience of how listening deeply is underpinned by our capacity to be fully present, receptive, attentive to internal and external experience, and attuning to what is emerging right now

■ *Different aspects of listening:* Encouraging clients to explore different aspects of listening can also be helpful to broaden their experience and understanding of listening. Just as we can do this ourselves as coaches, as we noted earlier, we can encourage clients to practise playing with different types of listening. We can invite them in and between sessions to bring attention to one or more of the following:

  ■ Content, words, information
  ■ Body language, gestures, facial expressions
  ■ Rhythm, tone, volume of the speech
  ■ Energy and emotion
  ■ Their felt sense and sensations in resonance with the speaker

Bringing in the guideline Speak the truth

- *Practising Listen deeply:* Encouraging clients to listen mindfully to themselves and to become aware of what is arising in the moment can help them identify and share things that they may not have even thought, let alone said, before. Our embodiment of listening deeply to the client and ourselves is a vital underpinning for this and we can provide guidance to support deep self-listening. Saima says that, since weaving RM into her coaching, she gets more comments such as, "*I don't think I'd have ever said that before', or 'I'm not quite sure where that comment came from'... 'That's really valuable for us both to be able to hear that. How did that pop out?' ... I think one person actually jokingly said: 'that was magic. How did you make me say that? I would have never said that in any other place'*"
- *Examining the different facets of Speak the truth:* Enabling clients to speak the truth in coaching is a good first step for helping clients translate this guideline to other contexts. We may find it helpful to guide clients to listen to their own embodied experience and explore choosing whether, what, and how to verbalise something to others. This might include guiding an understanding that:
  - 'Truth' in this context is not just factually true, but also the subjective truth of experience, which changes over time – helping them release a sense of one single and permanent truth
  - Speaking our truth involves discerning what to speak according to whether it is valuable, kind, and timely
  - Our speaking can get hijacked by habits, urges, and reactivity, so it is important to bring awareness and pause before speaking

The suggestions in this chapter have been about bringing the RM guidelines individually or collectively into our coaching work, including guiding practices directly for our clients (capacity Level Three). Offering formal mindful-dialogue-based practice in our coaching sessions takes this to a whole other level (capacity Level Four) and is the subject of the next chapter.

Chapter 18

Mindful dialogue in coaching

As set out in the framework of capacity levels in Chapter 14, we reach Level Four capacity when (a) our Relational Mindfulness (RM) practice is deeply embedded and embodied, (b) we have the capacity to directly offer individual mindfulness/compassion practice in our coaching, and (c) we have sufficient fluency with the RM guidelines and RM practice to take elements of mindful dialogue into our coaching work. In this chapter we provide suggestions about how those who are at this level of capacity might introduce elements of mindful dialogue into coaching sessions.

It is very important to say up front that the heart of mindful dialogue is not a structure or set of steps, it is relatedness, being fully with one another, and opening to insight that arises in these conditions. We hesitated even to give suggested formats because we know the risk is that the process could become formulaic, which would not be true RM and would not provide the benefits that RM has the potential to offer. We implore you to read this chapter and the resources in Appendix 2 (and on our dedicated website) with that in mind.

Not as easy as it looks

Our experience from teaching mindful dialogue to coaches, leaders, and others is that what seems simple as a participant is actually really complex to facilitate or teach. It takes a while to become fluent enough with the logistics to guide others through the steps of the practice and to embody the RM guidelines at the same time.

DOI: 10.4324/9781003390428-22

On reading through the suggestions below, it might be easy to assume we have done something sufficiently similar in coach training to make it totally familiar. Surely, the process of coaching in pairs and threes that we have all been through numerous times in our development as coaches is pretty much the same as first speaker/second speaker/shared dialogue or the speaker–listener loops described? However, whilst familiarity with coach training exercises may be an asset for engaging in mindful dialogue, there are important distinctions between the two. Indeed, we have seen seasoned coaches tumble into familiar 'coaching practice' mode and miss the subtleties of practising RM, let alone guiding such practices.

Distinctions between coaching and mindful dialogue

The first, most obvious, distinction between coaching and engaging in mindful dialogue with a coaching client is the degree of present-moment mindful awareness. In mindful dialogue, both coach and client engage in the interaction with as much mindfulness and gathering of their minds as possible – meditating together. The invitations to pause are not simply preambles or mechanical steps in the process. Pausing and bringing our attention into what is happening right now in our bodies and in the world around us is fundamental to mindful dialogue practice – more important than what is said or heard. Thus, if we are to support others to engage in mindful dialogue, we need to embody awareness as we facilitate the practice and to provide clear guidance to help those we are supporting to bring their attention into the present and become aware of their here-and-now experience.

The second distinction is the additional care and attention needed for setting up and guiding a mindful dialogue. RM practice can be unfamiliar in structure and unexpectedly intimate in nature, as we open to what is emerging internally and externally. It can lead to feelings of vulnerability and reactivity as well as great insights, which is why really good up-front contracting is vital, including agreements around safety, non-judgement, care for self and other, and so on (see Chapter 7). As a coach considering offering elements of mindful dialogue as part of a session, we need to discern a client's readiness, explaining what we are suggesting and why, and checking whether the client is willing to engage in this kind of dialogue.

Client readiness for elements of mindful dialogue

When discerning client readiness, we need to consider a number of factors. My (Emma's) doctoral research identified characteristics that would help participants to get the most out of RM-based development (see Box 18.1), the most important of which was deemed to be openness to change.

Box 18.1 What helps people get the most out of RM-based development?

■ Openness to change, including being ready to explore, experiment, and be challenged, being on a path of self-development, and being open-minded and open-hearted
■ Experience of meditation, mindfulness, and reflection in group settings
■ Resilience
■ Interest in the human experience, relationships, and personal patterns
■ Motivation and engagement

Source: Donaldson-Feilder et al (2022).

The research also highlighted some areas that might indicate a need to tread carefully (see Box 18.2), which might be warning signs to watch out for in coaching in general and are perhaps particularly important when considering introducing mindful dialogue.

Box 18.2 Potential warning signs of a need to tread carefully with RM-based development

When the client …

■ Is in a poor cognitive and emotional state
■ Has an unhelpful approach to life (e.g. needing to be the expert, high degrees of striving and agitation, dissociation, or experiential avoidance)
■ Has an unhelpful attitude to self-development (e.g. expecting a one-time fix or looking for technical expertise not self-development)

Source: Donaldson-Feilder et al (2022).

Based on the above, mindful dialogue might work better in coaching supervision than in coaching. It might also be helpful for those who are on an adult/vertical development journey and whose maturity, consciousness, meaning-making, and development are wide and deep enough to encompass dialogue as a source of embodied insight. We explore vertical development in Chapter 21.

We may want to explore a client's openness to RM by seeing how they respond to being guided in an individual mindfulness practice or two before suggesting mindful dialogue.

When and how to introduce elements of mindful dialogue

As well as client readiness, we need to discern when a mindful dialogue is most likely to be beneficial. It may be helpful to have had at least one or two coaching sessions (including individual mindfulness practice) before introducing the idea of engaging in mindful dialogue. It may also be helpful to wait until some time into a session before suggesting mindful dialogue – though not too near the end of the session as it is likely that some processing of the experience will be valuable. There may also be particular points in coaching where mindful dialogue is most helpful, for example, when a client is stuck or is not able to access new perspectives.

When introducing the possibility of engaging in a mindful dialogue, it is important that we position the suggestion as an 'experiment', engendering a sense of playfulness, curiosity, and lightness around it. In the same way as we might propose a Gestalt-based empty chair exercise or metaphor simile, when we offer elements of mindful dialogue, we can explain that what we are suggesting may seem a little strange or unfamiliar, but we have found it can be helpful.

The opportunities and risks of bringing in elements of mindful dialogue

At its best, mindful dialogue in coaching offers the client a chance to drop into a place of embodied awareness of self and other, allowing space and stillness from which new insights can emerge. Both coach and client are present, receptive, and open to what is arising (and vanishing) internally, externally, and between the two. There is a sense of collaboration, mutual care and respect, and connection – we might even call this love, interbeing, or interconnectedness. Both coach and client step out of the habitual rush of the thinking mind in order to come to the dialogue afresh moment-by-moment. Assumptions and habits are enabled to surface and be gently challenged. New perspectives emerge in the relational contact, and in the intersubjective 'We' space (Gunnlaugson & Brabant, 2016; Guenther, 2022).

Done poorly, attempting mindful dialogue in coaching could become formulaic, focussed on cognitive processing, or simply churn through old thinking, not opening to what is new and wants to emerge. The dialogue process could feel like a rigid structure that limits engagement, rather than a helpful 'holding' that creates space and awareness. The client could feel exposed and vulnerable, resulting in reactivity, defensiveness, or closing down. The coach might feel 'in charge' and responsible for generating insight rather than trusting in collaborative mindful dialogue to be a fertile substrate for insight to arise in the 'in-between' (Buber, 1970 – see Chapter 21).

Suggestions for coaching activities based on elements of mindful dialogue

Bringing elements of mindful dialogue into one-to-one coaching

To date, RM and ID have mostly been offered to groups. A facilitator or teacher shapes a contemplation or series of contemplations and provides guidance for individual and relational meditation, whilst embodying the RM guidelines and the wisdom potential of mindful dialogue. Having received guidance, the participants then engage in RM practice in pairs or small groups, with the teacher/facilitator holding the timings and process and offering further contemplations to develop and/or deepen the dialogue.

By contrast, offering RM practice on a one-to-one basis is not a familiar or well-established process. Thus, what we are suggesting is a new and emerging way of coaching, which may take time to mature and become established. Our suggestions below and in the accompanying resources are therefore tentative. We would welcome your engagement in this community of discovery and would very much value feedback you may have after experimenting with our suggestions.

In Appendix 2, we have provided three suggestions for integrating elements of mindful dialogue into coaching. Each of the three suggestions is on a separate page and also available for download from our dedicated website as a separate sheet, so you can use a single sheet to guide the process in a coaching session.

All the suggested formats require the coach to draw on all the RM guidelines to support the client to engage in a mindful, experiential exploration of a chosen coaching issue/topic. The dialogues proposed all involve listening deeply and speaking the truth, which are underpinned by the other four guidelines. In addition, to help frame each proposed format, we have indicated an RM guideline that the coach might particularly want to draw on for support: Open (particularly external aspect) for the first, Open (particularly internal aspect) for the second, and Attune to emergence for the third.

Before engaging in one of these formats, the coach will need to:

- Prepare themselves well to ensure they embody the RM guidelines – see Chapters 15 and 16
- Discern client readiness for this approach – see guidelines above
- Check whether the client is willing to engage in this kind of dialogue – see guidelines above
- Set the context for the client and let them know what to expect, including describing the steps of the process and clarifying that the coach will manage the timings and process so that the client doesn't need to attend to that
- Explain to the client that the dialogue is about mindful, experiential exploration of what is emerging in both their mind and their felt sense

We propose that the contemplation topic for these RM-based processes be determined by what the client is bringing to coaching. As mentioned, the contemplation in RM offers the opportunity to bring in wisdom at an experiential and felt level. It is important that the mindful dialogue is not seen as a forum for problem-solving, but instead as a chance to bring awareness, see clearly, generate different perspectives, and release any constrictions that may be obstructing flow and flexibility in a particular situation. The client and coach will need to agree together a contemplation question to guide the dialogue. Some possible contemplation questions might be the following:

- *Where is there tightening around this issue and where could there be release?*
- *In what ways are we seeing things as not changing when they are actually changing?*
- *What stress, distress, and/or pain are we ignoring in this situation? How does it feel to bring that into awareness and be with it?*
- *Where are we seeing things as personal, when in fact they are the result of multiple causes and conditions and not personal to us?*
- *What are we seeing as lovely, appealing, and/or desirable, when in fact that is just an appearance?*

Bringing elements of mindful dialogue into team/group coaching

For those with considerable experience in RM, mindfulness teacher training, and a mature level of coaching capacity, it may be feasible to bring elements of mindful dialogue into team/group coaching. For example, a coach and mindfulness teacher we spoke to talks about a team coaching intervention with a group of senior managers in a large organisation, in which RM strongly influenced how they worked. As well as RM practice supporting their own capacity to be present with emotions (Level Two capacity), they also invited the managers to pause (Level Three capacity) and to talk in pairs, and in the group, in a process that had a flavour of mindful dialogue (Level Four capacity).

They describe how, as the team was exploring the impact of climate change, they wanted to 'push away' their own unwanted emotions, which signalled what others were feeling. Bringing in the guideline Relax/allow, they say they realised, "*when I allow the tension, not adding to it, not pushing it away, I am allowing something very respectful and compassionate, for them, never mind for me.*" They invited the managers to talk about "*what is this feeling that we're feeling?*" joking that "*'If I'm feeling something, you're feeling something!'* They were feeling a sense of threat and it was really because of [my practice of RM] that we could go there.*"

This coach had been working with these managers for many years and had not showed much emotion before. "*But now I'm welling up in front of them because somehow when I was open to the relational space and the sadness of what had happened in the last year in the world and (with) climate change, I… really felt myself getting very emotional… I just sat there, and they all just looked at me. A couple of* *tears fell, and I was like, 'F***: this is not a therapy session; this is a high level, multi-million euro change process where I'm responsible for managing both the project and the team I brought in and I am about to cry.' And the CEO of the group just passed me the tissues; and he said, in front of his whole team, 'I knew you cared about this company but now we trust you absolutely.' Another team member said, 'Every bit of hesitancy I had about this process is gone, you were so real!'"*

They also share how RM helped them to be flexible in this work, dancing with what was in the room: *"A good few times last year, when I had everything prepared for a session... [I said] 'we've got to change everything in the next half an hour, because something is changing in the room... I feel we've entered a transitional space.'"* Trusting themselves, they asked the team whether anybody could *"give me a sense of what was going on in the room...?"*, informing the group that *"'We're going to use the pause again...to go around the room.'"* They would not have done that before *"not in that very concrete interruption way... but I trusted myself to pause and allow and listen and [let what truth there was emerge]... because the attunement and embodying of RM envelops the group and trust is built over time."*

Whilst they doubt the team would be able to name what RM is, they say, *"I think they'd say they felt more understood. They would say that they felt that I got it, I got the complexity very quickly... I picked up on the nuances. They would say, 'that really helps us to get there faster... You have a way of getting to the nub of things. You're not scared of getting us into the complex thinking.'...So it's very powerful... it has been a transformational way of working."*

This case study suggests that a couple of elements of mindful dialogue may be helpful in team/group coaching:

- *Pairs dialogue:* Inviting members of the team/group to pair up and engage in a mindful dialogue with separate speaker and listener, then shared dialogue, on the issue at hand. Inviting mindful discernment of their felt experience (physical sensations, emotions) and speaking of that, whilst bringing a sense of care for both self and other.
- *Formal group-go-round:* Inviting each member of the team/group to speak in turn, whilst others listen, encouraging people to bring their attention into the present moment and speak about what they are feeling/experiencing right now, whilst bringing a sense of care for both self and other. This process has a lot of similarities to Nancy Kline's (1999) Thinking Environment process (see Chapter 20) with an additional emphasis of bringing mindful awareness and present-moment attention to the speaking and listening.

Teaching RM requires teacher training

We would not expect or advise a coach to offer RM teaching unless they had undertaken training as an RM/Insight Dialogue (ID)/Interpersonal Mindfulness Program (IMP) teacher. Teaching RM requires a profound and embodied understanding not only of the guidelines, but also of the foundations and underpinnings of the practice. Even for those with RM/ID/IMP teacher training, the decision to bring RM teaching into coaching would require considerable additional discernment about the client's readiness, plus re-contracting with the client in order to ensure that the process was held safely and was of benefit to the client.

Maturing beyond the formal practice structure

Based on her work on how coaches learn embodied self-awareness and integrate it into their coaching, Blake (2023) suggests a helpful trajectory from beginner to mature embodied coaching. She observes that we start by getting the experiential and embodied learning for ourselves (in our levels model, this is about capacity Levels One and Two). In her next phase, we try experimenting with offering exercises/practices to our clients – perhaps those we have found beneficial ourselves (capacity Levels Three and Four in our levels model). Finally, as we mature in our own learning, we begin to understand the underlying principles, mechanisms, and vocabulary, allowing us to tailor what we offer to meet the needs of our client in a fluid and eclectic way that draws on but is not bound by the practices (moving beyond the capacity levels).

This trajectory aligns with the model of coaching maturity mentioned in Chapter 6 (Clutterbuck & Megginson, 2011). As coaches move to the most mature systemic eclectic level, they let go of reliance on particular models and processes and, if they do use a tool, they integrate it subtly into the coaching with an understanding of its origins and philosophy, and based on a holistic perspective of the client, their context, and the system within which they are operating.

As well as RM practice offering a way of increasing coaching maturity by shifting from 'doing' to 'being' and moving beyond tools and techniques (see Chapter 6), there is also the potential for growing our maturity through how we bring RM into coaching. After practising RM formally and informally for a while, we can get to a point where we are comfortable embodying RM. Then, with some mindfulness/compassion/RM/ID teacher training, we can experiment with bringing elements of mindful dialogue into our coaching. Finally, having understood the principles and mechanisms of RM at a deep and experiential level, we can start integrating what is covered in this book into our coaching in a way that is more fluid and dynamic, tailored to the client and their situation in the moment. For many of us, this will require not only considerable practice and experimentation, but also reflection and contextualisation. For those with prior experience of mindfulness and some of the other models covered in Chapters 19–21, and/or who have already reached a mature systemic eclectic level in their coaching, the integration of RM may be simpler and quicker than for others.

This final stage may take us into mindful dialogue with our coaching clients without the need for a formal mindful dialogue structure. As we pause with our client, let go of resistance, open our awareness, attune to what is emerging in the moment, move beyond needing to know, listen deeply to what arises, and speak with discernment, we naturally engage all the RM guidelines in our coaching. When we have this level of fluency with RM and have become a collaborator with our client in mindfully exploring the experiential and embodied learning possible for us both in the coaching encounter, we can engage in dialogue informed but not bound by our RM practice. Hawkins (2023) describes this as us as coaches stepping to the learning edge together with our client and, in a participatory and interconnected way, exploring questions that none of us can answer alone. With the foundation of RM, we can do this from a place of mindful presence and awareness.

As we mature, maybe we can begin to see that the principles and mechanisms at play in coaching, when supported by approaches such as RM, are not 'tools' we operate alone. We understand at an experiential and embodied level that there is an alchemy and a mystery when we enter fully into dialogue with another. With this level of openness, we can draw on the vast interconnected system in which we all operate to access a collective intelligence beyond any individual's meaning-making or frame of reference. This has similarities to Otto Scharmer's 'presencing', with client and coach both bringing an open mind/curiosity, open heart/compassion, and open will/courage (Scharmer, 2009 – see Chapter 21). Then, we may trust that we will draw on the power of a wider interrelated field to support our client, their system, and the wider world.

Having delved into RM in some depth, including how to practise RM and how we might bring RM into our coaching, next we want to take a step back and explore the wider field. In Section 5 we set out a selection of theories and approaches that align with and can potentially enrich RMEC and vice versa.

References

Blake, A. (2023). Interview on Coaches Rising Podcast. www.coachesrising.com/podcast/embodied-self-awareness-with-amanda-blake/

Buber, M. (1970). *I and Thou* (Vol. 243). Simon and Schuster.

Clutterbuck, D., & Megginson, D. (2011). Coach maturity: An emerging concept. In L. Wildflower & D. Brennan (Eds.), *The handbook of knowledge-based coaching: From theory to practice*, 299–313. John Wiley & Sons.

Donaldson-Feilder, E., Lewis, R., Yarker, J., & Whiley, L. (2022). Interpersonal mindfulness for managers: A Delphi Study exploring the application of interpersonal mindfulness to leadership development. *Journal of Management Education*, 46(5), 816–852.

Guenther, S. (2022). From me to we: A phenomenological inquiry into coherence. *Journal of Awareness-Based Systems Change*, 2(2), 149–171.

Gunnlaugson, O., & Brabant, M. (2016). Introduction: Background of we-space in the integral community. In O. Gunnlaugson & M. Brabant (Eds.), *Cohering the integral we space: Engaging collective emergence, wisdom, and healing in groups*, 11–18. Integral Publishing House.

Hawkins, P. (2023). Interview on Coaches Rising Podcast Coaches Rising Interview. www.coachesrising.com/podcast/systemic-coaching-in-a-time-of-transition/

Kline (1999). *Time to think*. Cassell Illustrated.

Scharmer, O. (2009). *Theory U: Leading from the future as it emerges*. Barrett-Koehler Publishers.

Information

Dedicated website accompanying this book: www.relationalmindfulness.net

Section 5

Indra's Net: A trove of additional gems to further enhance Relational Mindfulness

I draw on so many things now. I think RM slips in really well. It seems to be an amplifier of what I already know. I mean, I already knew about listening, but this is listening more deeply… it just… brings those sorts of things into perspective. It fits… it's a unifier.

Malcolm, ID teacher, management consultant and executive coach, and one of our interviewees for this book

In this section (Chapters 19–21), we share models, theories, frameworks, and approaches which can further enrich Relational Mindfulness (RM) and RM-Enhanced Coaching (RMEC), and vice versa. As we curated this collection, making tough choices about what to include and exclude, and what should go where, an ancient Buddhist metaphor came to mind to conceptualise the interbeing and inter-causality we saw: Indra's Net.

Indra's Net stretches in all directions, with a single glittering jewel hanging in each 'eye' of the net. As the net itself is infinite, the jewels are infinite in number. Every thing, every being, is a jewel in this net, each reflecting in its polished surface all the other jewels, and on and on. Each has its place, all interconnect, and all are part of the whole.

DOI: 10.4324/9781003390428-23

Thus, we are humbly aware that what we have outlined prior to this section are just some of the jewels in an infinite net representing RM, with all that entails and promises – including presence, awareness, attunement, resonance, compassion, courage, and wisdom – and that what we include in this section represents a small selection of other gems. We trust that in each the whole is accessible, yet each has something unique to offer.

In attempting to order this section's material, we were loosely guided by the three foundations for RM: meditative awareness, relationship, and wisdom (see Chapter 5); and by the RM benefits identified in our research: becoming fully present, finding connection, gaining insights around relational habits and choice, and new ways of thinking and perceiving (see Table 6.1, Chapter 6). So Chapter 19 is on Becoming fully present and aware, Chapter 20 on Relating and connecting, and Chapter 21 on Insight and wisdom. We have placed each offering according to where we felt it most sat well, but with awareness of the holographic nature of RM. Gestalt, for example, could easily have sat in all three.

We invite you to dance lightly with this flow, perhaps taking it, as we did, as an opportunity to embrace the deeper learning of the profound nature of being, including in our relationships: that of interbeing.

You are here!

Introduction

Section 1
- Setting the scene
- Exploring mindfulness and compassion: definitions and origins
- Benefits of individual mindfulness and compassion in coaching

Origins, underpinnings and benefits of RM

Section 2
- Exploring Relational Mindfulness (RM)
- Insight Dialogue-based RM
- Benefits of bringing RM into coaching

Practice and application

Section 3
- Foundations for practice and application
- Exploring each of the six guidelines in turn

Section 4
- Different levels of bringing RM into coaching
- Preparing with, embodying, drawing on RM

Additional gems to further enhance RM

Section 5
- Becoming fully present and aware
- Relating and connecting
- Insight and wisdom

Next steps and beyond

Section 6
- Where next for you?
- Vision for the future

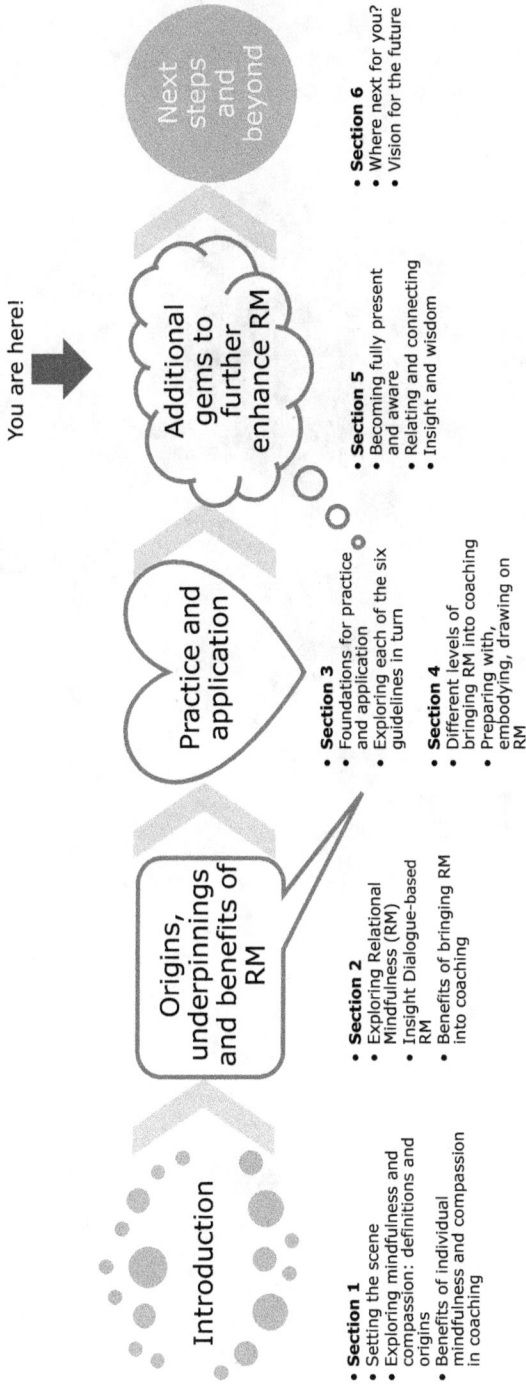

Figure S5 You are here!

Chapter 19

Becoming fully present and aware

Tear off your mask. Your face is glorious.

Rumi

This chapter explores 'jewels' that can deepen and broaden our understanding of what is happening in Relational Mindfulness (RM) in terms of becoming present and aware, inspire us as RM-Enhanced Coaching (RMEC) coaches in how we step into presence and awareness and bring these alive in our coaching practice, and perhaps inspire those using other approaches to draw on RM and RMEC to enhance presence and awareness. We will explore:

- Bodily awareness, including somatic coaching
- Gestalt

Dropping our masks

Therapist and physician Rachel Naomi Ramen (Ramen & Wisdom, 1996) movingly describes her first encounter with Carl Rogers, the humanistic psychotherapist who popularised the concept of unconditional positive regard (Rogers, 1957) – accepting the client unconditionally. Her exquisite account points to the quality of presence we seek to embody in RMEC.

Rogers apparently explained to the group of physicians and psychologists, which included Ramen, that before every session with a client, to become fully

DOI: 10.4324/9781003390428-24

attentive and present for his client, he paused to remember their shared humanity. He then conducted a demonstration with a volunteer doctor *"without saying a single word, conveying to this client simply by the quality of his attention a total acceptance of him exactly as he was"* (Ramen & Wisdom, 1996, p.219).

Ramen describes how *"in the safe climate of Roger's total acceptance, he began to shed his masks, hesitantly at first and then more and more easily."* And *"as each mask fell, Rogers welcomed the one behind it unconditionally, until finally we glimpsed the beauty of the doctor's face."* Ramen writes, *"I doubt that even he himself had ever seen it before"* (Ramen & Wisdom, 1996, p.219).

What a gift Rogers offered that doctor, and those who witnessed and felt the quality and potency of his attention and presence! In our experience, RMEC at its best offers a vehicle and container for 'unmasking', for encounters in which we truly and authentically meet our clients as fellow human travellers. Coming into and maintaining presence is key, and this requires high-level awareness of the body.

The body as a source of presence and present-moment awareness

In RMEC, we seek to become more nuanced around how we sense and experience ourselves, others, and the rest of the world, appreciating that we experience the present moment, including our relationships, through the body. Greater somatic awareness helps us become more present and aware and, in doing so, improves how we relate to and connect with others, and as coaches this supports others' growth. As Siegel (2010, p.xx) says, *"The way in which we are grounded in ourselves, open to others, and participate fully in the life of the mind are important aspects of our presence at the heart of relationships that help others grow."*

Mindfulness of the body helps us become more choiceful about what we attend to and helps to expand our meaning-making. Self-experiencing, including through the body, is one of the capacities we seek to develop in vertical adult development, for example (see Chapter 21).

Heightened somatic awareness helps us to access more wisdom and insights, with our 'antennae' picking up more data from what our body senses into, including others and the wider field. As Nicholas Janni (2022, p.99) says, *"The body is your primary gateway to a sense of aliveness. It is also the conduit through which you can access multiple layers of perception, information and inner knowing."*

More than just five senses

One way to fine-tune our 'self-as-instrument' is through a deeper understanding and awareness of our bodily sensations. In RMEC, we resonate with Blake's description of our entire body as a *"social and emotional sense organ"* (Blake, 2018, p.12), appreciating that we are more than just our five senses of sight, touch, smell, hearing, and taste. We fully embrace the holistic nature of the body, with not just a skull-based brain, but brains too in our heart and gut (e.g. Gershon, 1999 and McCraty et al, 2004), and appreciate that our thoughts, and our feelings and emotions leave their signatures in the body, they are not separate from the body.

In addition to *exteroception* (encompassing the five senses), other classes of sensations or senses which we experience (unless we suffer from alexithymia or alexisomia, where we have difficulty experiencing, identifying, and expressing emotions and bodily sensations) include:

- *Interoception*: our internal visceral experience. This is what Siegel, in his Wheel of Awareness, calls our 'sixth sense' (Siegel, accessed February 2024). Part of this awareness is an appreciation that our heart, gut, lungs, skin, and connective tissue all automatically send signals to the brain about our internal state. The vagus nerve (or tenth cranial nerve) connects our brain to our body, directly innervating the heart, gut, and lungs. Thus, communication is not just brain to body. Up to 90% of vagal nerve fibres send signals to the brain rather than receiving signals from the brain (Berthoud & Neuhuber, 2000)
- *Nociception:* the sense of pain
- *Proprioception:* the sense that lets us perceive the location, movement, and action of parts of the body and is about our sense of balance. This sense is linked to our mood: if we are able to stand tall, with an open posture, for example, this can change how we feel and how others perceive us (Carney et al, 2010)
- *Neuroception:* direct visceral perception of danger or safety

Interconnectedness

In his Wheel of Awareness, Siegel (accessed February 2024) names mental activities as a 'seventh sense' and also adds an eighth: interconnectedness. This eighth sense aligns well with the RM guidelines Open, Attune to Emergence, and Listen Deeply. With these guidelines we open and attune to the wider system whilst maintaining awareness of ourselves and of the relationship between the two. To access this interconnected attentional field, we need the stability of the guidelines Pause and Relax/allow as foundations.

We can learn a lot from African and other cultures when it comes to drawing on this 'eight sense' to cultivate heightened attunement to the body's wisdom. The Anlo-Ewe culture of West Africa, for example, has no word for senses. Instead, they have the word *seselelame* which translates as *"feel-feel-at-flesh-inside"* (Shepherd, 2017, p.17). Seselelame represents an embodied awareness, perception through bodily sensations associated with the five senses, but also intuition, sensing one's wellbeing levels and so on. To quote Shepherd (p.23), seselelame

"... *is a holistic, synthesised, noncategorical, subjective wakefulness to the world as it is perceived through the body.*"

The Anlo-Ewe culture places interoception at the centre and includes exteroception and proprioception too. 'Balance' is a primary sense for the Anlo-Ewe (Shepherd, 2017), cultivated and appreciated from an early age, and includes physical skills of balance but also a balanced personality, including a person's character and moral fortitude. It does not recognise boundaries, understanding instead that we are each in a dynamic relationship with everything and everyone, that we are not individual units separate from everything else but are a process. We see at work here a deep grasp of the holographic nature of being.

Somatic awareness is also about becoming aware of our bodily shape. Building somatic awareness seeks to help us connect more deeply with ourselves, with this process that we call 'I', with others and beyond, to come into the present moment, and to access alternative sources of knowledge and wisdom.

There are many other approaches that support somatic awareness, including Gestalt (which we explore in this chapter) and Theory U (Chapter 21). Below we explore somatic-based coaching, an approach which explicitly works on, with and through the body, supporting us not only to develop greater somatic awareness, including of our physical shape but also to work out what we can do with this awareness, taking action to shift how we show up somatically.

Somatic-based coaching

We agree with Eunice Aquilina that somatic awareness can be the missing piece, and that, as she says, "*we cannot think our way to being different*" (Aquilina, 2016, p.3). And also, as Strozzi-Heckler (2014, p.37) says, "*The body will reveal our predispositions to the qualities of awakening, self-collecting, dimming, expanding, recoiling, contracting, guardedness, and warmth...will relentlessly disclose our embodied strategies for belonging, for love, safety, and acceptance.*"

Many coaches explicitly 'bring' the body into coaching (as we all have bodies, in reality, we cannot avoid working somatically!). RMEC coaches will be more likely to do this than most, given the importance of the body in anchoring us into mindfulness. Somatic-based coaches include the late Wendy Palmer, who developed the Leadership Embodiment approach, drawing on mindfulness and Aikido, and Richard Strozzi-Heckler, who developed the somatic coaching approach, together with Aquilina, and Blake, whom we have already mentioned and who both trained with the Strozzi Institute.

Somatic coaching takes its name from the term somatics, which comes from the early Greek, *sōmatikōs*, meaning 'bodily' or 'pertaining to the body', and proposes that body and mind are not separate and are both part of a living process called the soma. Somatic coaching embraces this idea of the body as a process, as a whole, including "*the physical world of sensations, temperature, weight, movement, streamings, pulsation, and vibrations, as well as images, thoughts, attitudes, yearnings, dreams, and language*" (Strozzi-Heckler, 2014, p.33). It sees 'mind', 'body', and 'spirit' as united, describing "*the human form as the unified space in which humans act, perceive, think, feel, sense, express emotions and moods, and live their spiritual longing*" (Strozzi-Heckler, 2014, p.33).

The methodology

Somatic coaching works:

- *On the body* (e.g. stretching and effective breathing)
- *With the body* (e.g. unblocking emotional energy by bringing awareness to how someone holds themselves when with others)
- *Through the body* (e.g. building awareness of how we have been shaped, literally, by our experience, revealing how we relate to life and other people)

The core elements of the methodology are somatic awareness, somatic opening, and somatic practices.

Somatic awareness

According to Strozzi Heckler (2014, p.50), building greater somatic awareness "*allows us to begin to engage in more profound internal and interpersonal change, and to act more congruently with our values. This is a fundamental step toward authenticity and a satisfying embodiment of our values.*"

In somatic coaching, we pay attention to the shape of our client. Each of us is literally shaped by our experiences, the culture we live in, our activities and early relationships. Over time, we automate certain patterns and strategies, with our body becoming, as Blake (2018, p.7) puts it, "*a reflection of the person who lives within it.*" These patterns affect how we perceive the world and how we behave. Our body is, as Blake says, "*both a lens of perception and an instrument of action*" (Blake, 2018, p.33).

Contractions we repeat change our body's structure, which has an impact on how we show up. To organise around safety and protection is deeply wired in all of us, so sometimes, we compress our boundaries, stiffening, and tightening the stomach, physically making ourselves 'small' and 'narrow', narrowing or blocking our connection with others in order to protect ourselves. Or we may even disassociate and cut ourselves off from awareness, protecting ourselves from overwhelming sensory experiences, feelings, and moods.

Many of us as coaches will have embodied the role of 'helper', perhaps giving the impression of taking up little space and of not being grounded, perhaps leaning forwards as we ready ourselves to attend to others' needs.

Somatic awareness can be the first step in healing past wounds and traumas. As we begin to notice historical embodied patterns of habits and tendencies, including in relationship, we can begin to identify which may no longer serve us, which get in the way of us being present. We can begin to recognize where our unmet needs and unresolved feelings show up in our bodies, providing additional information and wisdom, again often in relationship. This is an important step for us as coaches and for our clients.

Building somatic awareness may not be an easy journey. Bringing in mindfulness and compassion, as we do in RMEC, can help to create a safe and spacious container for the client to feel more open to bringing in more awareness. We can shine the spotlight of mindfulness onto where there is resistance, clinging, numbing, and/or contracting, mindfully and compassionately enquiring into how somatic patterns and shape impact our interpersonal interactions.

Somatic opening

It is possible to consciously shift our embodied ways of being, which is part of the territory of somatic coaching, and which RMEC can also help address. Embodied shifts can be much more powerful than trying to effect change through cognitive engagement alone. Somatic opening can be a discombobulating process which deeply challenges our sense of identity, but it can be deeply rewarding personally and interpersonally.

Somatic coaching supports clients to undo, 'disorganise', and deconstruct their historically embodied shape to give birth to another shape, seeking to release the armouring bands we build up over time. Psychoanalyst Wilhelm Reich developed the theory of body armour (e.g. Hoff, 1978), seeing how we use physical contractions to suppress unwanted emotion, for example. Armouring bands, which can affect heartbeat, digestion, and breathing (e.g. Fogel, 2009), consistently appear in the areas of the eyes, jaw, mouth, throat, chest, diaphragm, pelvis, thighs, calves, and feet. One way to release such bands is through hands-on work with the client, though that is less likely to be the territory of coaching. In RMEC, we might use the guideline Relax/allow to offer a gentle softening of tension wherever possible.

Somatic practices

Somatic coaching includes 'generative practices' such as meditation which can include mindful movement. It also includes practices making a clear, powerful, and embodied 'declaration,' drawing on the combined power of language and embodiment to make and honour value-based commitments.

The declaration

The declaration is one of five 'speech acts' (the others are requests, offers, promises, and assessments and assertions) identified by Fernando Flores in his work on philosophy, workflow technology, and coaching (e.g. Flores, 2012). Flores drew on the work of philosopher Martin Heidegger, and his colleagues Humberto Maturana and Francisco Varela. Aquilina (2016, p.70) describes a declaration as "*a commitment to future action, a future way of being*", adding that "*when we declare the future we are moving to, it fuels our intention to transform.*"

Flores saw language as action rather than just words that transfer information from one place (the speaker) to another (the listener). When people engage in conversations, commitments are made, and spaces of possibilities are opened up – and this process is embodied. In a declaration, to represent the embodiment, the language used is 'I *am* a commitment to…' (rather than I commit to, or even I am committed to). This is very much about listening deeply and speaking the truth!

RMEC and somatic coaching

Whilst we would not recommend anyone untrained in bodywork to engage in such interventions, there is much that the RMEC coach can draw on to aid somatic opening. Other routes to somatic opening that somatic coaching works with include the following: directed attention, visualisations, breath patterns, and working with emotional processes. As RMEC coaches, we can support somatic awareness and opening by how we are with the client: non-judgmentally supporting them to turn towards difficulties with self-compassion, courage, and curiosity; allowing space for deep emotions; listening deeply to the client, ourselves, and the field for greater recognition of what is here, including embodied patterns, and what wants to unfold and shift, and playing this back – speaking the truth – to the client where appropriate.

As Level Three capacity RMEC coaches who teach individual mindfulness will know, mindfulness of the body is the first of four foundations of mindfulness, the starting point, and anchor into the present moment. We can introduce this bodily foundation to clients through practices such as the Body Scan, Mindful Eating, Mindfulness of Breathing, Mindfulness of Sound, and Mindful Walking (see our dedicated website), helping clients get better acquainted with their body and its wisdom. Having the body as the chosen object of focus can deepen an appreciation of *impermanence* in noticing the natural coming and going of sensations. It can offer a gateway to tuning into *interconnectedness*: starting with an appreciation that we breathe in air that others breathe too, for example, or that we are eating food that has been grown by others, moving on perhaps to feeling into a lack of a solid boundary between us and others, and 'nature', realising that we are part of the natural world.

If the message being received by our system is that we are not safe, this will negatively impact our capacity to connect and may lead to actions and reactions we may later regret. As Blake (2018, p.12) says, the body is "*the seat of a powerful intelligence that helps you navigate your most important experiences and relationships… the lens through which you perceive your relational world, and the instrument by which you act in it."*

As RMEC coaches, through practising RM, we can proactively strengthen vagal tone, boosting connection for ourselves and enabling us to help clients to do so too. We can become more aware of what our interoception is telling us about our physical manifestation, noticing knots in our stomach or hunched shoulders when there is no real danger, for example, giving us the opportunity to take care of our shape, and calm our nervous systems through mindfulness practices.

If we notice our own feelings such as anxiety showing up somatically in a coaching session, we can take action to take care of these. Perhaps, for example, we notice contractions in our abdomen, so we choose to sit back in our chair, and pay attention to our breathing, breathing into our belly, which allows us to then be more open and better connect with a client.

As we become more adept at this somatic awareness and opening, we are better placed to embody, role model, and suggest somatic shifts to our clients. For example, we can encourage clients to actively shift their posture which may help them relax and connect more deeply with us and others.

And as we and clients shift our shapes, we can draw on the RM guidelines to support new ways of being. For example, we can pause to come home to ourselves, noticing and settling into the 'shape-shifting.' We can invite Relax/allow to help release historical resistance, for example, or even fear if it shows up in our system. Open can bring us present to the internal, external, and both as we connect to how our shape influences and interacts with everything and everyone else. Attune to Emergence can help us feel less constrained, less cut-off, less constricted, and more part of the dance of life. Listen deeply points us to what really wants to be heard, and Speak our Truth can be expressed in our evolving body shape.

Next, we explore Gestalt, in which building awareness plays centre stage.

Gestalt

Fritz Perls (1893–1970) was one of the founders of Gestalt therapy, which has been practised since the 1950s. Gestalt draws on philosophical and psychological traditions including Kurt Lewin's field theory, Martin Buber's philosophy of dialogue, the existential philosophy of Søren Aabye Kierkegaard and Martin Heidegger, Taoism, and Zen Buddhism. As Perls spent time in Japanese Zen monasteries, it is perhaps unsurprising that his therapeutic techniques include mindfulness practices and focusing on the present moment.

Gestalt has been applied widely, including in management and leadership, politics, community building, social change, and coaching (e.g. Bolton, 2023; Allan & Whybrow, 2018; Francis & Parlett, 2016; Bluckert, 2015; Leary-Joyce, 2014).

Core beliefs, concepts, and foci of Gestalt

One of the core beliefs on which Gestalt coaching is based is that *building awareness of self, others and the system/s supports growth and transformation.*

As Bluckert (2015, p.7) says, in Gestalt, *"awareness is seen as the cornerstone of the developmental process. Growth and development occur when people expand what they can see and act on… from this perspective the role of the Gestalt coach is clear and unambiguous- it's to become an awareness-raising partner."*

In Gestalt, just as in RMEC, we are invited to notice what is going on internally and externally, including words used, mood, body language, energy levels, and emotion.

The Gestalt coach, like the RMEC coach, will tune into their interior world, noticing what they are sensing, thinking, and feeling so they can use 'self-as-instrument.' They will also tune into the external, for example: the quality of conversation and group dialogue, the nature of interaction and group dynamics, the quality of engagement and level of energy, the quality of awareness, contact and connection, the nature of the relationships, the emotional climate, the attention to good process and healthy self-regulation, and how difference is appearing or not, and whether it is celebrated or repressed (Bluckert, 2015). This comprehensive list may serve RMEC coaches as additional prompts for what we might pay attention to.

As Gestalt coaches – and RMEC coaches – we are both attending to the content of a coaching session and simultaneously helicoptering above it to notice the client's styles of relating and our own internal thoughts and feelings. However, in Gestalt coaching as well as in RMEC, we are invited to be open to emergence, rather than being prescriptive around where we place our attention.

Other core beliefs in Gestalt coaching include:

- *Healthy functioning depends on creatively adjusting to ever-changing circumstances* (Bluckert, 2015, pp.6–8)
- *Change happens in the present moment, organically and across multiple 'realities'* (e.g. Francis & Parlett, 2016)
- *Change occurs when we are in contact with, and accept, 'what is', rather than trying to be different*
- *Unfinished situations can deplete energy, interrupt focus, and impact motivation*
- *The relationship between coach and client is key – with a focus on embracing authenticity*
- *Exploration of the here-and-now – of direct, felt experience – provides opportunities for growth and learning, including through attending to what is unfolding live in the relationship* (e.g. Francis & Parlett, 2016; Bluckert, 2015)
- *People are always doing the best they can from how they see and experience the world* (Bluckert, 2015, pp.6–8)

These beliefs are in keeping with RMEC and certainly resonate with us and how we see coaching.

Key concepts in Gestalt coaching include:

■ *Emergence and the 'fertile void'* – the state of not-knowing, which can be generative. Gestalt coaching seeks to be unattached to outcome, and accepting of what is here, focusing on raising awareness, although still wanting to support clients to creatively adjust or adapt to their environment, to grow and develop. Francis and Parlett (2016, p.5) explain that "*a classic Gestalt stance is one of 'creative indifference' to outcomes… instead staying scrupulously close to what is actually happening between us as coach and client.*" The Gestalt coach seeks to stay "*as close as possible to how human beings experience their reality, which is in the form of complex and meaningful configurations of experience that are changing all the time*" (Francis & Parlett, 2016, p.3)

■ The Gestalt theory of change, *the Paradoxical Theory of Change* (Beisser, 1970), proposes that change occurs when one is fully in contact with 'what is', and when 'we become who we are.' Leary-Joyce has adapted this notion for coaching to: "*change happens when you accept who you are… change is effort when you want to be different from who you are*" (Leary-Joyce, accessed November 2023)

   In Gestalt, authentic change is believed to occur not by trying to be what we are not, but by fully embracing what we are in the present moment. It assumes that we first need to 'become our truth' before we can move from it, and in exploring and embracing that truth, a new configuration naturally arises. By becoming more deeply aware and accepting of our current thoughts, feelings, and behaviours, we set the stage for sustainable change

■ Aligned with the Paradoxical Theory of Change is the *Gestalt Cycle of Experience*, which offers clients a roadmap for understanding how people navigate experiences, facilitating personal growth and change. The process, according to Gestalt, sees us continuously cycle through six stages as we respond to arising needs. Each stage of the cycle – sensation, awareness, mobilisation, action, contact, satisfaction, and withdrawal – offers an opportunity for something new and unexpected to come into consciousness. As mentioned above, Gestalt describes the phase between these sensations in which much possibility and potential is deemed to lie, and which precedes something new emerging as *the fertile void*. Bolton (2023) describes the cycle as "*the natural, spontaneous process through which new insights, understandings, or behaviours surface and become integrated into an individual's experience.*"

Again, these concepts resonate well with RMEC and the RM guidelines – particularly Attune to emergence, Listen deeply, and Speak the truth – can support us in helping ourselves and our clients access this kind of change.

Core *foci* in Gestalt coaching include:

- *The whole and the components of the whole.* The German word *Gestalt*, whilst not easily translatable into English, approximately means a unified or meaningful whole, a pattern, shape, or configuration. In Gestalt coaching, it is important to both attend to the whole, and to what is incomplete, which may be draining energy. The Gestalt Cycle of Change shines a light on any unfinished business that may arise within the process. Working with the Cycle helps to dial up awareness, prompting the client to notice sensations, needs or desires that come up, and how these show up in the body, emotions, or cognition, then interpreting with curiosity and compassion what this all means. This may include noticing how needs and desires play out in relationship, including what happens when these are or are not satisfied

- *Whatever is arising in the present moment.* Just like RMEC, Gestalt coaching, rather than interpreting and analysing the here-and-now, invites us instead to notice and describe what is unfolding in the moment, *"staying grounded in real experience… founded on the belief that there is wisdom inherent in direct, felt experience"* (Bluckert, 2015, p.8). The Gestalt Cycle *"provides a potent framework for understanding and facilitating emergence in the coaching process"*, writes Bolton (July 2023). As such, it aligns with the RM guideline Attune to emergence and can help deepen our appreciation of impermanence and unfolding, arising and vanishing

- *The relationship.* In all coaching, a quality relationship between coach and client is an important part of the process, but this is particularly so in Gestalt coaching and RMEC. As Bluckert (2015, p.16) says, *"From a Gestalt perspective, the coaching relationship is the crucible for learning and change. For that crucible to be strong enough, it needs to contain three elements: trust, contact and authentic dialogue."* Gestalt coaching, just like RMEC, goes further than some approaches by explicitly working live with the relationship between the coach and client to enable learning. The relationship can be used *"as a microcosm of how the client relates and interacts elsewhere in their life"* (Francis & Parlett, 2016, p.5)

In Gestalt, the coach selectively shares what they observe and how they experience clients' behaviours, assumptions, unconscious habits, and patterns of interaction (Francis & Parlett, 2016; Bluckert, 2015). The purpose of the coach sharing their experience is to increase the client's awareness of themselves, how they behave and think. This can be very powerful. To quote Bluckert again (2015, p.127), *"skilfully delivered, and with good timing, these observations can be some of the most impactful and profound of all coaching interventions."*

Drawing on the relationship can also involve the coach using their presence to offer alternative ways of responding. This can mean having authentic frank

---

Box 19.1 Try this – Gestalt + RM

One classic Gestalt technique is the 'empty chair' exercise, which invites the client to move between two or more chairs, helping them speak from different spaces and notice what is emerging between the spaces.

We can be creative here – creative experimentation is after all a hallmark of a Gestalt approach – and bring in the RM guidelines. For example, each time the client moves to a new chair/space, the coach can invite them to bring in the six RM guidelines to explore what emerges.

Then the coach might invite a mindful dialogue between the various parties represented by the chairs, perhaps with a co-created contemplation, or even a series of contemplation rounds, depending on the coach's level of capacity.

---

interactions, both ways, to help to disrupt the client's familiar ways of thinking and relating (e.g. Francis & Parlett, 2016), with the coach perhaps modelling a different way of relating (attachment theory may be helpful here too, see Chapter 20).

Again, the resonances with RMEC are strong and the RM guideline Speak the truth can be a powerful underpinning for the types of sharing and interacting outlined above.

Next, we delve more deeply into relating and connecting, building on presence and awareness to help us attune with others.

References

Allan, J., & Whybrow, A. (2018). Gestalt coaching. In *Handbook of coaching psychology*, 180–194. Routledge.

Aquilina, E. (2016). *Embodying authenticity: A somatic path to transforming self, team and organisation.* Live It Publishing Ltd.

Berthoud, H. R., & Neuhuber, W. L. (2000). Functional and chemical anatomy of the afferent vagal system. *Autonomic Neuroscience*, 85(1–3), 1–17.

Blake, A. (2018) *Your body is your brain: Leverage your somatic intelligence to find purpose, build resilience, deepen relationships and lead more powerfully.* Trokay Press.

Bluckert, P. (2015). *Gestalt coaching: Right here, right now.* Open University Press.

Bolton, N. (July 2023). The Gestalt Cycle of Experience: An emergent approach to change in coaching. Animas Centre for Coaching, www.animascoaching.com/blog/gestalt-cycle-of-experience/

Carney, D. R., Cuddy, A. J., & Yap, A. J. (2010). Power posing: Brief nonverbal displays affect neuroendocrine levels and risk tolerance. *Psychological Science*, 21(10), 1363–1368.

Flores, F. (2012). *Conversations for action and collected essays: Instilling a culture of commitment in working relationships.* CreateSpace Independent Publishing Platform.

Fogel, A. (2009). *The psychophysiology of self-awareness: Rediscovering the lost art of body sense.* W.W. Norton & Co.

Francis, T., & Parlett, M. (Eds.). (2016). *Contact and context: New directions in Gestalt coaching* (Vol. 3). Taylor & Francis.

Gershon, M. D. (1999). The enteric nervous system: A second brain. *Hospital Practice*, 34(7), 31–52.

Hoff, R. (1978). Overview of Reichian therapy. *Holistic Health Handbook* (Berkeley, Calif.: And/Or Press, 1978), 205.

Janni, N. (2022). *Leader as healer.* LID Publishing.

Leary Joyce, J. (2014). *The fertile void: Coaching at work.* AOEC Press.

Leary-Joyce, J. (2023). The paradox of change. www.youtube.com/watch?v= oh2IoK5_YLA&list=PLopJ6a9y8nlPXTcFw6uS3PjxtEpy6_65o&index=5 (accessed November 2023).

McCraty, R., Atkinson, M., & Bradley, R. T. (2004). Electrophysiological evidence of intuition: Part 1. The surprising role of the heart. *The Journal of Alternative & Complementary Medicine*, 10(1), 133–143.

Remen, R. N., & Wisdom, K. T. (1996). *Stories that heal*, 217–219. River-head Books.

Rogers, C. R. (1957). The necessary and sufficient conditions of therapeutic personality change. *Journal of Consulting Psychology*, 21(2), 95.

Shepherd, P. (2017). *Radical wholeness: The embodied present and the ordinary grace of being.* North Atlantic Books.

Siegel, D. J. (2010). *The mindful therapist: A clinician's guide to mindsight and neural integration.* WW Norton & Company.

Strozzi-Heckler, R. (2014). *The art of somatic coaching: Embodying skillful action, wisdom, and compassion.* North Atlantic Books.

Information

Dedicated website accompanying this book: www.relationalmindfulness.net

Chapter 20

Relating and connecting

*You think because you understand 'one' you must also understand 'two',
because one and one make two. But you must also understand 'and.'*

Rumi

In this chapter, we explore more 'jewels' to deepen our understanding of what
happens when we relate to, connect, and communicate with one another, and
what hinders and supports deep connection. We will explore the following:

- Positivity resonance
- Attachment theory
- Nonviolent communication (NVC)
- Psychological safety
- The power of vulnerability
- Models for listening deeply
- Compassion as a resource – empathic distress versus compassion fatigue
- Compassion-Focused Coaching
- Coaching with compassion

Positivity resonance and the broaden-and-build theory of positive emotions

What happens when we connect with one another? In Box 20.1 we explore the
neurobiology of connection – brain synchronisation, the role of the hormone
oxytocin, and the importance of strong vagal tone.

DOI: 10.4324/9781003390428-25

Fredrickson's Positivity Resonance Theory of Co-experienced Positive Affect theory proposes that concepts such as desire, intimacy, and trust can be understood as products of the accumulation of momentary experiences of the emotion love. When such moments occur between and among individuals, they build and fortify enduring social bonds and become steady resources for individuals through good times and bad. Positivity resonance can arise between any pair or group where there is a shared positive emotion, including in coaching and coaching supervision relationships.

For positivity resonance to occur, we need real-time sensory connection – hearing, seeing, and sensing each other – and perceived safety (Fredrickson, retrieved November, 2024), with the presence of the following:

- *Shared positive affect:* A shared experiential component
- *Caring non-verbal synchrony:* A behavioural component marked by non-verbal movements and gestures associated with care and love that are linked in form and tempo across individuals, and
- *Biological synchrony:* A physiological component marked by shifts in affect-related biomarkers linked in form and tempo across individuals

Broaden-and-build theory

Positive emotions, which generally occur in safe contexts, *"stimulate expansive attention, and increase openness and receptivity to a range of experiences"* (Conway et al, 2013, p.19), presumably including in relationships.

Fredrickson's research around her broaden-and-build theory (Fredrickson, 2004) found that positive emotions, which include joy, interest, contentment, and love, appear to *broaden* peoples' momentary thought–action repertoires, promoting the discovery of novel and creative actions, ideas, and social bonds. They also *build* people's enduring personal physical, intellectual, psychological, and social resources, which function as reserves that can be drawn on later to improve the likelihood of successful coping and survival (Fredrickson, 1998, 2001).

Cultivating positive emotions

The inspiring message from Fredrickson's work is that we can shift mechanisms such as brain synchronisation, oxytocin production, and vagal tone. By increasing our levels of positivity resonance, through the various practices she has researched, we can create positive change across all these areas of our neurobiology.

As we suggest in Box 20.1, one way to actively cultivate positive emotions is through Loving Kindness Meditation (LKM). Participants practising LKM reported more positive emotion, associated with improvements in self-acceptance, physical health, competence, sense of purpose in life, and improved

Box 20.1 The neurobiology of connection – mutual support for stabilising attention

Neurobiological research is increasingly revealing the array of mechanisms by which humans communicate and influence each other. Fredrickson's work (2013) draws together a range of research evidence, which she summarises into three broad categories of neurobiological mechanisms for connection or 'positivity resonance':

1. ***Brain synchronisation:*** When we connect with another being, our brain waves mirror one another. Initial breakthrough studies of this phenomenon established the concept of 'mirror neurons' (Acharya & Shukla, 2012) and showed that when we see someone undertake an action, neurons in our brain light up as if we were completing that action ourselves. However, Fredrickson (2013) brings together research showing that this mirroring is much more extensive than isolated mirror neurons: that the resonances are 'penetrating and widespread.' She quotes the work of Hasson and colleagues (2012), whose brain imaging studies have shown that speaking and listening to the human voice can activate much of the same brain activity in speaker and listener.

   When we listen attentively and really grasp what another person is saying, our brain activity can virtually synchronise with the speaker's – even to the extent of anticipating what they are about to say. The key brain area for this synchrony is the insula, which is linked with conscious feeling states. Synchrony is more likely to happen when the two people share the same emotion. Fredrickson concludes that *"Shared emotions, brain synchrony and mutual understanding emerge together"* (2013, p.45) which she links to care and concern for one another

2. ***Oxytocin:*** Nicknamed the 'cuddle hormone', oxytocin has long been known to be important for social bonding and attachment, such as between intimate partners and between mother and baby. More recent research has shown that it also plays a key role in our more day-to-day interactions and social lives and that cuddling, or even touch, is not necessary for its release. Fredrickson (2013) summarises a range of research studies that show that oxytocin makes people more trusting of one another – and that trusting another with an important secret (having determined that they are trustworthy) increases levels of oxytocin

   In addition to its role in supporting mutual trust and bonding, oxytocin can also help us deal with stressful interpersonal situations by reducing the threat response of our amygdala, enabling us to behave more positively to others. In a beautiful positive feedback loop, behaving in a kindly way towards others also raises our oxytocin levels. Playing a key role in our 'calm-and-connect' response (which we explore later in this chapter when we look at Compassion-Focused Coaching), oxytocin can both calm the fears that might arise in novel social situations and help us more skilfully connect with others, while at the same time heightening our attunement to cues that indicate whether to trust another person

3. ***Vagal tone:*** The vagus nerve (or tenth cranial nerve) connects our brain to our body, particularly our heart. Signals from the vagus nerve are responsible for soothing us after experiencing a fight-or-flight response, by orchestrating our 'calm-and-connect' response (in which oxytocin also plays a part – see above). Signals from our vagus nerve help us make eye contact, synchronise our facial expressions with another person, and even track the other person's voice against background noise.

   The strength of our vagus nerve, or vagal tone, determines the effectiveness of our heart's response to stress and its routine efficiency and at the same time determines our flexibility across a range of domains, from internal bodily processes such as inflammation to regulation of attention and emotions. Socially, those with higher vagal tone are better able to navigate social exchanges and establish positive connections with others. It is good to know, therefore, that Fredrickson's own research (see Fredrickson, 2013 for a summary) shows that we can build our vagal tone through regularly engaging with practices such as Loving Kindness Meditation, a meditation practice originating in Buddhism which involves generating warm and tender feelings for self and others, gradually widening the circle (see our dedicated website)

relations (Fredrickson et al, 2008). It appears that LKM potentially increases positive emotion more than mindfulness meditation (Van Cappellen et al, 2020; Fredrickson et al, 2017).

Meanwhile, specifically in the coaching context, Heardman (2017) found that coaches practising the LKM benefitted through their inner critic being 'quietened', and they were able to be more present and listen more deeply to their client. His research found practising the LKM helped coaches create an environment that improved coaching outcomes.

Our belief is that Relational Mindfulness (RM) practices also serve to increase positivity resonance – we would love to conduct research on this!

There are some potential obstacles to connecting and staying in connection, and one of these is certain attachment styles, which we explore next.

Attachment theory

As mammals, we have highly developed attachment systems because we require nurturing for some time after being born, and our capacity to stay in connection has helped our species to survive and thrive (e.g. Cozolino, accessed 2023). Early healthy relationships help us think well of ourselves, trust others, regulate our emotions, maintain positive expectations, and use our intellectual and emotional intelligence (Cozolino, accessed 2023). However, many of us do not get a healthy start when it comes to relationships.

Attachment theory, first developed by psychologist, psychiatrist, and psychoanalyst John Bowlby (Bowlby, 1969), can help us shine a light in coaching on relational strategies and narratives, somatic reactions, and behavioural preferences we and our clients developed early on, which will play out in coaching and other relationships.

As RM-Enhanced Coaching (RMEC) coaches, attachment theory can help us understand how we show up with clients and can help to foster greater self and relational awareness and insight in our clients. In this way, it can help shift patterns which no longer serve, deepening connection, intimacy, trust, and psychological safety in coaching and other client relationships, enabling clients to better satisfy their own and others' needs, and removing relational obstacles to harnessing potential.

The theory

The internal 'working model' we develop early on of the self, others, and relationships drives how we experience and deal with stress or threat. Our early attachment bonds have a huge impact not only on our information processing but also on interpersonal functioning, including attitudes, emotions, affect regulation, and behavioural strategies (Mikulincer & Shaver, 2007).

We each develop a particular adult attachment style which reflects early relational experiences with carers:

■ *Secure*
  If, when infants perceive a threat, their need for proximity to and care from attachment figures is satisfied, they feel safe and able to engage in further exploration. They develop a secure attachment style. They have a positive model of themselves, others, and the world (Mikulincer & Shaver, 2007), greater capacity for empathy, and are thus more able to perceive and respond to others' needs (Begley, 2007). They have a high tolerance for ambiguity and tend to be less dogmatic in their thinking and communicating (Begley, 2007); they are mindful and mature enough to repair ruptures as needed in their rapport and communication with others (Siegel, 2007)

There are three insecure attachment patterns that develop when infants do not get satisfactory responses, leading them to deploy secondary strategies and engage in less (effective) exploration. These are as follows:

- *Avoidant*

Individuals whose caregivers were consistently emotionally unavailable, dismissing, unresponsive, and perhaps rejecting tend to score high in attachment avoidance. They may engage in deactivating strategies, pursuing self-reliance, avoiding discomfort with closeness, keeping a distance, and suppressing signs of vulnerability (e.g. Mikulincer & Shaver, 2007). Individuals with this style are low in anxiety, but high in avoidance. They have a positive model of themselves, but a more negative one of others

- *Anxious*

Individuals whose caregivers have been inconsistently available and responsive, enmeshed and entangled, frequently imposing their emotional state, will score highly in attachment anxiety. They will tend to manage their uncertainty about independence by stepping up efforts to seek closeness and protection and manage their anxiety by using hyperactivating strategies (Mikulincer & Shaver, 2007). People with this pattern often intensify bids for attention until a satisfying sense of attachment security is attained. They are low in avoidance, but high in anxiety, and have a positive model of others, but a lower one of themselves

- *Disorganised*

This is the least common attachment pattern, seen in individuals whose caregivers were frightening and frightened, disorienting and alarming. These individuals will have tended to approach their caregivers for security whilst at the same time avoiding them for safety, resulting in a conflicted and even disassociated state (Cozolino, 2006)

In coaching

An attachment perspective can be useful in coaching to understand clients' cognitive and interpersonal responses during and outside of sessions. Building on Bowlby's (1988) recommendations on supporting clients to shift insecure working models and achieve positive outcomes, Drake (2009) offers the following pointers for coaches to understand and facilitate clients' development using attachment (and narrative frames). We include some thoughts below on where RMEC might come in, and vice versa:

- *Provide clients with a sense that coaching sessions are safe havens, offering a secure base from which they can explore their defensive strategies* (both beliefs and behaviours). To quote Drake (2009, p.56), "*The goal is to move them to a 'sweet spot' where there is sufficient juice to activate their awareness and engage them but sufficient safety so they can stay present to their defences and make new choices.*"

As RMEC coaches, we are well-placed as discussed previously to offer a safe container for clients for this kind of exploration. A deeper understanding of psychological safety and compassion, both of which we explore in this chapter, can help here too.

- *Use the rapport gained to help clients examine how they currently relate to others and describe these relationships, and the biases inherent in their constructions*

    As we have explored, the RM guidelines can help us become present and attuned to our clients (see also the section in this chapter on positivity resonance), building rapport. In RMEC, we can support mindful, compassionate, and emergent exploration of topics, and depending on our coach capacity level, we might introduce RM contemplations around these areas.

- *Use coaching sessions as a laboratory for the study of clients' attachment-related behaviours,* including the transference and projection of their working models onto us as coaches and the coaching relationship, and the opportunity to experiment with new, more secure, relational patterns

    As RMEC coaches, we can draw on attachment theory alongside approaches such as Gestalt and somatics (both explored in Chapter 19) to help us to work in-the-moment with the client and our relationship as it unfolds, potentially offering clients the gift of experiencing a new way of relating that better serves them, others, and the wider system. If we think of ourselves as coaches as 'mirrors' for clients, it is vital that we do our own development work regularly *"so we remain compassionate, clean, and clear in our reflections"* (Drake, 2009, p.56). Having an individual mindfulness and compassion practice and infusing our coaching relationships with the RM guidelines will help us to do this

- *Help clients to reflect on how their working models and their subsequent interpersonal patterns – particularly around the roles and positions they tend to take relative to significant others – are rooted in childhood experiences with primary attachment figures*

    Again, the RM guidelines help us safely and emergently support such reflection.

- *Position ourselves as coaches as a 'good enough' and available caregiver to help (clients) experience other attachment orientations and behaviours.* Drake suggests we see coaching as a relationship in which coaches, as surrogate attachment figures, make room for experiences the client's original attachment figures were unable to make room for

    As RMEC coaches, we not only want to role model more helpful forms of relating but also tap into our shared common humanity, what it means to be a human being with all the difficulties that entails. Compassion-Focused Coaching (see later in this chapter) helps us support the client to be 'good enough' and us to role model that.

Working with different styles

We may have an inkling already of our client's attachment style or we can invite clients to fill in a free attachment style questionnaire such as therapist Diane Poole Heller's (https://traumasolutions.com/attachment-styles-quiz/) and explore the results in the coaching within an RMEC framework. We are not so much seeking to change their style – this very often is not possible. However, we can help the client widen their window of tolerance (Siegel, 2010), which as we saw in Chapter 3 is about our capacity to be with a range of emotions.

Clients with a secure style are the easiest to coach, says David Drake (Hall, 2011), who has researched attachment theory in coaching (e.g. Drake, 2009). In addition to the positive capacities we might see in such clients (see description of secure style above), they tend to be more open to engaging in new, growth-promoting, self-expanding experiences and addressing existential concerns (Mikulincer & Shaver, 2007).

Clients with a dismissing/avoidant style may find it hard to trust us, so we want to be consistently present. We want to support them to expand their window of tolerance around emotions and somatic experiences, including becoming more able to ask others emotive questions, alongside working with their existing strengths such as setting boundaries, and coping.

Clients with an anxious attachment style may be hypersensitive to signs of rejection and excessively ruminate on their shortcomings and immediate relationship threats (Mikulincer & Shaver, 2008). As coaches we want to help these clients make more room for autonomy, expanding their window of tolerance around independence and self-expression, alongside working with their existing strengths such as empathy, access to feelings, and sensitivity to the environment.

Mindfulness and attachment styles

Although there appears to be no research specifically into the benefit of RM on attachment issues, studies have pointed to the positive impact of individual mindfulness, suggesting that RM could potentially have a similar or even greater positive impact. A meta-analysis of 33 published research studies on mindfulness and attachment style (Stevenson et al, 2017) points to a link between dispositional mindfulness and adult attachment style, which may have implications for people's capacity for being relationally mindful. Stevenson et al (2017) suggest that the higher the level of mindfulness, the lower the levels of attachment anxiety and avoidance. These researchers found this to be true for total mindfulness score, and four of the five facets of mindfulness identified by Baer et al (e.g. 2006) – describing, acting with awareness, non-judging, and non-reacting. The other facet – observing – was not shown to be associated.

Authenticity

Often coaching is about surfacing and addressing gaps between who clients see themselves to be and who they are asked to be in their work role – the different 'masks' they feel they have put on to get through. Although it can also be for all sorts of other reasons such as racial discrimination, 'mask-wearing' can sometimes be traced back to relationships with carers in early childhood. A child may hide their 'True Self' if they feel it is risky to show their real personality, feelings, and needs, presenting instead a 'False Self' in a bid to get their needs met and protect themselves from re-experiencing developmental trauma, shock, and stress in close relationships (Winnicott, 1965). Coaching in a highly psychologically safe space, such as that provided in RMEC, can help clients discover or re-discover their True Self, from which they can be spontaneous, creative, and more authentic.

Defence mechanisms

Defence mechanisms, which can be linked to attachment styles, and to people's lived experiences, can often be blind spots for us and our clients and get in the way of connection. They include (Bolton, 2023) the following:

■ *Desensitisation*, where individuals numb or dampen their responses to certain sensations or emotions, disconnecting from the intensity of the experience to avoid repeated disappointment, for example, which might stop them recognising and taking care of a need for reliability or consistency in a relationship
■ *Retroflection*, when an individual acts towards themselves how they would like to towards others or vice versa, for example, criticising themselves harshly as a reflection of their internalised judgement of others, blocking their need for self-compassion and acceptance
■ *Confluence*, where there is no, or little, differentiation between the self and others, leading to people losing touch with their personal needs and desires, prioritising others' preferences over their own
■ *Egotism, or self-absorption*, where someone excessively focusses on their own needs and desires without considering the impact on others, leading to difficult relationships
■ *Projection*, attributing one's own feelings, thoughts, or impulses to another person, again stopping an individual from addressing their own needs, including in relationship
■ *Deflection*. Here the individual diverts attention away from themselves, for example, focussing on others or changing the subject, again potentially stopping them from identifying and meeting their needs

Next, we explore NVC as an approach to help us and our clients identify and act wisely on feelings and needs, supporting healthier relating and communicating.

Nonviolent communication

NVC is an approach to communication developed by the late clinical psychologist Marshall Rosenberg. Exposure at a young age to violence set Rosenberg on a mission to understand what causes violence and how it can be reduced. Much of his life's work focused on exploring what happens to disconnect humans from our compassionate nature, and what allows some people to stay connected to this nature under even the most trying circumstances (Rosenberg, 2015).

Rosenberg (accessed January 2024) has said that *"Nonviolent Communication is based on the principle of Ahimsa – the natural state of compassion when no violence is present in the heart."* As in RM, at NVC's core is the belief that humans are naturally compassionate and that it is possible to replace old communication patterns with more mindful, authentic, and compassionate ways of interrelating. And like RM, NVC proposes principles and a process to do just that. NVC and RMEC are highly complementary and at times overlapping, with a shared emphasis on awareness, compassion, and authenticity.

Drawing on his studies in clinical psychology and work supporting civil rights activists and others, Rosenberg developed NVC to spread peace-making skills, founding the Center for Nonviolent Communication (CNVC), a global non-profit organisation dedicated to sharing NVC around the world, including through training. NVC training is widely viewed as a tool for peacefully resolving differences, including in war-torn areas, healthcare, the military, and families, and increasingly in coaching (e.g. Cox & Dannahy, 2005; Deiorio et al, 2022; Moore et al, 2010).

The NVC approach

Rosenberg proposes a radically transformative and specific approach to *"communicating – both speaking and listening – that leads us to give from the heart, connecting us with ourselves and with each other in a way that allows our natural compassion to flourish"* (Rosenberg, 2015, p.2).

Whilst NVC may not explicitly discuss or prescribe mindfulness meditation, it is very much about mindful compassionate communication. NVC assumes that violent strategies – whether verbal or physical – are learned behaviours taught and supported by the prevailing culture. NVC also assumes that we all share the same, basic human needs, that all actions are a strategy to meet one or more of these needs, and that needs are never in conflict, only our strategies for meeting them (Rosenberg, 2015). NVC supports us so *"we come to hear our own deeper needs and those of others"* (Rosenberg, 2015, p.3).

Undoubtedly influenced by Rosenberg's friendship with and mentorship by fellow psychologist Carl Rogers, NVC emphasises the importance of empathetically and respectfully listening, just as we do in RMEC. And, like RM, NVC seeks to reframe *"how we express ourselves and hear others"* so we *"express ourselves with honesty and clarity, while simultaneously paying others a respectful and empathic attention*" (Rosenberg, 2015, p.3).

Expression in NVC is seen to arise as a conscious response from an awareness of what we are actually perceiving, feeling, and wanting, rather than reacting habitually and automatically, which again resonates with RMEC.

Awareness, presence, and attunement are key in NVC, just as they are in RMEC and in coaching in general. NVC invites us to become more aware and choiceful of where we place our attention. To quote Rosenberg again (Rosenberg, 2015, p.4), "*(NVC) is an ongoing reminder to keep our attention focused on a place where we are more likely to get what we are seeking.*"

A language and a way of being

While studying what affects our ability to stay compassionate, Rosenberg was struck by the crucial role of language and our use of words. However, like RMEC, although NVC proposes dialogical exchanges in which speakers draw on NVC principles, it is a way of showing up, with awareness, and may not even involve spoken words. As Rosenberg says, "*the consciousness and intent that (NVC) embraces may be expressed through silence, a quality of presence, as well as through facial expressions and body language*" (Rosenberg, 2015, p.12).

Additionally, it is worth noting that sometimes when we and our clients come to Speak the truth, perhaps having attuned to emergence and interconnectedness, we touch a deep truth that can be hard to put into words, or at least words may not suffice to describe our experience. Language can be enriching, and it can be limiting. And the nature of profound directly experienced truth is that it often defies description. That said, having a more nuanced vocabulary for feelings and needs can be very helpful in coaching, including RMEC, as we will explore.

The NVC process

The process has four components which are shared verbally or otherwise in a flow of communication back and forth. The aim is to express clearly, without evaluation and judgement:

■ 1. *Observations:* The concrete actions that we observe that affect our wellbeing
■ 2. *Feelings:* How we feel in relation to what we observe
■ 3. *Needs:* The needs, values, desires, etc. that create our feelings
■ 4. *Requests:* The concrete actions we request to enrich our lives

The focus in NVC on separating observation from evaluation, on communicating from a place of non-judgement and clarity, is of course very mindful and aligned with RMEC. Non-judgement, as we noted in Chapter 2, is a core mindfulness trait, and seeking to separate observation from evaluations and assumptions is integral to practising the RM guidelines, allowing us to become fully present and attuned to ourselves and others.

When we mix evaluation and judgement with observation, it becomes less likely that others will hear the message we want to convey. They are more likely to be resistant and believe they are being criticised. Developing a more nuanced vocabulary for feelings and emotions can help us avoid making assumptions.

Identifying and describing feelings and emotions

A note in passing: The terms feeling and emotion are often used interchangeably; however, to be clear, feelings are the subjective perceptions of emotions. We may or may not be conscious of emotions, but they will be there anyway.

There is still plenty of debate about how many human emotions and experiences exist. Brown, for example (Brown, 2021), explores 87 emotions and experiences, and Ekman (2016) points to evidence for 7 universal emotions or emotion families (with an additional 10 which may be universal and 11 more on which the jury is out): fear, anger, joy, sadness, contempt, disgust, and surprise.

This assumption that there are commonly shared feelings – and needs – is central to the NVC approach. The CNVC's extensive inventory of feelings and needs can be downloaded for free or a donation from the CNVC website (www. cnvc.org/). However, below is a flavour of some of these.

Basic universal feelings

Feelings we might typically experience when our needs are met include affectionate, engaged, excited, exhilarated, grateful, hopeful, inspired, joyful, peaceful, and refreshed.

Feelings we might typically experience when our needs are not satisfied include afraid, angry, annoyed, aversion, confused, disconnected, disquiet, embarrassed, fatigue, pain, sad, tense, vulnerable, and yearning.

Basic universal needs

These include autonomy, connection, honesty, physical wellbeing, play, peace, and meaning. The CNVC inventory includes other needs nestled under each of these. Given our focus on relationships, here are those listed under the heading of connection: acceptance, affection, appreciation, belonging, cooperation, communication, closeness, community, companionship, compassion, consideration, consistency, empathy, inclusion, intimacy, love, mutuality, nurturing, respect/self-respect, safety, security, stability, support, to know and be known, to see and be seen, to understand and be understood, trust, and warmth.

Whilst we do not want to quote lists of needs and feelings (although sharing these with clients can be helpful), we can support clients to get greater emotional granularity, with many benefits, including for relationships. Learning to label emotions with a more nuanced vocabulary can be transformative, helping us identify and communicate our needs and get the support we require from others, supporting greater emotion regulation and psychosocial wellbeing (David, 2016).

Getting in touch with our feelings can help us have a greater appreciation of our shared common humanity, which boosts connection. And it can build clients' courage, motivation, and capacity to take constructive action and make behaviour changes (Moore et al, 2010).

Surfacing feelings

Despite the potential benefits, many of us struggle to identify our feelings and needs, let alone communicate them courageously and clearly to others or even to ourselves.

Rosenberg (2015, p.98) underlines the importance of ensuring the other person feels heard and understood, suggesting techniques we are familiar with in coaching, such as reflecting back messages that are emotionally charged, and para-phrasing "*only when it contributes to greater compassion and understanding*", using a tone that communicates that we are checking to see if we have understood rather than claiming we have understood.

Using specific words rather than generic terms helps us to speak our truth clearly and without assuming the other person will have the same experience or interpretation.

Identifying needs versus wants

NVC can also help coaches and their clients gain a deeper appreciation of the difference between wants and needs, so that the coaching becomes about what really matters to the client and their system. Such an appreciation can help us as RMEC coaches to be more open to emergence, and to avoid colluding thought-lessly with clients' desires, which can sometimes be at odds with what is really needed.

Difficulties in identifying and expressing needs

Rosenberg (2015) identifies and explores different types of communication that block compassion, obscuring our awareness that we are each responsible for our own thoughts, feelings, and actions. These include denial of responsibility, com-municating our desires as demands, and moralistic judgements that imply there is something wrong on the part of people not acting in alignment with our values. The latter can take the form of blame, insults, put-downs, criticism, comparisons, and diagnoses, which are actually "*tragic expressions of our own values and needs*" (Rosenberg, 2015, p.16), increasing defensiveness and resistance.

Some coaching clients will struggle more than others to listen deeply to and speak the truth about their needs. Some have been socialised to prioritise others' needs and ignore their own, for example; they may have been criticised for expressing their needs and can struggle to express them clearly and respectfully. Sometimes they become desperate, with their unmet needs shouting louder and louder until they burst out. See Box 20.2 for an example of how this might manifest and how RM and NVC might help.

Many of our clients will also struggle to identify and express their feelings and needs. They might share how resentment builds, sometimes leading to overwhelm

---

Box 20.2 Liz's experience: combining RM with NVC

For years, I (Liz) would keep quiet about housework piling up and then either suddenly have what might be described as a tantrum – it certainly was not mature mindful compassionate communication – or offer a monologue about everything I had been doing, making what I felt was a strong case for having a rest or getting some support, but to no avail with my family! According to NVC, this is a classic unhealthy way people try to get needs met.

I would get to the point of feeling overloaded and resentful, bashing about in the kitchen and eventually would mutter something like, "It would be great if SOMEONE would at least stack the dishwasher."

How much more effective and authentic it is these days for me to say, for example, "I am feeling tired and overwhelmed, I'd love some support. Would you mind helping me?"

Combining NVC with RM is very powerful, I and some clients with whom I have started sharing this have found. Instead of blurting something out with desperation or even aggression, we can bring in the RM guidelines. Pausing to come into the present moment and into our body, taking a few deep breaths and feeling our feet on the ground, Relaxing/Allowing, lowering our shoulders and relaxing our belly, Opening to the space in between ourselves and the other, and beyond, Attuning to emergence. Then *observing* without judgement or evaluation what is actually here, Listening deeply to what we are *feeling*, and what our *needs* are, before articulating mindfully and compassionately any *request* we have, drawing on Speak the truth (not just ours!).

I find this combined approach makes it easier for me to self-regulate, to find out and tune into what I am feeling and what I need, and to express myself and speak the truth in a grounded, kindly way. It works! And sometimes I find I do not want to speak; there was just something about checking in with myself and self-soothing.

or even burnout, and to conflict in their relationships. At work, they may fear being labelled 'neurotic' or 'overly emotional.'

Culture can have an impact here too. A number of my (Liz's) clients are Asian females who have been socialised not to express needs, and who as a result struggle to get in touch with their needs, let alone articulate them. Meanwhile, Black female clients have told me they fear that expressing their needs in a primarily white organisational culture may see them labelled troublemakers, as 'the angry Black woman.'

Helping clients get more in touch with their feelings and needs and communicate these in ways more likely to land well, drawing on both NVC and RM, can bear welcome fruit. And developing courage and willingness to be honest and vulnerable can help develop fertile conditions for psychological safety to take root. Next, we explore this burgeoning field of research and practice.

Psychological safety

Psychological safety is currently enjoying much justified attention in leadership, organisational development, and coaching. However, the concept is sometimes misunderstood. A more nuanced understanding of psychological safety and of how we can build psychological safety can help us and our clients to create conditions in which RM can flourish, while drawing on RM can support the co-creation of psychologically safe conditions.

Defining psychological safety

Amy Edmondson, author of *The Fearless Organization* (Edmondson, 2018) and a prominent researcher on psychological safety, defines psychological safety as a climate in which people tend to trust and respect each other, *"are comfortable being and expressing themselves…(and) feel comfortable sharing concerns and mistakes without fear of embarrassment or retribution"* (p.xvi).

Psychological safety is about reframing failure, which Edmondson (2018) categorises into three different types: preventable, complex, and intelligent, stressing that it is impossible to avoid failure. The main thing is to learn from them, which requires speaking about them.

Psychological safety is not about lowering performance standards, nor about cultivating an environment in which people are not held accountable, nor about avoiding conflict. It is not about being nice, agreeing with each other and/or offering praise and support for everything everyone says.

The terms psychological safety and trust are often used interchangeably. However, Edmondson says (p.17) that psychological safety is experienced at group level, whereas *"trust refers to interactions between two individuals or parties;*

trust exists in the mind of an individual and pertains to a specific target individual or organization."

Benefits of psychological safety

Being clear about the potential benefits of building psychological safety can help us make a case for establishing RM practice in coaching and workplace contexts, providing us with a compelling entry point.

Google's in-depth two-year study involving 180 teams, Project Aristotle, found that psychological safety was the number one factor differentiating their highest performing teams from other teams (Rozovsky, 2015). Other important factors were clear goals, dependable colleagues, personally meaningful work, and a belief that the work has impact: psychological safety is the underpinning of these four.

Psychologically safe teams are more likely to learn from failures, hold courageous conversations, and draw on 'power with' rather than 'power over', enhancing diversity, inclusion, and belonging, to be innovative (Huang & Jiang, 2012), and to have high employee engagement (e.g. Chughtai & Buckley, 2013; May et al, 2004).

Building psychological safety

Edmondson (2018) sets out three important dimensions of a culture of psychological safety: 'setting the stage' (framing the work, including welcoming failure as part of learning, and emphasising why the work matters), 'inviting participation', and 'responding productively', which could include sanctions in extreme circumstances.

With 'inviting participation', just as with Kline's Thinking Rounds (see later in this chapter), sharing circles such as in Buddhist and Indigenous cultures, and RM mindful dialogue, it is vital that participants understand that their voice matters and is welcome. While someone speaks, others are invited to listen 'intensely.'

Given psychological safety is about candour and free exchange of ideas, RM can help by supporting honest, authentic, and courageous exchanges, including through the RM guideline Speak the truth, underpinned by listening deeply to ourselves, others, and the system, thus enabling people on different 'sides' to speak openly and wisely, including about failures.

Being prepared to be open about where we have messed up requires courage and vulnerability, particularly for leaders operating in more traditional command and control cultures, where they may be always expected to be directive and have all the answers. The RM guidelines can help people speak up with courage and discernment about failure and avoid playing the blame game – of ourselves as well as others.

Responding productively should include expressing appreciation of others, which may feel difficult given our negativity bias, which means we are more likely to focus on negative feedback and dismiss or not even hear positive feedback. In many cultures, we are not used to being appreciated or offering appreciative comments. The RM guidelines can help us be more receptive to appreciation and to offer something that is succinct, sincere, and genuine.

Also important in building psychological safety Edmondson (2018) is emphasising uncertainty, being curious and alert, picking up on early indicators of change, which can then be expressed back into the system. The RM guidelines help us do that, including Attune to emergence, Listen deeply, and Speak the truth. This can be supported by other frameworks too, such as Theory U (see Chapter 21).

Edmondson (2018) also points to the importance of appreciating our inter-dependence, encouraging more regular conversations, including about how people's work is impacting on others and vice versa. This can involve taking inter-personal risks and sharing concerns as well as ideas, so the more mindful we are individually and in relationship, the easier this will be – the RM guidelines can be helpful here too.

Brown's research on vulnerability, which we explore briefly next, can also be helpful when it comes to building connection, including around the co-creation of psychological safety.

The power of vulnerability

Brené Brown (2021, pp.13–14) describes vulnerability as *"the emotion that we experience during times of uncertainty, risk and emotional exposure"*, stressing that *"vulnerability is not weakness; it's our greatest measure of courage."* Her research (Brown, 2021) on courage and leadership suggests that the ability to embrace vulnerability enables leaders to handle uncertainty, risk, and emotional exposure in a way that aligns with values and furthers organisational goals.

In addition to the myth that vulnerability is weakness, Brown (2019) highlights five other myths:

- *I can go it alone.* We need relationships to be able to express vulnerability
- *I don't do vulnerability*
- *You can engineer the uncertainty and discomfort out of vulnerability*
- *Trust comes before vulnerability.* Being vulnerable helps to create trust
- *Vulnerability is disclosure.* We need to be intentional and discerning when it comes to sharing with others: it *"takes discipline and self-awareness to understand what to share and with whom…vulnerability is not oversharing, it's sharing with people who have earned the right to hear our stories and our*

experiences" (Brown, 2021, p.14). As we have explored elsewhere, this discernment is highly relevant in RM when it comes to Speak the truth. The RM guidelines including the latter can help us and our clients be wise around disclosure

As we indicated above, the capacity to listen deeply helps to cultivate climates in which there is trust and psychological safety. Next, we look at some models for ramping up and deepening our listening.

Models for listening deeply

As Remen points out, "*listening is the oldest and perhaps the most powerful tool of healing. It is often through the quality of our listening and not the wisdom of our words that we are able to effect the most profound changes in the people around us*" (Remen & Wisdom, 1996, pp.219–220).

Many of us are rather shocked to discover when we train as a coach that we are not as good at listening as we thought we were, and it is rare for any of us, including coaches, to be able to listen really deeply, to really let go of attachment to ideas and desired outcomes, trusting emergence and the intelligence of the client and the system. To quote Thich Nhat Hanh (2011, p.92), "*Listening with empathy means you listen in such a way that the other person feels you are really listening, really understanding, hearing with your whole being – with your heart. … But, in fact, how many of us can listen like that?*"

Nancy Kline, who developed the Thinking Environment and whose work we explore shortly, finds that it continues to be a stretch for coaches to listen fully with presence. She says that (Hall, 2021a) "*the contrast between even the most client-centred coaching and the Thinking Environment is still vast*" and that "*(coaches) find that they still need to take a giant, and different kind of, step to achieve this level of generative presence with a client.*"

Different levels of listening

Well-known models which describe progressively deeper levels of listening include the following:

- Covey's (1989) five levels: Ignoring, pretending, selective listening, attentive listening, and empathic listening
- Co-active Coaching's (Kimsey-House et al, 2018) three levels: Internal listening, focused listening, and global listening
- Scharmer's four levels (Scharmer, 2018): Downloading, factual, empathetic, and generative

▪ Lawrence's (Lawrence, 2020, 2021) five ways we can listen: To noise, for content, for intention, for identity, to influence

All levels of listening serve a purpose. However, in RMEC, we are interested in being able to listen at the levels which enable the most depth and breadth of presence, awareness, and attunement.

Out of the afore-mentioned, in Covey's model, we want to reach the fifth level, empathic listening, where we are listening with intent to really understand. Here, to quote Covey (1989, p.241) it is about getting *"inside another person's frame of reference. You look through it, you see the world the way they see the world, you understand their paradigm, you understand how they feel"* where you are *"focused on receiving the deep communication of another human soul."*

In Co-active's model, we aim to be able to flex into the third level, global listening, with a wider focus than just the other person. To quote Kimsey-House et al (2018, p.45), at this level, *"You listen as if you and the coachee are at the center of the universe, receiving information from everywhere at once. It's as though you are surrounded by a force field that contains you, the coachee, and an environment of information."*

And as we attune to emergence increasingly, we want to be able to flex into Scharmer's fourth level of generative listening, connecting to the emerging future (see Chapter 21).

With Lawrence's model, again, the other ways of listening serve their purpose but in RMEC, we want to be able to step into the active mode of listening for intention. Not just listening for content, to which we might add our own meaning and make assumptions, and certainly not merely listening for when others are speaking, to assess when we can easily jump in.

▪ *Listening for intention* requires a conscious effort to understand what the other person is trying to say, making sure as best we can that our own narratives, lived experiences, prejudices, and projections are not getting in the way. Listening for intention outside of RM formal dialogue can include, as in Lawrence's model, checking in because we are curious and really want to establish whether we have really understood what the other person is trying to say

▪ We might want to be able to *listen for identity* too, seeking to understand who the other person is, their values, motivations, and life experiences

▪ Lawrence's fifth way of listening, *listening to influence,* may not sound like a way of listening that is appropriate in RMEC, in which we tend to be seeking to be unattached to outcome. However, if we delve deeper into Lawrence's model, we may see that this level can offer a gateway to the systemic. Lawrence (2021, p.4) notes that the first four ways of listening *"offer us a language through which we can be much more specific as to how we choose* to listen in any given situation." However, these forms of listening "*encourage us to think individualistically, to regard others as autonomous and discrete.*" The fifth way of listening is about explicitly opening to systemic perspectives, in particular those emerging from theories of complex adaptive systems which (p.4) "*explicitly recognise the role of interaction and relationship in shaping change, including individual change.*" Through this lens, listening to influence becomes about collective meaning-making of both external events and internal events – who we are as people. This lens allows for the fact that we cannot control change as it is constant and emergent, a theme that we have picked up elsewhere in this book and which is central to RMEC. However, it holds that we can seek to influence change "*through engaging in purposeful dialogue. Through this lens sense-making is a social process. We make meaning together*" (Lawrence, 2021, p.4). Whilst this latter lens may not necessarily sit perfectly in a formal RM dialogue, unless the chosen enquiry question aligns, it can be adopted in RMEC in general, particularly where this has a wider vision. We further explore this potential in Chapter 23

Nancy Kline's Thinking Environment

Let silence take you to the core of life.

Rumi

The power of silence, quality attention, and not being interrupted

Nancy Kline (1999, 2009) developed the Thinking Environment approach to help people access high-quality thinking through high-calibre generative presence. With its emphasis on deep listening, being comfortable with silence, and using language with discernment, and presence, it is an approach very aligned with RMEC. Kline's work has been shared through her books and Time to Think, the leadership development and coaching company she founded. Her work is based on the premise that the quality of everything we do depends on the quality of the thinking we do first, that the quality of our thinking is ignited by high-quality attention of those listening to us. Attention generates thinking. As Kline says (Kline, 2020, p.36) "*…your continuous, generous attention may be the dearest gift you can give anyone. Or that they can give you.*"

The approach draws partly on the power of silence on the part of the listener, with a commitment to the speaker that they will not be interrupted. As we know if we have had the fortune to engage in an RM dialogue, it can be utterly delicious to have the space to think, speaking as and when feels appropriate, with no fear of being judged for being silent or of being interrupted, knowing the other person is listening deeply and helping to hold a mindful container. Such a luxury seems even more precious in these times we live in where we can feel bombarded by noise and distractions.

Creating a Thinking Environment

Creating a Thinking Environment requires paying attention to 'ten components':

- *Attention:* Listening without interruption and with interest in where the person will go next in their thinking
- *Equality:* Regarding each other as thinking peers, giving equal time to think
- *Ease:* Discarding internal urgency
- *Appreciation:* Noticing what is good and saying it
- *Feelings:* Welcoming the release of emotion
- *Encouragement:* Giving courage to go to the unexplored edge of our thinking by ceasing competition as thinkers
- *Information:* Absorbing all the relevant facts
- *Difference:* Prioritising diversity of group identities and understanding their lived experience
- *Incisive Questions™:* Freeing the human mind of an untrue assumption lived as true
- *Place:* Producing a physical environment – the room, the listener, our body – that says, 'You matter'

The process

In one-to-one coaching, the Thinking Partnership is created between the 'thinker' (client) and their 'partner' (coach). However, a Thinking Environment can be created between more than two people. The Thinking Pair refers to the timed short Pairs used in groups (usually timed for 3–7 minutes each way), as one of four key building blocks. The others are Dialogue, Rounds, and Open Discussion. In Rounds, all those present have equal turns to speak without being interrupted. An enquiry question is usually agreed before embarking upon the round.

Depending on RMEC coach capacity, the RM guidelines can be fruitfully interwoven implicitly and potentially explicitly into a Thinking Round, perhaps starting with a collective pause, for example, and/or inviting pauses when these feel natural and helpful.

Next, we look at a relational framework with Buddhist roots that may inspire us as we seek to integrate and embody deep listening in all areas of our lives, including in coaching.

Thich Nhat Hanh's approach

The teachings, practices, and community of the late Zen Buddhist monk Thich Nhat Hanh (affectionately known as Thầy – 'teacher' in Vietnamese) have been a very significant influence for me (Liz) in developing mindfulness and compassion individually and in relationship, including in my coaching practice.

Thầy established the first Plum Village, a Zen Buddhist spiritual community, in France after being exiled from his homeland Vietnam. There are now others, including in the US, Vietnam, and Thailand. The communities regularly open to lay people to promote mindful compassionate approaches, including in relationships. In Plum Village, RM guidelines, although they are not named such, are naturally and seamlessly embedded into both formal and informal practices.

Thầy's monastic order proposes various sets of precepts by which people can aspire to live and 'mindfulness trainings' (5 for beginners, or 14 for those who wish to go deeper). The fourth of the five mindfulness trainings (Plum Village, accessed October 2023), 'Loving Speech and Deep Listening' (Hanh, 2022), encapsulates a relationally mindful stance beautifully, reminding us that RM is a practice which we need to cultivate and be committed to.

Thầy describes deep listening as "*the kind of listening that helps us to keep compassion alive while the other speaks*", going on to say that "*During this time you have in mind only one idea, one desire: to listen in order to give the other person the chance to speak out and suffer less*" (Hanh, 2011, p.93). In the Loving Speech and Deep Listening training, we are invited to practise compassionate listening and "*knowing that words can create happiness or suffering, to be committed to speaking truthfully using words that inspire confidence, joy, and hope*" and to "*speak and listen in a way that can help myself and the other person to transform suffering and see the way out of difficult situations*" (for full text of this training, see our dedicated website).

The Plum Village community is increasingly applying its practices of deep listening and loving speech, of being mindful together, to good effect in a range of settings. In a podcast recorded to mark Climate Coaching Action Day 2023, an annual initiative launched by *Coaching at Work* magazine in 2020, Jo Confino, leadership coach, journalist, and lay Zen Buddhism practitioner, describes some of the work he has been involved in with climate leaders. This has included a five-day retreat for people involved in climate including climate justice leaders and oil and gas lobbyists, at Plum Village, France. Confino shares that to foster greater connection, attendees were invited to just show up as human beings rather than in their particular roles, to practise mindfulness together, to listen deeply to one another. Many of these leaders have stayed in touch since the retreat. For us, this inspires us to think of ways we might bring RM alive beyond one-to-one conversations, a topic we explore in Chapter 23.

Whilst we will not describe these in detail (see our dedicated website for more), we would like to touch briefly on some of Plum Village's formalised practices, as they can naturally enhance a deepening of mindfulness and compassion in relationship, including in coaching and among those not immersed in this tradition.

The bell and the pause

In Plum Village, there is a beautiful practice of ringing a bell from time to time with the intention of inviting people to pause. When any bell 'is invited' to sound (to use the language of Plum Village), everyone pauses. The bell signals it is time for sitting meditation practice, walking meditation, food or some other activity, or simply to 'come home' to our body and breath, to ourselves.

When people first arrive in Plum Village, particularly if it is their first time, they may take a while to notice the bell has sounded, continuing their chatter or whatever else they are doing. They can be visibly irritated by having to interrupt doing mode. Very quickly, though, most people relax into this practice and come to welcome it. A settling, a steadying, a sense of tranquillity, of grounding, of being in community, of mindfully being in relationship becomes palpable. Looking around, you can see all these people just stop, some closing their eyes, some taking deeper breaths, many smiling contentedly.

Plum Village's app, which includes plenty of resources and practices, includes an audio of its bell (see our dedicated website) which can be listened to on demand, or automated to sound regularly. And, as we explore earlier in the book, there are other ways to puncture our days with reminders to pause, including with other sounds (see our dedicated website).

Deep listening and loving speech practices

BEGINNING ANEW

Deep listening and loving speech are encouraged both informally and formally including through Beginning Anew (Hanh, 2006), a profoundly relational mindful compassionate ceremony, which offers a container for people to safely speak the truth with courage and discernment.

Typically practised once a week in Plum Village, Beginning New invites people to appreciate and amplify the good things, as well as allowing a chance to air difficulties, and to begin over with those they are having a difficulty with. Outside of the community, many lay practitioners, including myself (Liz), report drawing on Beginning Anew as a mindful way to nourish and build relationships, ritualising mutual appreciation, allowing space to express regret and for nipping little niggles in the bud before they fester and grow into problematic issues.

The Beginning Anew ceremony has three parts: flower watering, expressing regrets, and expressing hurts and difficulties. Flower watering is about appreciating and acknowledging the wholesome, wonderful qualities of the others, not flattering but speaking the truth. Then after expressing regrets for anything we have done to hurt others, we have the chance to express ways we feel that others have hurt us. Here, the RM guideline Speak the truth, with compassion, and wisdom, comes alive as we speak frankly but avoiding being destructive. Listen deeply is alive too, listening to another's hurts and difficulties with the willingness to relieve the suffering of the other person. If someone feels what has been said is not true, they can seek to correct this another time, privately and calmly.

Beginning Anew can be a very powerful group or one-to-one practice. I (Liz) have attended a number of Plum Village retreats and I cannot recall a Beginning

Anew ceremony in which nobody has cried. I have witnessed an estranged father and adult son reconnecting deeply after many years, young children profoundly hearing their parents speak the truth about regretting not spending more time with them and what they appreciate about their children, a couple who had grown apart reconnecting once again, and two brothers resolving a conflict that had been poisoning their family for years.

We can adapt this beautiful practice for team/group coaching, as long as the coach is trained in team coaching dynamics and is preferably operating at or above RM coach capacity Level Two, embodying mindfulness and compassion. The RM guidelines, depending on coach capacity, can be woven into the process seamlessly.

Touching the Earth

This practice helps us reconcile and be in mindful compassionate relationship with everyone in our lives, past, present, and even future, helping us to connect to limitless life across time and space. Again, I (Liz) have experienced and witnessed the power of this practice, and many tears have been shed.

Whilst the spiritual nature of these ceremonies will not be for everyone, they can inspire the creation of similar practices to help heal and transform relationships and adopt a longer time horizon. Plum Village offers other practices along the lines of Touching the Earth, which encourage us to bring our antecedents into our present moments – for example, inviting us to have our mother and father 'breathe with us.' These practices of touching in with our ancestors can enable us to rewrite narratives we are holding around our relationships which no longer serve us, helping us heal difficult relationships.

Of course, Plum Village is by no means the only tradition offering practices for connecting with ancestors – this is embedded in many cultures including Eastern and Indigenous cultures. Indigenous wisdom is increasingly being honoured and woven into Western approaches, offering gifts around how we relate not only to past and future generations, but to Mother Nature, of which we are of course a part.

Whilst compassion has been relevant to many of the 'jewels' we have covered so far in this chapter, it deserves specific attention. Below we explore more approaches with compassion at their heart, namely Compassion-Focused Coaching and coaching with compassion. However, first, we will build on what we touched on in Chapter 3, seeking to debunk what we and some prominent compassion researchers see as a troublesome myth: that we can have too much compassion.

Compassion as a resource – empathic distress versus compassion fatigue

As Kelly McGonigal (2021) says, *"caring for others triggers the biology of courage and creates hope"*, which we very much welcome in coaching. However, a more nuanced understanding of compassion and empathy can help us as RMEC coaches to minimise the risk of tipping into a depleting and disconnecting state which will hinder our capacity to be relationally mindful and present for our clients. In turn, we will be better able to support clients to access the wonderful resource that is compassion.

Compassion fatigue and empathic distress

Figley coined the term *compassion fatigue* to describe a form of burnout among caregivers (Figley, 1995). This term implies it is compassion itself that is fatiguing whilst many, including us, believe – and experience – that compassion is potentially an unlimited resource, and that the higher someone's compassion levels, including towards self, the less likely they are to tip into burnout.

Research (e.g. Klimecki et al, 2013) suggests that compassion fatigue is a misnomer and that it is empathy that fatigues helpers, not compassion. Many other prominent researchers agree, including Davidson, Neff, and Brach:

Speaking at the Compassion in Therapy Summit online in 2021, Davidson (2021) says,"*From a neuroscientific perspective and in contemplative traditions, there's no such thing as compassion fatigue – instead it's empathy fatigue which happens when we haven't learnt how to transform empathy into compassion.*" He continues "*empathy can be very toxic, especially when you're with people who are suffering.*"

At the same summit, Kristin Neff said (Hall, 2021b), "*(Figley's) choice of term was a bit unfortunate. Compassion is not fatiguing. Empathy is fatiguing… because it activates lots of pain centres in our brain.*"

And Tara Brach (Brach, 2021) explained that "*empathy involves activity in the limbic system so we can get burnt out. Compassion involves activity in the pre-frontal cortex – it's pleasant and rewarding because it serves our species.*"

So, when we think we are tipping into compassion fatigue, we may instead be experiencing 'empathic distress.' This is a strong aversive and self-oriented response to the suffering of others, accompanied by the desire to withdraw from a situation in order to protect oneself from excessive negative feelings (Singer & Klimecki, 2014). These researchers associate empathic distress with negative feelings such as stress, with poor health including burnout, and with withdrawal and non-social behaviour, whereas compassion is associated with positive feelings, including love, with good health, and with approach and pro-social motivation.

Whilst McGonigal (2021) agrees that when people talk about compassion being overwhelming or draining, often what they are thinking about is the intensity of empathy. She warns that denying the existence of compassion fatigue can have a potentially negative impact, including "*when people hold the value of compassion, and something happens so they can no longer sustain it and [then they] hear someone say, compassion fatigue doesn't exist, you're just doing it wrong.*"

As RMEC coaches, or indeed any coaches, we believe we should be able to understand what empathic distress looks and feels like, and what we can do to nip it in the bud, shifting where possible into a more resourceful and compassionate response, and supporting clients to do likewise. We want to avoid or reduce empathic distress, given its negative impact on building connection, presence, self- and other-compassion, and resourcefulness in relationship.

'Antidotes' to empathic distress include, as McGonigal (2021) suggests, accessing support and community, seeking out joy, and engaging in moral elevation "*to counteract the moral outrage you feel about the world*", seeing and celebrating the compassion around us.

Being able to distinguish self from other is key. In coaching, we want to be able to empathise with our client, attuning to them and their experiences, having a sense of what it is like to be in their shoes, yet we do *not* want to 'get in the pit' of suffering with them. To do so would mean we are no longer able to be of service to them. So we want to have a sense of where we start and they end, without blurring.

However, this is nuanced and complex territory, partly because of the philosophy that sometimes comes with mindfulness, and certainly is present in Buddhism, including in ID, which promotes a sense of interconnectedness. Meditative practice alone and in relationship can lead us to question whether there is indeed a boundary between us and others, discovering that actually there is not. Such a beautiful awakening to our interrelatedness, to our "*place in the family of things*", to quote the late poet Mary Oliver from her poem, *Wild Geese*, can be one of the most profound gifts we ever receive from individual mindfulness and RM.

As we have pointed to before, there is something about 'both/and', about holding both a sense of us individually, this little 'process' right here that we call ourselves, *and* of the collective; of the internal landscape, the external landscape, and both. We do not want to lose sight totally of a boundary between self and other, however unreal this may be on one level. We want to avoid what McGonigal (2021) calls "*idealising compassion*" with "*a total lack of distinction between self and other [there being] no more separation and [a sense of] we're all one.*" She says the neuroscience for sustainable compassion and non-overwhelming empathy shows "*increased activation in the brain areas that help you distinguish self from other. We have a brain system that helps us create boundaries so we're not merged but we can [still] have... mindful relationship and engagement.*"

Staying within our 'window of tolerance' (Siegel, 2010), working with personal preferences and tendencies, taking into account our own and others' attachment styles, histories of trauma, whether we or a client is neurotypical or neurodivergent (the latter may mean more sensitivity to emotional cues, potential overwhelm, heightened sensitivity to rejection, and so on), for example, can all help in the reduction or prevention of empathic distress. Drawing on mindfulness strategies in the moment if we do become empathically distressed can help us self-regulate, as we have seen.

How else might we be to develop compassion – combined with awareness and wisdom – in coaching? There is much we can learn as RMEC coaches from the last two 'jewels' we explore in this chapter.

Compassion-Focused Coaching

Compassion-Focused Coaching (CFC) has evolved from Compassion-Focused Therapy (CFT), a psychotherapeutic approach first developed by Gilbert (2009) and colleagues to support people experiencing very high levels of shame and self-criticism. Research suggests CFT increases self-compassion and reduces symptoms in individuals with a range of mental health problems; it is now applied within a broad range of clinical and non-clinical contexts and has been adapted for coaching (e.g. Irons et al, 2018).

CFT is an integrated multimodal approach which draws on scientific and psychological theories and approaches including neuroscience, evolutionary, developmental, Buddhist, and social psychology. It seeks to understand the evolved functions of social relationships and caring connections and their physiological regulating abilities, placing the importance of caring, sharing, and supportive relationships with self and others at the centre of the therapeutic process (Gilbert & Simos, 2022).

Broadly speaking, CFC aims to build awareness, compassion, and wisdom, helping individuals, groups, and organisations become more aware of and skilful in engaging with difficulties, distress, and suffering and in finding ways to alleviate difficulties and promote growth (Irons et al, 2018). It does this by helping coaching clients develop a particular type of soothing-affiliative emotion that may help them to better manage their difficulties and, over time, develop a 'compassionate mind' that may be used to deal with external difficulties or internal struggles (Irons et al, 2018). External difficulties may include difficult relationships or a toxic culture in the organisation where the client works, while internal struggles may include high levels of rumination, self-criticism, or fear of failure. It uses 'compassionate mind training' (Gilbert, 2009) to help people develop and work with experiences of inner warmth, safeness, and soothing, via compassion and self-compassion.

As an aside, having more self-compassion does not necessarily mean we have more compassion for others, according to Neff (2015, p.187). Her research (2015, p.188) has shown that people who lack self-compassion can be just as kind to others as those who are self-compassionate. Other research (Neff, 2003) also shows that women tend to have slightly lower levels of self-compassion than men do, tending to be harsher self-critics. Women are socialised to be caregivers to others but not themselves.

CFC: Insights and underpinnings

CFC and CFT are held within a broad evolutionary psychology framework of understanding what it means to be human, including our capacity for distress and happiness. Core concepts are as follows:

■ *Our brains have evolved over millions of years with limitations*

Whilst we are each unique in many ways, we share common features, some helpful, some not, unless we come to understand and work with them. For example, our brains are wired to act on certain motives, including seeking status or attachment, we typically have access to emotions such as anxiety, anger, sadness which have served a purpose in our evolution, helping us to connect and stay safe, and we share with other animals behavioural repertoires including flight, fight, and freeze.

As humans, we have also evolved complex cognitive systems which have allowed us to harness the power of imagination, plan for the future, learn from the past, experience meta-cognition, and monitor ourselves amongst others. However, our 'newer brain' – these more recently developed capacities – can sometimes interact unhelpfully with our 'older brain' – the long-established motives, emotions, and behavioural repertoires outlined above, leading us to get caught in negative loops of thinking, for example. The point, says CFC, is that it is *not our fault,* it is just how our minds work.

■ *Social constructionism* (how our sense of self is shaped by our experiences in life)

Helping the client to reflect on the type of person they might have been if they had been born into different lives can help them to appreciate that they have been shaped socially by factors and events outside their control. Their lived experience will have contributed to struggles such as lack of confidence, high levels of self-criticism, low sense of self-worth, propensity for anger, aggression, anxiety, or submissiveness. Again, it is not their fault. Building awareness is not about taking away the client's agency, rather to reduce their sense of shame and self-blame. They can then be freed up to work out how to take responsibility for developing an alternative version of themselves, including how they show up in relationship.

As we explored in the last chapter, RMEC can help us as coaches to role model what 'good enough' interrelating looks like, and to support our clients to embody vulnerable, courageous, and authentic interrelating. Helping clients forgive themselves for how they have been shaped can be a brilliant first step.

■ *Our emotions are linked to basic motives and behaviours*

Drawing on the work of others, including Depue and Morrone-Strupinsky (2005), CFC/CFT suggests that we have three types of emotion regulation systems:

- *The threat and self-protection system:* This system, the most dominant, has evolved so we can identify threats and react accordingly. Its focus on the negative, including 'negative' emotions, in its bid to keep us safe, fuels our negativity bias, which helps us survive. As Rick Hanson, author of the *Buddha's Brain*, has said, "*the brain is like Velcro for negative experiences, but Teflon for positive ones. That shades 'implicit memory' – your underlying expectations, beliefs, action strategies, and mood – in an increasingly negative direction*" (Hanson, retrieved January 2023)
- *The drive, seeking, and acquisition system* has the purpose of propelling us to seek out and take advantage of resources, mobilising us to make the effort to acquire these. Emotions involved here are 'positive' emotions such as excitement
- *The contentment, soothing, and affiliative system* (which we have referred to elsewhere), which is linked with the so-called rest and digest response, sees us and other animals slow down, rest, and recover. It involves 'positive' emotional states including calmness. It is associated with the parasympathetic nervous system and facilitates experiences of safeness and soothing. As humankind has evolved, this system has enabled us to be highly attuned to others extending affection, care, and attachment

In supporting clients to understand the evolved function of emotions and how these link to basic motives and behaviours, we can also help them reflect on what happens when these get out of balance. We need to be able to access all these systems, but we can end up spending too much time in the drive, seeking, and acquisition system, for example, which can lead to overwhelm and see us 'tip over into' the threat and self-protection system. Given the role the hormone dopamine plays in this system, clients may become addicted to this way of being and may resist operating from the contentment system, which can feel dull. Yet this means they miss out on intimacy.

The consumerist society in which so many of us live can fuel a desire to keep chasing more and more, which does not help.

Meanwhile, many face intense pressure from their employers, the system and/or themselves to work long, hard hours, or are susceptible to overwhelm for other reasons. They may 'get stuck' in the threat system and may easily become defensive with others.

In both cases, we can help clients appreciate the value in operating mainly from the contentment, soothing, and affiliative system, with 'departure' into the other systems only when appropriate. We can bring in the RM guidelines implicitly or explicitly, and individual mindfulness practices to help them downregulate. This may not always be easy or even possible.

Treading carefully

Some clients may be suffering from trauma, for example, perhaps with relational causes. CFT is widely used to support people who have experienced trauma, drawing amongst others on attachment theory, offering individuals an evolutionary-based understanding of interpersonal difficulties which can be helpful (Lucre & Clapton, 2021). We would not recommend addressing trauma in coaching, but we do believe it is important for coaches to be trauma-informed (e.g. Francis, 2023; Roques, 2023). And for those psychologically informed coaches for whom working with trauma is within their capacity, CFC can offer a framework for doing so, helping to heal trauma ruptures in relationships.

Practices

In addition to psycho-education, sharing the concepts outlined above, and inviting reflection (which RMEC can support through mindful contemplations, depending on the coach's capacity level), CFC draws on a variety of practices. These seek to help clients notice and understand the impact of certain emotions, self-criticism, rumination, worry, and self-monitoring, including on how they relate to and connect with themselves and with others.

Practices include compassion-focused imagery (Gilbert, 2009; Palmer, 2009) such as imagining a compassionate other, or compassionate self, and soothing rhythm breathing. CFC aims to help people to create a different, more supportive, encouraging, and compassionate relationship with themselves (Irons et al, 2018). Building self-compassion (which we explored in Chapter 3) is key. In addition to those suggested by CFT/C, Neff (https://self-compassion.org/, accessed January 2024) and colleagues have developed many resources, many of which are free. See Box 20.3 for a few to try out:

Box 20.3 Examples of self-compassion practices

Whenever a client is (or we are) distressed, we might suggest they repeat to themselves the following words or find some similar words that feel appropriately soothing personally (Neff, 2015, p.119):

> *This is a moment of suffering*
> *Suffering is a part of life*
> *May I be kind to myself in this moment*
> *May I give myself the compassion I need*

Or we can suggest a 'hugging practice' (Neff, 2015, p.49), giving oneself a hug or some other caring and soothing touch, thus boosting the love hormone oxytocin, helping the individual to feel more secure, soothing any distressing emotions, and calming their nervous system.

We might like to try the Three Chair Dialogue: The Criticizer, The Criticised, and The Compassionate Observer, which Neff (Neff, 2015, pp.35–37) adapted from Gestalt therapy, and which invites people to get in touch with different parts of themselves which may be in conflict. (See also Chapter 19.)

One tried-and-tested practice is the three-step Self-compassion Break (Neff, 2015), which encourages mindfulness, tapping into shared common humanity, and self-kindness, which we can guide clients through.

Another coaching approach which draws on the power of cultivating 'positive' emotions, including compassion, is that proposed by Boyatzis and colleagues, which we explore below.

Coaching with compassion

Boyatzis and colleagues' evidence-based 'Coaching with compassion' model offers further compelling evidence for the effectiveness of a highly relational coaching approach rooted in compassion and mindfulness, which of course RMEC is.

As Boyatzis et al (2019, pp.129–130) say, *"inspiring, meaningful coaching moments and high-quality, trusting coaching relationships don't just happen. They take intention, preparation and practice… Effective developmental conversations are shaped by the quality of the discrete connections we form, our ability to listen deeply and remain fully present."*

Like us, Boyatzis and his colleagues (2019) believe that building resonant relationships in coaching requires the experience of mindfulness, the arousal of hope, and the demonstration of compassion, and that the relationships that help the most are characterised by shared vision and shared compassion. Van Oosten (2013) showed that the stronger the relationship to the coach was, in terms of shared vision and compassion, the greater the impact of executives' emotional and social intelligence on their effectiveness, engagement in their work, and career satisfaction.

Boyatzis et al (2019) contrast the coaching with compassion approach with a 'Coaching with compliance' approach. For Boyatzis and colleagues, compassion involves noticing another's need, empathising, and acting to increase the other's hedonic wellbeing (related to pleasure) or reduce their pain, while in response to another's desire to grow, the motivation is to increase eudemonic wellbeing (related to finding meaning and purpose) or helping them develop.

Boyatzis and colleagues (2019) adopt a broad definition of coaching with compassion as follows: *"coaching with a genuine sense of caring and concern, focusing on the other person, providing support and encouragement, and facilitating the discovery and pursuit of the person's dreams and passions*" (Boyatzis et al, 2019, p.6). They define coaching for compliance, on the other hand, as where the coach "*attempts to facilitate the person's movement toward some externally defined objective*" (Boyatzis et al, 2019, p.6). Their research over many decades shows that the latter rarely leads to sustained change for individuals, nor does it help them reach their full potential, whereas the former does.

For Boyatzis and colleagues (Boyatzis et al, 2019), the object of coaching with compassion is "*to establish a resonant relationship between the coach and the person being coached, which is crucial to creating sustained transformation*" (Boyatzis et al, 2019, p.14). They describe resonant relationships as characterised "*by (1) an overall positive emotional tone and (2) a genuine authentic connection with the person being coached. There is a sense of the flow in the relationship, with the coach being in tune with the person she is intending to help*" (Boyatzis et al, 2019, p.21). This description feels perfectly aligned with how we would describe the kind of relationships we seek to cultivate in RMEC.

The coaching with compassion approach involves stimulating 'positive' emotions, activating the parasympathetic nervous system and what proponents (e.g. Boyatzis et al, 2019) call the 'positive emotional attractor' (PEA). Their research has shown that the PEA opens up clients to possibilities and the excitement that comes with change, which is vital for change to happen, particularly lasting change. They contrast the PEA with the 'negative emotional attractor' (NEA) which is usually triggered by 'shoulds' and 'oughts', and which can hinder the process of change, greatly diminishing creativity and openness to new ideas. They suggest that in coaching, we need to emphasise the PEA state as much as possible. There is a place for the NEA, as it helps people survive, but there needs to be the right balance between the NEA and PEA.

Boyatzis et al (2019) agree that both mindfulness and compassion stimulate the PEA. Emotional contagion "*allows the coach and the person she is coaching to literally affect and infect each other with feelings of hope, compassion, mindfulness and exciting possibilities in life and work*" (Boyatzis et al, 2019, p.24).

Boyatzis' and colleagues' Intentional Change Theory (ICT) (Boyatzis, 2008, 2019) proposes that behavioural change is not linear but instead tends to occur in discontinuous bursts or 'discoveries.' They propose that five such discoveries must occur for an individual to make a sustained change in behaviour, all of which we believe RM can support. These are as follows:

- *Exploring and articulating the Ideal Self*, inviting the client to answer questions such as 'who do I really want to be?', articulating a personal and/ or shared vision. The RM guidelines Attune to emergence, Listen deeply, and Speak the truth in particular come to mind here
- *Uncovering an accurate view of their real self*, identifying where their ideal and real self are aligned and unaligned, including considering how others see them. Research by Taylor (2010) suggests that rather than gauging

self-awareness by comparing one's self-assessment to the assessment of others, a better indicator is people's prediction of how others see them compared with how people actually see them

- *Crafting a learning agenda*
- *Experimenting and practising new behaviours*
- *Cultivating resonant relationships and social identity groups* – in addition to the coach, the client is encouraged to have a network of resonant supportive relationships, "*although emotional and social intelligence is needed at every stage in coaching, establishing and maintaining resonant relationships is perhaps the most crucial*" (Boyatzis, 2019, p.43)

Boyatzis and colleagues' approach highlights the importance of asking questions that invite reflection and uncover what is most important and meaningful to the individual, and of building hope. One fMRI study carried out by Boyatzis and colleagues showed that spending 30 minutes talking about someone's vision or dream activates their brain regions associated with imagining new things and creates more activity in the parasympathetic nervous system, which is associated with emotions such as awe, gratitude, and curiosity (Boyatzis et al, 2019).

Even when people are in touch with a deep sense of meaning and purpose, they argue, unless they also feel hope about achieving the future they envision, they will find it hard to move forward. This brings to mind the mindful contemplations an RMEC coach at later capacity levels might introduce into coaching, or at the very least a spacious mindful space for enquiry infused by the RM guidelines.

In the next chapter, we explore more approaches that help to develop wisdom and insight in ourselves and our clients.

References

Acharya, S., & Shukla, S. (2012). Mirror neurons: Enigma of the metaphysical modular brain. *Journal of Natural Science, Biology and Medicine*, 3(2), 118–124.

Ainsworth, M. S., & Bowlby, J. (1991). An ethological approach to personality development. *American Psychologist*, 46(4), 333.

Baer, R. A., Smith, G. T., Hopkins, J., Krietemeyer, J., & Toney, L. (2006). Using self-report assessment methods to explore facets of mindfulness. *Assessment*, 13(1), 27–45.

Begley, S. (2007). *Train your mind, change your brain*. Ballantine Books.

Bericat, E. (2016). The sociology of emotions: Four decades of progress. *Current Sociology*, 64(3), 491–513.

Brown, B. (2021). *Atlas of the heart: Mapping meaningful connection and the language of human experience*. Random House.

Bolton, N. (July 2023). *The Gestalt Cycle of experience: An emergent approach to change in coaching*. Animas Centre for Coaching, www.animascoaching.com/blog/gestalt-cycle-of-experience/

Bowlby, J. (1969), *Attachment and loss: Attachment*. Hogarth.

Bowlby, J. (1988). During the first third of this century there were two great proponents of developmental psychiatry–Adolf Meyer and Sigmund Freud. Both believed that. *The American Journal of Psychiatry*, 145, 1–10.

Boyatzis, R. (2008). Leadership development from a complexity perspective. *Consulting Psychology Journal Practice and Research*, 60(4):298–313. doi: 10.1037/1065-9293.60.4.298

Boyatzis, R. E. (2019). Coaching with intentional change theory. In *Professional coaching: Principles and practice*, 221–230. Springer Publishing Company.

Brach, T. (2021). Compassion in Therapy Summit online. www.coaching-at-work.com/2021/03/02/the-pain-and-reward-of-compassion/

Brown, B. (2019). Brené Brown's Netflix special busts six vulnerability myths. *Psychology Today*. www.psychologytoday.com/intl/blog/shyness-is-nice/201905/bren-browns-netflix-special-busts-six-vulnerability-myths

Brown, B. (2021). *Atlas of the heart: Mapping meaningful connection and the language of human experience*. Random House.

Cameron, C. D., & Fredrickson, B. L. (2015). Mindfulness facets predict helping behavior and distinct helping-related emotions. *Mindfulness*, 6, 1211–1218.

Chughtai, A. A., & Buckley, F. (2013). Exploring the impact of trust on research scientists' work engagement: Evidence from Irish science research centres. *Personnel Review*, 42(4), 396–421.

Conway, A. M., Tugade, M. M., Catalino, L. I., & Fredrickson, B. L. (2013). The broaden-and-build theory of positive emotions: Form, function and mechanisms. In *The Oxford handbook of happiness*, 17–34. Oxford University Press.

Covey, S. R. (1989). *The 7 habits of highly effective people: An extraordinary step-by-step guide to achieving the human characteristics that really create success*. Simon and Schuster.

Cozolino, L. (2006). *The neuroscience of human relationships: Attachment and the developing brain*. W.W. Norton.

Cozolino, L. (retrieved January 2023). Survival of the nurtured. Dr Lou Cozolino website. (excerpt from book, www.drloucozolino.com/trauma/survival-of-the-nurtured).

Cox, E., & Dannahy, P. (2005). The value of openness in e-relationships: Using Nonviolent Communication to guide online coaching and mentoring. *International Journal of Evidence Based Coaching and Mentoring*. 3 (1), 39–51.

David, S. (2016). *Emotional agility: Get unstuck, embrace change, and thrive in work and life*. Penguin.

Davidson, R. (2021). Compassion in Therapy Summit online. www.coaching-at-work.com/2021/03/02/the-pain-and-reward-of-compassion/

Deiorio, N. M., Moore, M., Santen, S. A., Gazelle, G., Dalrymple, J. L., & Hammoud, M. (2022). Coaching models, theories, and structures: An overview for teaching faculty in the emergency department and educators in the offices. *AEM Education and Training*, 6(5), e10801.

Drake, D. (2012). Great pretenders. *Coaching at Work*. May/June. www.coaching-at-work.com/2012/05/02/great-pretenders/

Drake, D. B. (2009). Using attachment theory in coaching leaders: The search for a coherent narrative. *International Coaching Psychology Review*, 4(1), 49–58.

Ekman, P. (2016). What scientists who study emotion agree about. *Perspectives on Psychological Science*, 11(1), 31–34.

Edmondson, A., (2018), *The fearless organization*. John Wiley & Sons.

Figley, C. (1995). *Compassion Fatigue: Coping with secondary traumatic stress disorder in those who treat the traumatized*. Brunner-Routledge.

Francis, T. (2023). Trauma and coaching: blind spot. Coaching at Work, March/April. www.coaching-at-work.com/2023/03/02/trauma-and-coaching-blind-spot/

Fredrickson, B. L. (1998). What good are positive emotions?. *Review of General Psychology*, 2(3), 300–319.

Fredrickson, B. L. (2001). The role of positive emotions in positive psychology: The broaden-and-build theory of positive emotions. *American Psychologist*, 56(3), 218.

Fredrickson, B. L. (2004). The broaden–and–build theory of positive emotions. *Philosophical Transactions of the Royal Society of London. Series B: Biological Sciences*, 359(1449), 1367–1377.

Fredrickson, B. (2013). *Love 2.0*. Hudson Street Press.

Frederickson, B. (retrieved November, 2024). www.peplab.web.unc.edu/research/

Fredrickson, B. L., Cohn, M. A., Coffey, K. A., Pek, J., & Finkel, S. M. (2008). Open hearts build lives: Positive emotions, induced through loving-kindness meditation, build consequential personal resources. *Journal of Personality and Social Psychology*, 95(5), 1045.

Fredrickson, B. L., Boulton, A. J., Firestine, A. M., Van Cappellen, P., Algoe, S. B., Brantley, M. M., … , & Salzberg, S. (2017). Positive emotion correlates of meditation practice: A comparison of mindfulness meditation and loving-kindness meditation. *Mindfulness*, 8, 1623–1633.

Gilbert, P. (2009). Introducing compassion-focused therapy. *Advances in Psychiatric Treatment*, 15(3), 199–208.

Gilbert, P., & Simos, G. (Eds.). (2022). *Compassion focused therapy: Clinical practice and applications*. Routledge.

Hall, L. (2011). Narratives begin in childhood. *Coaching at Work*, 6, 2.

Hall, L. (2021a). The pain and reward of compassion. *Coaching at Work*, 16(2), 10–11.

Hall, L. (2021b). A promise to you - a profile of Nancy Kline. *Coaching at Work*, 16, 3.

Hanh, T. N. (2006). *Reconciliation: Healing the inner child*. Parallax Press.

Hanh, T. N. (2011). *Anger: Buddhist wisdom for cooling the flames*. Random House.

Hanh, T. N. (2022). Loving speech and deep listening (transcript). Plum Village app. https://plumvillage.app/loving-speech-and-deep-listening-transcript/

Hanson, R., retrieved January 2023. Take in the good. Rick Hansen website. www.rickhanson.net/take-in-the-good/

Hasson, U., Ghazanfar, A. A., Galantucci, B., Garrod, S., & Keysers, C. (2012). Brain-to-brain coupling: a mechanism for creating and sharing a social world. *Trends in Cognitive Science*, 16(2), 114–121.

Heardman, P. (2017). What's love got to do with it? *Coaching at Work*, 12, 3.

Huang, C. C., & Jiang, P. C. (2012). Exploring the psychological safety of R&D teams: An empirical analysis in Taiwan. *Journal of Management & Organization*, 18(2), 175–192.

Irons, C., Palmer, S., & Hall, L. (2018). Compassion focused coaching. In *Handbook of coaching psychology: A guide for practitioners* (2nd ed.). Routledge.

Kimsey-House, H., Kimsey-House, K., Sandahl, P., Whitworth, L., & Phillips, A. (2018). *Co-active coaching: The proven framework for transformative conversations at work and in life*. Hachette UK.

Klimecki, O. M., Leiberg, S., Lamm, C., & Singer, T. (2013). Functional neural plasticity and associated changes in positive affect after compassion training. *Cerebral cortex*, 23(7), 1552–1561.

Kline, N. (1999). *Time to think: Listening to ignite the human mind*. Hachette UK.

Kline, N. (2009). *More time to think: A way of being in the world*. Fisher King Publishing.

Kline, N. (2020). *The Promise that changes everything: I won't interrupt you*. Penguin UK.

Lawrence, P. (2020). Learning to listen. August 2020. Centre for Coaching in Organisations.

Lawrence, P. (2021). The 5th way to listen. June 2021. Centre for Coaching in Organisations.

Lucre, K., & Clapton, N. (2021). The compassionate Kitbag: A creative and integrative approach to compassion-focused therapy. *Psychology and Psychotherapy: Theory, Research and Practice*, 94, 497–516.

May, D. R., Gilson, R. L., & Harter, L. M. (2004). The psychological conditions of meaningfulness, safety and availability and the engagement of the human spirit at work. *Journal of Occupational and Organizational Psychology*, 77(1), 11–37.

McGonigal, K. (2021). Quoting from her book, The Upside of Stress (Vermillion, 2015), speaking at the 2021 Compassion in Therapy Summit, quoted in *Coaching at Work* (2021). www.coaching-at-work.com/2021/03/02/the-pain-and-reward-of-com passion/

Mikulincer, M., & Florian, V. (1998). The relationship between adult attachment styles and emotional and cognitive reactions to stressful events. In J. A. Simpson & W. S. Rholes (Eds.), *Attachment theory and close relationships*, 143–165. Guilford Press.

Mikulincer M., & Shaver P.R. (2007), *Attachment in adulthood: Structure, dynamics, and change*. Guilford Press.

Mikulincer, M., & Shaver, P. R. (2008). Adult attachment and affect regulation. In J. Cassidy & P. R. Shaver (Eds.), *Handbook of attachment: Theory, research and clinical applications* (2nd ed.), 503–531. Guilford Press.

Moore, M., Tschannen-Moran, B., Silvero, G., & Rhode, R. (2010). Nonviolent communication and motivational interviewing in coaching. In *Coaching psychology manual*, 63–73. Wellcoaches®.

Neff, K. D. (2003). The development and validation of a scale to measure self-compassion. *Self and Identity*, 2(3), 223–250.

Neff, K. (2015). *Self-compassion: Stop beating yourself up and leave insecurity behind*. Yellow Kite Books (Hodder & Stoughton).

Palmer, S. (2009). Compassion-focused imagery for use within compassion focused coaching. *Coaching Psychology International*, 2(2). Available at SSRN: https://ssrn.com/abstract=1525814 or http://dx.doi.org/10.2139/ssrn.1525814

Remen, R. N., & Wisdom, K. T. (1996). *Stories that heal*, 217–219. Riverhead Books.

Roques, A. (2023). Post-traumatic growth. *Coaching at Work*. 18(3). 32–36 www.coach ing-at-work.com/2023/04/30/post-traumatic-growth/

Rosenberg, M. S. (2015). *Nonviolent communication: A language of life* (3rd ed.). Puddle Dancer Press.

Rosenberg, M. (2024). Center for Nonviolent Communication website, accessed January 2024. www.cnvc.org

Rozovsky, J. (2015). Five keys to a successful team. *The Water Cooler*.

Scharmer, S. (2018). How are you listening as a leader. Medium. https://medium.com/presencing-institute-blog/how-are-you-listening-as-a-leader-a1acdbea5cbf

Siegel, D. J. (2007). *The mindful brain: Reflection and attunement in the cultivation of well-being*. W.W. Norton.

Siegel, D. J. (2010). *The mindful therapist: A clinician's guide to mindsight and neural integration*. W. W. Norton & Company.

Singer, T., & Klimecki, O. M. (2014). Empathy and compassion. *Current Biology*, 24(18), R875–R878.

Taylor, S. N. (2010). Redefining leader self-awareness by integrating the second component of self-awareness. *Journal of Leadership Studies*, 3(4), 57–68.

Stevenson, J. C., Emerson, L. M., & Millings, A. (2017). The relationship between adult attachment orientation and mindfulness: A systematic review and meta-analysis. *Mindfulness*, 8, 1438–1455.

Van Cappellen, P., Catalino, L. I., & Fredrickson, B. L. (2020). A new micro-intervention to increase the enjoyment and continued practice of meditation. *Emotion*, 20(8), 1332.

Van Oosten, E. B. (2013). *The impact of emotional intelligence and executive coaching on leader effectiveness*. Case Western Reserve University.

Winnicott, D. W. (1965). A clinical study of the effect of a failure of the average expectable environment on a child's mental functioning. *The International Journal of Psycho-Analysis*, 46, 81.

Information

Dedicated website accompanying this book: www.relationalmindfulness.net

Chapter 21

Insight and wisdom

Out beyond ideas of wrongdoing and rightdoing,
there is a field. I'll meet you there.
When the soul lies down in that grass,
the world is too full to talk about.
Ideas, language, even the phrase 'each other'
doesn't make any sense.

Rumi

As coaches, we often speak about aiming to help our clients gain more insight, or even cultivating wisdom. It seems we are not alone: a quick search online (February 2024) for 'wisdom in coaching' brought up 310,000 results, including Webb (2020) and Kilburg (2000).

We have explored at various points in this book how Relational Mindfulness (RM) can help us, as coaches, access greater awareness, insight and wisdom and support our clients to do so too. Indeed, for coaches, the potential for cultivating insight is perhaps one of the most tantalising benefits of RM, as Emma has previously pointed out (Donaldson-Feilder, 2020).

As we have seen, RM encourages in-the-moment shared exploration and questioning of assumptions, habits, patterns, meaning-making, and other aspects of our experience of being human, supporting triple loop learning (which we explore very briefly below). RM helps us and our clients to broaden our perspectives and get better at living with paradox and handling complexity, interdependence, uncertainty, and ambiguity. In short, it helps us become wiser and more insightful, which is desperately needed in these times, as we explore in Chapter 23 when we step back to look at the wider picture.

DOI: 10.4324/9781003390428-26

In this chapter, we explore the following models and theories that can help us gain greater understanding of wisdom and insight. And we look at how to integrate them into our coaching, supporting and aligning with Relational-Mindfulness-Enhanced Coaching (RMEC) and vice versa:

- ▪ Vertical development
- ▪ Theory U
- ▪ Parts work

Before we delve into the models, we want to pause to contemplate what we mean by wisdom and insight.

Exploring wisdom and insight

Germer and Siegel (2012) define wisdom as "*simply knowing deeply how to live*" (p.21). For many, however, wisdom is along the lines of *The Cambridge Dictionary's* (accessed January 2024) definition of wisdom as "*the ability to use your knowledge and experience to make good decisions and judgments.*"

In the context of RMEC, we draw on knowledge and expertise including of coaching, mindfulness, and RM. Yet, wisdom is really about seeing things as they are right now, not through our own filters and biases, our attachment wounds and traumas, or from the socialised mind. As Kramer (2007) says, "*Interpersonal nondelusion, and its active expression as interpersonal wisdom, manifest in relationships as compassion, skilfulness, and perceptivity...One sees oneself, others, and the social situation as they are*" (p.63).

At times, knowledge and expertise, or at least our or our clients' attachment to these, can even get in the way of wisdom arising. In RMEC, wisdom is about letting go, trusting emergence, and letting compassion flow. We seek to drop our attachment to getting it 'right', dancing instead in the ebbs and flow of impermanence and emergence. We realise we cannot 'know' everything as everything is constantly changing. We embrace the interrelatedness of wisdom and compassion that we have noted before, such as in Chapter 2. To quote Kramer again (2007), "*When wisdom encounters others, it manifests as compassion. Interpersonal wisdom is compassion, together with unshakably knowing the empty nature of social self-concept*" (p.74).

One way we can expand our capacity to be wise, holding knowledge increasingly lightly is through vertical development, which we now explore.

Vertical development

Unlike horizontal development, which is about gaining new skills and competencies and acquiring more knowledge and information, vertical development is about gaining new mindsets, insights and practices, and sometimes unlearning too, to shift and expand thinking, behaviour, and way of being. Horizontal development is rather like adding new apps and programmes to a computer operating system, while vertical development is more like upgrading the entire operating system so it can cope with more complexity and demands. And then potentially doing this again and again through a series of overlapping 'stages.'

Adult development theory is complex, and models/frameworks abound. What they have in common is an assumption that it is not just children who go through developmental stages, but adults too, with shifts over time in adults' moral reasoning and meaning-making, amongst other aspects (e.g. Kegan, 1982; Fisher and Torbert, 1991; Graves, 1970; Cook-Greuter, 1999; Wilber, 2000; O'Fallon, 2020).

Bachkirova and Cox (2018) identify two developmental dimensions: cognitive-reflective – the degree of the complexity of thought and reflective judgement – with origins in Piaget's (1976) work and others; and ego-development, with origins in Loevinger (Hauser, 1976) and which focuses on the development of self-identity, maturity of interpersonal relationships, and engagement in action (Kegan, 1982; 1994; Cook-Greuter, 2004; Bachkirova, 2011, 2014).

Each developmental stage represents increasingly complex emotional and mental capacities and involves certain sense-making processes, which structure into patterns of action and coherent worldviews. These are called Action Logics in Torbert and Rooke's framework (2005). Our Action Logic impacts our ability to make sense of our experiences, solve problems, and interact with our environment, including in our relationships. Each evolution offers the potential for more choice, flexibility, and capacity for transforming.

Meaning-making influences people's development in at least three core areas (Harthill Consulting, accessed January 2024):

- Self-awareness
- Developing oneself, others, and relationships
- How to lead well within complex systems

Learning loops

With vertical development, and in RMEC, we are concerned primarily with triple loop learning (e.g. Flood & Romm, 1996), drawing on the work of Argyris and Schön (Argyris, 1977, Argyris & Schön, 1997) on double loop learning.

Single loop learning is when someone gathers information and knowledge to improve their competence and reflects on the outcomes of their actions, making adjustments to behaviour, tactics and skills as appropriate, and potentially leading to expertise (Kolb, 1984). As RMEC coaches, we can step up our expertise in bringing RM into coaching through single-loop learning to some degree, and there are times when single-loop learning is appropriate to support clients' goals. However, single-loop learning is highly limited in its potential for transformation. It does not allow for making sense and acting in a world with wildly varying perspectives and blindspots; it does not help us shift mindsets.

Shifting mindsets requires double-loop learning (Argyris & Schön, 1997), where we encourage the client to reflect on patterns and assumptions, not only learning but thinking about learning, and making any necessary corrections. This is not easy given the filters we all have in place individually and collectively. Group-think is often alive and kicking, with collective resistance to seeing, let alone addressing, uncomfortable issues. If someone does speak up, as the proverbial canary in the mine, they can be scapegoated.

Triple-loop learning goes much deeper, exploring issues such as what is behind our motivation, what our purpose and values are. It is about changing how we think and behave, shifting our way of doing and our way of being. If there is collective engagement in triple-loop learning, groups and organisations benefit from diversity of thinking (Flood & Rohm, 1996).

Triple-loop learning is what many coaching programmes promise, yet they do not always deliver – change is hard! RMEC makes no promises; however, in our experience, it can indeed support transformational shifts, as we saw in the case study in Chapter 18. And bringing in a vertical development lens can be very helpful, as can bringing in mindfulness when exploring through this framework.

Vertical development, coaching, and mindfulness

Coaching is well-established as a means to develop vertically (e.g. Petrie, 2015; Berger & Atkins, 2009). As Petrie says (2015), *"In many ways, coaching can be the ultimate vertical practice as it pulls on nearly all the levers of development (heat challenges, different perspectives, and new mapmaking)"* (p.18).

So too is mindfulness meditation (e.g. Petrie, 2015, Wilber, 2016, Frizzell & Banner, 2018 and Frizzell, 2015). To quote Petrie again (2015, p.20)*"There are few practices that produce as many benefits on as many levels (physical, mental, emotional, spiritual) as mindfulness and meditation…From a vertical perspective, the regular practice of turning inward and observing one's own thoughts helps leaders observe the constant process of their own mean-making."*

Many point to the power of an approach combining mindfulness with coaching when it comes to vertical development (Lee, 2021; Chaskalson & McMordie, 2017; Petrie, 2015; Siminovitch, 2018) which aligns with our experience too. Adamson and Brendgen (2021) highlight how supervision drawing on RM can support vertical development. Just as it matters which stage of meaning-making a client is at, the coach's or coach supervisor's stage of development is relevant (Bachkirova & Cox (2018). If we are operating from a later stage of development, we can *"offer up new and higher frames of thinking for the person to try on"* (Petrie, 2015, p.18).

Creating conditions for growth, insight, and wisdom

Petrie sets out conditions that can act as levers for vertical development:

■ *Accessing heat experiences (the 'what' that initiates the development)*

Some of the most intense heat experiences can come from being in relationship. Staying with discomfort, being courageous, and turning towards difficulty in relationships can offer significant developmental stretches. As RMEC coaches, we can draw on the power of mindfulness to help us and our clients be better able to sit with difficult emotions, which can point to where an individual is up against a developmental edge, where they are being 'had by' something. We can then support clients to identify appropriate new ways of being.

Not running away from feelings and emotions allows us the best chance of harnessing learning and growth opportunities, while doing the opposite can mean we regress developmentally (Anagnostakis, 2023).

■ *Colliding perspectives (the 'who' that enable the development)*

This includes peer coaching, engaging in frame-breaking experiences, stepping into another worldview – deep listening – and holding two opposing ideas in our minds, polarity thinking: moving from either/or thinking to 'both/and' thinking (Petrie, 2015).

RMEC can help clients simply be with the 'both/and', avoiding black and white thinking. It can also help us and clients be more open to the potential wisdom of other perspectives without feeling threatened, helping us to avoid 'othering.' Practising deep listening is *"one of the most direct ways"* to *"go against the grain of our brain and instead stretch to take on more perspectives"*, which is what is needed for development to take place (Petrie, 2015, p.15).

As we have explored, mindfulness can help us be less reactive when we are exposed to perspectives that are different to ours, and even to start to question who and what 'we' are. As Petrie (2015) says, *"Stick with (mindfulness and meditation) long enough and you start to notice that who you think 'you' are is mainly just a story you are constructing and reconstructing moment to moment"* (p.20).

Developing a systems perspective is another aspect of expanding perspectives. Here there is plenty of potential for RM to help individuals build positive relationships with key stakeholders, reducing the risk of blaming and othering, instead rising above interpersonal biases and boosting the chance of collaboration. All the RM guidelines can help, particularly Open (to others), Attune to Emergence (trusting what lies beyond petty egos), Listen deeply (to ourselves and our needs, to others and their needs), and Speak the truth (being courageous, ensuring we speak not just for ourselves but for others and the system, and only doing so if this is appropriate, compassionate and wise).RM, and mindfulness in general, can help us and our clients remain grounded when our world view is challenged, which can be highly discombobulating, particularly in certain stage shifts.

- *Elevated sensemaking (the 'how' – integrating the development)*

  This includes learning from the 'gurus', using vertical development 'stage maps', coaching with a vertical lens, making sense with a late-stage mentor, and teaching mindfulness and meditation (Petrie, 2015). RM can support us and our clients to engage with this integration both through the meta-perspective it encourages and through supporting authentic and open-hearted engagement with others.

Different stages

We will not explore different developmental stage maps in this chapter, given space constraints. However, we do want to highlight differences in how we might coach clients profiling at different stages, and for the purposes of that, we explore through Torbert and Rooke's (2005) framework. In this framework, the stages that most correspond to adult development are as follows: Opportunist, Diplomat, Expert, Achiever (all which classify as 'conventional' meaning-making) and Individualist, Strategist, Alchemist, and Ironist ('post-conventional' meaning-making).

The later the post-conventional stage, the fewer people there will be who have 'evolved' to that stage. In Harthill's mixed international sample of 10,000 professional profiles, 13% profiled as Expert, 53% as Achiever, 26% as Individualist, and 7% as Strategist. Only 1% profiled as Alchemist.

Note to readers: We are *not* saying that later stages of development are always necessarily better, or appropriate – but we are suggesting that the more variety of meaning-making there is, the more choice we have individually and collectively in how we respond. And that we do need a mass of people, particularly leaders, who have greater capacity for complexity, for self- and other-awareness, and so on, to meet the challenges we face. Often, the metaphor of the Russian doll with a number of doll sizes nestled within is used to point to how as we develop, we can add more Action Logics to choose from, whilst not rejecting earlier meaning-making. There may be times when earlier meaning-making makes the most sense in a particular context. There is also a school of thought – one which one of my (Liz) vertical development supervisors, Ian Mitchell, proposes as a possibility – that suggests that as we expand and nuance our meaning-making, so too can our shadow become more sophisticated. Yikes! As Mitchell in one of our group supervision sessions said so eloquently, "*just because someone has profiled as Alchemist, doesn't mean they're not an a******e!*" For us, this again highlights the contribution that RM can make here, not only helping people develop vertically, but helping them to build compassion and wisdom so that they show up ethically and can work with their shadow material.

As coaches we are most likely to encounter clients profiling at Expert, Achiever, and Individualist stages, with some perhaps at Strategist stage. And this is likely to be mirrored pretty much when it comes to the developmental stage of coaches. However, given the potency of both mindfulness and coaching to support vertical development, promoting greater awareness and insight, we hypothesise that a higher proportion of RMEC coaches compared to all coaches will potentially profile at later stages.

Bachkirova and Cox (2018) offer a six-level earlier-to-late developmental stage model of coach development: the Teller, the Helper, the Questioner, the Acceptor, the Cultivator, and the Playwright. The latter three seemingly correspond respectively to Individualist, Strategist and Alchemist in Torbert and Rooke's framework.

Bachkirova and Cox (2018) identify stage-specific patterns of working with clients as well as developmental tasks coaches might be most equipped for. For example, at the Cultivator stage, the coach has a systems view of reality, accepts the shadow, is aware of mutual interdependency and its role in individual development, and takes responsibility for relationship and helping others grow. Their working pattern includes exploring the self and coming to terms with conflicting needs. However, they may be impatient with slowness of the growth of others. As well as boosting awareness in general, RM may help coaches profiling at this stage be more patient with others who are at earlier stages of meaning-making!

When it comes to introducing mindfulness explicitly to clients, having a sense of their meaning-making can be helpful. Individuals and teams profiling at Achiever stage, for example, will tend to be impatient when it comes to slowing down to reflect (Torbert & Rooke, 2005). There may be some resistance to mindfulness as it may be perceived as getting in the way of getting things done. However, if it is possible to introduce clients profiling at this stage to mindfulness, this will help them be more reflective, and to develop their capacity for self-experiencing, building awareness, and connection. Developing awareness of self and other worldviews is particularly key to vertical development beyond Achiever action logic, which requires a different approach to that necessary to bring about the Expert-to-Achiever transformation (Torbert & Rooke, 2005).

As we expand our meaning-making, we are likely to become more in touch with the interconnectedness of all things, including in our relationships. For the Alchemist or the Playwright, reality is understood as undivided unity, truth as ever illusive because all thoughts are constructed, and language is inevitably used for mapping of reality. Playwrights are self-critical about their own ego-attachments, and not only understand others in developmental terms but are able to express genuine compassion and adjustment to the individual's ways of meaning-making. Their working pattern will include empathetic listening, and "*transformational non-distorted feedback*" (Bachkirova & Cox, 2018, p.556). Bachkirova and Cox (2018) suggest that coaching topics or tasks here might include working with conflict around existential paradoxes and creating a new story of one's life.

I and Thou

The capacity to see beyond 'self' is one which grows as we expand our meaning-making. This brings to mind the work of philosopher Martin Buber (Buber, 1970), who distinguishes between two modes of existence or perception: I-Thou and I-It. He suggests we see ourselves as 'it' or 'I' and others as 'it' or 'thou.' With I-It, we are more likely to objectify the other, which can in extreme cases lead to exploitation. Buber believed humankind was losing its ability to orient towards the Thou (Martin & Cowan, 2019).

For Buber, the concept of Thou refers to people as unbounded beings, parts of the universe they inhabit, and when two people engage with each other authentically in the present moment, they can tap into a relational dimension Buber called the 'in-between' (Martin & Cowan, 2019). When this in-between dimension is called forth, the relationship becomes greater than the individual contributions of the parties involved. This is what Buber described as an I-Thou relationship, characterised by mutuality, directness, presentness, intensity, and ineffability, one in which the uniqueness and separateness of the other is acknowledged without obscuring the relatedness or common humanness that is shared (Martin & Cowan, 2019, p.47). Buber believed that our innate capacity to 'confirm' others – participating with and accepting another's essential being – and to be confirmed in one's own uniqueness by others is the source of our humanity (Martin & Cowan, 2019).

In many cultures, seeing the other not only as the other, but as part of the whole is embedded, for example, in South Africa's concept of Ubuntu. In the Zulu language, the greeting *Sawubona* (plural, *Sanibonani*) means "*I see you, I see all that you are and what you represent.*"

Another theory which helps shift sense-making, and evolve consciousness, accessing deeper wisdom and insight, is Theory U, which we look at next.

Theory U

Otto Scharmer, senior lecturer at Massachusetts Institute of Technology (MIT), developed the method and framework of Theory U and Presencing to explore how we learn and lead in times of disruption when we cannot rely on the experiences of the past.

Theory U (Scharmer, 2018) is an awareness-based method for changing systems, which blends systems thinking, innovation, and leading change from the viewpoint of an evolving human consciousness. It offers a tried-and-tested methodology to support mindful exploration by individuals and the collective, enhancing individuals', groups', and the system's capacity to listen deeply and see themselves. Its approach is in part mindfulness-based and thus aligns well with RMEC, and vice versa.

The Presencing Institute was founded in 2006 by Scharmer and colleagues to create an action research platform at the intersection of science, consciousness, and profound individual, social, and organisational change, while the u-school for Transformation is a platform and network of partners that supports capacity-building, research, action labs, and movement-building for the advancement of awareness-based systems change to address the critical social and environmental challenges of our times.

Theory U integrates a range of methods and lineages for effecting change, including mindfulness:

- *Action research and organisational learning* in the tradition of Peter Senge, Ed Schein, Donald Schoen, Chris Argyris, and Kurt Lewin
- *Civil society movements* in the tradition of Martin Luther King Jr., Nelson Mandela, Mahatma Gandhi, and millions of others who are mobilising change in their local contexts
- *Design thinking* in the tradition of Tim Brown and Dave Kelly
- *Mindfulness, cognition science, and phenomenology* in the tradition of Francisco Varela, Jon Kabat-Zinn, Tanja Singer, Arthur Zajonc, and David Bohm

At its core, Theory U (U-school for transformation, accessed November 2024) comprises three main elements:

- *A framework for seeing the blind spot of leadership and systems change*: the 'interior condition' from which we operate
- *A method for implementing awareness-based change:* practical methods and tools for change makers, with a focus on building the collective capacity to shift the inner place from which we operate
- *A new narrative for evolutionary societal change*: updating our mental and institutional operating systems to redesign society in ways that address the pressing challenges of our time, and to apply the power of mindfulness and awareness to the transformation of the collective system

Theory U seeks to draw our attention to what it sees as the invisible source dimension of the social field, to the quality of relationships that we have with each other, the system, and ourselves. In this it supports the access to profound wisdom, for individuals and for the collective.

The U

Theory U is thus called because the methodology and framework is represented in the form of a U, mapping out a journey down one side to the bottom of the U, then up the other side, moving from open mind to open heart (beyond the habitual ego to the eco-system) to open will (courage to engage). Below is the journey (Scharmer, 2008), with some thoughts about where RM might fit in.

Going down means moving through:

■ *Suspending* (downloading past patterns) – holding the space for listening to others, oneself and what emerges from the collective (the RM guidelines support listening deeply), to

■ *Redirecting* (observing) – suspending the 'voice of judgement' (RM is supportive here too, helping us to let go of past patterns and critical voices). Suspending this voice means shutting down the habit of judging based on past experience, opening up a new space of inquiry and wonder. Without suspending this voice, argues Theory U, any attempts to get inside the places of most potential will be futile, then to

■ *Sensing* from the field and connecting with the heart, letting go (RM helps us open, and listen to our heart, and to let go) before reaching the bottom of the U, which is

■ *Presencing* (the blending of sensing and presence) – connecting to the 'source' of the highest future possibility and bringing it into the now. Scharmer (accessed February 2024) says presencing happens when our perception begins to come from the source of our emerging future (the RM guideline, Attune to emergence is helpful here). The boundaries between three types of presence collapse: the presence of the past (current field), the presence of the future (the emerging field of the future), and the presence of one's authentic Self. Scharmer describes how when this co-presence, or merging of the three types of presence, begins to resonate, we experience a profound shift, a change of the place from which we operate. In essence, the difference is about a shift of the heart on the level of the individual and the collective.

Then moving up the other side of the U to bring forth into the world whatever has emerged, going through:

■ *Crystallising*, accessing the power of intention, letting come, to
■ *Prototyping*, enacting, linking head, heart and hand, to
■ *Performing*, operating from the whole

According to Theory U, the process of letting go (of our old ego and current self) and letting come (our highest future possibility) establishes a subtle connection to a deeper source of knowing, of wisdom. These two selves meet at the bottom of the U and begin to listen to and resonate with each other. And then individuals and the group they are in, if the framework is used in a collective setting, can function as an intentional vehicle for an emerging future.

RMEC is perfectly placed to accompany an individual, group, or team to move with attention and awareness around the U, supporting the development of the capacities outlined above, particularly holding the space, observing, sensing, and presencing. The RM guidelines, particularly Attune to Emergence, support an opening to what wants to unfold, to a letting go of assumptions, to trusting the wisdom of the system.

Another element of Theory U's approach is Social Presencing Theater (SPT), which was developed by Arawana Hayashi, who has a background in the arts, meditation, and social justice, with colleagues at the Presencing Institute. SPT offers somatic and mindful practices which help to make visible both current reality and emerging future possibilities for individuals and groups, and which can easily be combined with RM or drawn on in RMEC.

Finally, we explore parts work, in particular Internal Family Systems (IFS), another systemic approach which can help us gain insight and wisdom about ourselves, others, and how we interrelate.

Parts work

The concept of multiplicity – that we contain lots of different 'sub-personalities' – is core to coaching approaches such as transpersonal and psychosynthesis coaching, and coaching informed by IFS.

As RMEC coaches, an appreciation of multiplicity as the inherent nature of the human mind can act as a gateway to greater insight generally and into how we show up in coaching and other relationships. Being open to multiplicity, to parts work, offers the potential for individual and relational healing, supporting greater connection, which can help co-create fertile conditions for effective outcomes through RMEC. In turn, we can adapt practices from RMEC (depending on our familiarity with and experience of RM) to support parts work, drawing on deep listening, for example. As Naomi Remen (Remen & Wisdom, 1996) writes, "*When we listen, we offer with our attention an opportunity for wholeness. Our listening creates sanctuary for the homeless parts within the other person. That which has been denied, unloved, devalued by themselves and by others*" (p.220).

We focus here just on IFS to get an idea of how RMEC and parts work in coaching can be mutually supportive.

Internal family systems

IFS is an evidence-based therapeutic model developed over four decades by Richard Schwartz, which assumes and seeks to de-pathologise the multi-part personality. It is increasingly being adapted for coaching (e.g. Rydings, 2022).

If we call to mind a dilemma we have faced, we will probably have heard at least one part urging us to go for it, and at least one other telling us not to, even if we are unfamiliar with parts work. Approaches such as IFS make what is going on behind the scenes more explicit.

IFS values our parts and assumes they all have a positive intention, although their 'burdens' may sometimes mean they seem harmful and destructive. IFS also believes that we each have an agenda-less 'Wise Self.' The qualities we seek to access and cultivate in RM are very much the qualities that, in IFS terms, we see in the Wise Self, which Schwartz describes as *"an essence of calm, clarity, compassion, and connectedness"* (2021, p.1).

IFS coaching can help parts feel safe, and to relieve themselves of their burdens, trusting the curious, compassionate Self, and assuming or returning to valuable constructive roles, with the person's 'internal family system' becoming more balanced and harmonious.

A note on Self: Those of us who have been meditating for some time, if we have turned our minds to finding the self, are likely to have found it rather elusive. Many Buddhist teachings invite us to explore, for example, where the self is located – is it in our feet, our hands, our chest, and so on – with the aim of highlighting that it seems impossible to locate a solid Self, that we will not be able to locate a Self residing permanently in any part of our body. Just as we hold the concept of a solid 'self' lightly in RMEC, we equally hold the idea of rigid parts with lightness.

Types of parts

In IFS, there are three types of parts:

- *Managers,* who are 'protectors', are focused on avoiding difficult experiences. They run our lives, often very effectively, but have tough methods such as the inner critic, and may be rigid in their views. They include parts such as the planner, the striver, the caregiver, the over-functioner, the judge of self and others, and the hypervigilator
- *Firefighters,* also 'protectors', step in when managers are struggling. Rydings (2022) tends to refer to them in coaching as 'reactors' or 'distractors', which describes their main strategies. These include avoidance, distraction, binge-eating, substance misuse, and disassociation
- *Exiles:* psychologically we split from our most painful experiences, particularly if these were when we were young. In coaching, we can refer to these 'burdens' as the feelings, memories, and beliefs that have come from difficult past experiences. Exiles mobilise protectors to stop us experiencing uncomfortable sensations and emotions

  The more extreme the feelings and wounds of the exiled parts, the more extreme the protectors become, trying to suppress and contain these feelings which may include terror, shame, and rage. When we see the negative impact of these protectors' strategies, it can be hard to remember their positive intent. But if we build a mindful and compassionate relationship with these parts, enquiring into their intention, we will discover that they are trying to take care of something for the individual and to heal something from the past.

The IFS Institute's policy is that only those who have completed at least Level One training can attempt to unburden parts. However, parts often spontaneously unburden and transform, choosing a new role in the client's system. In this case coaches can celebrate and spend time deepening and integrating the change.

Rydings (2022) identifies three primary goals in coaching through IFS:

- Freeing parts from extreme roles so they can return to their preferred naturally valuable states
- Re-establishing trust of parts in the leadership of the self
- Re-harmonising and balancing the system so parts co-exist without conflict

The aim is to update the system, bringing parts into the present, so they know they have survived, overcome or left that past event, and are now protected by the wise adult Self.

RM and IFS

Many IFS practitioners embrace mindfulness, for example, guiding clients through an individual practice at the beginning of a session so they can enter a mindful state. Once in this state, they will typically learn from their parts that they are suffering and/or at trying to protect the client, *"shifting from the passive-observer state to an increasingly engaged and relational form of mindfulness that naturally exists within"* (Schwartz, 2011, online). Schwartz says that, in his experience over decades, this state – the Wise Self in IFS terms – is accepting of all the parts and has an innate wisdom about how to relate to them in an attuned, loving way.

We explored attachment theory in Chapter 20, which calls upon the coach to be an important attachment role model for the client. With IFS, it is more that the coach holds the space, offering a non-judgemental container of awareness in which the client's own Wise Self can show up. The IFS coach will be conscious of their own parts showing up in coaching too. RM can help shine a light on which parts are present and help the coach self-manage and self-regulate.

RM can not only support the client and coach to enter into and remain in a mindful state but also support mindful, compassionate interrelating between parts. As RMEC coaches, we might even want to experiment with guided RM dialogue between parts. We might like to hold in mind Schwartz's words (2021, p.7): *"parts are sacred, spiritual beings and they deserve to be treated as such."*

Interweaving RM and IFS can also bring insights and wisdom around how we relate in the 'outer' world, building compassion too. To quote Schwartz (2021):

> *"If we can appreciate and have compassion for our parts, even for the ones we've considered to be enemies, we can do the same for people who*

resemble them. On the other hand, if we hate or disdain our parts, we'll do the same with anyone who reminds us of them."

(p.17)

We agree with Schwartz (2021) that love is what we need: *"Love is the answer in the inner world, just as it is in the outer world. Listening to, embracing, and loving parts allows them to heal and transform as much as it does for people"* (p.17).

References

Adamson, F., & Brendgen, J. (2021). *Mindfulness-based relational supervision: mutual learning and transformation*. Routledge.

Anagnostakis, A. (April 2023). The way OUT is THROUGH: Contrasting Emotions and Vertical Development. Vertical Development Education www.verticaldevelopm ent.education/p/the-way-out-is-through-contrasting-emotions-vertical-developm ent?r=h9bul&utm_campaign=post&utm_medium=email

Argyris, C. (1977). Double loop learning in organizations. *Harvard Business Review*, 55(5), 115–125.

Argyris, C., & Schön, D. A. (1997). Organizational learning: A theory of action perspective. *Reis*, 77/78, 345–348.

Bachkirova, T. (2011). *Developmental coaching: Working with the Self*. Open University Press.

Bachkirova, T. (2014). Psychological development in adulthood and coaching. In E. Cox, T. Bachkirova, & D. Clutterbuck (Eds.), *The complete handbook of coaching*, 131–144. Sage.

Bachkirova, T., & Cox, E. (2018). A cognitive-developmental approach for coach development. In *Handbook of coaching psychology: A guide for practitioners*, 548–561. Routledge.

Berger, J., & Atkins, P. (2009). Mapping complexity of mind: Using the subject-object interview in coaching. *Coaching: An International Journal of Theory, Research and Practice*, 2(1), 23–36.

Buber, M. (1970). *I and Thou* (Vol. 243). Simon and Schuster.

Chaskalson, M., & McMordie, M. (2017). *Mindfulness for coaches: An experiential guide*. Routledge.

Cook-Greuter, S. (1999). Postautonomous ego development: Its nature and measurement. Doctoral dissertation. Cambridge, Harvard Graduate School of Education.

Cook-Greuter, S. R. (2004). Making the case for a developmental perspective. *Industrial and Commercial Training*, 36(7), 275–281.

Donaldson-Feilder, E. (2020). An anchored connection. Coaching at Work. May/June 2020. www.coaching-at-work.com/2020/05/05/relational-mindfulness-part-2-an-anchored-connection/

Fisher, D., & Torbert, W. (1991). Transforming managerial practice: Beyond the achiever stage. *Research in Organizational Change and Development*, 5, 143–173.

Flood, R. L., & Romm, N. (1996). Diversity management. In *Critical systems thinking*, 81–92. Springer.

Frizzell, D. (2015). The perceptions and lived experiences of leaders practicing mind-fulness meditation: A phenomenological investigation. PhD dissertation, Walden University.

Frizzell, D., & Banner, D. K. (2018). Leader self-development, maturation, and medita-tion: Elements of a transformative journey. In *Handbook of personal and organiza-tional transformation* (Vol. 1), 427–441. Springer.

Germer, C. K., & Siegel, R. D. (2012). *Wisdom and compassion in psychotherapy: Deepening mindfulness in clinical practice*. Guilford Press.

Graves, C. (1970). Levels of existence: An open system theory of values. *Journal of Humanistic Psychology*, 10(2), 131–155. Sage Journals.

Hauser, S. T. (1976). Loevinger's model and measure of ego develop-ment: A critical review. *Psychological Bulletin*, 83(5), 928–955. https://doi.org/10.1037/0033-2909.83.5.928

Harthill Consulting (2024). Harthill Consulting's Leadership Development Profile report, accessed January 2024. Harthill Consulting. www.harthill.co.uk/

Kegan, R. (1982). *The evolving self: Problem and process in human development*. Harvard University Press.

Kegan, R. (1994). *In over our heads: The mental demands of modern life*. Harvard University Press.

Kilburg, R. R. (2000). *Executive coaching: Developing managerial wisdom in a world of chaos*. American Psychological Association.

Kolb, D. A. (1984). *Experiential learning: Experience as the source of learning and develop-ment*. Prentice-Hall.

Kramer, G. (2007). *Insight dialogue: The interpersonal path to freedom*. Shambhala Publications.

Lee, G. (2021). *Breakthrough conversations for coaches, consultants and leaders*. Routledge.

Martin, M., & Cowan, E. W. (2019). Remembering Martin Buber and the I-Thou in counseling. *Counseling Today*, 61, 46–48.

O'Fallon, T. (2020). States and STAGES: Waking up Developmentally. *Integral Review: A Transdisciplinary & Transcultural Journal for New Thought, Research, & Praxis*, 16(1), 13–38.

Petrie, N. (2015). The how-to of vertical leadership development–Part 2. 30 experts, 3 conditions and 15 approaches. Center for Creative Leadership, 26.

Piaget, J. (1976). *The psychology of intelligence*. Adams & Co.

Remen, R. N., & Wisdom, K. T. (1996). *Stories that heal*, 220. River-Head Books.

Rydings, B. (2022). All parts welcome. *Coaching at Work*, 17 (5), 36–38.

Scharmer, C. O. (2008). Uncovering the blind spot of leadership. *Leader to Leader*, 2008(47), 52–59.

Scharmer, O. (2018). *The essentials of Theory U: Core principles and applications*. Berrett-Koehler Publishers.

Scharmer, C.O. (2024). Presencing. U-school for transformation, accessed February 2024. www.u-school.org/presencing

Schwartz, R. (2011). When meditation isn't enough. *Psychotherapy Networker*, September/October 2011 www.psychotherapynetworker.org/article/when-meditation-isnt-enough/

Schwartz, R. (2021). *No bad parts: Healing trauma & restoring wholeness with the internal family systems model*. Random House.

Siminovitch, D. E. (2018). *The coach as awareness agent: A process approach*. Principles and Practice.

Torbert, W. R., & Rooke, D. (2005). Seven transformations of leadership. *Harvard Business Review*, 83(4), 66–76.

U-school for transformation (2024). Theory U, accessed November 2024. www.u-school. org/theory-u

Webb, P. J. (2020). Coaching for wisdom: System 3 thinking in complex decision making. *Philosophy of Coaching: An International Journal*, 5, 113–128.

Wilber, K. (2000). *Integral psychology*. Shambala.

Wilber, K. (2016). *Integral meditation: Mindfulness as a way to grow up, wake up, and show up in your life*. Shambhala Publications.

Section 6

Next steps and beyond

I think there's an astounding amount that RM can [contribute]… to our well-being, our sacred spaces… where we feel compelled to speak the truth and then act, bring about change from a place of courage, from a place of vulnerability, knowing that there are others around us that can also support us.

(Saima, Coach and Facilitator, Change Advantage,
and one of our interviewees for this book)

Having delved deeply into Relational Mindfulness (RM) in Sections 2–4, then broadened out to show links to the enormous Indra's Net that includes the field of awareness, relating, and wisdom in Section 5, in this final section, we point our minds to the future. In Chapter 22, we aim to give some pointers and suggestions for where you might take RM into your lives, including your work. Finally, in Chapter 23, we share a vision of how RM and RM-Enhanced Coaching (RMEC) could contribute to navigating the challenging times in which we live. We hope to inspire and support you to step into your own development and to contribute to the world in ways that bring greater presence, awareness, wisdom, compassion, and courageous collaboration.

DOI: 10.4324/9781003390428-27

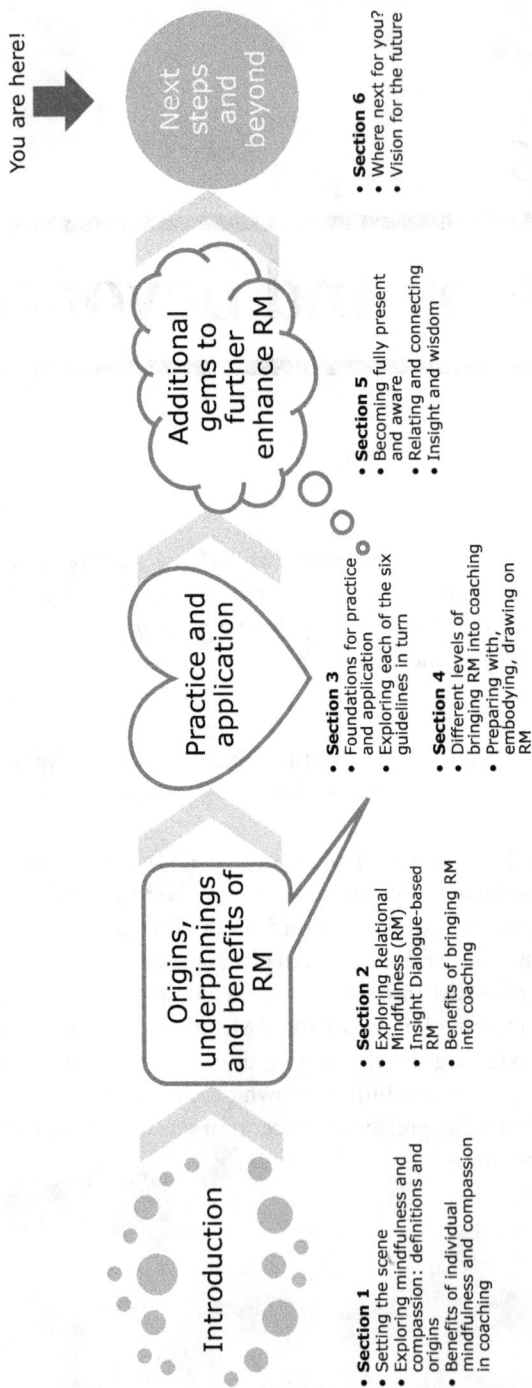

You are here!

Next steps and beyond

Section 6
- Where next for you?
- Vision for the future

Additional gems to further enhance RM

Section 5
- Becoming fully present and aware
- Relating and connecting
- Insight and wisdom

Practice and application

Section 3
- Foundations for practice and application
- Exploring each of the six guidelines in turn

Section 4
- Different levels of bringing RM into coaching
- Preparing with, embodying, drawing on RM

Origins, underpinnings and benefits of RM

Section 2
- Exploring Relational Mindfulness (RM)
- Insight Dialogue-based RM
- Benefits of bringing RM into coaching

Introduction

Section 1
- Setting the scene
- Exploring mindfulness and compassion: definitions and origins
- Benefits of individual mindfulness and compassion in coaching

Figure S6 You are here!

Chapter 22

Where next?

The real journey is right here. The great excursion starts from exactly where you are. You are the world. You have everything you need.

Rumi

Thank you for reading the first 21 chapters of this book! We hope doing so has inspired and enlightened you. Perhaps, like us, you have come to believe that Relational Mindfulness (RM) has a huge amount to offer coaches, the coaching community, and the wider world. So, what next? In this chapter, we give our thoughts on how RM might support you further on your journey as a coach.

Every reader will have their own unique context, development needs, capacities, and motivation for developing their coaching approach and way of being. It would therefore be impossible to set out a 'where next' to suit you all. What we aim to do here is give some pointers and suggestions for you to consider.

Where are you now?

You may agree that we can only work out where to go next when we have a good sense of where we are now. Not that our lives or our professional and personal development are simple linear journeys. They are clearly much more complex and multi-dimensional than that. However, the analogy of a development journey can help when planning next steps based on a review of our current capacity.

RM is a powerful way to engage in self-reflection and develop self-awareness, and these are both fundamental to taking RM into our lives, including our work. We invite you to take a pause to reflect and to review your current capacity for using RM to underpin your practice.

DOI: 10.4324/9781003390428-28

Useful reflection questions to include in your review might include the following:

- *Where do I sit in the framework of levels of coach capacity for bringing mindfulness, compassion, and RM into coaching?* (See Chapter 14)
- *What is my level of coach maturity?* (See Clutterbuck & Megginson, 2011)
- *To what extent have I grasped and embodied the practice of RM and RM-Enhanced Coaching (RMEC)?* (See Chapters 8–13 and 14–18)
- *Where am I on a journey of practising individual mindfulness and bringing it into my life?*
- *What is my vision going forward?*

Below we share some ideas for keeping up and building any momentum you have started to build.

Engaging in regular RM practice

The practices set out in Chapters 8–13 and Appendix 1 can be engaged with as a lifelong journey. We strongly recommend establishing a habit of formal RM practice as well as engaging with the RM guidelines in day-to-day interactions. We both find that regular formal and informal RM practice are invaluable parts of our ongoing personal and professional development.

Formal RM practice helps us grow our capacity to embody RM in all parts of our life. As mentioned in Chapter 7, our development depends on somatic as well as intellectual learning. When we spend time in mindful dialogue with another or others, we are building new patterns and habits of bringing full attention, receptivity, and attunement to what is emerging both within our own body, heart, and mind, and in the external world, particularly our dialogue partners. We are learning at a visceral level how to do that, which makes the learning more embedded, natural, and easy to draw upon in other contexts.

Formal RM practice is also a way of learning experientially about the nature of being human. By bringing our awareness into the moment of interacting with another person, we shed light on the experience of the relational process. By engaging with contemplation questions in this mindful and relational context, we can gain insights of the kind that our interviewees identified, both into our own relational habits and into new ways of thinking and perceiving (see Chapter 6). As mentioned elsewhere, the wisdom we can access in RM practice offers the potential for freedom, helping us step beyond cultural norms and constructs to a more interconnected and clearer sense of who we are.

In our experience, the learning from our formal RM practice cannot help but change how we are in our daily lives. The new patterns of relating that we establish, the insights we gain, and the shifts in understanding and perception we experience alter how we show up in all our relationships. However, if we circumscribe our conscious practice of RM to the times we set aside for mindful dialogue, we are limiting the transfer of learning into our other relationships. Consciously engaging in the informal practices outlined in Chapters 8–13 and actively choosing to bring RM into our coaching as described in Chapters 14–18 will greatly enhance our capacity to change and embed our learning more powerfully and sustainably.

In order to establish a regular formal RM practice, we need to identify people with whom we can do this. We are both fortunate to have people in our lives – including each other – who also believe in the value and power of RM to support growth, insight, and wisdom, with whom we can practise mindful dialogue. Hopefully, the guidelines provided in Chapter 7 can help you choose dialogue partners to provide you with this support. It may help to draw on the resources available on the dedicated website accompanying this book as we explore next.

Drawing on the resources on the RM website

As mentioned, we have created a website to accompany this book (see link below) to provide resources to support you on your RM journey. There you will find a range of documents, audios, videos, and links all related to RM and RMEC.

The documents we provide on the website include downloadable PDFs of the resource sheets from the appendices to this book. This is in case you find it easier to have a PDF in front of you rather than the whole book. There is also a document about the informal research we conducted for this book.

The audios on the website are designed to help you weave the RM guidelines into your formal individual practice and support your formal relational practice. The video aims to give you a sense of how mindful dialogue works.

We have also identified and provided links to resources on other websites that we believe are relevant to RM and can provide you with additional support.

Attending a group RM programme can be a further resource, as we explore next.

Attending an organised group RM programme

As we mentioned in Chapter 7, we recommend attending an organised RM programme. This is not just because we would love to see you on one of our RM programmes (which we would!) but also because we feel there are multiple benefits to engaging with a group to learn about and practice RM. There is something very powerful about being part of a group learning process, both due to the shared intention and shared interest that comes with such a group experience and through the multiple perspectives, comments, and questions that emerge in a group setting.

Group development programmes bring together the shared learning process of the group with input from an experienced facilitator or teacher. In the case of RM, it will be important to look for a teacher who not only has deep understanding and experience of RM practice and of bringing RM into their coaching but also embodies RM in their way of being and teaching. Being guided into mindful dialogue practice by someone like this will support your somatic learning as the neurobiological mechanisms described in Chapter 20 help connect and transmit messages at an embodied level. It will bring the practices to life in a way that simply reading and self-guiding cannot do. The most rewarding feedback on our programmes, which we get regularly, is that we embody what we are teaching.

Participating in one of our group RM programmes gives you the experience of learning about and practising with the ID-based RM guidelines in pairs, small groups, and the whole group. By practising with different participants in each session and buddying up with them between sessions (for which we provide support and guidance), you get to experience engaging in mindful dialogue with a range of different people. This diversity of dialogue partners can be enlightening in terms of multiple perspectives and also learning about our different responses, likes, challenges, etc. in relationship. We encourage participants on our programmes to continue practising with one another after the programme ends, so you can end up with a number of people with whom you can establish a regular formal practice.

Joining the RM for coaches community of practice

Bringing RM into coaching is still in its early stages. At the time of writing in 2024, there are approaching 100 people who have participated in one of our RM for coaches programmes and maybe several more hundred people who have attended our taster sessions and conference presentations. We intend to swell this number dramatically over the years ahead and build an active community of those working in coaching – and other relevant fields – with an interest and engagement in RM.

We are hoping that this book will help draw coaches to become part of this growing community. As a reader, we would like to invite you to join the community, which you can do via the dedicated website accompanying this book (see link below). Our plan is to offer resources and events for this community, and we would love to establish a dialogue about how RM can support greater wisdom, courage, compassion, and collaboration in us as coaches, in our clients, and in the wider world.

We would really like to hear from you about how you get on with establishing an RM practice, how it fits with your approach and experience of coaching, and any benefits or changes you notice as you bring RM into your life and work.

As we mentioned in Chapter 18, the ideas we present for bringing elements of mindful dialogue into coaching are new, tentative, and emerging. We are keen to hear feedback about how you get on with experimenting with our suggestions and anything else you are trying out. You can give us your feedback via our dedicated website (see link below).

Working through the coach capacity levels

The model we set out in Chapter 14 suggests that bringing mindfulness, compassion, and RM into coaching is a multi-faceted and multi-level process. These are qualities that take time to develop and require regular practice to embed into our way of being. Our intention in providing the model is to help you, the reader, identify where you are and where you aspire to be. It may be that you are not interested in moving through all the levels, which is, of course, a valid choice.

Moving from Level One in the model (where our coaching capability is enhanced by our experience of mindfulness, compassion, and/or RM) to Level Two (where we are embodying a mindful and compassionate presence) is a significant step. In our experience, this transition happens gradually and is non-linear in nature, including slipping back and losing confidence as well as jumping forward. Considerable practice – both formal and informal – is involved in building the habits of being present, compassionate, and insightful. Given all that we know about somatic learning and the way we connect in relationships, we would suggest that embodying these qualities is a powerful support for our clients. Certainly, the coaches we interviewed would appear to be seeing benefits through embodiment.

Moving to Level Three (where we are competent to directly offer mindfulness and/or compassion practices) and Level Four (where we are competent to directly offer elements of mindful dialogue) probably involve undertaking specific programmes of development on top of the regular practice needed for Levels One and Two. The capacity to guide practice and hold space for that is not simply acquired through our own practice; it requires skill-building and a deep understanding of the ethical implications and of what is and is not good practice in this field. We are aware that some of our readers already have training and skill in guiding mindfulness and/or compassion practices and may already be operating at Level Three; for you, RM is more of an additional support at this level and an invitation to consider moving to Level Four.

Whatever your current level and aspiration for development, we wish you well for your journey and would be really interested to hear how you get on and what you are taking away from this book. Please do get in touch with us via our dedicated website (see link below).

Having set out our thoughts on the next steps you might take as an individual coach, we are ready now to round off the book by exploring our vision for a future in which RM plays a vital role in the world.

Reference

Clutterbuck, D., & Megginson, D. (2011) Coach maturity: An emerging concept. In L. Wildflower & D. Brennan (Eds.), *The handbook of knowledge-based coaching: From theory to practice*, 299–313. John Wiley & Sons.

Information

Dedicated website accompanying this book: www.relationalmindfulness.net

Chapter 23

Vision for the future

To be or not to be is no longer the question. It's to inter-be.

Thich Nhat Hanh

In this chapter, we share a vision for how Relational Mindfulness (RM) in general and RM-Enhanced Coaching (RMEC) in particular might positively contribute as we navigate these challenging times, beyond the immediacy of one-to-one, team, or group coaching engagements.

The wider system

As we all know only too well, we face a host of 'wicked' (Rittel & Webber, 1973) problems. A global mental health crisis. The climate emergency and related issues, such as food insecurity, increasing numbers of refugees, and the possibility of the sixth mass extinction in our lifetimes. Increased polarisation which results in wars and divisive nationalism. Growth in wealth disparity. A sharp decline in trust of institutions and leaders. Fake news, deepfake, and other worrying misuses of new technology. Bombardment with data. We could go on and on.

From a systemic perspective, we can see that the issues we are grappling with are interconnected, that the three divides that Scharmer (2018) highlights are interwoven: social, ecological, and what he calls spiritual (such as hopelessness, anxiety, and depression). We agree with Scharmer that these divides get in the way of awareness-based social change. However, there is unfathomable complexity. To many of us it seems that humankind is in 'over our heads', to pick up on the title of a book by adult development researcher Robert Kegan published decades ago (Kegan, 1998).

DOI: 10.4324/9781003390428-29

It may be that everything is just as it should be and serves some greater purpose. Yet, even if there is some greater intelligence at play, taking responsibility, stepping in, and stepping up still makes sense to us. As long as we can do so without overly taking on roles of the 'Fixer', the 'Helper', or the 'Saviour', much though these may be enticing, particularly among those of us in helping professions.

Capacities

Collectively, humankind seems not to have in sufficient quantities the capacities we require to adapt and thrive in these challenging times. As Kegan (in Bachkirova, 2009, p. 17) says, *"A great deal of individual and collective suffering arises from the mismatch between the complexity of the world's demands and the complexity of our mindsets."*

We do not want to fuel the widespread tendency to create hierarchies, where we may put those with greater capacity for complexity and later state meaning-making (see Chapter 21 on vertical development) on a pedestal. However, given the collective changes we face, there is a compelling argument for investing in helping to enable an expansion in our own and clients' meaning-making, expanding our worldviews, and increasing capacity to manage complexity, for building greater awareness of self, others, and systems, and facilitating a shift from what some have called 'ego-centric' to 'eco-centric' – individually and collectively. In this context, some of us might say that the crux of our work as RMEC practitioners is to support individual and collective evolution of consciousness.

RM can contribute to addressing these collective challenges

Enhancing key qualities and capacities in the wider world through RM was one of the themes that emerged from the interviews we carried out as part of our research for this book. We asked our coach interviewees how they saw RM contributing to coaching going forward and in the wider world, including areas such as in leadership, climate change, social injustice, and dialogue in public life.

Analysis of interview data suggests (and we agree) that RM can contribute to the wider system by introducing and ramping up much-needed qualities and capacities, such as inner and vertical development, listening deeply to others, opening to new perspectives, kindness and compassion, high-quality conversation, connection, and collaboration.

As one of our interviewees, Jane, says, *"We're faced with significant systemic challenges. One of the symptoms of this is the increasing polarization of thought. It's such a vital capacity, to be able to sit with another human being who has an opposing view to ours and to pause, relax, allow, stay in the body, feel and hold the reactivity rather than shutting down, judging and 'othering.' The practice of RM can support the cultivation of this capacity because it develops an awareness of relational reactivity, and also by its very nature it ignites the compassionate heart through the insights that are born in the process. We see the vulnerable human being sitting opposite us who is just like us. We are less caught in ourselves. There is capacity to appreciate another person's perspective and, as a consequence, grow our own mind. This is the principle of vertical development."*

The responses also suggest – and, once again, we agree – that RM can enhance coach training, leadership, education, and parenting, and support and enable systemic change in the wider world, for example, helping to address the social impact of climate change and widespread suffering due to mental health struggles.

As Shenaz says, *"I think [the contribution of RM is] potentially huge. I think it's on a societal level. I think if we go back to any of the mental health and anxiety statistics, that one in five in the world will become mentally ill, and one in four will have issues, these are unbelievable statistics. And then there's climate change and anxiety... all the challenges of humanity in a way, and now we've got all this talk about AI. And the actual thing is that people believe their thoughts. That's the biggest, most fearful thing."*

Malcolm also sees the potential of RM: *"I think [RM is] part of something that is emerging... it's pointing to the next thing... far more about community focus. And so that's the trajectory... My hope is it might bring in a greater focus on the whole, as in a whole community... organisation or society, as in a whole world. We are all totally interconnected and when one suffers or succeeds, all are affected in some way. Unless we wake up to that soon, I think we're in terrible trouble as a planet, as humankind... RM is one of the things that maybe can help address that."*

Another interviewee, Saima, says, *"...I think there's something at a much greater systemic level... to me, RM is about the quality of dialogue we all want to aspire to, to be able to be in charge of the change we want to see and have a just civil society where everybody belongs, a planet that we all take care of – 'there isn't a planet B, there isn't an alternative.' And for me, the health in how we speak with each other and ourselves has a parallel trait across the health of our planet and our ecosystems and our societal systems. And the wiser we are, the faster, the more effective we are around how we can have those integral conversations at this level with the benefit of RM, the more effectively we can get to the crux of what wants to happen and how we can bring about change and well-being."*

As Malcolm and Saima imply, there is something important about how RM can bring us together. In mindful dialogue, we meet and explore contemplation topics in ways that dissolve barriers and generate both better understanding and a sense of the wider interconnected system. By building opportunities for courageous collaboration, RM can help us realise that we are all interrelated. The fact that we are not alone and that we are stronger together was something that we (Liz and Emma) tapped into when we engaged in mindful dialogue as we neared completion of this book (see Box 23.1).

Box 23.1 Highlights from Liz and Emma's mindful dialogue

The following are some highlights from a mindful dialogue we engaged in to explore how RM can contribute more widely, beyond coaching. We meditated together in silence first, then meditated relationally taking 5 minutes each to speak and be listened to, ending with 5 minutes in shared dialogue.

Liz as speaker (Emma listening): *"So what I'm first feeling into is that what's out there is in here, and I'm just conscious of how much pain and suffering there is, so my greatest hope is that RM can help to minimize, to reduce suffering.*

We know suffering is part of life but there's something about helping to increase levels of wisdom so that people aren't unnecessarily suffering... The wisdom [element] does feel really important and... it's like we don't know how to relate... we somehow learn really difficult, unhelpful ways of relating. So there's something about that, helping people unlearn, to really feel into different ways of relating and connecting and into interconnectedness and then what becomes different, what becomes possible? [Evolution of] consciousness...

I'm conscious of not quite striving but a desire, a want that's pulling me forward, there's something about the whole nature of RM really being about not striving yet having purpose. So I think really it's just about helping make the world a better place in some small way. Knowing that that's a big ask, but [there's] a conviction that this is a tried and tested methodology or whatever you want to call it, and just wanting more people to have access to it...

I fundamentally do actually believe everyone's doing their best... If that's the case, then what else is getting in the way? ...RM can help shift how people show up...so it's something about a vision about this becoming the way things are done... becoming embedded... like individual mindfulness has started to be...

I listened to a podcast the other day from Jess Serrante... saying that the opposite of goodness is not evil, it's a deadened response... How can certain people who are committing atrocities possibly be capable of doing that? And it feels to me less about evil than being cut off from others... There's something around... bringing [people] into connectedness... for a more compassionate world."

Emma as speaker (Liz listening): *"I so resonate with what you say about there being so much suffering out there and if only we could make a difference. And it does feel like there's so much within RM that could contribute... [the] whole idea of being fully present with one another, receptive, and in particular the capacity to see that our view is just one way of seeing the world and that there are multiple perspectives, none of which is... intrinsically right...*

[From] trolling on social media, and all the horribleness right up to wars and violence… how do we overcome that….

I've been listening to Dan Siegel and he talks about the error of the separate self and how we're all actually striving to get back to wholeness. And yet so many people are doing it in a way that is actually dividing and divisive… There's just so much that needs courage and collaboration – courageous collaboration – and needs genuine listening and receptivity and openness to insight and to new perspectives, and willingness to have our constructs shaken, and the capacity for compassion, kindness. It's needed everywhere. And as I say that, there's also something about not taking ourselves too seriously as well, you know, that tendency to get too rigid and caught."

(Both speaking and listening)

Liz: *"What's coming up for me hearing you speak is something about what Dan Siegel is referring to, or Tara Brach's 'trance of unworthiness', or Deborah Tull's 'myth of separation', all these things. There's something about [how] on some level we all yearn [for connection], don't we? We know on some level that actually that [separation] is just not how it is and so there's a kind of yearning, but we don't know how [to be different]. So for me, what RM offers is a 'how.'"*

Emma: *"Yes, there's something about enabling people. And it is swimming against a tide, a very human tide of thinking that if we could only have more or do more then we'd be happy, and that we are separate and we need to maintain our identity. Those are strong human urges and RM is an antidote."*

Liz: *"Totally! And that wisdom piece is important here for me because there's something about forgiving ourselves, understanding those urges… and saying, "okay, there you are, I see you", and being in touch with the yearning, with [how the separation] is not serving us …So, yeah, we need an antidote… [seeing that] we're caught in these ways of being, forgiving ourselves – the compassion and the wisdom – and not expecting it to go away."*

Emma: *"…and we're not doing it alone, are we?… We all have our own work to do but there's also something [with RM] about not doing it alone, because it's such a beautiful relational practice…"*

Liz: *"I think that can build. I'm hoping it could be even a tipping point, who knows?"*

Emma: *"I love that. That really touches me."*

Inner Development Goals

The recognition of the afore-mentioned capacity chasm prompted a group of thought leaders, including adult development scholars Kegan and Susanne Cook-Greuter, to gather on the Ekskäret island in the Stockholm archipelago in April 2019. The momentum for the gathering came from the sense that greater knowledge and wisdom from adult development research are sorely needed

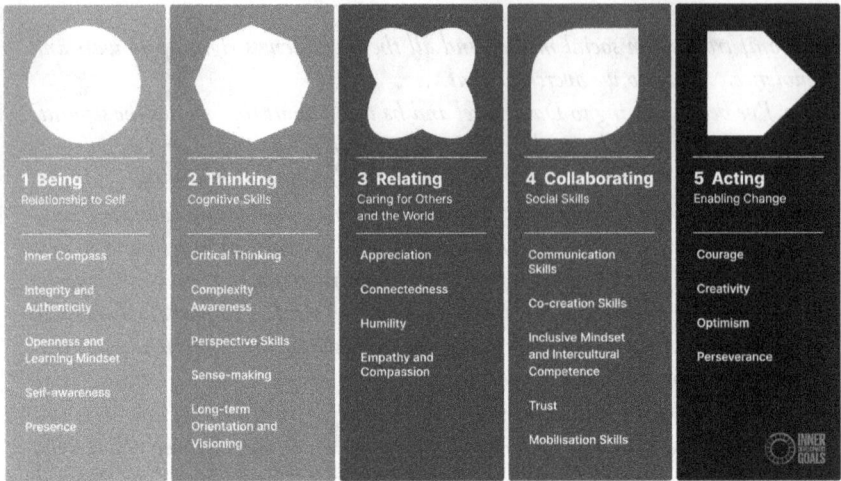

Figure 23.1 The Inner Development Goals framework.

https://innerdevelopmentgoals.org/framework/

for humankind to move towards a more sustainable world. In addition to this gathering, surveys were carried out among professionals, including coaches, and exploratory conversations and consultations were held among prominent thought leaders, including Kegan, Cook-Greuter, Peter Senge, Otto Scharmer, Amy Edmondson, and Jennifer Garvey Berger.

Following this meeting, the Growth that Matters Manifesto was launched, stating the urgent need to work systemically with growth in adults to better meet the accelerating complexity of societal challenges. Next, a not-for-profit initiative, The Inner Development Goals (IDGs), was launched, with the remit of researching, collecting, and communicating science-based skills and qualities that help us all to live purposeful, sustainable, and productive lives. The IDGs identified a set of five dimensions organising 23 skills and qualities of human inner growth and development, aligned with the United Nations' 17 Sustainable Development Goals for creating a sustainable world by 2030. As we can see from Figure 23.1, the five IDG dimensions are being, thinking, relating, collaborating, and acting, with a number of capacities nested under each.

Vertical development

The inner development capacities highlighted by the IDGs require a shift in an individual's sense-making: vertical rather than horizontal development (the term *vertical* still sticks in our craw as it implies later is better – see Chapter 21 for more on vertical development). The capacities have much to do with cultivating our interior condition, but also how we interrelate. Vertical development is frequently the outcome of RM and RMEC: supporting the development of capacities highlighted by the IDGs, including presence, integrity and authenticity, self-awareness, perspective skills, empathy and compassion, communication skills, trust, courage, and creativity.

As Jane says, *"I think RM is a practice that can help to cultivate many of the capacities associated with [the IDGs]... The reality is that we're far from achieving this because of a lack of inner capacity to deal with the increasing complexity we are faced with. If we, as a global coaching community, engage with RM, we're taking an active part in shifting in our relationship to ourselves, to others and the world around us. It can make a huge contribution."*

Another interviewee, Shenaz, says, *"...the quality of awareness, quality of consciousness, quality of conversation. I think the [IDGs] are very exciting. I think there's a direct application of RM into developing inner goals... [they] are for everything... not just for climate change. I think the question [is] how do we develop the vertical development of people... create more agency, more quality of thought?"*

Explicitly aligning with the IDG roadmap and offering RM as a way to navigate and travel the territory is work in progress, but it is very much underway (see Box 23.2).

Box 23.2 Building the IDG qualities through RM

Since learning about the IDGs, we have been convinced that RM could offer a route to developing the qualities they set out. Some of the coaches attending our RM programmes echoed this conviction. One group in particular (the 4Ss, all of whom we interviewed for this book) felt that they wanted to bring the IDGs into the next RM programme I (Emma) offered them – and I was delighted to oblige!

The programme I designed has three distinct phases:

- *Phase 1 (sessions 1 and 2) – Introduction:* These first two sessions focus on setting the scene, mapping the territory, and setting development intentions. Providing brief input on the distinction between 'doing' and 'being', the 'knowing-doing gap' and the significance of embodiment, the aim is to set a context for the IDGs in the broader field of inner and outer development. I include an introduction to the IDGs themselves, invite a reflection on agile change, and offer a question posed by the IDG authors about which IDG would make the biggest difference in participants' lives.
- *Phase 2 (sessions 3–7) – Exploring the IDGs:* In these sessions, we work our way through the five IDG dimensions, focussing one session on each: being, thinking, relating, collaborating, and acting. We explore the skills that make up each dimension, the processes that help us develop them, and links to other aligned/relevant models, theories, and research.

> ■ *Phase 3 (sessions 8 and 9) – Taking RM and the IDGs out into the world:* These final two sessions aim to translate all that has been covered in the first seven sessions into tangible shifts in participants' work, relationships, and impact in the world. The threads of inner and outer development that run through the programme are woven together to create an invitation and springboard for participants to make changes in their way of being and what they are doing in the world.
>
> Each session in the programme includes individual and RM practices as well as some brief input/slides to point participants' minds towards relevant concepts, models, and research. Participants practice mindful dialogue in pairs and in the group as a whole – generally two pair and two group practices per session. Each mindful dialogue is framed by drawing on one or more of the ID-based RM guidelines and a contemplation topic that invites an experiential and embodied exploration of a question/subject based on the theme of the session.
>
> Bringing together the IDG framework and RM practice makes for a powerful combination and a catalyst for both inner and outer development. I am very grateful to the coaches who made this possible.

On the theme of bringing key qualities to the world, the responses from our interviewees fell into three groups: really listening to others and opening to new perspectives, kindness and compassion, and quality of conversation and collaboration, which are of course all connected. We explore these further below.

Really listening to others and opening to new perspectives

So many of the ills in the world come from 'othering', from believing that we are separate from each other and from the rest of nature. RM can help to dispel the myth of separation, acknowledging how much we have in common whilst being open to others' perspectives and to new ideas.

As Rhonda says, "*I think we could all benefit from listening more and talking less in general… I think that RM and the whole element of not prejudging what people are thinking or saying… is really critical.*"

Beth says, "*I think there's all sorts of benefits to being in equal dialogue… where I see the most conflict is where people are just unwilling or unable to access another person's perspective.*"

And Emma R points to RM's potential for "*… freeing the mind of all these narrow-minded views and our prejudices… helping to put all those things aside and then people… come up with far better decisions.*"

And Stephanie asks, *"[In politics] how much listening, proper listening is there, how much proper dialogue is there, how much emergence, how much wisdom? All sorely lacking. So, imagine if these people were equipped with some of these things, the world would be wonderful."*

Opening up to new perspectives and listening deeply gives rise to kindness and compassion.

Kindness and compassion

The environmental activist and Buddhist scholar Joanna Macy reminds us that *"of all the dangers we face, from climate chaos to nuclear war, none is so great as the deadening of our response"* (Macy, retrieved April 2024).

Increasing our capacity to let ourselves really feel, to dial up our response, to turn towards suffering, and to be kind and compassionate towards ourselves and others is one of the biggest contributions RM can make in these times. As interviewee Malcolm points out, one way RM helps is by highlighting shared common humanity (not to forget commonality with all the other beings with which we share this planet). He says, *"...when people get together and are honest... about themselves and their own experiences, the first thing that happens is that they begin to recognise how similar they are, and as people begin to recognise how similar they are, a sense of community, compassion or goodwill develops. And then, when there is suffering involved, that is perceived and there's a wish to do something about it."*

He continues, *"It's a progression from me as a self to me as a part of something much bigger... Once you become aware of being connected to the whole, then actually what emerges is compassion and a sense of empathy with other people and when we get to that point, then the relationship becomes something different... RM supports the relationship to become something different and then we feel connected to something bigger, and we develop empathy and compassion and... I think it's what the world needs."*

When it comes to pro-social behaviour, RM amplifies the impact of individual mindfulness, as Becky says: *"...there's a lot of fascinating and wonderful things written about the potential contribution of individual mindfulness to society... a lot of it is about pro-social behaviour, isn't it? And acting with compassion; and RM just kind of does that on steroids... It's not that RM has something different and new to offer, but it's that it would amplify those societal benefits that are already being talked about."*

Quite simply, says Pirjo, *"Any context could benefit from RM ... We would be much kinder towards each other."*

Quality of conversation and collaboration

Given that RM is about mindful dialogue, clearly this is another area where interviewees see it making a difference. As Shenaz says, *"I think that anything to do with speech and the quality of speech, RM will catalyse that."*

Saima highlights the co-created element of RM: *"…there's that sense of co-ownership through RM… It's a beautiful asset to the important conversations we want to be having around the world. And it's fostering the opportunity to have real, quality, meaningful dialogue so that people and the planet start to notice the differences that we need. I'm not sure how else we're going to get to where we need to be other than by having the quality and safety of feeling part of a conversation, a dialogue that's grounded in RM."*

Another interviewee says, *"RM can [contribute to] … positive progress to humanity and especially… whatever is specifically about communication, conflict, understanding. It can be useful in all the range of… communication from the most conflictual… to the least conflictual… It has a place and [can make] a huge contribution… especially [for] those who have specific roles in dealing with others."*

Malcolm points to how RM can enable quick connection: *"RM enables people to connect quite quickly at a very personal human level and, particularly in today's interconnected world, it's even more important that we get on with and understand people quite quickly. We don't have much time to form relationships."*

Speaking the truth

Although the capacity to speak the truth, which we develop through RM practice, was not highlighted specifically by our interviewees, we believe it deserves a mention as we cast our minds to the future, and how we need to show up in these times.

For us, developing the capacity to speak the truth – our own, others' in the system, and that of the system/s we operate in (these will often, maybe even always, be aligned if we speak with discernment and love) – is vital in these times. The film, *Don't Look Up*, comes to mind. In the film (spoiler alert), all life on Earth is extinguished as a result of a meteor crashing into the planet, but, despite urgent warnings from scientists, people did not want to listen in the lead-up to the catastrophic event. Sound familiar? There are lots of reasons why people do not want to or cannot listen to the 'truth', but we need discerning truth-sayers. We need people with courage to call things out. And we need this speaking up to be done wisely and compassionately.

Next, we look at the potential of RM to contribute within specific contexts.

Contributing to particular contexts

Training for coaches (and other helping professionals)

We explored in earlier chapters some different coaching approaches with which RM can be interwoven. And there are many more approaches we could have delved into. For us, the future is very rosy when it comes to the potential of RM to enhance coaching practice.

One area in which we foresee and hope for more engagement is in bringing RM more widely into coach training. This is something our interviewees were positive about too.

Some, including Saima, are already using RM in coach training. Meanwhile, Stephanie asks, *"Why is this not part of core training [for coaches]? ...as coaches, we're being asked to do these relatively tangible things and you're marked on them in your competencies. But where is the guidance and the structure for learning this in a way that isn't a tool-based, surface-based approach?"*

Stephanie continues, *"What is coaching mastery? ...it's the self of the coach, and RM is an integral part of that, especially because the coaching is the relationship. It's the relationship we're creating with the clients. So it's almost, 'well, of course it's integral. How could it not be?'"*

Emma R says, *"...whatever coaching model you use, or whether you use an integrated model like I do, I think RM is a great backdrop for all of those things. I don't think it's another model that you'd say, right, I use this. It's very much something that all coaches would really benefit from using. And I think it's so powerful in terms of... the increases in thinking that can come from it... that's what we're trying to do, isn't it? We're trying to help people think better... freeing the mind to come up with better solutions... to come up with far better decisions."*

Jane sees huge potential: *"I think RM has a huge contribution to make to... coaching becoming more relational, to coaches having the courage to be present, to be grounded in the awareness of their body, in relationship with another. That's the tender territory, if we're not used to being grounded in our bodies because that's where... we feel things deeply. RM supports a letting go of trying to control the relationship and opening to the free-flowing chaos that is relationship and being okay with this because we're grounded in the sense of presence."*

For Pirjo, it is about supporting a shift in coaches' being: *"'Who you are being as a coach', how you are with your clients, is essential. In coaching work, the doing is built on the being. I see RM as kind of a basis for being. So I think it's essential because it supports the being part."*

Of course, these areas of development are relevant not only for training coaches but also for training other helping professionals, from psychotherapists and psychologists to social workers, paramedics, and other health professionals.

Leadership

The potential of RM to contribute in the leadership space was also highlighted. One of the authors of this book (Emma) is already doing work in this arena, including research on how to bring RM into leadership development and offering RM modules within leadership development programmes – particularly development of compassionate leadership. And our interviewees saw the potential here too.

Becky, who works in workplace wellbeing, says, *"...I am immediately thinking about how if leaders were to understand and embody RM... workplace well-being would go through the roof. Because so many of the difficulties that I see in my day job could be solved by leadership behaviour of this nature... Mindful leadership is a recognised thing, isn't it? I think RM could take that to the next level... I remember reading something saying, imagine if a member of your staff comes to you with a problem and you listen without judgement and you try and understand what that really feels like for them. And then instead of jumping to a solution, you explore options and make a bigger space in which for the problem to exist. And doesn't that sound like good leadership? Hey, well, guess what? It's called mindfulness. And I'm now thinking about that through the lens of RM. Well, if you would then put RM on top of that, it would just expand."*

Becky continues, *"I have a bit of a thing about how I believe the further up the organisation you get, ...the more important it is that you consider others in your behaviour. So I can show up and be a bit grumpy and not conduct myself very well, but I only manage one person, so that's only going to affect her and that's it. But if I am a leader of thousands of people, then I think I need to work a bit harder not to be like that. And that involves, of course, being more aware of my feelings... better able to manage them. And therefore, I think mindfulness is more important the higher you get. And then if you think about RM, well, if leaders are thinking about the impact on others in their interactions and their decisions and their behaviour, wow! Organisational life would be pretty different."*

Rhonda also sees the need for leaders to change their behaviour, *"A lot of my coaching is with leaders who need to shut up more, to put it very abruptly. They need to hear what's going on around them and they don't understand why they're having these issues, but it's because they're not listening to what's happening. And in fact, I've had conversations with some of them about RM and the value of working in that way and listening and being part of a dialogue where you're not the main character."*

Shenaz sees RM as naturally integrating with leadership development: *"The most natural space where RM integrates for me is in leadership development...My favourite way of integrating it is looking at what I've always looked at, which is the whole dimension of what's the inner game... and the outer goals and the outer ways of looking at leadership. And my belief that leadership always happens at two levels, internally and externally."*

The possibilities of RM in leadership and leadership development probably merit a whole book to itself – a book we hope to one day write ourselves.

Other contexts

Interviewees saw the potential for RM to also contribute positively in other arenas, such as politics and international relations, and education and parenting.

Shenaz says, *"...anything to do with international relations, anything to do with facilitating very difficult conversations. I could see RM as a module within so many of those kinds of international relations programmes."* We would certainly love to see

RM applied in a way that could address some of the political and international divides and the polarisation that seems to have become endemic on our world over recent decades. Perhaps RM could help us step out of our 'bubbles' and find greater scope for collaboration and peace.

Ideally, RM could contribute to establishing these capacities early in life. Saima asks, *"How can we get this into every single school around the world and every single learning centre or institute around the world? I would sign up to [that] today because that's what we need."* Another interviewee believes that *"RM should be part of the basics at school or at work."*

Shenaz shares how she is *"thinking of bringing it in now to teacher training, because one of my colleagues trains teachers at a school of teacher training in Dublin. And I have worked with quite a few schools and done leadership development for teachers, and I'm thinking, can you imagine the poor teachers, what's coming to them in the next 20 years?"*

Shenaz concludes, however, that *"Perhaps for me most importantly is how RM has transformed my parenting and also opened up a deeper listening within my relationship with my husband when managing a difficult home situation."*

Conclusion

> By letting go, it all gets done.
>
> (Lao-Tzu)

There is so much we can engage with, drawing on the power of RM to seek to make a positive difference in this world we share. And yet, it feels important to take a pause and to remind ourselves that RM is not about striving; it is about allowing, about being with. There is something here about simplicity, about re-connecting and deepening our connection with ourselves, other beings, and our planet, about re-wilding our hearts, about relaxing and letting go, about stripping things away so we get to the core of what it means to be human: love.

We do not know what the future holds. If we knew everything was going to hell in a handcart tomorrow, we would still plant an apple tree today, as Martin Luther is said to have responded when asked what he would do if the world were to end tomorrow. We would still want to be relationally mindful and compassionate, probably even more so.

Perhaps we do indeed collectively face, or perhaps we are already deeply mired in, irrevocable societal collapse, and our best approach is the 'deep adaptation' proposed by the likes of Jem Bendell (2023). Perhaps we can turn things around with 'deep transformation', as Jeremy Lent (2021) proposes. Perhaps together we can bring about *"small islands of coherence in a sea of chaos"*, which *"when a complex system is far from equilibrium, …have the capacity to shift the entire system to a high order"*, to use the words of Nobel laureate Ilya Prigogine (cited in a blog by Scharmer, 2023).

We hold no illusions that RM on its own can change the world (and we note some attachment to wanting to change it, which may be misplaced!) We do not see ourselves as experts with all the answers (thank goodness) nor saviours waltzing in with the panacea for all ills (we wish). However, we believe whole-heartedly that RM can definitely make a difference, helping us to, in the words of Margaret Wheatley, *"create islands of sanity – places of possibility and refuge where the human spirit can thrive"* (2024, p.5). As Wheatley (2024, p. 13) asks, *"Can we use our power and influence to create sanctuaries to awaken and restore our finest human qualities?"* We believe we can, and that RM can help us co-create such sanctuaries through our coaching and beyond. Why would we not? We invite you to join us in this endeavour, in a mindfully relaxed, unattached way!

References

Bachkirova, T. (2009). Cognitive-developmental approach to coaching: An interview with Robert Kegan. *Coaching: An International Journal of Theory, Research and Practice*, 2(1), 10–22.

Bendell, J. (2023). *Breaking together: A freedom-loving response to collapse*. Good Works.

Inner Development Goals (2024). Accessed November 2024. https://innerdevelopme ntgoals.org/

Kegan, R. (1998). *In over our heads: The mental demands of modern life*. Harvard University Press.

Lent, J. (2021). *The web of meaning*. New Society Publishers.

Macy, J. (2024). Joanna Macy website, accessed April 2024. www.joannamacy.net/main

Rittel, H. W., & Webber, M. M. (1973). Dilemmas in a general theory of planning. *Policy Sciences*, 4(2), 155–169.

Scharmer, O. (2018). Three stages of global movement building: soil, seed, & eco-system. *Field of the Future blog*. Medium https://medium.com/presencing-institute-blog/ three-stages-of-global-movement-building-soil-seed-eco-system-activation-a383a 6d3fc8b

Scharmer, O. (2023). 2023 in eight points: Meditating on our planetary moment. *Field of the Future Blog*. Medium. https://medium.com/presencing-instit ute-blog/2023-in-eight-points-meditating-on-our-planetary-moment-3081c f51ed5d

Wheatley, M. (2024). *Restoring sanity: Practices to awaken generosity, creativity and kindness in ourselves and our organizations*. Berrett-Koehler Publishers.

Information

Dedicated website accompanying this book: www.relationalmindfulness.net

Appendices

Appendix 1

Resources accompanying Chapters 8–13

Formal Relational Mindfulness practice with each of the Relational Mindfulness guidelines

The following resource sheets provide a step-by-step process for each of the Relational Mindfulness (RM) guidelines to help you undertake mindful dialogue with that particular guideline. You can also find downloadable PDFs of each of these sheets on our dedicated website (www.relationalmindfulness.net) together with audios to support your individual practice and other resources relevant to RM.

Resource sheet for Chapter 8: Formal RM practice with the guideline Pause

In this resource sheet, we provide a step-by-step process to help you undertake mindful dialogue with the guideline Pause. Before you start, it is vital to read Chapter 7 to set the context for your practice. In particular:

Before you engage in mindful dialogue it is important to:

- Understand the parameters of the practice – its form and intention
- Be aware of the potential for discomfort to arise and the importance of establishing safety for the practice, underpinned by ethics, integrity, and care
- Choose your dialogue partner carefully
- Set clear agreements with your dialogue partner to create the safety needed to engage in mindful dialogue together

At the beginning of the practice period, you and your dialogue partner will need to:

- Revisit/remind yourselves of the agreements you have made to support safety for the practice
- Agree logistics around timing and order of speaking
- Choose a contemplation question or topic

Possible contemplation topics: when practising with a focus on the guideline Pause, suitable contemplation topics could be:

- *Pausing to attend to sensations in the body, seeing what sensations are arising – then speaking aloud about what you notice, tracking your experience of body sensations moment-by-moment with awareness. Not looking for anything particular, staying connected to body, noticing what comes up*
- *Attending to where your awareness is drawn and what sensations, mind activity, and emotions are arising moment-by-moment, noticing whether they feel pleasant, unpleasant, or neither – then speaking aloud about what you notice and naming your experience of pleasant, unpleasant, and neutral*
- *Noticing sounds and sights, becoming aware of the moment of contact where a sound reaches your ears or a sight reaches your eyes; what is the experience as a sound/sight comes into your awareness? Speaking aloud about that process as it happens*
- *Exploring and describing your energy levels in this moment – looking at physical, emotional, and mind-state energy – where is energy high, low, middling, what does that feel like?*

Structuring the practice: we suggest practising in a pair and following the simple process as set out in Chapter 7, with a focus on Pause as follows:

- *Step 1:* Start with a 5-minute silent individual practice: you can bring in the guideline Pause silently in your mind or use the Pause audio provided on the dedicated website accompanying this book (see link at the start of Appendix 1) to guide you both through a practice and support you to come into the present moment with awareness
- *Step 2:* After the silent practice, the first speaker takes 5 minutes to speak, during which the intention is that ...
  - ... the speaker pauses to attend to sensations in the body and speaks from the felt sense of what arises in response to the chosen contemplation topic, drawing on further pauses to support mindful speaking
  - ... the listener rests in receptive awareness, staying connected to the sensations in the body and receiving the speaker's sharing, pausing internally to support mindful listening
- *Step 3:* After 5 minutes, you both pause briefly to settle into moment-to-moment experience in silence
- *Step 4:* Then, the second speaker takes 5 minutes to speak with the same intentions for both speaker and listener as set out for the first speaker's turn
- *Step 5:* After 5 minutes, you both take a further pause
- *Step 6:* Then, you release the form of separate speaker and listener and take a further 5 minutes to engage in shared dialogue, either continuing the same contemplation or developing the contemplation question slightly, with the same intentions for speaking and listening as when the roles of speaker and listener were separate
- *Step 7:* Finally, you round off your dialogue and, unless you are continuing into a further dialogue, express your appreciation of one another (recognising that you could not do this practice without each other)

The above sequence will take 20–25 minutes. As you get more experienced, you may want to extend the duration of the sections to increase the time of each speaking phase and/or of the silent practice before, between, and after the dialogue.

Resource sheet for Chapter 9: Formal RM practice with the guideline Relax/allow

In this resource sheet, we provide a step-by-step process to help you undertake mindful dialogue with the guideline Relax/allow. Once again, before engaging in formal RM practice, do please read Chapter 7 to set the context for your practice. In particular:

Before you engage in mindful dialogue it is important to:

- Understand the parameters of the practice – its form and intention
- Be aware of the potential for discomfort to arise and the importance of establishing safety for the practice, underpinned by ethics, integrity, and care
- Choose your dialogue partner carefully
- Set clear agreements with your dialogue partner to create the safety needed to engage in mindful dialogue together

At the beginning of the practice period, you and your dialogue partner will need to:

- Revisit/remind yourselves of the agreements you have made to support safety for the practice
- Agree logistics around timing and order of speaking
- Choose a contemplation question or topic

Possible contemplation topics: when practising with a focus on the guideline Relax/allow, suitable contemplation topics could be:

- *Noticing and describing any tension or discomfort in your body and then exploring how it is to invite a softening and a sense of allowing things to be as they are, bringing as much kindly receptivity as you can towards the sensations*
- *Thinking of someone (e.g. grandparent, close friend, partner) or something (e.g. a pet or a tree/favourite place in nature) that you experience as being fully present with you in a non-judgemental way – with whom you can be exactly as you are. The invitation is to describe how it feels to be in their presence and how it feels now as you reflect*
- *How is it to allow, receive, and turn towards a current challenge in your coaching/work or elsewhere in your life?*
- *Reflecting on an aspect of your relational life or a recent moment in a relationship that gives you a sense of ease, gratitude, and/or contentment, exploring and describing how that feels*

Structuring the practice: we suggest practising in a pair and following the simple process as set out in Chapter 7, focusing on Relax/allow as follows:

- *Step 1:* Start with a 5-minute silent individual practice: you can bring in the guideline Relax/allow silently in your mind, or you can use one of the audios provided on the dedicated website accompanying this book (see link at the start of Appendix 1) to guide you both through a practice. Either way the aim of this time is to support you to bring a kindly receptivity to whatever is arising in your body, heart, and mind
- *Step 2:* After the silent practice, the first speaker takes 5 minutes to speak, during which the intention is that …
  - … the speaker pauses to attend to sensations in the body and invites a relaxing and allowing, bringing kindness and receptivity to whatever is present, then speaks from the felt sense of what arises in response to the chosen contemplation topic, drawing on further pauses and invitations to relax/allow to support mindful speaking
  - … the listener rests in receptive awareness, staying connected to the sensations in the body and receiving the speaker's sharing, pausing, relaxing, and allowing internally to support mindful listening
- *Step 3:* After 5 minutes, you both pause briefly to settle into moment-to-moment experience in silence
- *Step 4:* Then, the second speaker takes 5 minutes to speak with the same intentions for both speaker and listener as set out for the first speaker's turn
- *Step 5:* After 5 minutes, you both take a further pause
- *Step 6:* Then, you release the form of separate speaker and listener and take a further 5 minutes to engage in shared dialogue, either continuing the same contemplation or developing the contemplation question slightly, with the same intentions for speaking and listening as when the roles of speaker and listener were separate
- *Step 7:* Finally, you round off your dialogue and, unless you are continuing into a further dialogue, express your appreciation of one another (recognising that you could not do this practice without each other)

The above sequence will take 20–25 minutes. As you get more experienced, you may want to extend the duration of the sections to increase the time of each speaking phase and/or of the silent practice before, between, and after the dialogue.

Resource sheet for Chapter 10: Formal RM practice with the guideline Open

In this resource sheet, we provide a step-by-step process to help you undertake mindful dialogue with the guideline Open. As we will continue to repeat for each of these resource sheets, before engaging in formal RM practice, it is vital to read Chapter 7 to set the context for your practice. In particular:

Before you engage in mindful dialogue it is important to:

- Understand the parameters of the practice – its form and intention
- Be aware of the potential for discomfort to arise and the importance of establishing safety for the practice, underpinned by ethics, integrity, and care
- Choose your dialogue partner carefully
- Set clear agreements with your dialogue partner to create the safety needed to engage in mindful dialogue together

At the beginning of the practice period, you and your dialogue partner will need to:

- Revisit/remind yourselves of the agreements you have made to support safety for the practice
- Agree logistics around timing and order of speaking
- Choose a contemplation question or topic

Possible contemplation topics: when practising with a focus on the guideline Relax/allow, suitable contemplation topics could be:

- *Pausing to attend to sensations in the body, then expanding awareness to include the whole body, then expanding further to include the external environment: noticing where your awareness is drawn, internally, externally, both. When you are ready, describing out loud your present-moment experience, for example, what sensations are arising internally and what you are noticing externally, and exploring whether you can hold both in awareness*
- *Describing a recent experience of compassion or kindness – as the giver, receiver, or witness of a compassionate/kind act – focusing less on the story and more on what is happening within you as you recall that moment*
- *How does it feel to be in a good, collaborative, connected relationship? What have you experienced in moments of relating in this way? (You can develop this for the shared contemplation to explore: What is showing up in the relational field now?)*
- *Explore any gratitude you feel in your life right now: perhaps your appreciation for the place where you live, for having food to eat, for the people you care about and the people who care about you, or any other aspect of your life in general*

or this moment in particular. How does it feel in the body as you explore your experience of gratitude?

Structuring the practice: we suggest practising in a pair and following the simple process as set out in Chapter 7, adapted to Open as follows:

1. *Step 1:* Start with a 5-minute silent individual practice: you can bring in the guideline Open silently in your mind, to support you to bring an awareness of internal sensations arising in your body, heart, and mind and external stimuli in the environment. Alternatively, you can use the audio provided on the dedicated website accompanying this book (see link at the start of Appendix 1) to guide you both through a practice of Open
2. *Step 2:* After the silent practice, the first speaker takes 5 minutes to speak, during which the intention is that …
    ■ … the speaker pauses to attend to sensations in the body and the external environment, inviting a spacious awareness that holds internal, external, and both, then speaks from the felt sense of what arises in response to the chosen contemplation topic, drawing on the guideline Open to support mindful speaking
    ■ … the listener rests in receptive awareness, staying connected to the sensations in the body and receiving the speaker's sharing, pausing, relaxing, and allowing and attending to what is arising internally, externally, and both to support mindful listening
3. *Step 3:* After 5 minutes, you both pause briefly to settle into moment-to-moment experience in silence
4. *Step 4:* Then, the second speaker takes 5 minutes to speak with the same intentions for both speaker and listener as set out for the first speaker's turn
5. *Step 5:* After 5 minutes, you both take a further pause
6. *Step 6:* Then, you release the form of separate speaker and listener and take a further 5 minutes to engage in shared dialogue, either continuing the same contemplation or developing the contemplation question slightly, with the same intentions for speaking and listening as when the roles of speaker and listener were separate
7. *Step 7:* Finally, you round off your dialogue and, unless you are continuing into a further dialogue, express your appreciation of one another (recognising that you could not do this practice without each other)

The above sequence will take 20–25 minutes. As you get more experienced, you may want to extend the duration of the sections to increase the time of each speaking phase and/or of the silent practice before, between, and after the dialogue.

Resource sheet for Chapter 11: Formal RM practice with the guideline Attune to emergence

In this resource sheet, we provide a step-by-step process to help you undertake mindful dialogue with the guideline Attune to emergence. Again, before engaging in formal RM practice, it is vital to read Chapter 7 to set the context for your practice. In particular:

Before you engage in mindful dialogue it is important to:

- Understand the parameters of the practice – its form and intention
- Be aware of the potential for discomfort to arise and the importance of establishing safety for the practice, underpinned by ethics, integrity, and care
- Choose your dialogue partner carefully
- Set clear agreements with your dialogue partner to create the safety needed to engage in mindful dialogue together

At the beginning of the practice period, you and your dialogue partner will need to:

- Revisit/remind yourselves of the agreements you have made to support safety for the practice
- Agree logistics around timing and order of speaking
- Choose a contemplation question or topic

Possible contemplation topics: when practising with a focus on the guideline Attune to emergence, suitable contemplation topics could be:

- *Noting and describing out loud your experience of change moment-by-moment – naming experiences that are arising and vanishing, internally and externally – physical sensations, sounds, sights, thoughts, emotions*
- *Thinking of a time when you encountered something new, when you were exploring afresh without assumptions, and describing the sensations associated with that at the time and in this moment of recalling it. Focusing less on the story and more on the felt experience*
- *Sharing your experience of change in your life at the moment: exploring what is emerging and vanishing. Focusing on how this experience of change feels – what is the felt sense, the physical sensations, emotions?*
- *Exploring any resistance to change your experience – somewhere in your life or in this moment where change is happening, and you do not want it to. This might be in any area of your life – coaching, work, personal life, physical changes as you age ....*

Structuring the practice: we suggest practising in a pair and following the simple process as set out in Chapter 7, adapted to Attune to emergence as follows:

■ *Step 1:* Start with a 5-minute silent individual practice: you can bring in the guideline Attune to emergence silently in your mind, to support you to become aware of what is emerging, arising and vanishing in your body, heart and mind. Alternatively, you can use the audio provided on the dedicated website accompanying this book (see link at the start of Appendix 1) to guide you both through a practice of Attune to emergence

■ *Step 2:* After the silent practice, the first speaker takes 5 minutes to speak, during which the intention is that …

  ■ … the speaker pauses to attend to sensations in the body and the external environment, inviting awareness of the constant arising and vanishing of experience, then speaks from the felt sense of what arises in response to the chosen contemplation topic, drawing on the guideline Attune to emergence to support mindful speaking

  ■ … the listener rests in receptive awareness, staying connected to the sensations in the body and receiving the speaker's sharing and bringing awareness to the constant arising and vanishing of experience to support mindful listening

■ *Step 3:* After 5 minutes, you both pause briefly to settle into moment-to-moment experience in silence

■ *Step 4:* Then, the second speaker takes 5 minutes to speak with the same intentions for both speaker and listener as set out for the first speaker's turn

■ *Step 5:* After 5 minutes, you both take a further pause

■ *Step 6:* Then, you release the form of separate speaker and listener and take a further 5 minutes to engage in shared dialogue, either continuing the same contemplation or developing the contemplation question slightly, with the same intentions for speaking and listening as when the roles of speaker and listener were separate

■ *Step 7:* Finally, you round off your dialogue and, unless you are continuing into a further dialogue, express your appreciation of one another (recognising that you could not do this practice without each other)

The above sequence will take 20–25 minutes. As you get more experienced, you may want to extend the duration of the sections to increase the time of each speaking phase and/or of the silent practice before, between, and after the dialogue.

Resource sheet for Chapter 12: Formal RM practice with the guideline Listen deeply

In this resource sheet, we provide a step-by-step process to help you undertake mindful dialogue with the guideline Listen deeply. As always, before engaging in formal RM practice, please read Chapter 7 to set the context for your practice. In particular:

Before you engage in mindful dialogue it is important to:

- Understand the parameters of the practice – its form and intention
- Be aware of the potential for discomfort to arise and the importance of establishing safety for the practice, underpinned by ethics, integrity, and care
- Choose your dialogue partner carefully
- Set clear agreements with your dialogue partner to create the safety needed to engage in mindful dialogue together

We would also encourage you to read (or re-read) Chapter 12 before you engage in a practice with the guideline Listen deeply to remind yourselves of the importance of meta-perspective and of balancing exploration and receptivity. And we strongly recommend that you become familiar with mindful dialogue before engaging in the practice suggested below as it involves a more complex process than the previously suggested practices, which makes it harder to maintain meditative awareness.

When we practice with a focus on the guideline Listen deeply, listening starts to take centre stage. Provided you are familiar with mindful dialogue, it is a good moment to introduce other formats of practice and include listener feedback as part of the process. The guidance below therefore suggests loops which include time for the listener to feed back what they have 'received' from the speaker.

It is vital to ensure that this process is a relational meditation, rather than a 'feedback exercise.' To support this, when you are the listener you are encouraged not to treat listening as a memory test. Instead, the invitation is to allow the speaker's communication to land fully in each moment. When listening in this way, the significant elements will be easy to recall later.

At the beginning of the practice period, you and your dialogue partner will need to:

- Revisit/remind yourselves of the agreements you have made to support safety for the practice
- Agree logistics around timing and order of speaking and whether you will do both the speaker/listener 'loops' (A and B) described below or just one of them.

Contemplation topics: In the suggested process set out below, we have provided a suggested pair of contemplation topics. If you engage in both speaker/listener 'loops', the process involves a progression from listening to content in loop A to listening to body language and the music of the voice in loop B and the contemplation topics indicated in italics are designed to support this process.

Structuring the practice: we suggest structuring the practice in a format of speaker/listener 'loops.' You will need a mindfulness bell ready to time: 6 minutes, then 2 minutes, then 1 minute for each speaker/listener 'loop.'

A. First speaker/listener 'loop'

- *Step 1:* Starting with a 6-minute silent individual practice: you can bring in the guidelines Pause, Relax/allow, and Open silently in your mind, or you can use one of the audios provided on the dedicated website accompanying this book. (see link at the start of Appendix 1) to guide you both through a practice. Either way the aim of this time is to support you to bring awareness to your moment-by-moment experience
- *Step 2:* After the silent practice, the first speaker takes 6 minutes to speak, during which the intention is that ...
  - ... the speaker pauses to listen deeply to sensations in the body and to what is arising in the mind, then speaks from the felt sense of what arises in response to the question: *What roles do I play in my coaching and other work, and my professional community?*
  - ... the listener rests in receptive awareness, staying connected to the sensations in the body and listening deeply to the speaker's sharing, drawing on all the RM guidelines to support this listening. The focus for the listening is on the content of what the speaker is saying – words, phrases, verbal expression – knowing that you will be feeding back what you hear, but not treating this as a memory exercise, but instead a chance to let the speaker's words land fully, so that they are easy to recall later
- *Step 3:* After 6 minutes, you both pause briefly to settle into moment-to-moment experience in silence
- *Step 4:* Then, the first listener takes 2 minutes to offer back *what you heard in terms of content, words, phrases*
- *Step 5:* After 2 minutes, you both pause briefly to settle into moment-to-moment experience in silence
- *Step 6:* Then, the first speaker takes 1 minute to 'close the loop', offering any reflections, additions, adjustments to what the listener has said
- *Step 7:* After 1 minute, you both pause briefly to settle into moment-to-moment experience in silence
- *Steps 8–13:* Then you repeat steps 2–7 above for the second speaker/listener: the second speaker speaks for 6 minutes, the second listener offers back for 2 minutes, and the second speaker takes 1 minute to 'close the loop' as described

- *Step 14:* Once both speaker/listener loops have been completed, you both pause briefly and
  - If you are only doing the first loop/contemplation, express your appreciation of one another
  - If you are doing both loops/contemplations, take 6 minutes to practise individually – supported by the guidelines Pause and Relax/allow – before you start the second loop

B.Second speaker/listener 'loop'

- *Step 1:* After the silent practice, the person who spoke first becomes the first listener for this second loop. The new first speaker takes 6 minutes to speak, during which the intention is that …
  - … the speaker once again pauses to listen deeply to sensations in the body and to what is arising in the mind, then speaks the truth from the felt sense of what arises in response to the question: *What roles do I play in my close relationships with family and friends?*
  - … the listener rests in receptive awareness, staying connected to the sensations in the body and listening deeply to the speaker's sharing, drawing on all the RM guidelines to support this listening. The focus for the listening is on the speaker's gestures, facial expressions, and other body language, and what you hear in their tone of voice, volume, etc. – knowing that you will be feeding back what you observe, but not treating this as a memory exercise, but instead a chance to let the speaker's embodiment touch you, so that it is easy to recall later
- *Step 2:* After 6 minutes, you both pause briefly to settle into moment-to-moment experience in silence
- *Step 3:* Then, the first listener takes 2 minutes to offer back *what you saw in the speaker's gestures, facial expressions, and other body language, and what you heard in their tone of voice, volume, and so on*
- *Step 4:* After 2 minutes, you both pause briefly to settle into moment-to-moment experience in silence
- *Step 5:* Then, the first speaker takes 1 minute to 'close the loop', offering any reflections, additions, adjustments to what the listener has said
- *Step 6:* After 1 minute, you both pause briefly to settle into moment-to-moment experience in silence
- *Steps 7–12:* Then you repeat steps 1–6 above for the second speaker/listener: the second speaker speaks for 6 minutes, the second listener offers back for 2 minutes, and the second speaker takes 1 minute to 'close the loop' as described
- *Step 13:* Finally, you round off your dialogue and express your appreciation of one another (recognising that you could not do this practice without each other)

Resource sheet for Chapter 13: Formal RM practice with the guideline Speak the truth

In this resource sheet, we provide a step-by-step process to help you undertake mindful dialogue with the guideline Speak the truth. As always, before engaging in formal RM practice, it is vital to read Chapter 7 to set the context for your practice. In particular:

Before you engage in mindful dialogue it is important to:

■ Understand the parameters of the practice – its form and intention
■ Be aware of the potential for discomfort to arise and the importance of establishing safety for the practice, underpinned by ethics, integrity, and care
■ Choose your dialogue partner carefully
■ Set clear agreements with your dialogue partner to create the safety needed to engage in mindful dialogue together

To explore Speak the truth, we suggest speaker/listener loops with time for the listener to feed back what they have 'received' from the speaker. In this case, the listener's feedback is focussed on what the speaker's communication has evoked for them. As before, we strongly recommend that you become familiar with mindful dialogue before engaging in speaker/listener loops due to the complexity of following the process whilst also maintaining a meditative awareness.

As explained for the dialogue for Listen deeply, it is vital to ensure that this process is a relational meditation, rather than a 'feedback exercise.' To support this, when you are the listener you are encouraged not to treat listening as a memory test. Instead, the invitation is to allow the speaker's communication to land fully in each moment and attend to what is evoked as that happens. When listening in this way, the significant elements will be easy to recall later.

At the beginning of the practice period, you and your dialogue partner will need to:

■ Revisit/remind yourselves of the agreements you have made to support safety for the practice
■ Agree logistics around timing and order of speaking
■ Choose a contemplation question or topic

Possible contemplation topics: when practising with a focus on the guideline Speak the truth, suitable contemplation topics could be:

■ *Exploring the process of speaking – feeling into the physical process and naming out loud what comes before speaking and how it feels to emit speech/words/ sounds – opening to the miracle of communication*

- *How do we discern what is to be spoken that is true in the moment, and also beneficial, timely, and said with goodwill (rather than just speaking whatever is on our mind or speaking out of habit) – how do we know the difference in the body? Thinking of specific moments when you have done this and focusing particularly on the felt experience*
- *Exploring your experience of seeking pleasure and enjoyment in relationships. How does this pleasure-seeking manifest in your life? What aspects of your coaching work are motivated by this desire for pleasure?*
- *What are you learning at an experiential level about yourself, your coaching, and the nature of being human?*

Structuring the practice: we suggest structuring the practice in a format of speaker/listener 'loops.' You will need a mindfulness bell ready to time: 6 minutes, then 2 minutes, then 1 minute for each speaker/listener 'loop.'

- *Step 1:* Start with a 6-minute silent individual practice: you can bring in the guidelines Pause, Relax/allow, and Attune to emergence silently in your mind, or you can use one of the audios provided on the dedicated website accompanying this book. (see link at the start of Appendix 1) to guide you both through a practice. Either way, the aim of this time is to support you to bring awareness to your moment-by-moment experience
- *Step 2:* After the silent practice, the first speaker takes 6 minutes to speak, during which the intention is that ...
  - ... the speaker pauses to listen deeply to sensations in the body and to what is arising in the mind, then speaks the truth from the felt sense of what arises in response to the contemplation topic, what is emerging moment-by-moment and what is most relevant, beneficial, and kind
  - ... the listener rests in receptive awareness, staying connected to the sensations in the body, listening deeply to the speaker's sharing and drawing on all the RM guidelines to support this listening. The focus for the listening is on what is evoked in you as the speaker speaks. You will be feeding back what is evoked for you, but not treating this as a memory exercise. Instead this offers a chance to let the experience of listening land fully, so that it is easy to recall later
- *Step 3:* After 6 minutes, you both pause briefly to settle into moment-to-moment experience in silence
- *Step 4:* Then, the first listener takes 2 minutes to offer back *what has been evoked in you as you listened*: drawing on the guideline Speak the truth to help you speak of what is emerging now and what is most relevant, beneficial, and kind
- *Step 5:* After 2 minutes, you both pause briefly to settle into moment-to-moment experience in silence

- *Step 6:* Then, the first speaker takes 1 minute to 'close the loop', offering any reflections, additions, adjustments to what the listener has said
- *Step 7:* After 1 minute, you both pause briefly to settle into moment-to-moment experience in silence
- *Steps 8–13:* Then you repeat steps 2–7 above for the second speaker/listener: the second speaker speaks for 6 minutes, the second listener offers back for 2 minutes, and the second speaker takes 1 minute to 'close the loop' as described
- *Step 14:* Finally, you round off your dialogue and, unless you are continuing into a further dialogue, express your appreciation of one another (recognising that you could not do this practice without each other)

Appendix 2

Resources accompanying Chapter 18

Suggestions for coaching activities based on elements of mindful dialogue

The following resource sheets provide suggested step-by-step processes for bringing elements of mindful dialogue into coaching.

The suggestions we provide should only be used by coaches who have reached Level Four capacity in bringing mindfulness and compassion into coaching (see Chapter 14). This means (a) our Relational Mindfulness (RM) practice is deeply embedded and embodied, (b) we have the capacity to directly offer individual mindfulness/compassion practice in our coaching, and (c) we have sufficient fluency with the RM guidelines and RM practice to take elements of mindful dialogue into our coaching work.

It is very important to recognise that the heart of mindful dialogue is not a structure or set of steps; it is relatedness, being fully with one another and opening to insight that arises in these conditions. To support this, it is essential that we embody the RM guidelines when offering any of these suggestions in coaching – see Chapters 15 and 16.

It is also vital to read Chapter 18 before engaging with any of the suggested formats below, in order to understand the following:

- The distinctions between coaching and mindful dialogue

- ■ The importance of client readiness and how we might determine whether a particular client is ready for elements of RM or not
- ■ When and how to introduce elements of RM
- ■ The opportunities and risks of bringing in elements of RM
- ■ The context and purpose of bringing elements of mindful dialogue into coaching

The ideas we present here are still tentative and at pilot stage. This is a new and emerging way of coaching which may take time to mature and become established. We would welcome your engagement in this community of discovery and would very much value feedback you may have after experimenting with the following suggestions.

All these suggestions draw on all the RM guidelines to support the client to engage in a mindful exploration of a chosen coaching issue/topic. The dialogues proposed all involve listening deeply and speaking the truth, which are underpinned by the other four guidelines. In addition, to help frame each proposed format, we have indicated an RM guideline that you might particularly want to have in mind.

You can find downloadable PDFs of each of these sheets on our dedicated website (www.relationalmindfulness.net) together with audios to support your individual practice, other resources relevant to RM, and ways of getting in touch with us.

Suggestion 1: Bringing in elements of mindful dialogue, supported particularly by the RM guideline Open (external aspect)

The following format has similarities to the relational formal practice speaker–listener loop set out in the resource sheet for Chapter 12 (see Appendix 1), adapted into a coaching activity. A key distinction between a mutual mindful dialogue and this activity is that we propose only engaging in the loop with the coach as the listener, not having a loop with the coach in speaker role. The risk to this is that it leads to loss of mutuality and a constriction around the roles of coach and client, so the coach will need to be skilful about how to wisely bring their presence and humanity into the dialogue.

Another key distinction is that the contemplation topic will be determined by what the client is bringing to coaching: the client and coach will need to agree together what particular coaching issue is to be the focus for the dialogue and a specific contemplation question. As mentioned, the contemplation in RM offers the opportunity to bring in wisdom at an experiential and felt level. It is important that the mindful dialogue is not seen as a forum for problem-solving, but instead as a chance to bring awareness, see clearly, generate different perspectives, and release any constrictions that may be obstructing flow and flexibility. Some possible contemplation questions might be the following:

- *Where is there tightening around this issue and where could there be release?*
- *In what ways are we seeing things as not changing even though they are actually doing so?*
- *What stress, distress, and/or pain are we ignoring in this situation? How does it feel to bring that into awareness and be with it?*
- *Where are we seeing things as personal, when in fact they are the result of multiple causes and conditions and not personal to us?*
- *What are we seeing as lovely, appealing, and/or desirable, when in fact that is just an appearance?*

The following steps assume that the coach has already discerned client readiness, explained what they are suggesting and why, and checked whether the client is willing to engage in this kind of dialogue along the lines set out in Chapter 18.

In addition, the coach needs to set the context for the client by the following:

- Explaining that the dialogue is about mindful, experiential exploration of what is emerging in both their mind and their felt sense
- Describing the feedback-loop process so the client knows what to expect
- Deciding together which aspect of the client's communication the coach will be particularly attending to and feeding back, selecting one of the following:

- Content, words, information
- Body language, gestures, facial expressions
- Rhythm, tone, volume of the speech

Once the context is set, the suggestion is to progress through the following steps:

- *Step 1:* The coach guides the client in a mindful Pause, perhaps also bringing in the guidelines Relax/allow and Open if that feels supportive, depending on how the coaching session has gone so far
- *Step 2:* After the silent practice, the client is invited to listen deeply to sensations in the body and to what is arising in the mind in response to the chosen contemplation question, and to take 5 or 6 minutes to speak of what is emerging moment-by-moment …
  - … during this time the coach rests in receptive awareness, staying connected to the experience and listening deeply to the client's sharing, drawing on all the RM guidelines to support this listening. The focus for the coach's listening is on the agreed element of the client's communication (content, body language, or vocal music), not treating this as a memory exercise, and instead letting the client's words land fully, as an embodied experience, so that they are easy to recall later
- *Step 3:* After 5 or 6 minutes, both coach and client pause briefly to settle into moment-to-moment experience in silence
- *Step 4:* Then, the coach takes 2 minutes to offer back *what they heard in terms of the agreed element of the client's communication (content, body language, or vocal music)*
- *Step 5:* After 2 minutes, both coach and client pause briefly to settle into moment-to-moment experience in silence
- *Step 6:* Then, the client takes a minute or two to 'close the loop', offering any reflections, additions, adjustments to what the listener has said
- *Step 7:* After a minute or two, both coach and client pause briefly to settle into moment-to-moment experience in silence
- *Step 8:* Client and coach reflect together on what has emerged in the dialogue and continue the coaching session from there

Suggestion 2: Bringing in elements of mindful dialogue, supported particularly by the RM guideline Open (internal aspect)

The following format has similarities to the relational formal practice speaker–listener loop set out in resource sheet for Chapter 13 (see Appendix 1), again adapted for coaching. As in suggestion 1, we propose only engaging in the loop with the coach as the listener, so the coach will need to be skilful about how to wisely bring their presence and humanity into the dialogue to counterbalance the loss of mutuality and avoid constriction around the roles of coach and client.

As before, we suggest that the contemplation topic be determined by what the client is bringing to coaching, with both parties agreeing together the focus for the dialogue and the contemplation question. As mentioned, it is important that the mindful dialogue is not seen as a forum for problem-solving, but instead as a chance to bring awareness, see clearly, generate different perspectives, and release any constrictions that may be obstructing flow and flexibility in a particular situation – and as an opportunity to bring in wisdom at an experiential and felt level. Again, some possible contemplation questions might be the following:

- *Where is there tightening around this issue and where could there be release?*
- *In what ways are we seeing things as not changing even though they are actually doing so?*
- *What stress, distress, and/or pain are we ignoring in this situation? How does it feel to bring that into awareness and be with it?*
- *Where are we seeing things as personal, when in fact they are the result of multiple causes and conditions and not personal to us?*
- *What are we seeing as lovely, appealing, and/or desirable, when in fact that is just an appearance?*

Again, the following steps assume that the coach has already discerned client readiness, explained what they are suggesting and why, and checked client's willingness to engage in this kind of dialogue (see Chapter 18). In addition, the coach needs to set the context for the client by the following:

- Explaining that the dialogue is about mindful, experiential exploration of what is emerging in both their mind and their felt sense
- Describing the feedback-loop process so the client knows what to expect, including what the coach will be providing in the way of feedback

Again, once the context is set, the suggestion is to progress through the following steps:

- *Step 1:* The coach guides the client in a mindful Pause, perhaps also bringing in the guidelines Relax/allow and Open if that feels supportive and depending on how the coaching session has already gone

- *Step 2:* After the silent practice, the client is invited to listen deeply to sensations in the body and to what is arising in the mind in response to the chosen contemplation question, and to take 5 or 6 minutes to speak of what is emerging moment-by-moment …
  - … during this time the coach rests in receptive awareness, staying connected to the experience and listening deeply to the client's sharing, drawing on all the RM guidelines to support this listening. The focus for the coach's listening is what is evoked for them as the client speaks, so it will be particularly helpful to draw on the guideline Open to notice what is arising internally and externally and in the space between
- *Step 3:* After 5 or 6 minutes, both coach and client pause briefly to settle into moment-to-moment experience in silence
- *Step 4:* The coach takes 2 minutes to offer back *what has been evoked in them as they listened*: drawing on the guideline Speak the truth to speak of what is emerging now and what is most relevant, beneficial, and kind
- *Step 5:* After 2 minutes, both coach and client pause briefly to settle into moment-to-moment experience in silence
- *Step 6:* The client takes a minute or two to 'close the loop', offering any reflections, additions, adjustments to what the listener has said
- *Step 7:* After a minute or two, both pause briefly to settle into moment-to-moment experience in silence
- *Step 8:* Client and coach reflect together on *what has emerged in the dialogue* and continue the coaching session from there

Suggestion 3: Bringing in elements of mindful dialogue, supported particularly by the RM guideline Attune to emergence

The following format has similarities to the relational formal practices set out in resource sheets for Chapters 8–11 (see Appendix 1), again adapted for coaching. This time, we propose that the coach and client both play speaker and listener roles. However, the coach will still need to be skilful about how to wisely bring their presence and humanity into the dialogue to avoid constriction around the roles of coach and client.

This dialogue format may be particularly helpful when a client is stuck on a particular issue/problem. The aim here is to draw on the guideline Attune to emergence as a way to touch into a wider collective intelligence, drawing on the interconnected nature of the field in which we are operating, opening beyond our individual meaning-making and releasing a sense of knowing the answers.

As in the other suggestions, the contemplation topic will be determined by what the client is bringing, with both parties agreeing together the focus for the dialogue and a specific contemplation question. Since the contemplation in RM offers the opportunity to bring in wisdom at an experiential and felt level, it is important that the mindful dialogue is not seen as a forum for problem-solving, but instead as a chance to bring awareness, see clearly, generate different perspectives, and release any constrictions that may be obstructing flow and flexibility in a particular situation. As before, some possible contemplation questions might be the following:

- *Where is there tightening around this issue and where could there be release?*
- *In what ways are we seeing things as not changing even though they are actually doing so?*
- *What stress, distress, and/or pain are we ignoring in this situation? How does it feel to bring that into awareness and be with it?*
- *Where are we seeing things as personal, when in fact they are the result of multiple causes and conditions and not personal to us?*
- *What are we seeing as lovely, appealing, and/or desirable, when in fact that is just an appearance?*

Again, we assume that the coach has discerned client readiness and willingness to engage in this kind of dialogue and explained what they are suggesting and why (see Chapter 18). In addition, the coach needs to set the context for the client by the following:

- Explaining that the dialogue is about mindful, experiential exploration of what is emerging in both their mind and their felt sense

- Describing the feedback-loop process so the client knows what to expect, emphasising that the speaking is about what is arising and vanishing moment-by-moment, noticing how that is constantly changing

Again, once the context is set, the suggestion is to progress through the following steps:

- *Step 1:* The coach guides the client in a mindful Pause, perhaps also bringing in the guidelines Relax/allow, Open and Attune to emergence if that feels supportive and depending on how the coaching session has gone so far
- *Step 2:* After the silent practice, the client is invited to listen deeply to sensations in the body and to what is arising in the mind in response to the chosen contemplation question, and to take 5 or 6 minutes to speak of what is emerging moment-by-moment ...
    - ... during this time the coach rests in receptive awareness, staying connected to the experience and listening deeply to the client's sharing, drawing on all the RM guidelines to support this listening, particularly the guideline Attune to emergence to support awareness of the constantly changing process of arising and vanishing
- *Step 3:* After 5 or 6 minutes, both pause briefly to settle into moment-to-moment experience in silence
- *Step 4:* The coach takes 5 or 6 minutes to speak of what is emerging moment-by-moment in terms of sensations in the body and what is arising in the mind in response to the chosen contemplation question
    - ... this time, the client is invited to rest in receptive awareness and listen deeply to the coach's sharing, and to bring awareness to the constantly changing process of arising and vanishing in their own felt sensations and mind in response to the coach's words
- *Step 5:* After 5 or 6 minutes, both pause briefly to settle into moment-to-moment experience in silence
- *Step 6:* Client and coach release the form of separate speaker and listener and take a further 5 minutes to engage in shared dialogue, exploring *what is emerging now after having both spoken and listened*
- *Step 7:* After 5 minutes, both pause briefly to settle into moment-to-moment experience in silence
- *Step 8:* Client and coach reflect together on what has emerged in the dialogue and continue the coaching session from there

Index

Note: Page numbers in *italic* indicate figures and in bold indicate tables.

coaching maturity and 204–205; distinction between coaching and 198; introducing elements of 199–200; opportunities and risks 200; suggestions for coaching activities 200–203, 319–326; teacher training for 203–204; in team/group coaching 202–203
mindfulness: attitudinal foundations 21; benefits of RM for mindfulness practice 55–56; compassion and 22–24, 66; defining 19–21; origins and applications 17–19; self-compassion and 22; *see also* individual mindfulness and compassion; Relational Mindfulness (RM)
Mindfulness Initiative 23, 31, 34
Mindfulness-Based Cognitive Therapy (MBCT) 18, 23
Mindfulness-Based Stress Reduction (MBSR) 17–18, 23, 71
mind-states 118, 150
mind-wandering 37
mirror neurons 227
mirroring 55, 64, 69, 117–118, 182, 227
Mitchell, I. 268
multiplicity 273

National Health Service, UK 18
National Institute for Health and Care Excellence, UK 18
natural world 138
Neff, K. 22, 31, 36, 249, 251, 254–255
negative emotional attractor (NEA) 256
negative emotions 35–37, 253
negativity bias 241, 253
nervous system 33–35; parasympathetic 33, 253, 256, 257
neurobiology of connection 66, 175, 226–228; brain synchronisation 99, 226, 227; interpersonal resonance 36, 55, 64; mirroring 55, 64, 69, 117–118, 182, 227; oxytocin 99, 226, 227–228; vagal tone 99, 226, 228; *see also* brain
neuroception 218
nociception 213
non-judgemental, use of term 48
non-judgemental acceptance 90, 91
non-reactivity 90, 91
non-verbal communication 90, 102, 150, 151, 153, 154, 187, 194, 226
nonviolent communication (NVC) 234–239
nucleus accumbens 29

O'Fallon, T. 60
online practice 103

Open guideline 133–139; defining 67, 68–69, 133–135; directly offering individual practice of 192–193; embodying 183–184; formal individual practice 136–137; formal relational practice 137, 308–309; informal individual practice 138; informal relational practice 138–139; integrating into coaching preparation 178–179; links to coaching competencies 88; suggestions for coaching activities 319–322; supporting ourselves 135–136
Ormston, R. 23, 31, 34
oxytocin 99, 226, 227–228

Palmer, W. 214
Paradoxical Theory of Change 220
parasympathetic nervous system (PNS) 33, 253, 256, 257
parenting 49, 299
Parker, S. K. 21
Parlett, M. 220, 221
parts work 273–276
Pause guideline 115–123; defining 67, 68, 115–117; directly offering individual practice of 192, 193; embodying 181–182; formal individual practice 118–119; formal relational practice 120, 304–305; informal individual practice 120–121; informal relational practice 120–123; integrating into coaching preparation 178; links to coaching competencies 88; supporting ourselves 117–118
perceiving, new ways of 52, 54–55, 77, 83–85
perceptual narrowing 34, 37
periaqueductal grey matter 29
Perls, F. 218
Petrie, N. 266, 267
Piaget, J. 265
Plum Village community 245–248
politics 298–299
Porges, S. W. 66
positive emotional attractor (PEA) 256
positive emotions 35–36, 226, 228, 253
positivity resonance 225–228
posterior cingulate cortex 28
Pratscher, S. D. 49, 90–91
prefrontal cortex 28, 29
presence 211–212; becoming more fully present 51, 52, 76–79, 77, 88; body as a source of 212–214; in coaching competency frameworks 88; Gestalt 218–222; quantitative data on 90; somatic-based coaching 214–218

For Product Safety Concerns and Information please contact our EU
representative GPSR@taylorandfrancis.com
Taylor & Francis Verlag GmbH, Kaufingerstraße 24, 80331 München, Germany